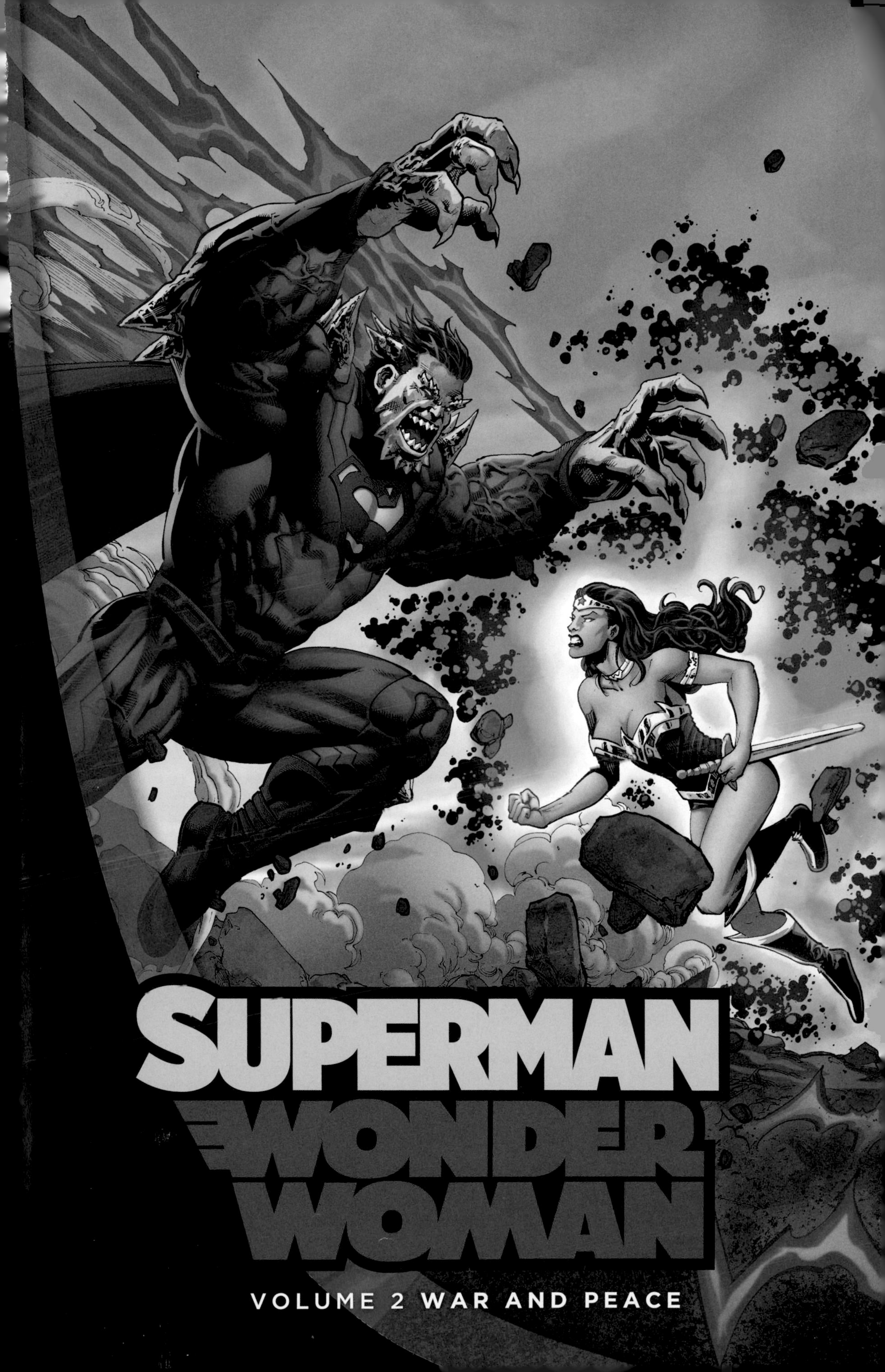
SUPERMAN
WONDER
WOMAN
VOLUME 2 WAR AND PEACE

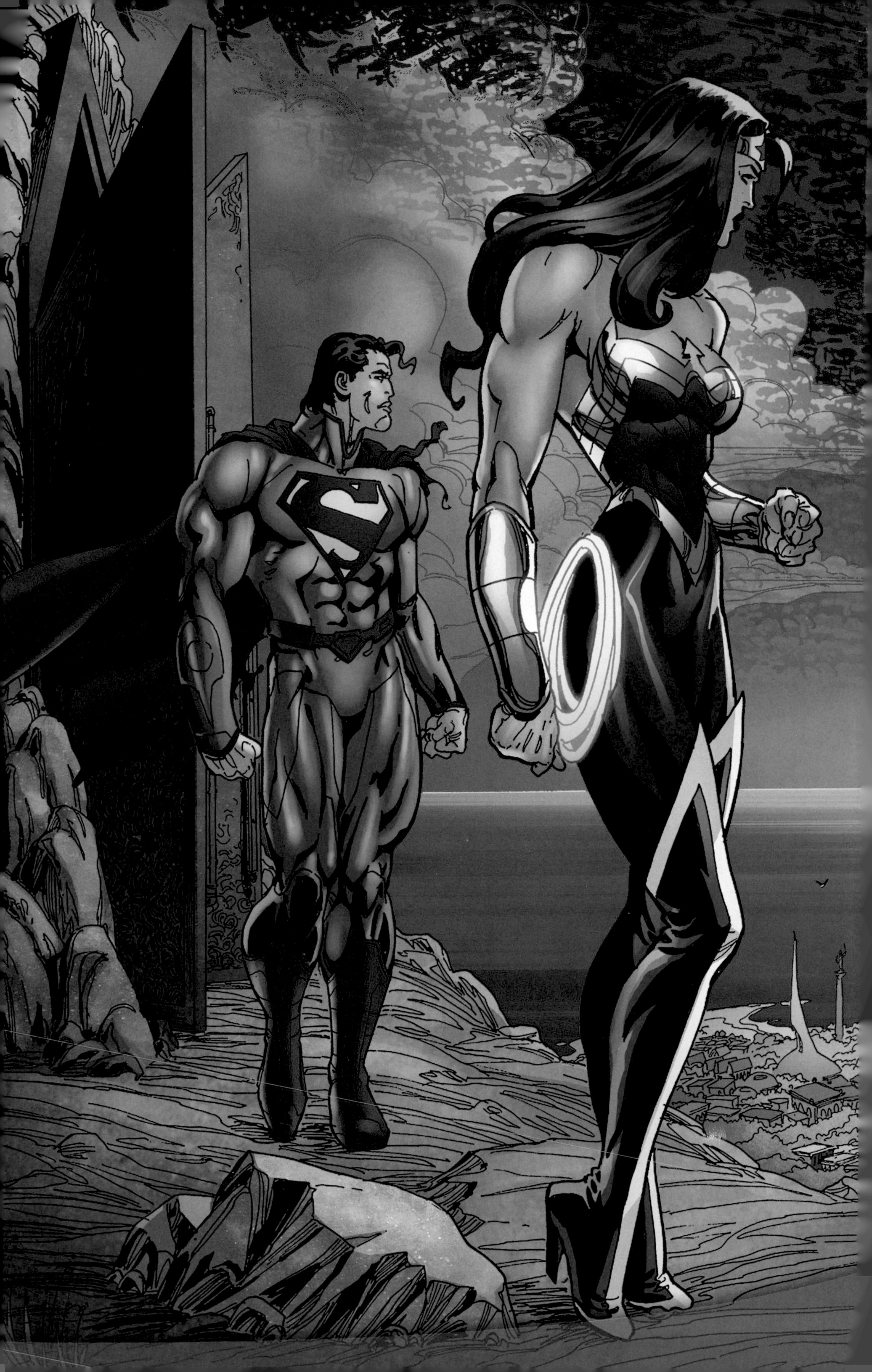

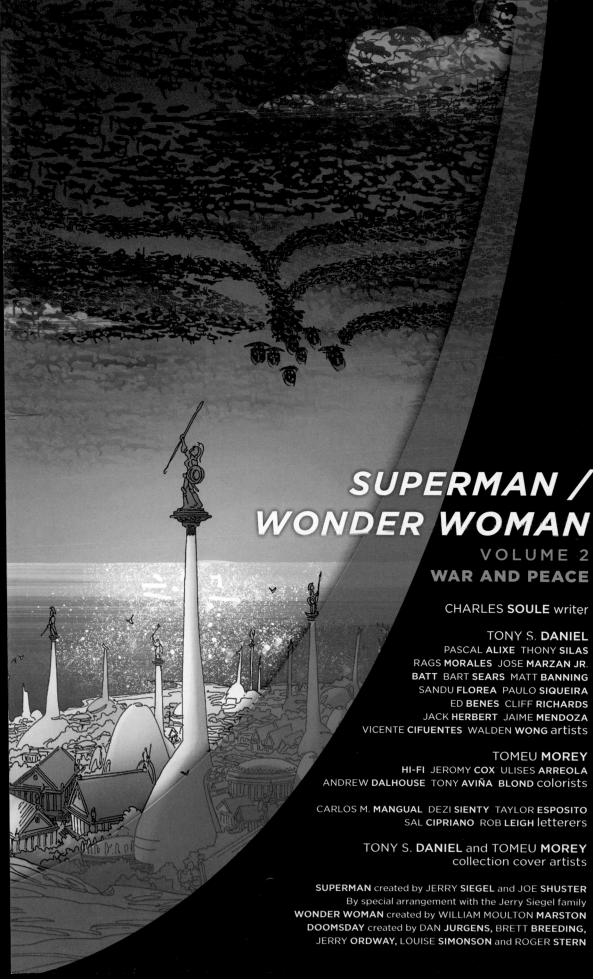

SUPERMAN / WONDER WOMAN

VOLUME 2
WAR AND PEACE

CHARLES **SOULE** writer

TONY S. **DANIEL**
PASCAL **ALIXE** THONY **SILAS**
RAGS **MORALES** JOSE **MARZAN JR.**
BATT BART **SEARS** MATT **BANNING**
SANDU **FLOREA** PAULO **SIQUEIRA**
ED **BENES** CLIFF **RICHARDS**
JACK **HERBERT** JAIME **MENDOZA**
VICENTE **CIFUENTES** WALDEN **WONG** artists

TOMEU **MOREY**
HI-FI JEROMY **COX** ULISES **ARREOLA**
ANDREW **DALHOUSE** TONY **AVIÑA** **BLOND** colorists

CARLOS M. **MANGUAL** DEZI **SIENTY** TAYLOR **ESPOSITO**
SAL **CIPRIANO** ROB **LEIGH** letterers

TONY S. **DANIEL** and TOMEU **MOREY**
collection cover artists

SUPERMAN created by JERRY **SIEGEL** and JOE **SHUSTER**
By special arrangement with the Jerry Siegel family
WONDER WOMAN created by WILLIAM MOULTON **MARSTON**
DOOMSDAY created by DAN **JURGENS**, BRETT **BREEDING**,
JERRY **ORDWAY**, LOUISE **SIMONSON** and ROGER **STERN**

EDDIE BERGANZA MATT IDELSON Editors – Original Series RICKEY PURDIN DARREN SHAN Associate Editors – Original Series
ANTHONY MARQUES Assistant Editor – Original Series   LIZ ERICKSON Editor
ROBBIN BROSTERMAN Design Director – Books ROBBIE BIEDERMAN Publication Design

BOB HARRAS Senior VP – Editor-in-Chief, DC Comics

DIANE NELSON President DAN DIDIO and JIM LEE Co-Publishers GEOFF JOHNS Chief Creative Officer
AMIT DESAI Senior VP – Marketing and Franchise Management
AMY GENKINS Senior VP – Business and Legal Affairs NAIRI GARDINER Senior VP – Finance
JEFF BOISON VP – Publishing Planning MARK CHIARELLO VP – Art Direction and Design
JOHN CUNNINGHAM VP – Marketing TERRI CUNNINGHAM VP – Editorial Administration
LARRY GANEM VP – Talent Relations and Services ALISON GILL Senior VP – Manufacturing and Operations
HANK KANALZ Senior VP – Vertigo and Integrated Publishing JAY KOGAN VP – Business and Legal Affairs, Publishing
JACK MAHAN VP – Business Affairs, Talent NICK NAPOLITANO VP – Manufacturing Administration SUE POHJA VP – Book Sales
FRED RUIZ VP – Manufacturing Operations COURTNEY SIMMONS Senior VP – Publicity BOB WAYNE Senior VP – Sales

SUPERMAN/WONDER WOMAN VOLUME 2: WAR AND PEACE

DC Comics, 1700 Broadway, New York, NY 10019
A Warner Bros. Entertainment Company.
Printed by RR Donnelley, Salem, VA, USA. 2/13/15. First Printing.

ISBN: 978-1-4012-5347-9

Library of Congress Cataloging-in-Publication Data

Soule, Charles.
Superman/Wonder Woman. Volume 2, War and Peace / Charles Soule, Tony Daniel.
pages cm. — (The New 52!)
ISBN 978-1-4012-5247-9 (hardback)
1. Graphic novels. I. Daniel, Tony S. (Antonio Salvador) II. Title. III. Title: War and Peace.
PN6728.S9S65 2014
741.5'973—dc23
                        2014018207

SUSTAINABLE
FORESTRY
INITIATIVE

Certified Chain of Custody
20% Certified Forest Content,
80% Certified Sourcing
www.sfiprogram.org
SFI-01042
APPLIES TO TEXT STOCK ONLY

EVOLUTIONS

TONY S. DANIEL penciller **MATT BANNING SANDU FLOREA** inkers
cover by **TONY S. DANIEL & TOMEU MOREY**

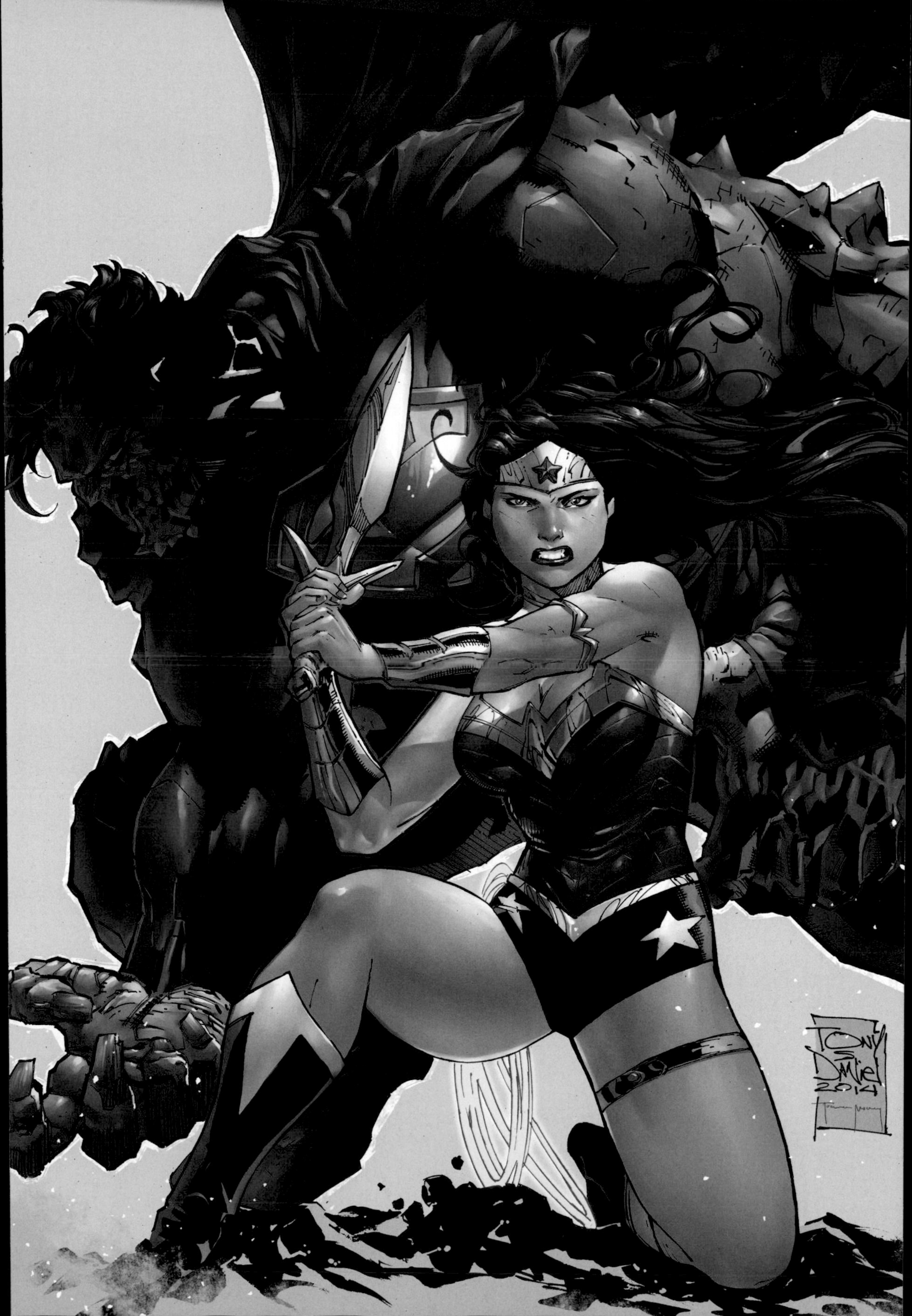

WORLD   U.S.   METROPOLIS   BUSINESS   OPINION   SPORTS   ARTS   STYLE   VIDEO

May 14, 2014

Daily Planet

QUARANTINED!

Photo by James Olsen

SMALLVILLE, KANSAS, QUARANTINED BY U.S. GOVERNMENT

By Lois Lane

The small Midwestern town of Smallville, Kansas, has been quarantined by the U.S. Department of Health after residents abruptly began falling into apparent comas.

Authorities in the area have launched an official investigation into the cause of the outbreak but have speculated that it was linked to the reemergence of the creature Doomsday before its horrific defeat at the hands of the Man of Steel.

An official close to newly appointed Senator Sam Lane who asked not to be identified stated that "Due to the lack of data in regard to what is causing the people of this town to remain in these comas, we must proceed with extreme caution

Photo by James Olsen

until we have a way of knowing that this town does not represent a threat to the surrounding areas."

Neighboring towns have been put on high alert to keep all windows closed and not to leave their homes unless necessary.

Tempers have flared as family members have complained that information is being withheld from them.

Families Mourn Loss of their Loved One
Moving forward after "Doomsday
Where is Superman?
Plane Crash in the Alaskan Wilderness

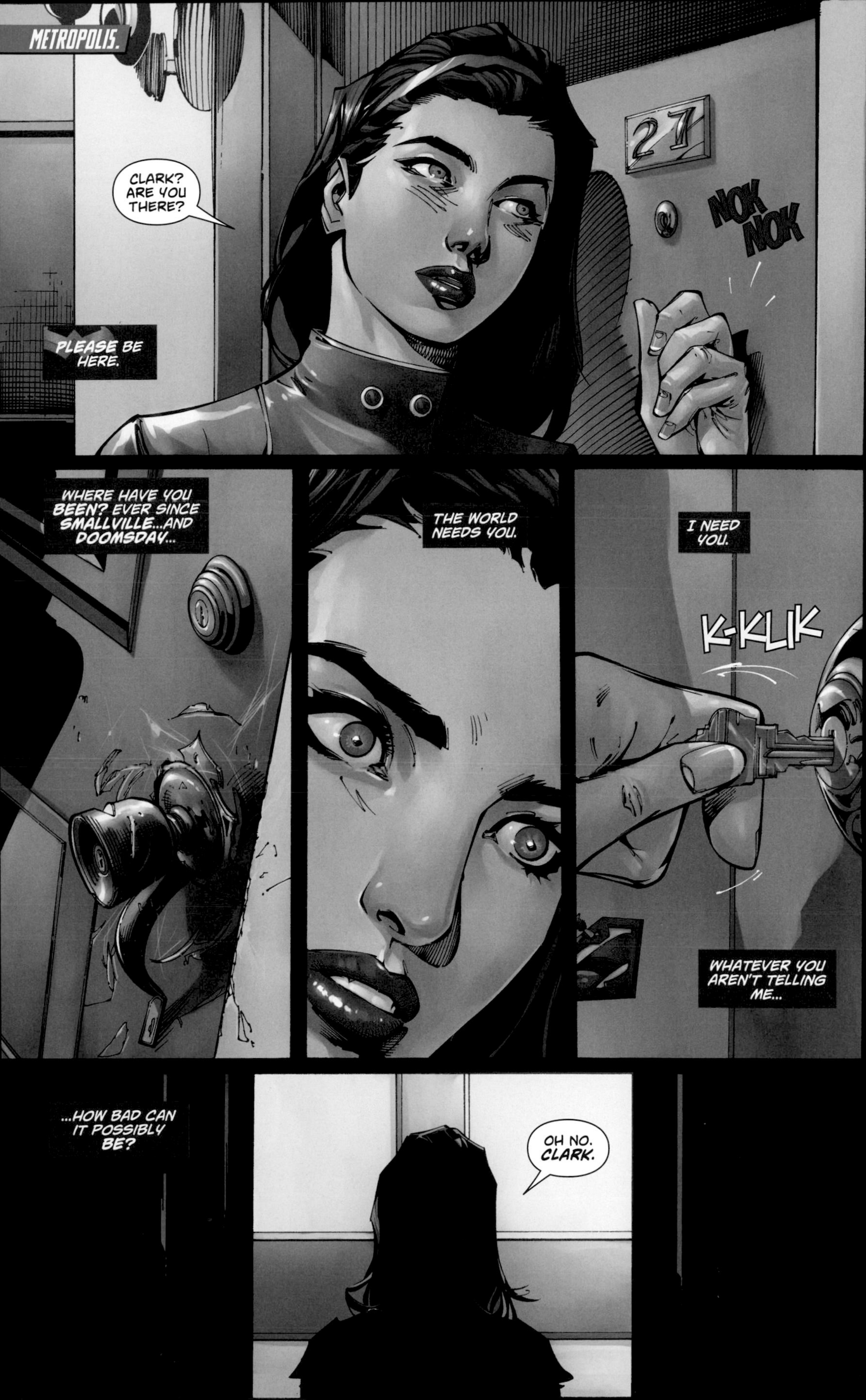
METROPOLIS.
CLARK? ARE YOU THERE?
27
NOK NOK
PLEASE BE HERE.
WHERE HAVE YOU BEEN? EVER SINCE SMALLVILLE...AND DOOMSDAY...
THE WORLD NEEDS YOU.
I NEED YOU.
K-KLIK
WHATEVER YOU AREN'T TELLING ME...
...HOW BAD CAN IT POSSIBLY BE?
OH NO. CLARK.

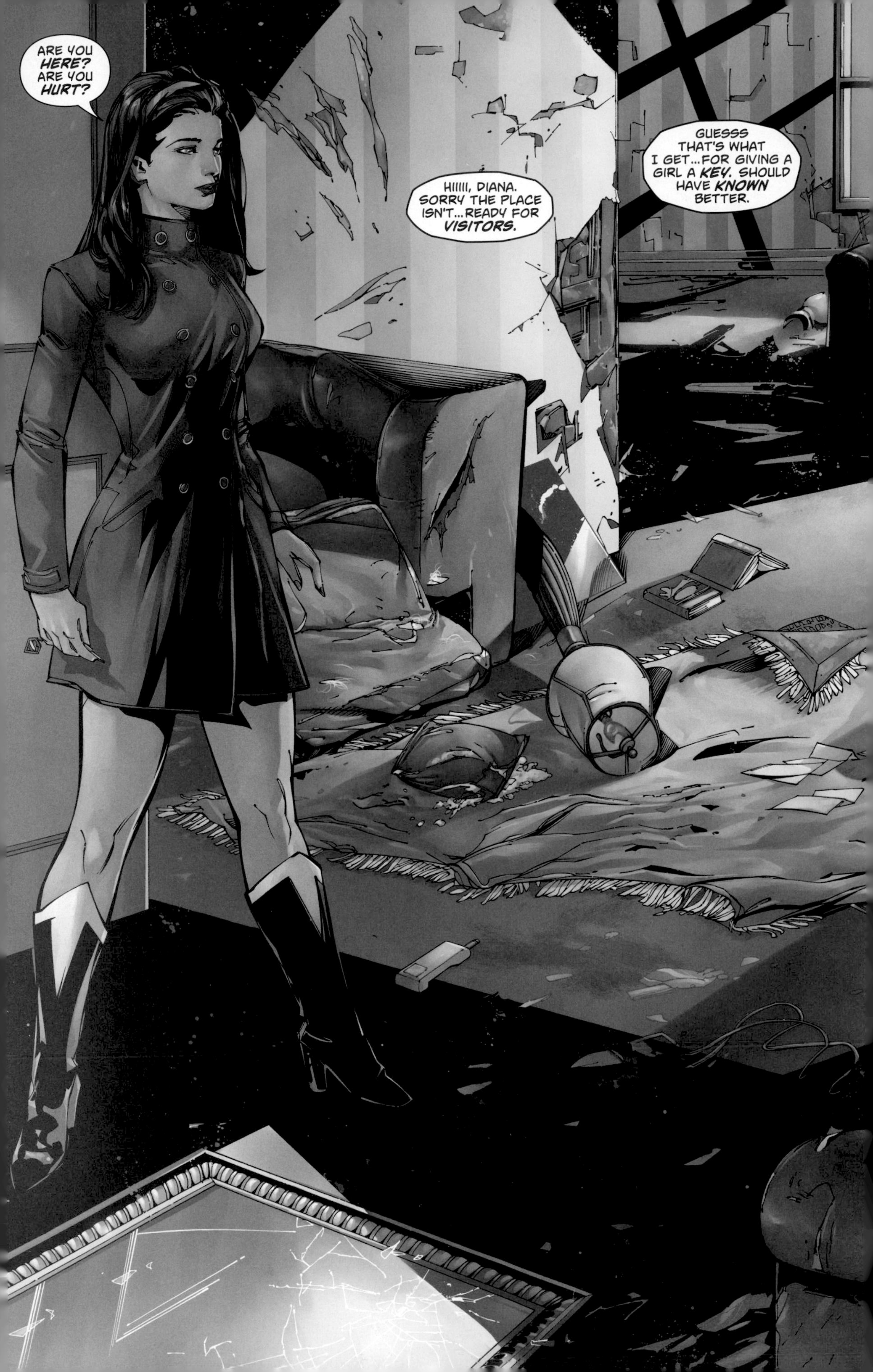
ARE YOU HERE? ARE YOU HURT?
HIIIII, DIANA. SORRY THE PLACE ISN'T...READY FOR VISITORS.
GUESSS THAT'S WHAT I GET...FOR GIVING A GIRL A KEY. SHOULD HAVE KNOWN BETTER.

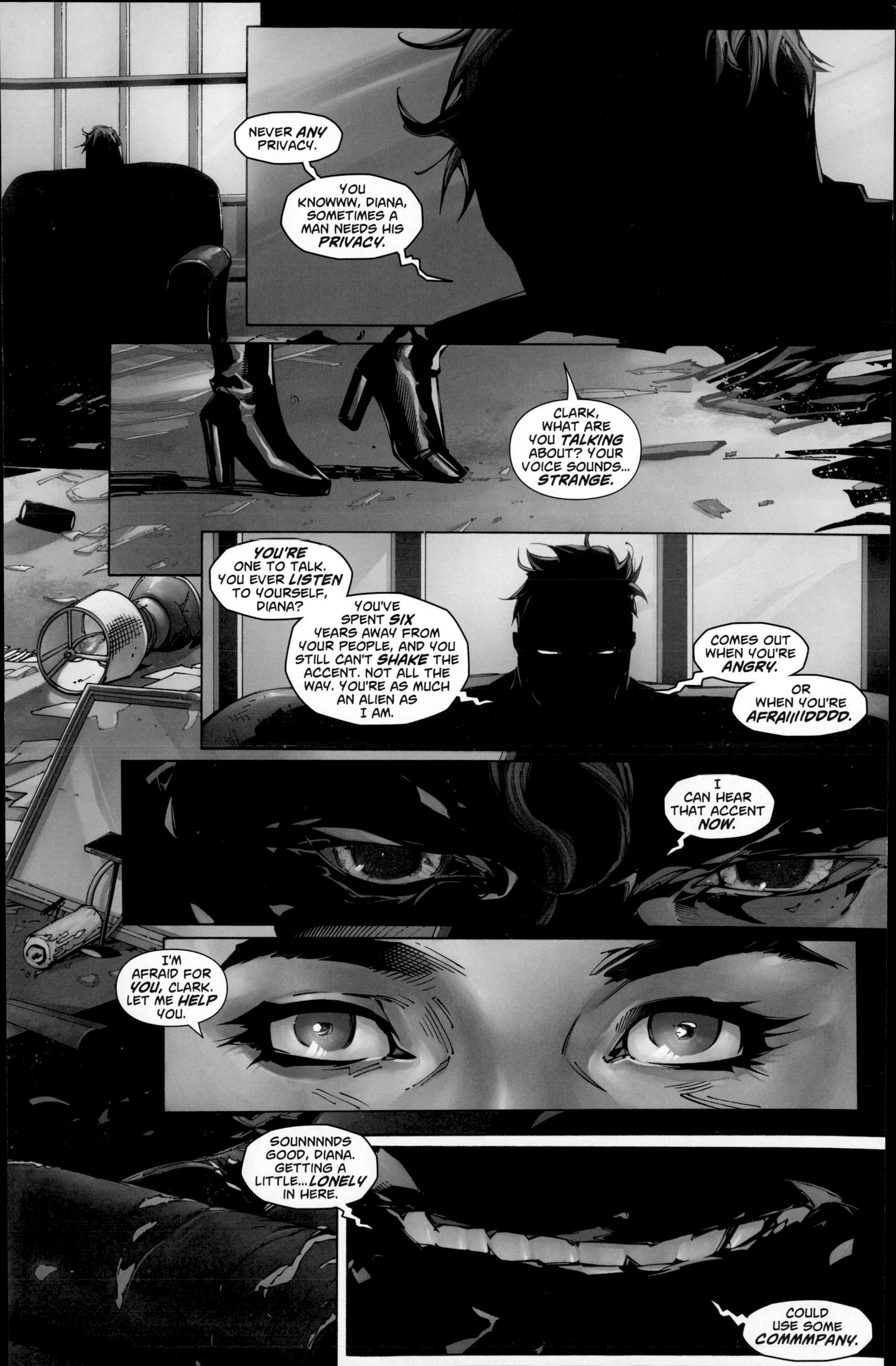
NEVER ANY PRIVACY.
YOU KNOWWW, DIANA, SOMETIMES A MAN NEEDS HIS PRIVACY.
CLARK, WHAT ARE YOU TALKING ABOUT? YOUR VOICE SOUNDS... STRANGE.
YOU'RE ONE TO TALK. YOU EVER LISTEN TO YOURSELF, DIANA?
YOU'VE SPENT SIX YEARS AWAY FROM YOUR PEOPLE, AND YOU STILL CAN'T SHAKE THE ACCENT. NOT ALL THE WAY. YOU'RE AS MUCH AN ALIEN AS I AM.
COMES OUT WHEN YOU'RE ANGRY.
OR WHEN YOU'RE AFRAIIIIDDDD.
I CAN HEAR THAT ACCENT NOW.
I'M AFRAID FOR YOU, CLARK. LET ME HELP YOU.
SOUNNNNDS GOOD, DIANA. GETTING A LITTLE... LONELY IN HERE.
COULD USE SOME COMMMPANY.

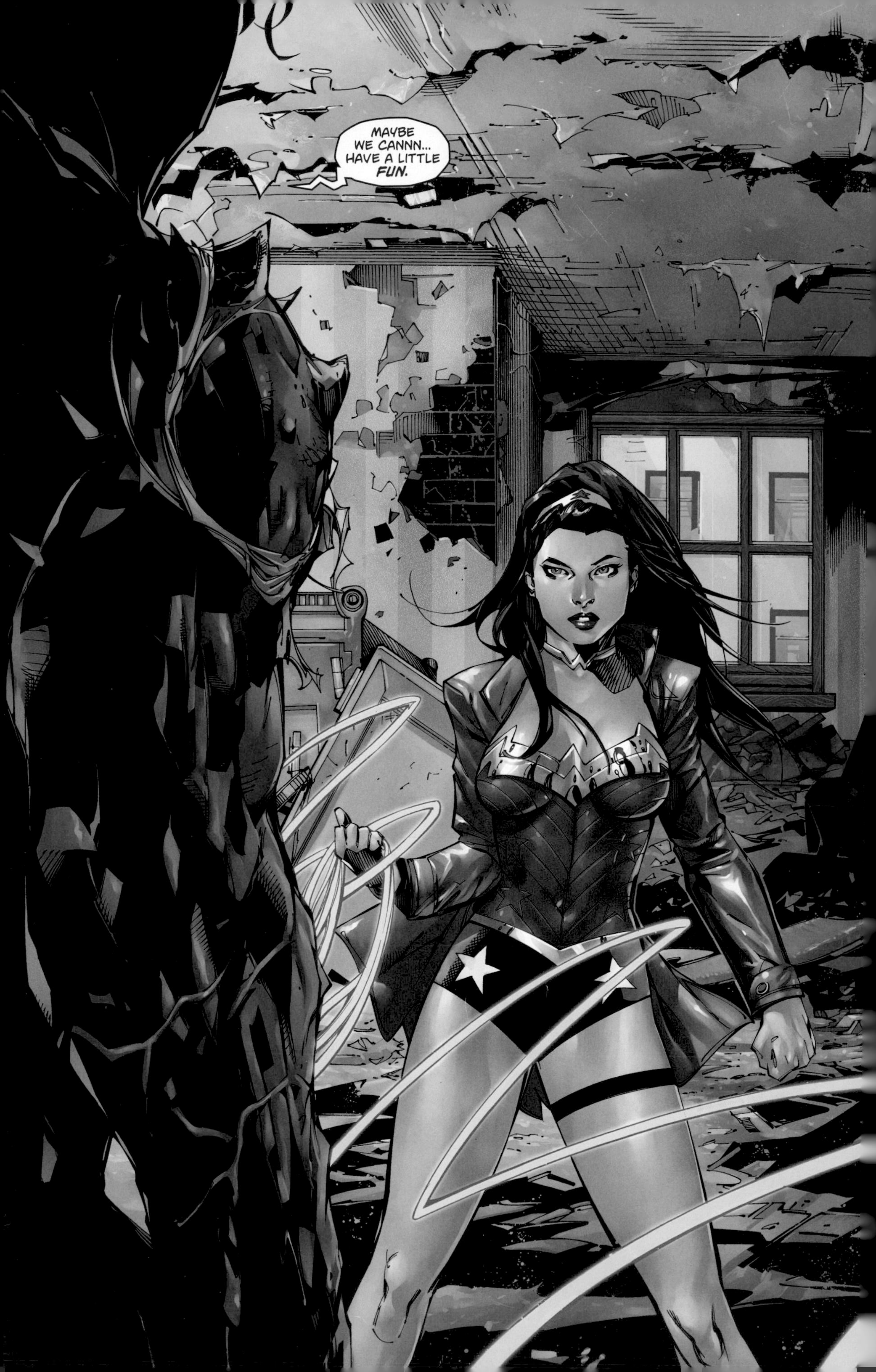
MAYBE WE CANNN... HAVE A LITTLE FUN.

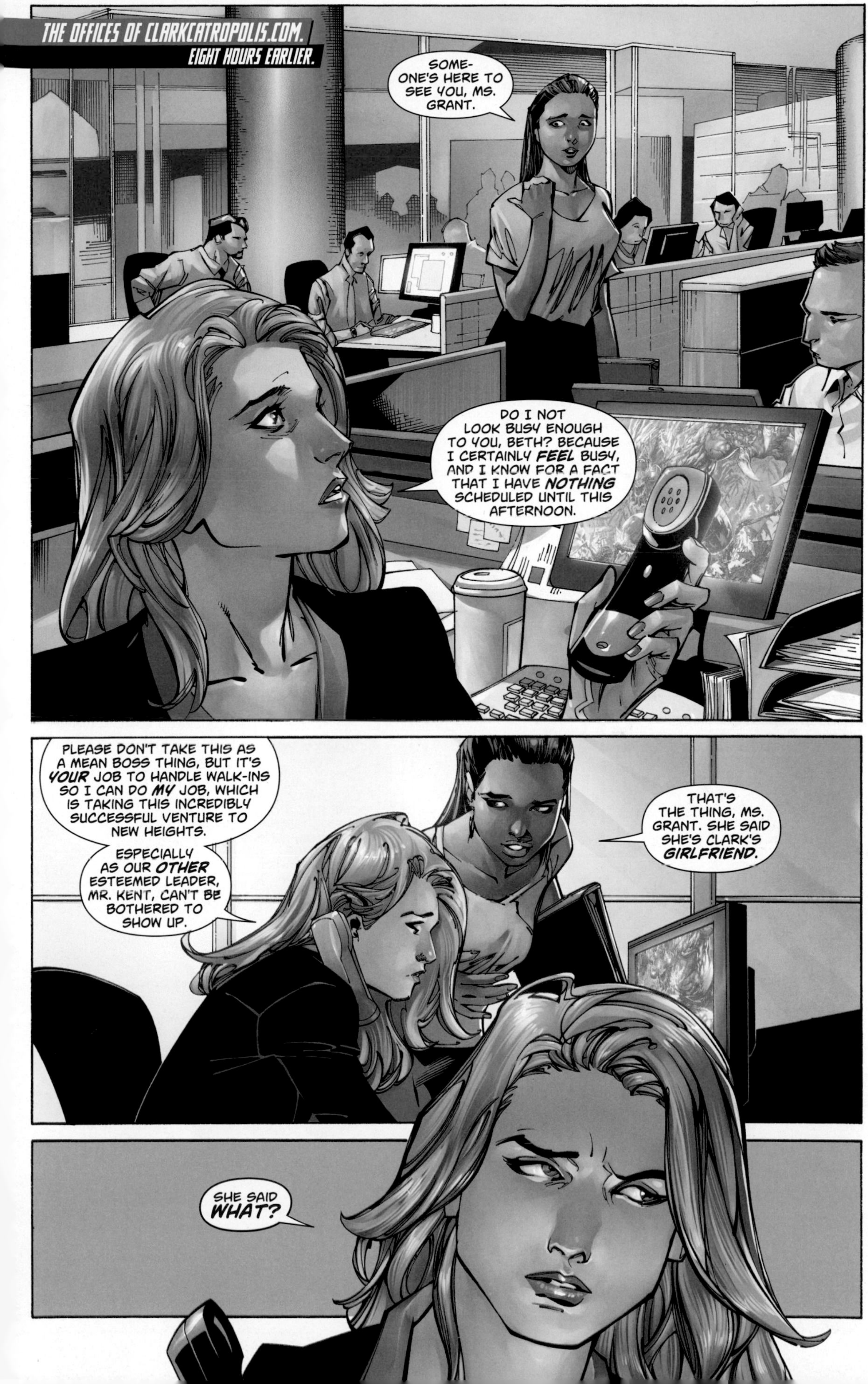
THE OFFICES OF CLARKCATROPOLIS.COM.
EIGHT HOURS EARLIER.
SOME-ONE'S HERE TO SEE YOU, MS. GRANT.
DO I NOT LOOK BUSY ENOUGH TO YOU, BETH? BECAUSE I CERTAINLY FEEL BUSY, AND I KNOW FOR A FACT THAT I HAVE NOTHING SCHEDULED UNTIL THIS AFTERNOON.
PLEASE DON'T TAKE THIS AS A MEAN BOSS THING, BUT IT'S YOUR JOB TO HANDLE WALK-INS SO I CAN DO MY JOB, WHICH IS TAKING THIS INCREDIBLY SUCCESSFUL VENTURE TO NEW HEIGHTS.
ESPECIALLY AS OUR OTHER ESTEEMED LEADER, MR. KENT, CAN'T BE BOTHERED TO SHOW UP.
THAT'S THE THING, MS. GRANT. SHE SAID SHE'S CLARK'S GIRLFRIEND.
SHE SAID WHAT?

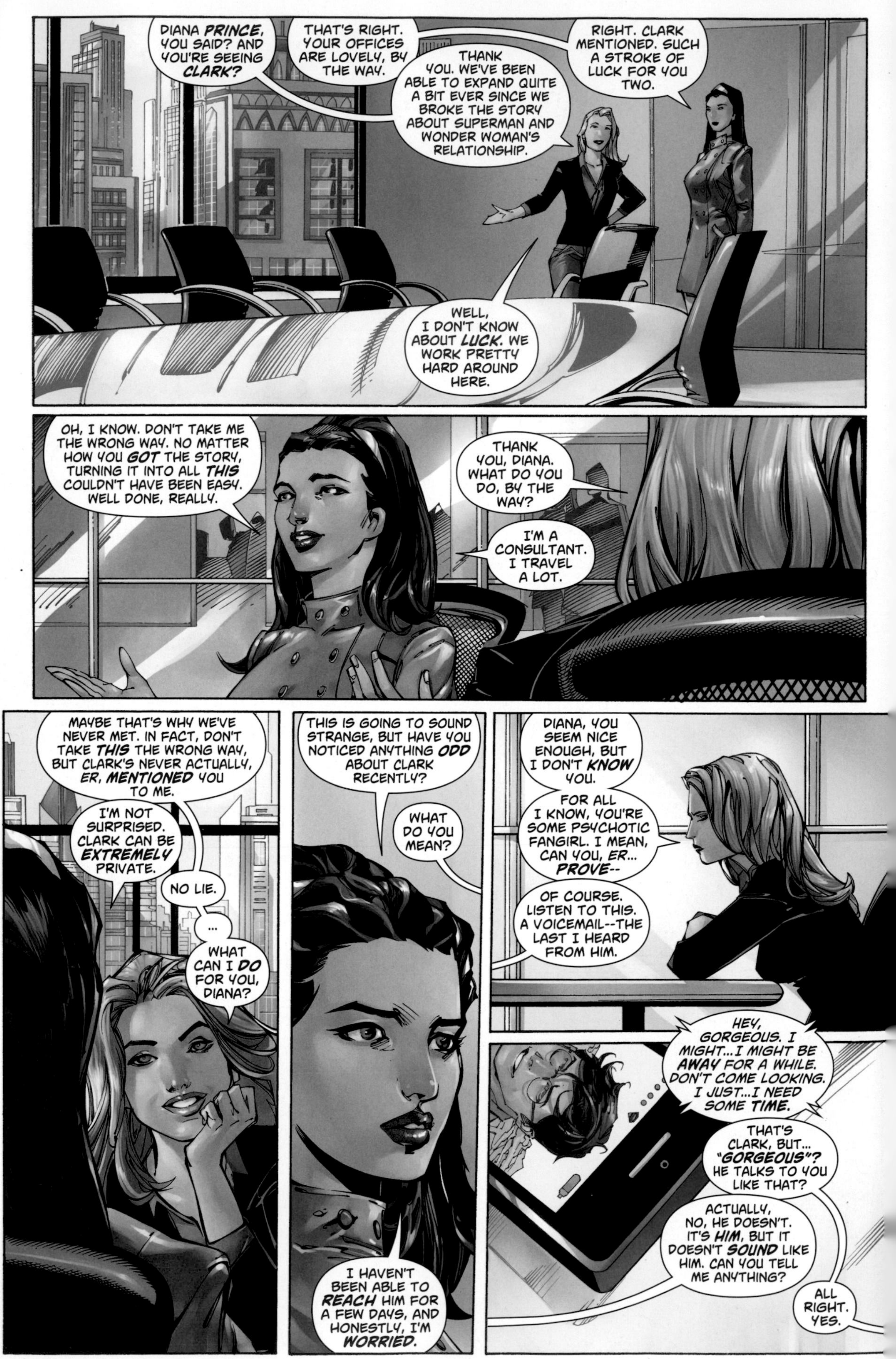
DIANA PRINCE, YOU SAID? AND YOU'RE SEEING CLARK?
THAT'S RIGHT. YOUR OFFICES ARE LOVELY, BY THE WAY.
THANK YOU. WE'VE BEEN ABLE TO EXPAND QUITE A BIT EVER SINCE WE BROKE THE STORY ABOUT SUPERMAN AND WONDER WOMAN'S RELATIONSHIP.
RIGHT. CLARK MENTIONED. SUCH A STROKE OF LUCK FOR YOU TWO.
WELL, I DON'T KNOW ABOUT LUCK. WE WORK PRETTY HARD AROUND HERE.
OH, I KNOW. DON'T TAKE ME THE WRONG WAY. NO MATTER HOW YOU GOT THE STORY, TURNING IT INTO ALL THIS COULDN'T HAVE BEEN EASY. WELL DONE, REALLY.
THANK YOU, DIANA. WHAT DO YOU DO, BY THE WAY?
I'M A CONSULTANT. I TRAVEL A LOT.
MAYBE THAT'S WHY WE'VE NEVER MET. IN FACT, DON'T TAKE THIS THE WRONG WAY, BUT CLARK'S NEVER ACTUALLY, ER, MENTIONED YOU TO ME.
I'M NOT SURPRISED. CLARK CAN BE EXTREMELY PRIVATE.
NO LIE.
...
WHAT CAN I DO FOR YOU, DIANA?
THIS IS GOING TO SOUND STRANGE, BUT HAVE YOU NOTICED ANYTHING ODD ABOUT CLARK RECENTLY?
WHAT DO YOU MEAN?
I HAVEN'T BEEN ABLE TO REACH HIM FOR A FEW DAYS, AND HONESTLY, I'M WORRIED.
DIANA, YOU SEEM NICE ENOUGH, BUT I DON'T KNOW YOU.
FOR ALL I KNOW, YOU'RE SOME PSYCHOTIC FANGIRL. I MEAN, CAN YOU, ER... PROVE--
OF COURSE. LISTEN TO THIS. A VOICEMAIL--THE LAST I HEARD FROM HIM.
HEY, GORGEOUS. I MIGHT...I MIGHT BE AWAY FOR A WHILE. DON'T COME LOOKING. I JUST...I NEED SOME TIME.
THAT'S CLARK, BUT... "GORGEOUS"? HE TALKS TO YOU LIKE THAT?
ACTUALLY, NO, HE DOESN'T. IT'S HIM, BUT IT DOESN'T SOUND LIKE HIM. CAN YOU TELL ME ANYTHING?
ALL RIGHT. YES.

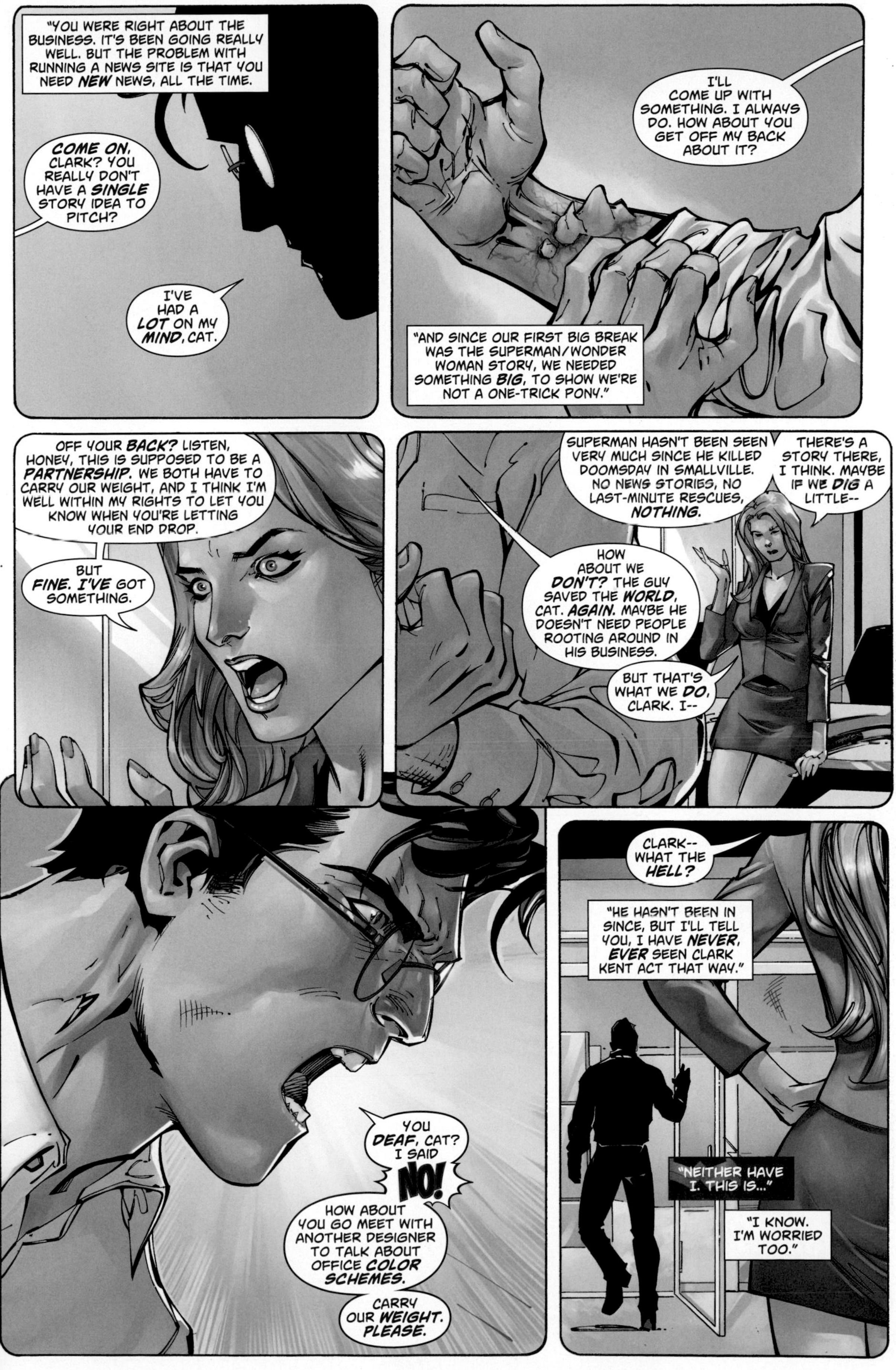
"YOU WERE RIGHT ABOUT THE BUSINESS. IT'S BEEN GOING REALLY WELL. BUT THE PROBLEM WITH RUNNING A NEWS SITE IS THAT YOU NEED NEW NEWS, ALL THE TIME.
COME ON, CLARK? YOU REALLY DON'T HAVE A SINGLE STORY IDEA TO PITCH?
I'VE HAD A LOT ON MY MIND, CAT.
I'LL COME UP WITH SOMETHING. I ALWAYS DO. HOW ABOUT YOU GET OFF MY BACK ABOUT IT?
"AND SINCE OUR FIRST BIG BREAK WAS THE SUPERMAN/WONDER WOMAN STORY, WE NEEDED SOMETHING BIG, TO SHOW WE'RE NOT A ONE-TRICK PONY."
OFF YOUR BACK? LISTEN, HONEY, THIS IS SUPPOSED TO BE A PARTNERSHIP. WE BOTH HAVE TO CARRY OUR WEIGHT, AND I THINK I'M WELL WITHIN MY RIGHTS TO LET YOU KNOW WHEN YOU'RE LETTING YOUR END DROP.
BUT FINE. I'VE GOT SOMETHING.
SUPERMAN HASN'T BEEN SEEN VERY MUCH SINCE HE KILLED DOOMSDAY IN SMALLVILLE. NO NEWS STORIES, NO LAST-MINUTE RESCUES, NOTHING.
THERE'S A STORY THERE, I THINK. MAYBE IF WE DIG A LITTLE--
HOW ABOUT WE DON'T? THE GUY SAVED THE WORLD, CAT. AGAIN. MAYBE HE DOESN'T NEED PEOPLE ROOTING AROUND IN HIS BUSINESS.
BUT THAT'S WHAT WE DO, CLARK. I--
YOU DEAF, CAT? I SAID
NO!
HOW ABOUT YOU GO MEET WITH ANOTHER DESIGNER TO TALK ABOUT OFFICE COLOR SCHEMES.
CARRY OUR WEIGHT. PLEASE.
CLARK-- WHAT THE HELL?
"HE HASN'T BEEN IN SINCE, BUT I'LL TELL YOU, I HAVE NEVER, EVER SEEN CLARK KENT ACT THAT WAY."
"NEITHER HAVE I. THIS IS..."
"I KNOW. I'M WORRIED TOO."

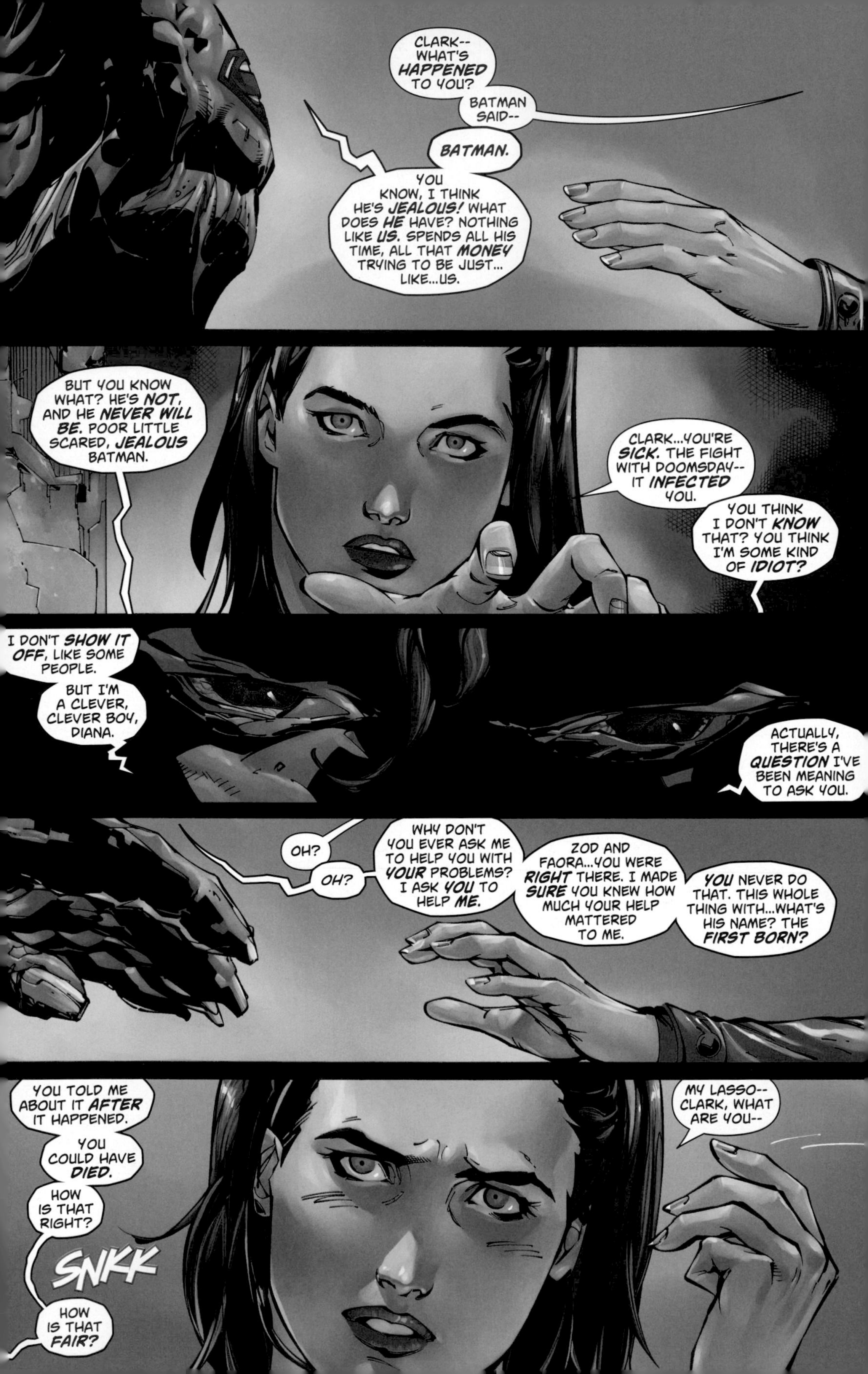
CLARK-- WHAT'S HAPPENED TO YOU?
BATMAN SAID--
BATMAN.
YOU KNOW, I THINK HE'S JEALOUS! WHAT DOES HE HAVE? NOTHING LIKE US. SPENDS ALL HIS TIME, ALL THAT MONEY TRYING TO BE JUST... LIKE...US.
BUT YOU KNOW WHAT? HE'S NOT, AND HE NEVER WILL BE. POOR LITTLE SCARED, JEALOUS BATMAN.
CLARK...YOU'RE SICK. THE FIGHT WITH DOOMSDAY-- IT INFECTED YOU.
YOU THINK I DON'T KNOW THAT? YOU THINK I'M SOME KIND OF IDIOT?
I DON'T SHOW IT OFF, LIKE SOME PEOPLE.
BUT I'M A CLEVER, CLEVER BOY, DIANA.
ACTUALLY, THERE'S A QUESTION I'VE BEEN MEANING TO ASK YOU.
OH?
OH?
WHY DON'T YOU EVER ASK ME TO HELP YOU WITH YOUR PROBLEMS? I ASK YOU TO HELP ME.
ZOD AND FAORA...YOU WERE RIGHT THERE. I MADE SURE YOU KNEW HOW MUCH YOUR HELP MATTERED TO ME.
YOU NEVER DO THAT. THIS WHOLE THING WITH...WHAT'S HIS NAME? THE FIRST BORN?
YOU TOLD ME ABOUT IT AFTER IT HAPPENED.
YOU COULD HAVE DIED.
HOW IS THAT RIGHT?
SNKK
HOW IS THAT FAIR?
MY LASSO-- CLARK, WHAT ARE YOU--

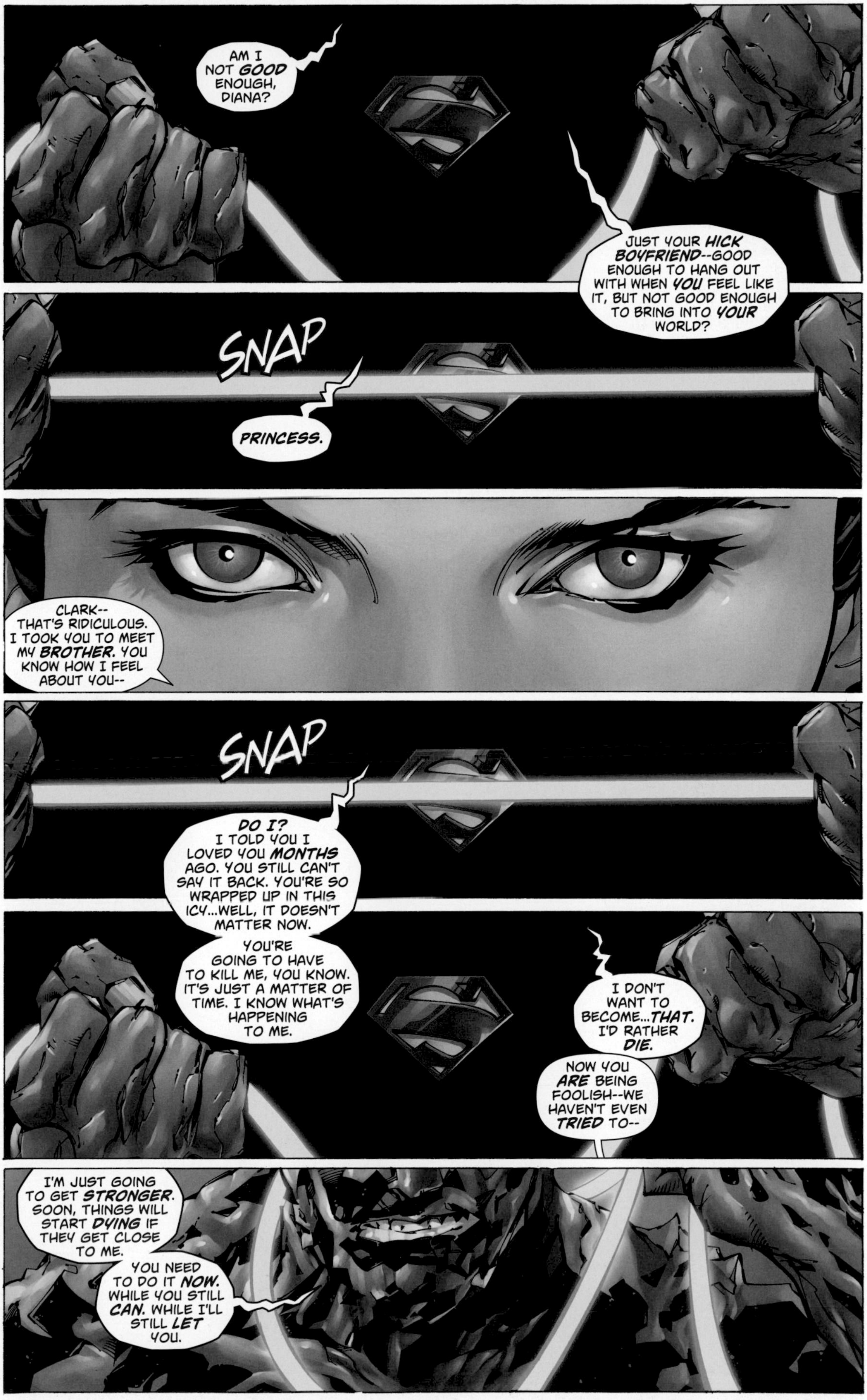

AM I NOT GOOD ENOUGH, DIANA?
JUST YOUR HICK BOYFRIEND--GOOD ENOUGH TO HANG OUT WITH WHEN YOU FEEL LIKE IT, BUT NOT GOOD ENOUGH TO BRING INTO YOUR WORLD?
SNAP
PRINCESS.
CLARK-- THAT'S RIDICULOUS. I TOOK YOU TO MEET MY BROTHER. YOU KNOW HOW I FEEL ABOUT YOU--
SNAP
DO I? I TOLD YOU I LOVED YOU MONTHS AGO. YOU STILL CAN'T SAY IT BACK. YOU'RE SO WRAPPED UP IN THIS ICY...WELL, IT DOESN'T MATTER NOW.
YOU'RE GOING TO HAVE TO KILL ME, YOU KNOW. IT'S JUST A MATTER OF TIME. I KNOW WHAT'S HAPPENING TO ME.
I DON'T WANT TO BECOME...THAT. I'D RATHER DIE.
NOW YOU ARE BEING FOOLISH--WE HAVEN'T EVEN TRIED TO--
I'M JUST GOING TO GET STRONGER. SOON, THINGS WILL START DYING IF THEY GET CLOSE TO ME.
YOU NEED TO DO IT NOW. WHILE YOU STILL CAN. WHILE I'LL STILL LET YOU.

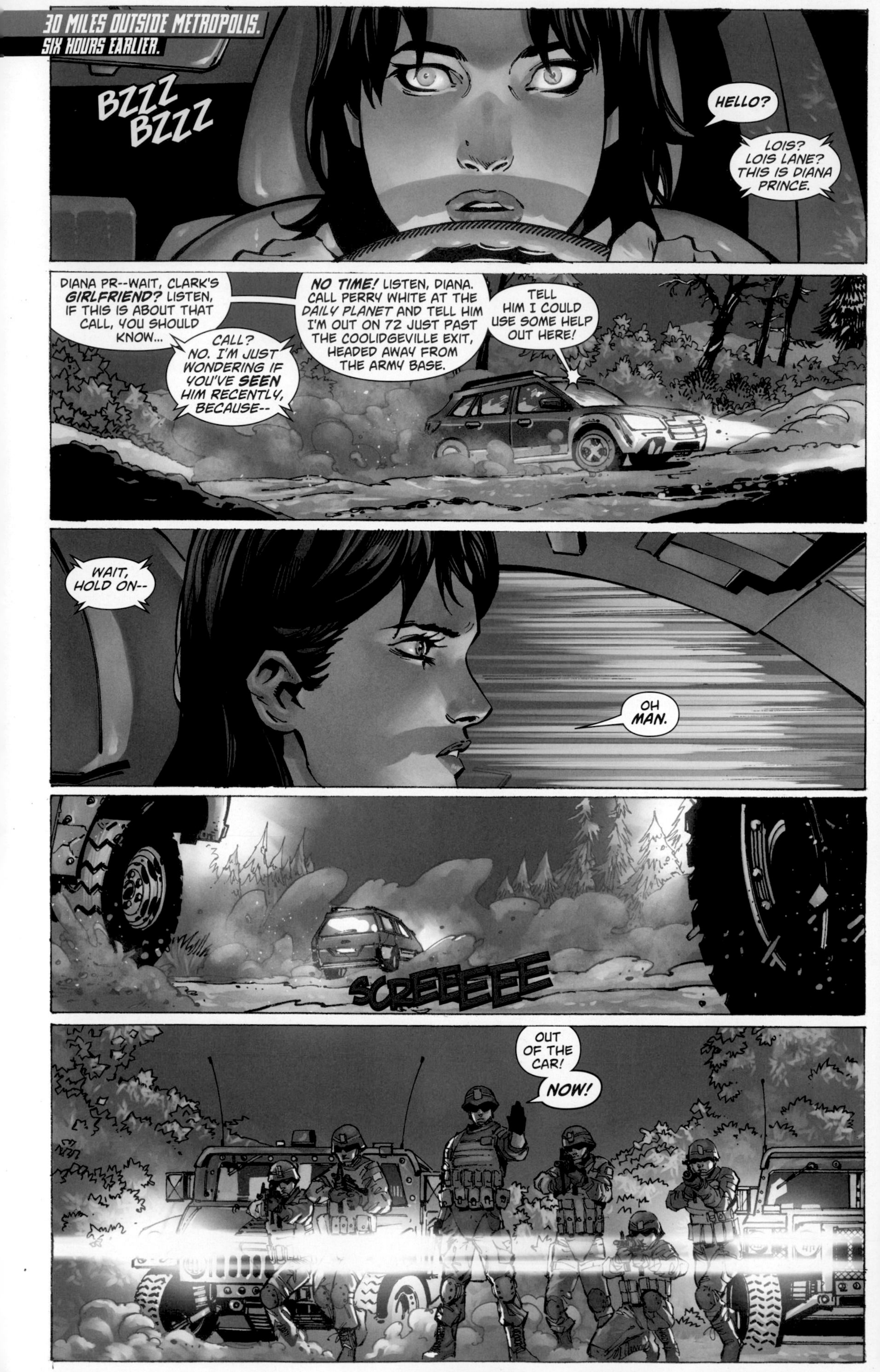
30 MILES OUTSIDE METROPOLIS.
SIX HOURS EARLIER.
BZZZ BZZZ
HELLO?
LOIS? LOIS LANE? THIS IS DIANA PRINCE.
DIANA PR--WAIT, CLARK'S GIRLFRIEND? LISTEN, IF THIS IS ABOUT THAT CALL, YOU SHOULD KNOW...
CALL? NO. I'M JUST WONDERING IF YOU'VE SEEN HIM RECENTLY, BECAUSE--
NO TIME! LISTEN, DIANA. CALL PERRY WHITE AT THE DAILY PLANET AND TELL HIM I'M OUT ON 72 JUST PAST THE COOLIDGEVILLE EXIT, HEADED AWAY FROM THE ARMY BASE.
TELL HIM I COULD USE SOME HELP OUT HERE!
WAIT, HOLD ON--
OH MAN.
SCREEEEEE
OUT OF THE CAR!
NOW!

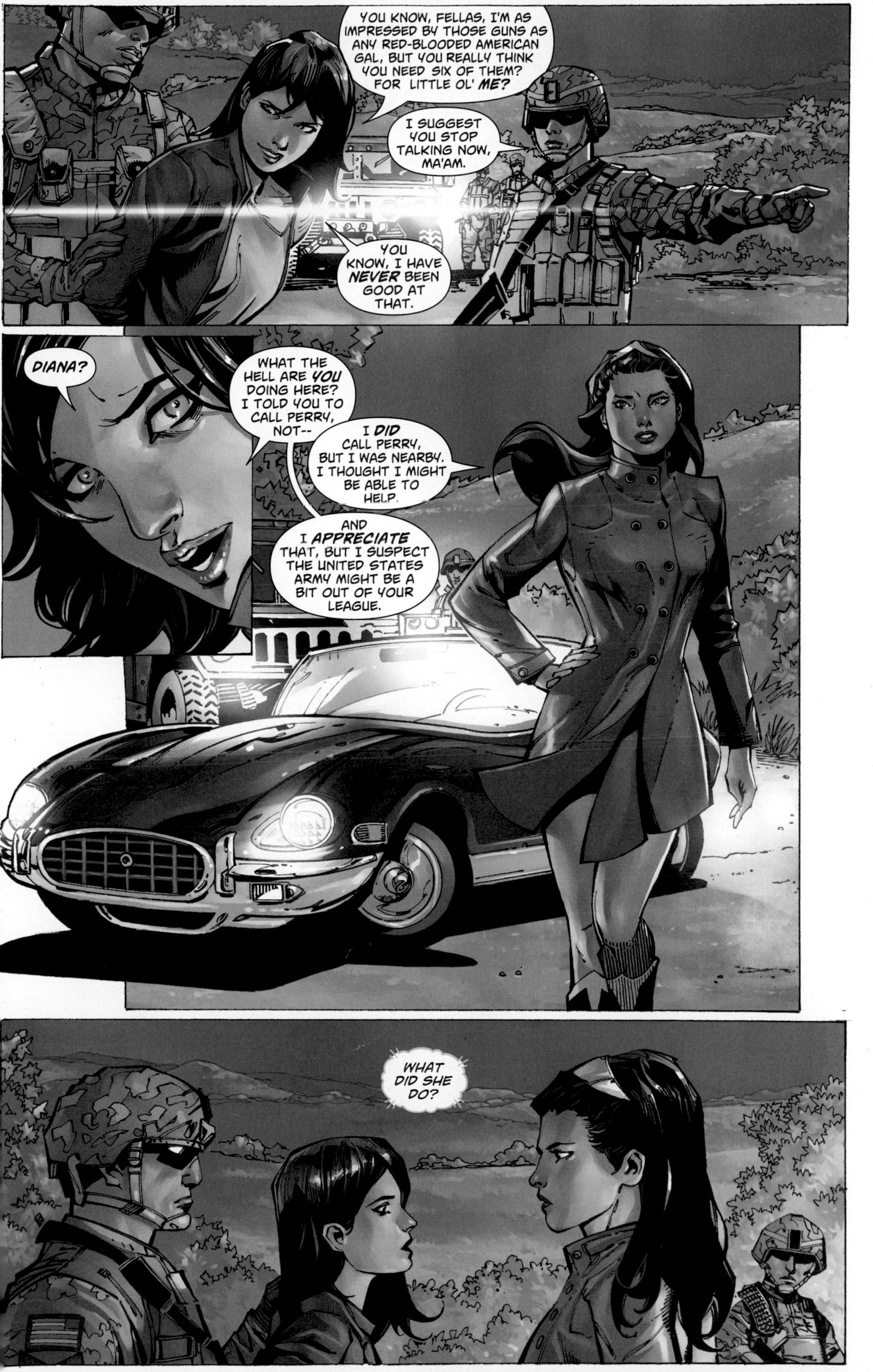
YOU KNOW, FELLAS, I'M AS IMPRESSED BY THOSE GUNS AS ANY RED-BLOODED AMERICAN GAL, BUT YOU REALLY THINK YOU NEED SIX OF THEM? FOR LITTLE OL' ME?
I SUGGEST YOU STOP TALKING NOW, MA'AM.
YOU KNOW, I HAVE NEVER BEEN GOOD AT THAT.
DIANA?
WHAT THE HELL ARE YOU DOING HERE? I TOLD YOU TO CALL PERRY, NOT--
I DID CALL PERRY, BUT I WAS NEARBY. I THOUGHT I MIGHT BE ABLE TO HELP.
AND I APPRECIATE THAT, BUT I SUSPECT THE UNITED STATES ARMY MIGHT BE A BIT OUT OF YOUR LEAGUE.
WHAT DID SHE DO?

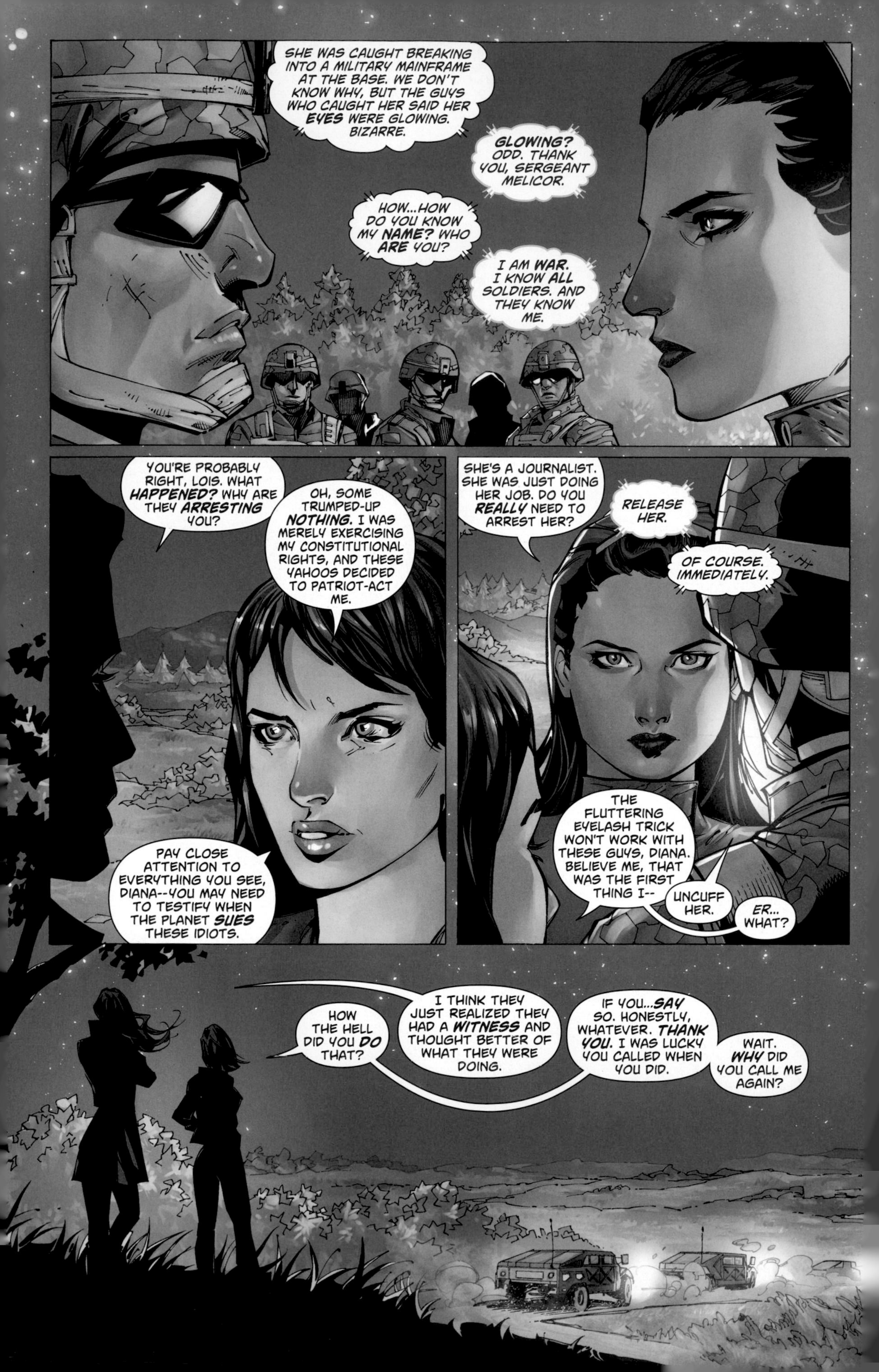
SHE WAS CAUGHT BREAKING INTO A MILITARY MAINFRAME AT THE BASE. WE DON'T KNOW WHY, BUT THE GUYS WHO CAUGHT HER SAID HER EYES WERE GLOWING. BIZARRE.
GLOWING? ODD. THANK YOU, SERGEANT MELICOR.
HOW...HOW DO YOU KNOW MY NAME? WHO ARE YOU?
I AM WAR. I KNOW ALL SOLDIERS. AND THEY KNOW ME.
YOU'RE PROBABLY RIGHT, LOIS. WHAT HAPPENED? WHY ARE THEY ARRESTING YOU?
OH, SOME TRUMPED-UP NOTHING. I WAS MERELY EXERCISING MY CONSTITUTIONAL RIGHTS, AND THESE YAHOOS DECIDED TO PATRIOT-ACT ME.
PAY CLOSE ATTENTION TO EVERYTHING YOU SEE, DIANA--YOU MAY NEED TO TESTIFY WHEN THE PLANET SUES THESE IDIOTS.
SHE'S A JOURNALIST. SHE WAS JUST DOING HER JOB. DO YOU REALLY NEED TO ARREST HER?
RELEASE HER.
OF COURSE. IMMEDIATELY.
THE FLUTTERING EYELASH TRICK WON'T WORK WITH THESE GUYS, DIANA. BELIEVE ME, THAT WAS THE FIRST THING I--
UNCUFF HER.
ER... WHAT?
HOW THE HELL DID YOU DO THAT?
I THINK THEY JUST REALIZED THEY HAD A WITNESS AND THOUGHT BETTER OF WHAT THEY WERE DOING.
IF YOU...SAY SO. HONESTLY, WHATEVER. THANK YOU. I WAS LUCKY YOU CALLED WHEN YOU DID.
WAIT. WHY DID YOU CALL ME AGAIN?

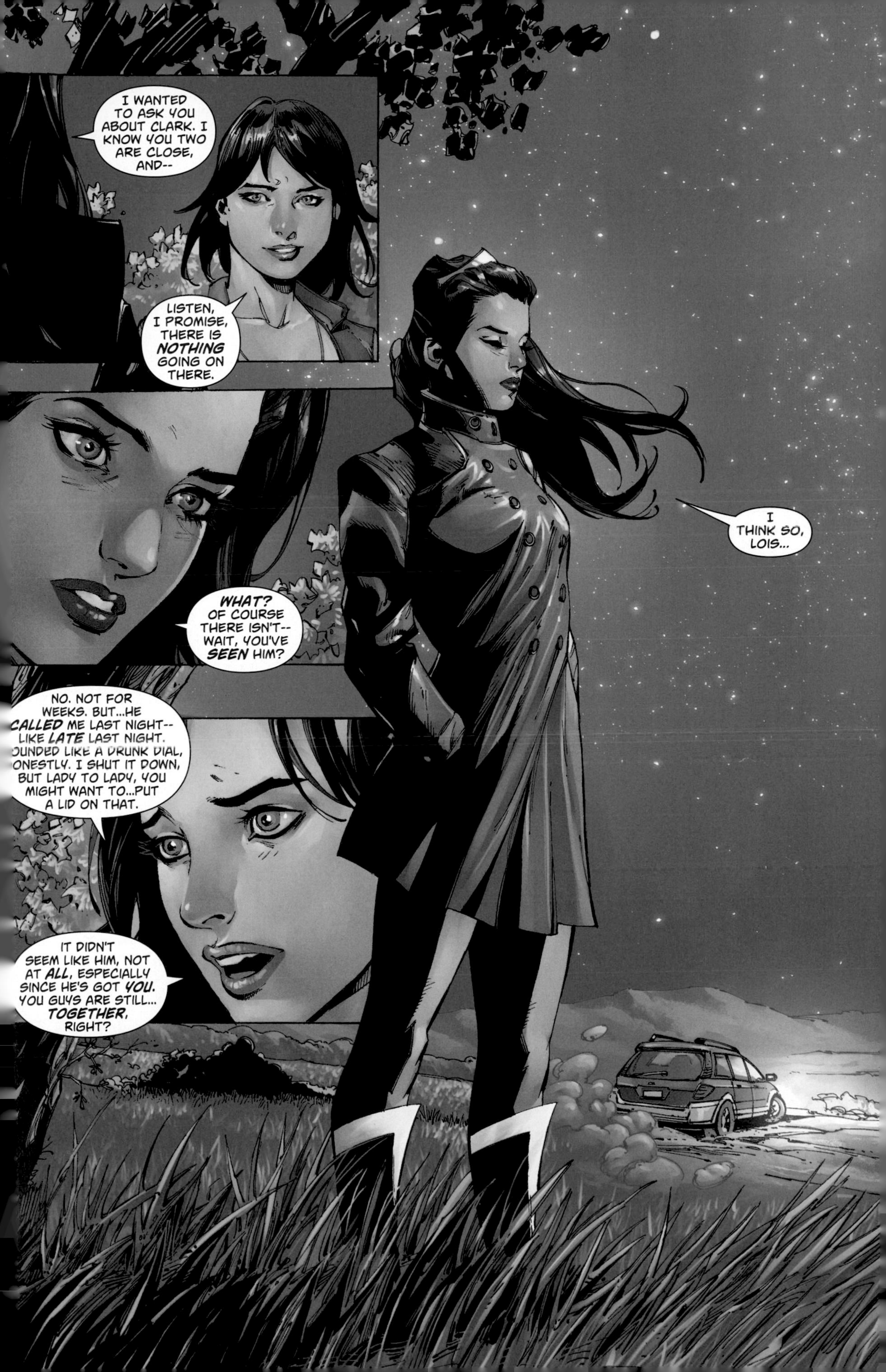
I WANTED TO ASK YOU ABOUT CLARK. I KNOW YOU TWO ARE CLOSE, AND--
LISTEN, I PROMISE, THERE IS NOTHING GOING ON THERE.
WHAT? OF COURSE THERE ISN'T-- WAIT, YOU'VE SEEN HIM?
NO. NOT FOR WEEKS. BUT...HE CALLED ME LAST NIGHT-- LIKE LATE LAST NIGHT. OUNDED LIKE A DRUNK DIAL, ONESTLY. I SHUT IT DOWN, BUT LADY TO LADY, YOU MIGHT WANT TO...PUT A LID ON THAT.
IT DIDN'T SEEM LIKE HIM, NOT AT ALL, ESPECIALLY SINCE HE'S GOT YOU. YOU GUYS ARE STILL... TOGETHER, RIGHT?
I THINK SO, LOIS...

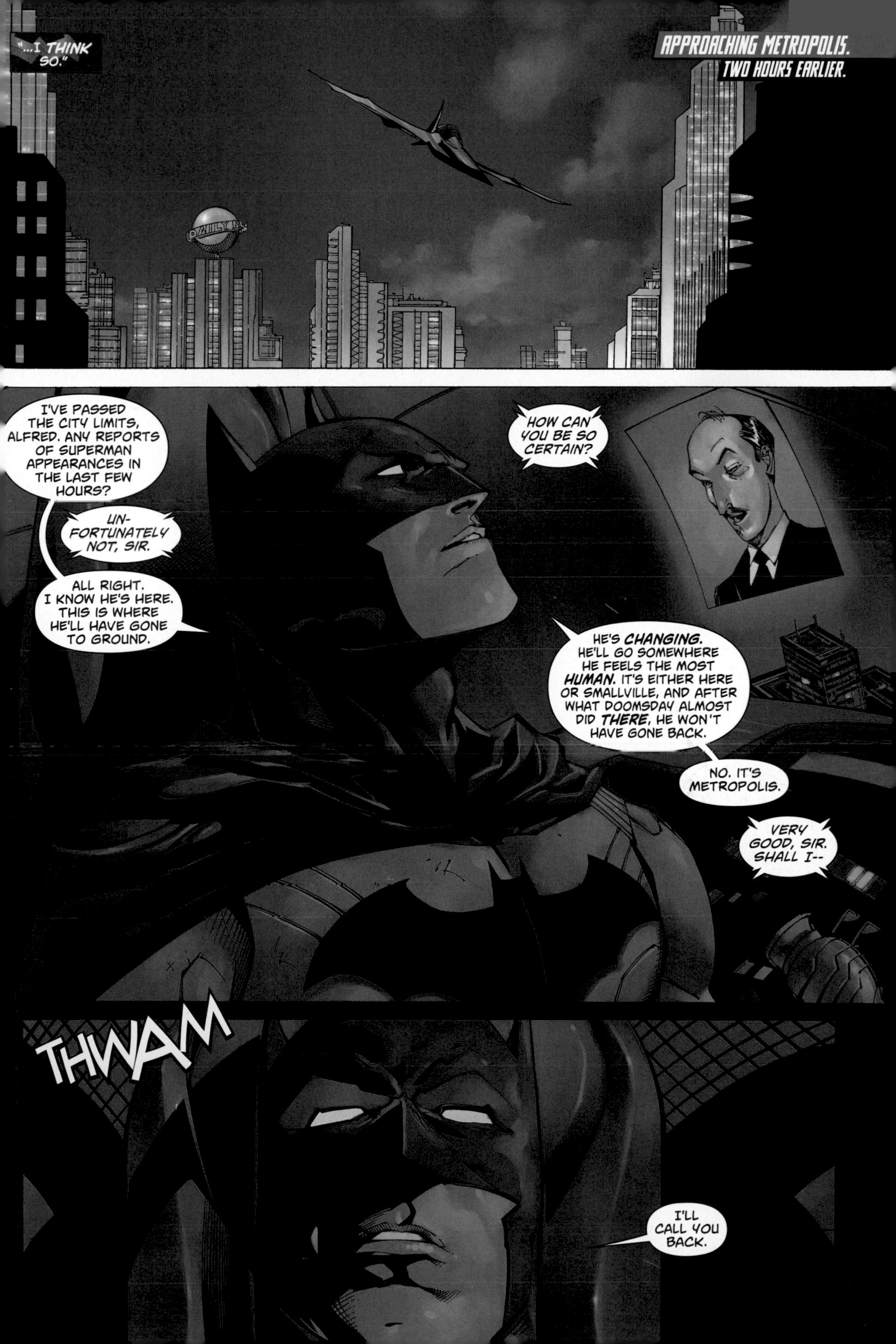
"...I THINK SO."
APPROACHING METROPOLIS.
TWO HOURS EARLIER.
I'VE PASSED THE CITY LIMITS, ALFRED. ANY REPORTS OF SUPERMAN APPEARANCES IN THE LAST FEW HOURS?
UN-FORTUNATELY NOT, SIR.
ALL RIGHT. I KNOW HE'S HERE. THIS IS WHERE HE'LL HAVE GONE TO GROUND.
HOW CAN YOU BE SO CERTAIN?
HE'S CHANGING. HE'LL GO SOMEWHERE HE FEELS THE MOST HUMAN. IT'S EITHER HERE OR SMALLVILLE, AND AFTER WHAT DOOMSDAY ALMOST DID THERE, HE WON'T HAVE GONE BACK.
NO. IT'S METROPOLIS.
VERY GOOD, SIR. SHALL I--
THWAM
I'LL CALL YOU BACK.

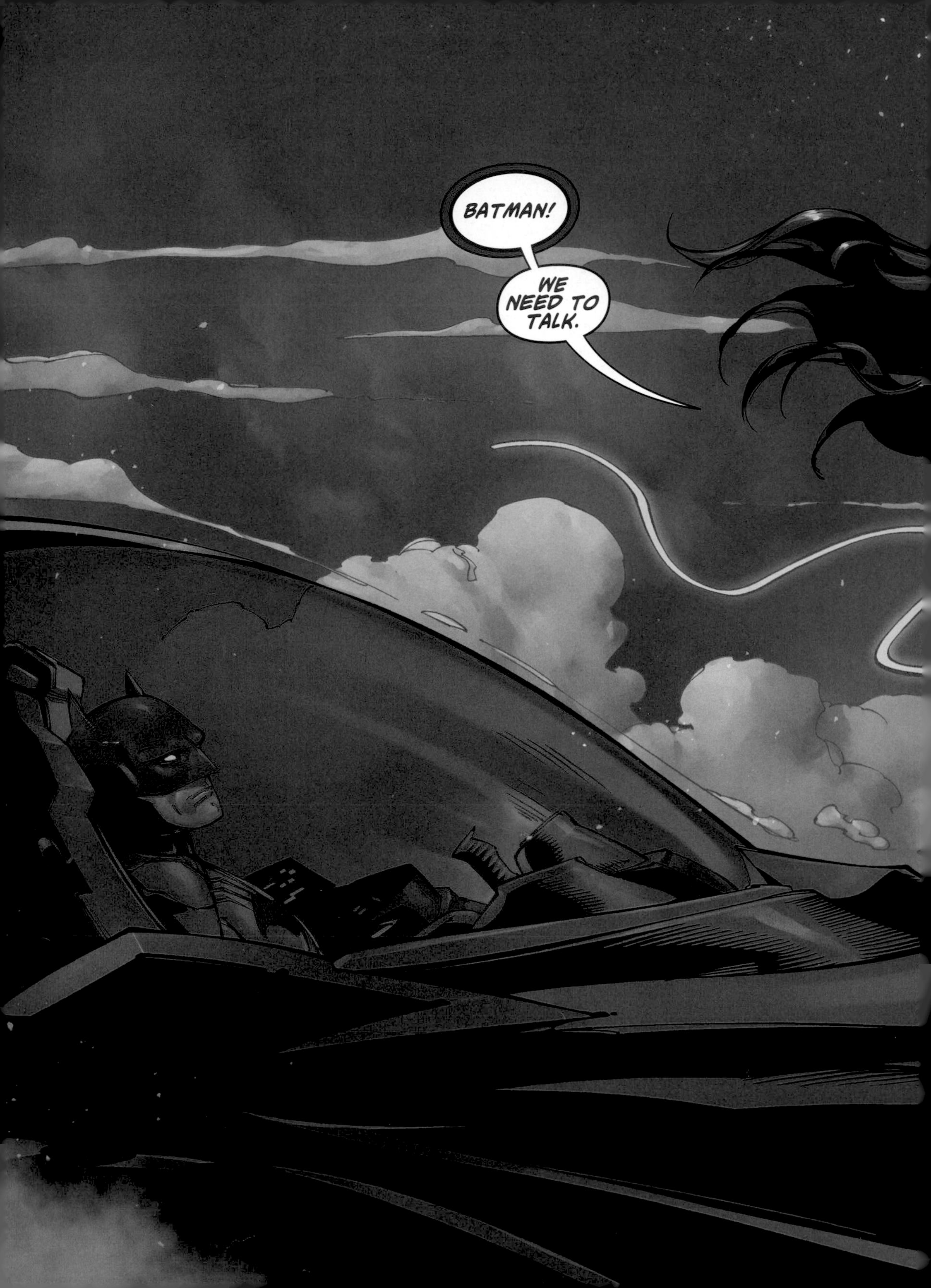
BATMAN!
WE NEED TO TALK.

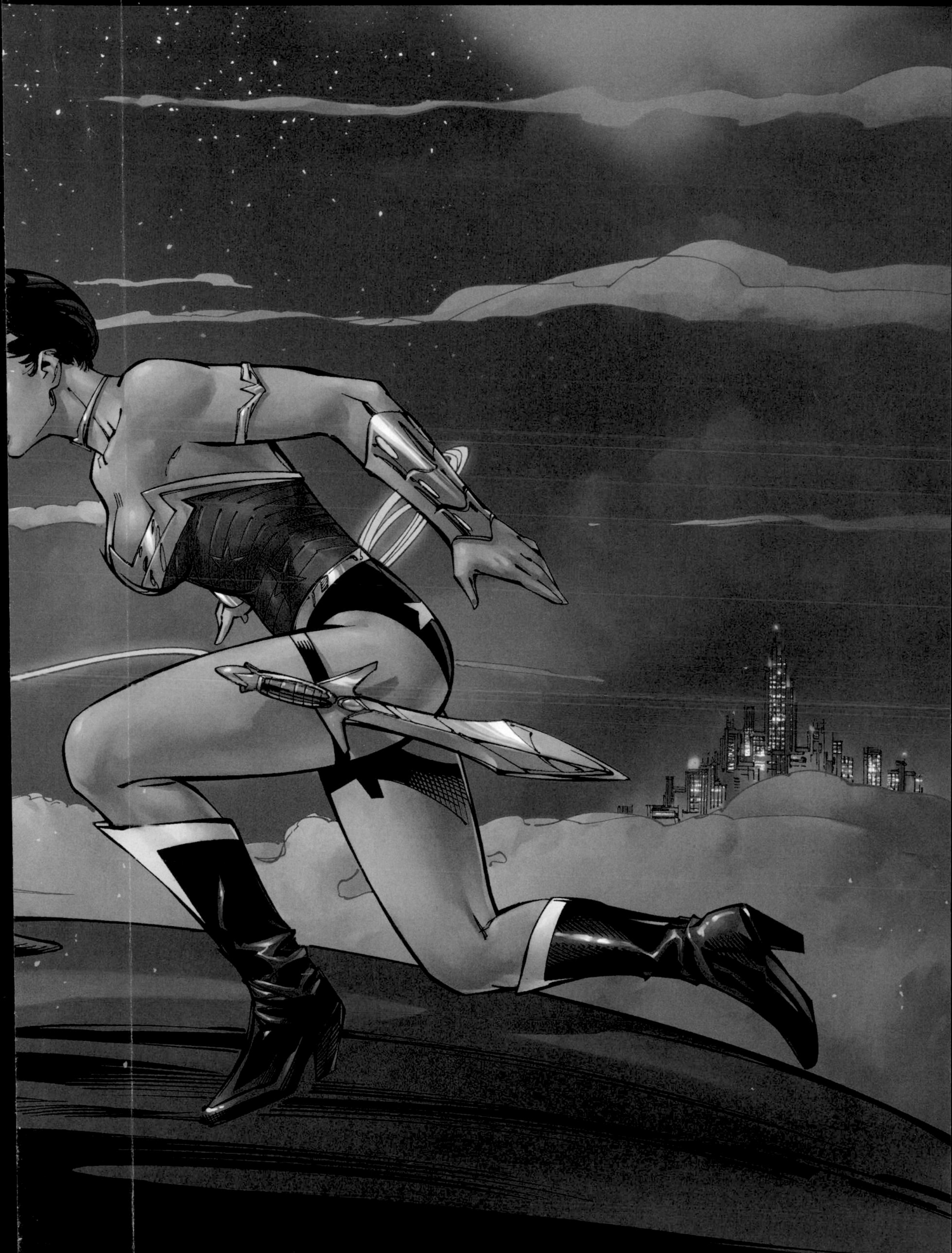

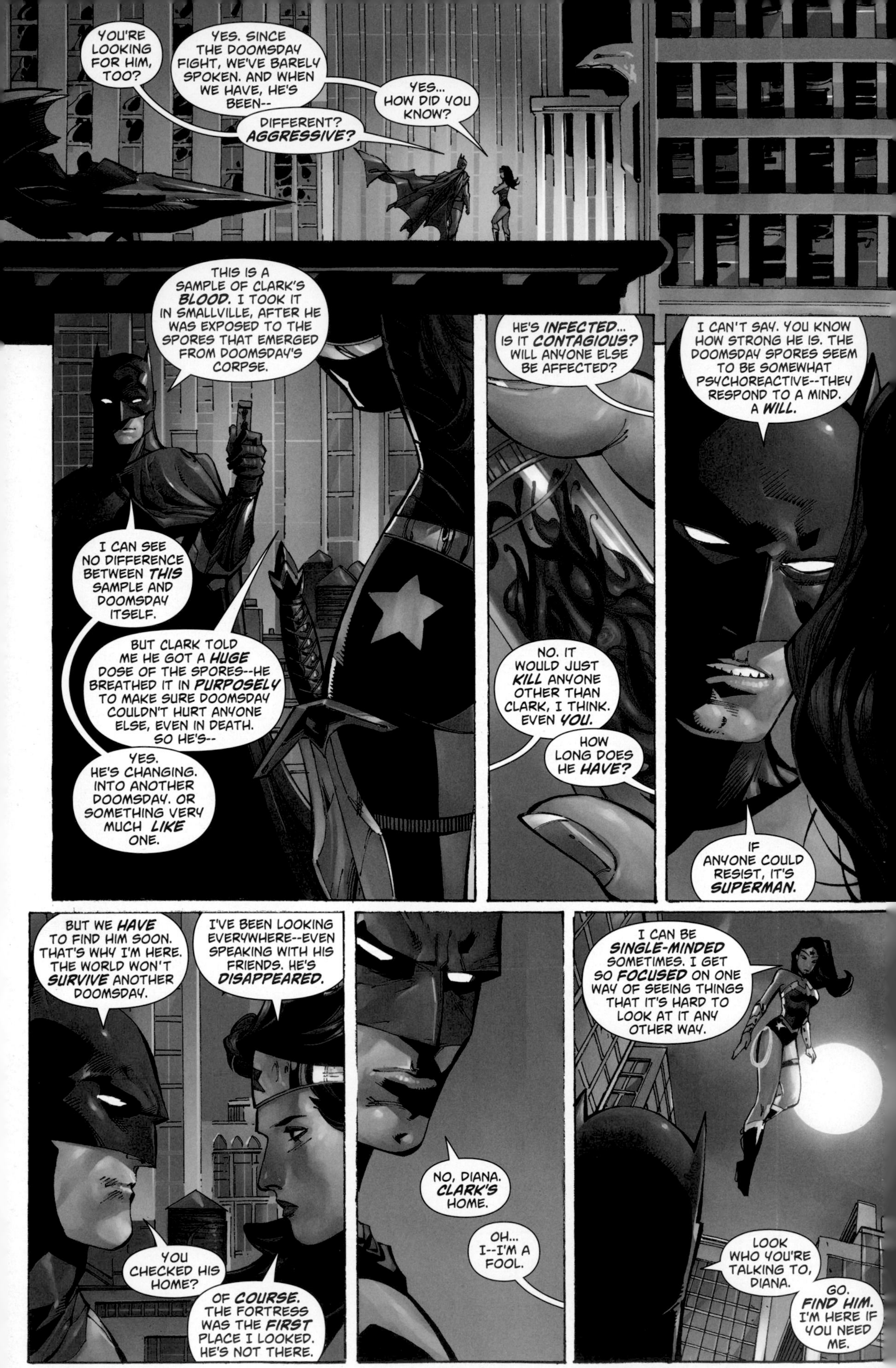
YOU'RE LOOKING FOR HIM, TOO?
YES. SINCE THE DOOMSDAY FIGHT, WE'VE BARELY SPOKEN. AND WHEN WE HAVE, HE'S BEEN--
DIFFERENT? AGGRESSIVE?
YES... HOW DID YOU KNOW?
THIS IS A SAMPLE OF CLARK'S BLOOD. I TOOK IT IN SMALLVILLE, AFTER HE WAS EXPOSED TO THE SPORES THAT EMERGED FROM DOOMSDAY'S CORPSE.
I CAN SEE NO DIFFERENCE BETWEEN THIS SAMPLE AND DOOMSDAY ITSELF.
BUT CLARK TOLD ME HE GOT A HUGE DOSE OF THE SPORES--HE BREATHED IT IN PURPOSELY TO MAKE SURE DOOMSDAY COULDN'T HURT ANYONE ELSE, EVEN IN DEATH. SO HE'S--
YES. HE'S CHANGING. INTO ANOTHER DOOMSDAY. OR SOMETHING VERY MUCH LIKE ONE.
HE'S INFECTED... IS IT CONTAGIOUS? WILL ANYONE ELSE BE AFFECTED?
NO. IT WOULD JUST KILL ANYONE OTHER THAN CLARK, I THINK. EVEN YOU.
HOW LONG DOES HE HAVE?
I CAN'T SAY. YOU KNOW HOW STRONG HE IS. THE DOOMSDAY SPORES SEEM TO BE SOMEWHAT PSYCHOREACTIVE--THEY RESPOND TO A MIND. A WILL.
IF ANYONE COULD RESIST, IT'S SUPERMAN.
BUT WE HAVE TO FIND HIM SOON. THAT'S WHY I'M HERE. THE WORLD WON'T SURVIVE ANOTHER DOOMSDAY.
I'VE BEEN LOOKING EVERYWHERE--EVEN SPEAKING WITH HIS FRIENDS. HE'S DISAPPEARED.
YOU CHECKED HIS HOME?
OF COURSE. THE FORTRESS WAS THE FIRST PLACE I LOOKED. HE'S NOT THERE.
NO, DIANA. CLARK'S HOME.
OH... I--I'M A FOOL.
I CAN BE SINGLE-MINDED SOMETIMES. I GET SO FOCUSED ON ONE WAY OF SEEING THINGS THAT IT'S HARD TO LOOK AT IT ANY OTHER WAY.
LOOK WHO YOU'RE TALKING TO, DIANA.
GO. FIND HIM. I'M HERE IF YOU NEED ME.

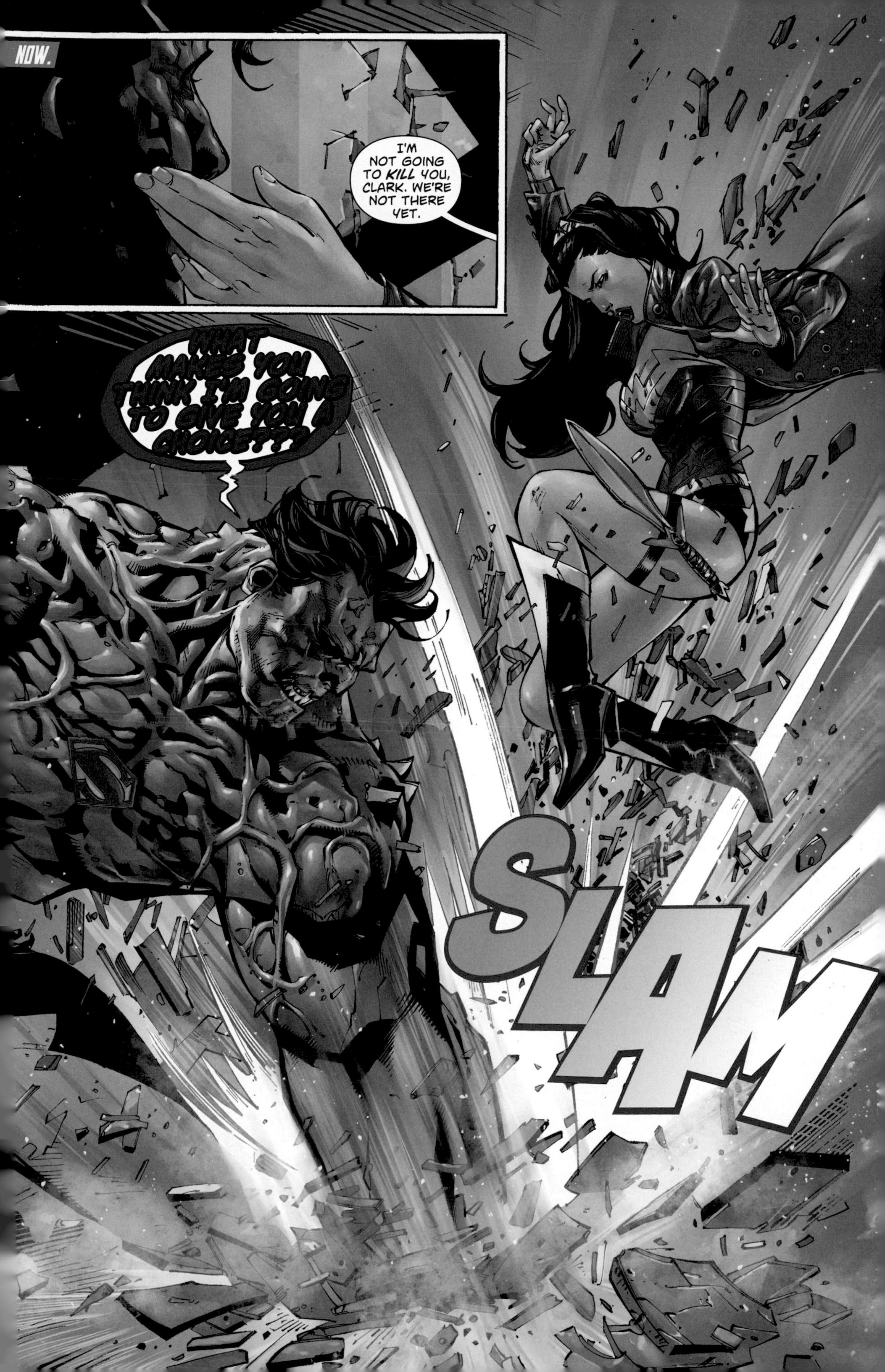
NOW.
I'M NOT GOING TO KILL YOU, CLARK. WE'RE NOT THERE YET.
WHAT MAKES YOU THINK I'M GOING TO GIVE YOU A CHOICE???
SLAM

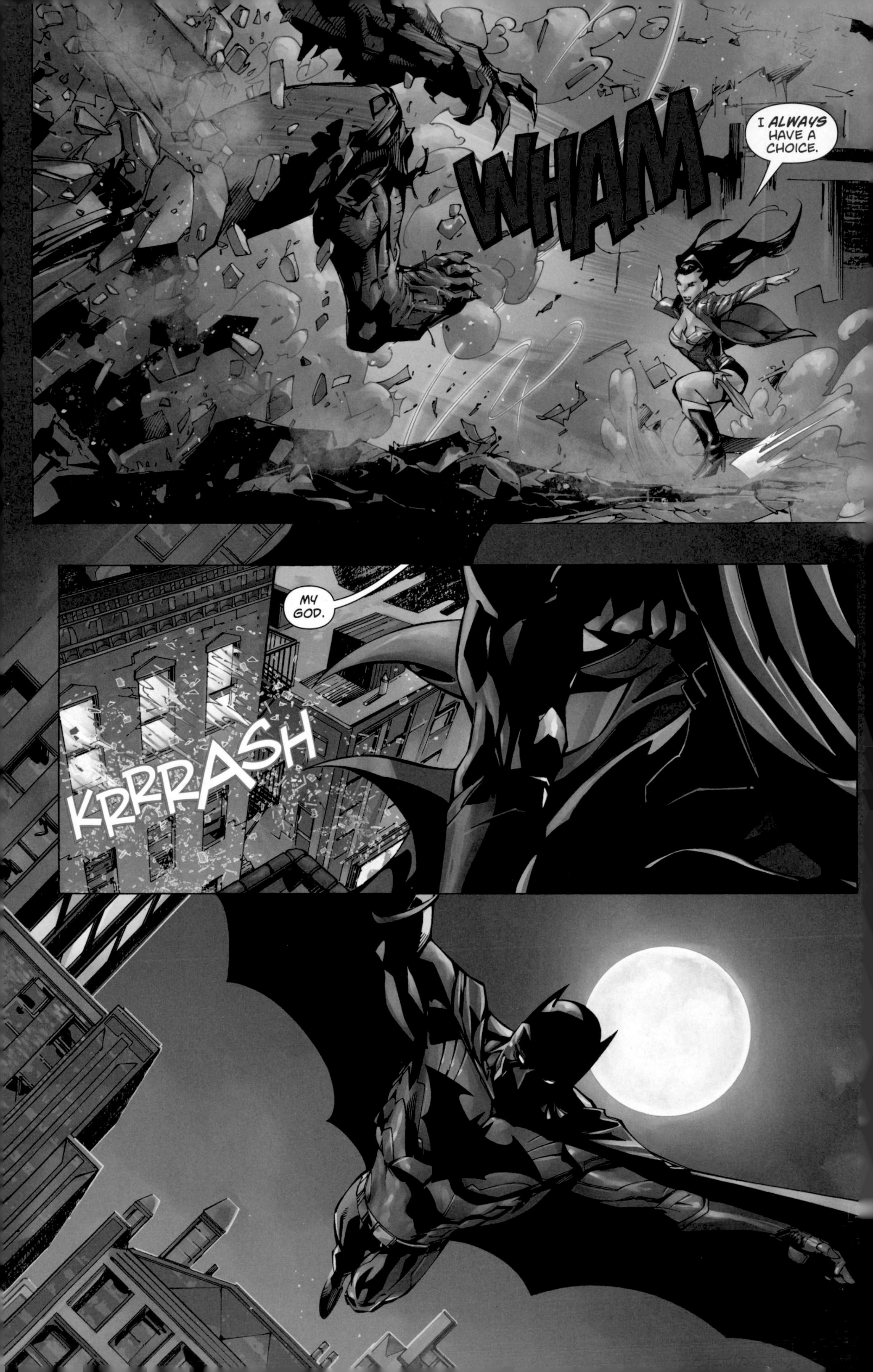
WHAM
I ALWAYS HAVE A CHOICE.
MY GOD.
KRRRASH

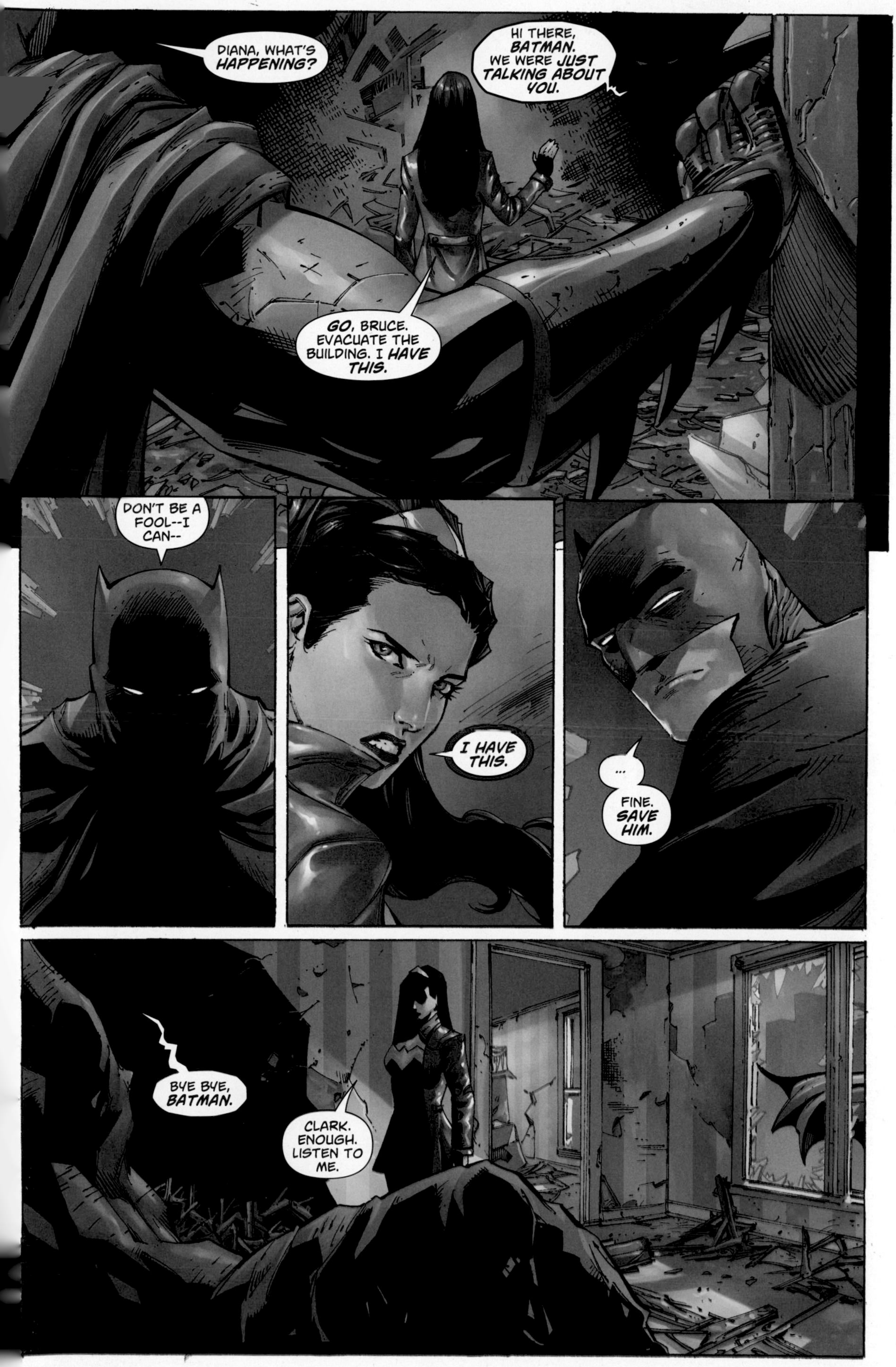
DIANA, WHAT'S HAPPENING?
HI THERE, BATMAN. WE WERE JUST TALKING ABOUT YOU.
GO, BRUCE. EVACUATE THE BUILDING. I HAVE THIS.
DON'T BE A FOOL--I CAN--
I HAVE THIS.
...
FINE. SAVE HIM.
BYE BYE, BATMAN.
CLARK. ENOUGH. LISTEN TO ME.

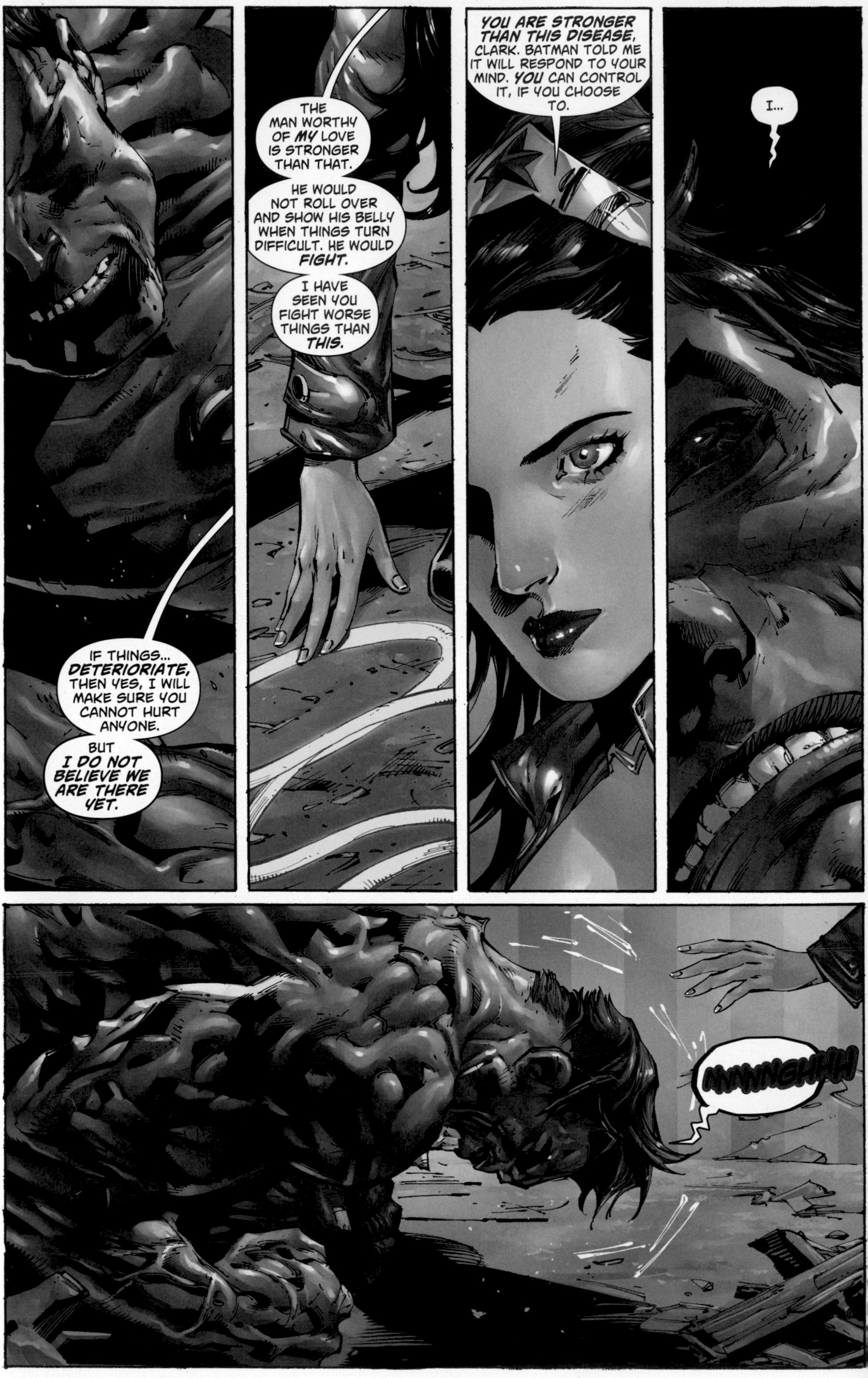
THE MAN WORTHY OF MY LOVE IS STRONGER THAN THAT.
HE WOULD NOT ROLL OVER AND SHOW HIS BELLY WHEN THINGS TURN DIFFICULT. HE WOULD FIGHT.
I HAVE SEEN YOU FIGHT WORSE THINGS THAN THIS.
IF THINGS... DETERIORIATE, THEN YES, I WILL MAKE SURE YOU CANNOT HURT ANYONE.
BUT I DO NOT BELIEVE WE ARE THERE YET.
YOU ARE STRONGER THAN THIS DISEASE, CLARK. BATMAN TOLD ME IT WILL RESPOND TO YOUR MIND. YOU CAN CONTROL IT, IF YOU CHOOSE TO.
I...
NNNNNGHHH

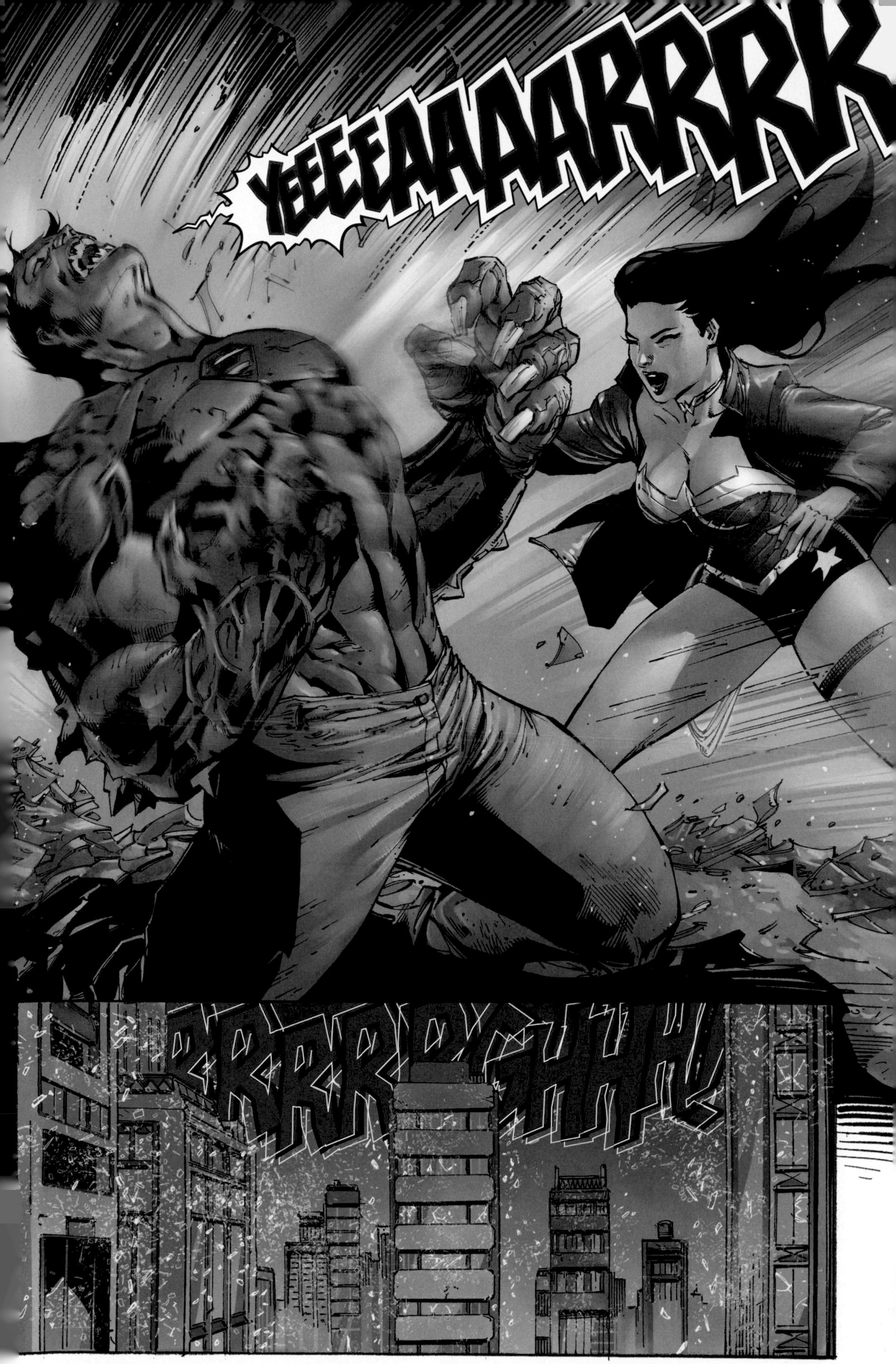
YEEEAAAARRRK

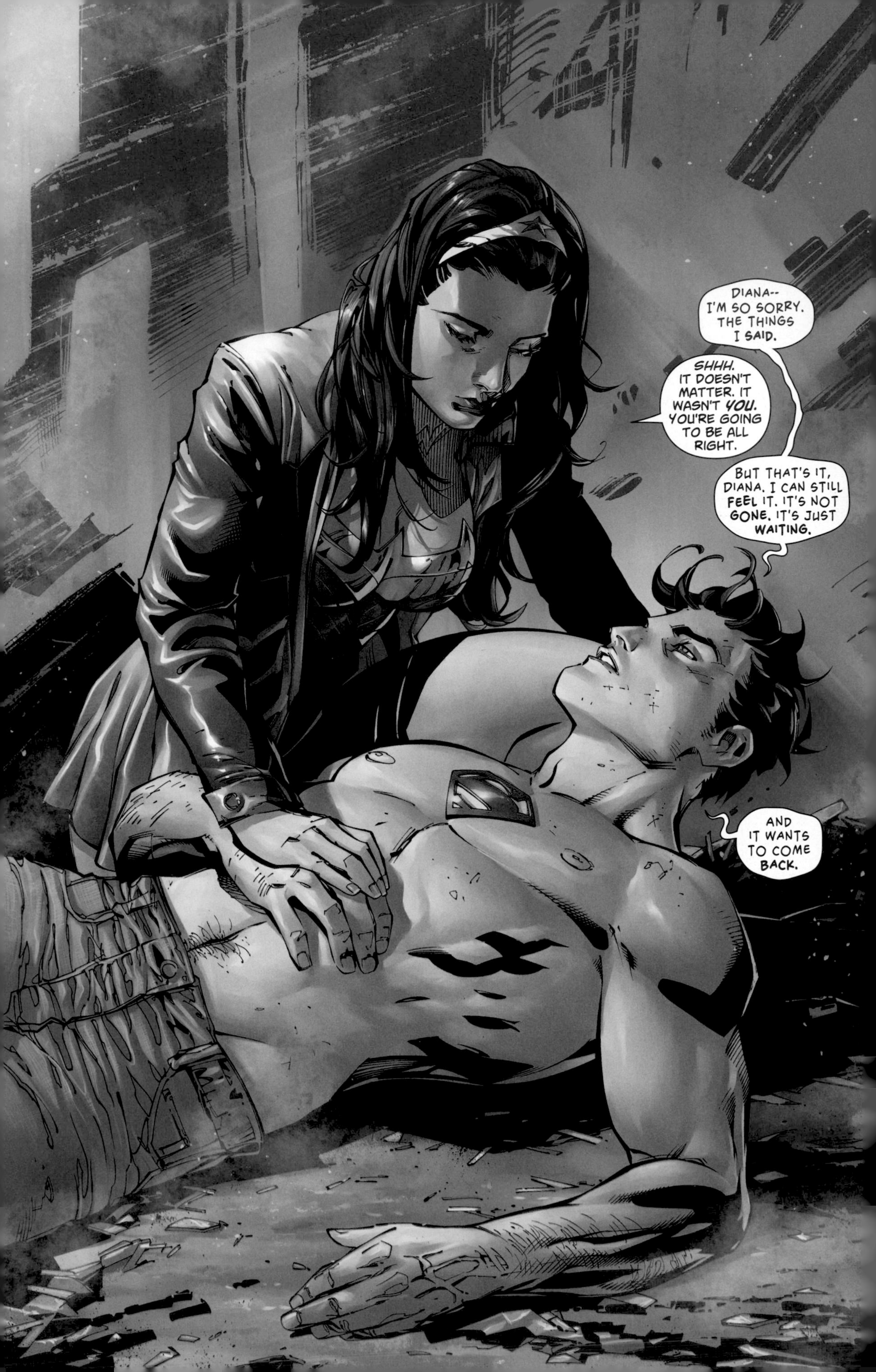
DIANA-- I'M SO SORRY. THE THINGS I SAID.
SHHH. IT DOESN'T MATTER. IT WASN'T YOU. YOU'RE GOING TO BE ALL RIGHT.
BUT THAT'S IT, DIANA. I CAN STILL FEEL IT. IT'S NOT GONE. IT'S JUST WAITING.
AND IT WANTS TO COME BACK.

ESCAPE

TONY S. DANIEL penciller **MATT BANNING SANDU FLOREA** inkers
cover by **TONY S. DANIEL & TOMEU MOREY**

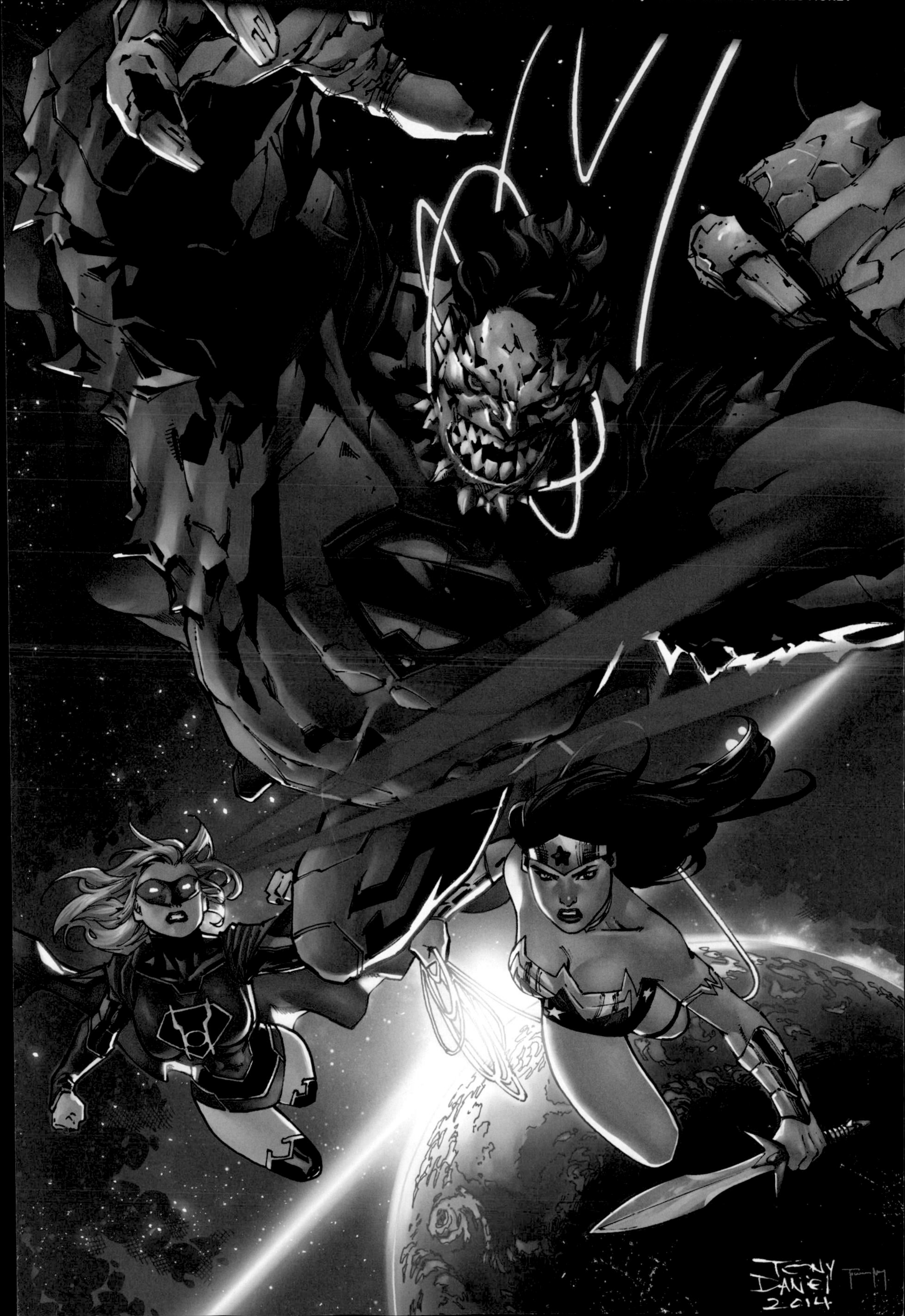
TONY DANIEL 2014

SUBSCRIBE NOW | SIGN IN | SEARCH | SECTIONS

CADMUS
WE MAKE YOU FEEL... BETTER!

The new Q-Pad5 available this Fall from Queen Industries

WORLD U.S. METROPOLIS BUSINESS OPINION SPORTS ARTS STYLE VIDEO

June 13, 201

Daily Planet

REMAIN CALM AND BREATHE EASY!

By Lois Lane

In a surprise move to help combat the threat of Super Doom, the United States government, along with the support of all nations, dropped a kryptonite bomb in the atmosphere above the Atacama Desert in Chile.

The kryptonite that was released from the bomb was in a concentrated mist form that spreads rapidly when coming in contact with oxygen. Once the mist is carried by the Earth's wind currents, it creates a world incapable of sustaining anyone of Kryptonian origin.

It has also resulted in the green hue that is currently in the skies.

The Center for Disease Control (CDC) maintains that the mist is not harmful to human beings and that we can breathe easy.

The deployment of the bomb came after Superman escaped from a secret holding facility where scientists were hoping to find a cure to reverse his transformation into Superdoom.

S.T.A.R. Labs Im

What do we know about about the Kryptonite mist?

The Long term effects on crops in South America

Is Superman still on the planet?

The man who developed the mist

BIG BELLY BURGER
NOW OFFERING TURTLE BOY TOYS WITH THEIR KIDS' MEALS!

FERRIS AIR

TURTLE BOY THE MOVIE
COMING SOON TO A THEATER NEAR YOU

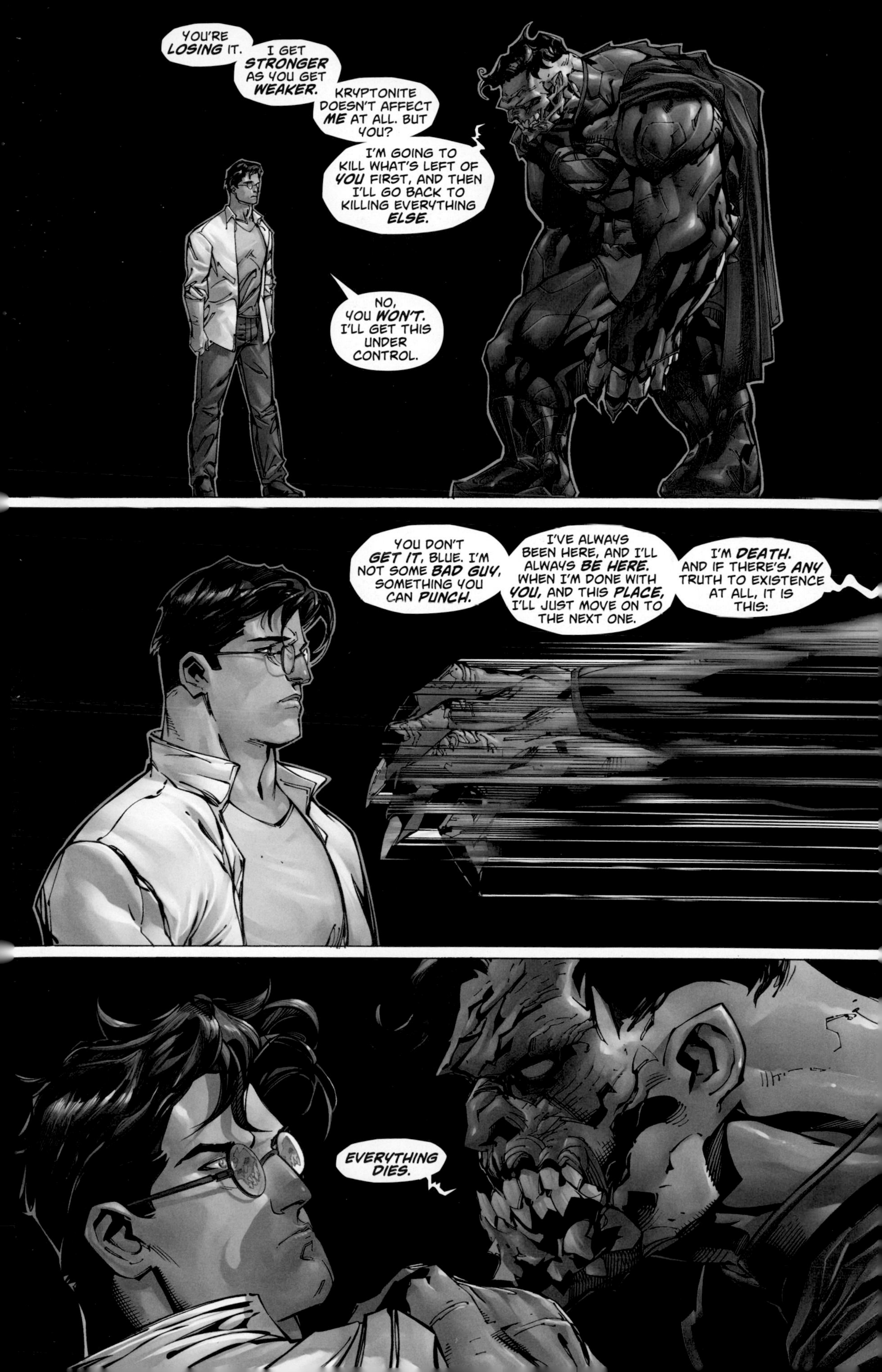

YOU'RE LOSING IT.
I GET STRONGER AS YOU GET WEAKER.
KRYPTONITE DOESN'T AFFECT ME AT ALL. BUT YOU?
I'M GOING TO KILL WHAT'S LEFT OF YOU FIRST, AND THEN I'LL GO BACK TO KILLING EVERYTHING ELSE.
NO, YOU WON'T. I'LL GET THIS UNDER CONTROL.
YOU DON'T GET IT, BLUE. I'M NOT SOME BAD GUY, SOMETHING YOU CAN PUNCH.
I'VE ALWAYS BEEN HERE, AND I'LL ALWAYS BE HERE. WHEN I'M DONE WITH YOU, AND THIS PLACE, I'LL JUST MOVE ON TO THE NEXT ONE.
I'M DEATH. AND IF THERE'S ANY TRUTH TO EXISTENCE AT ALL, IT IS THIS:
EVERYTHING DIES.

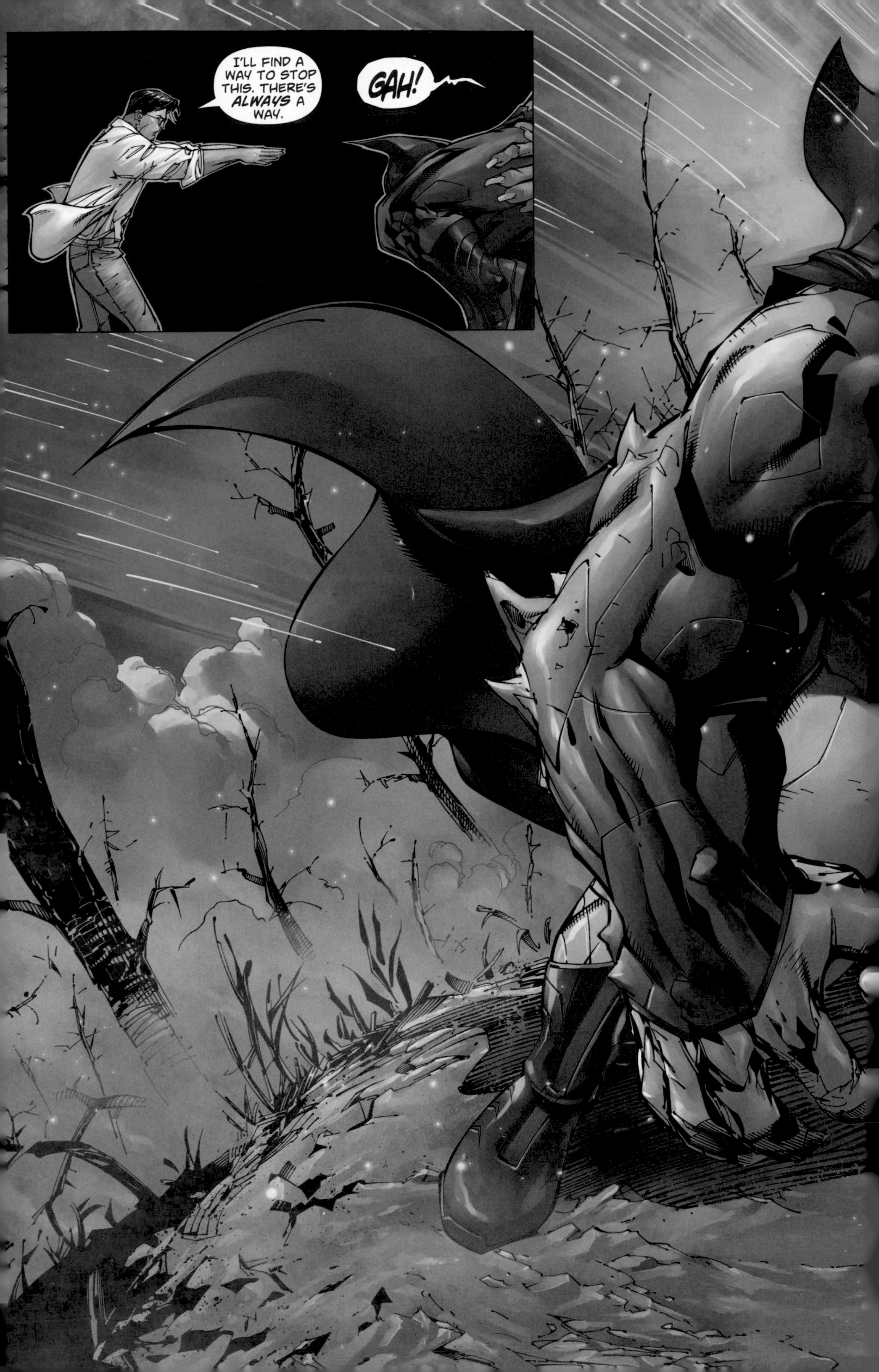
I'LL FIND A WAY TO STOP THIS. THERE'S ALWAYS A WAY.
GAH!

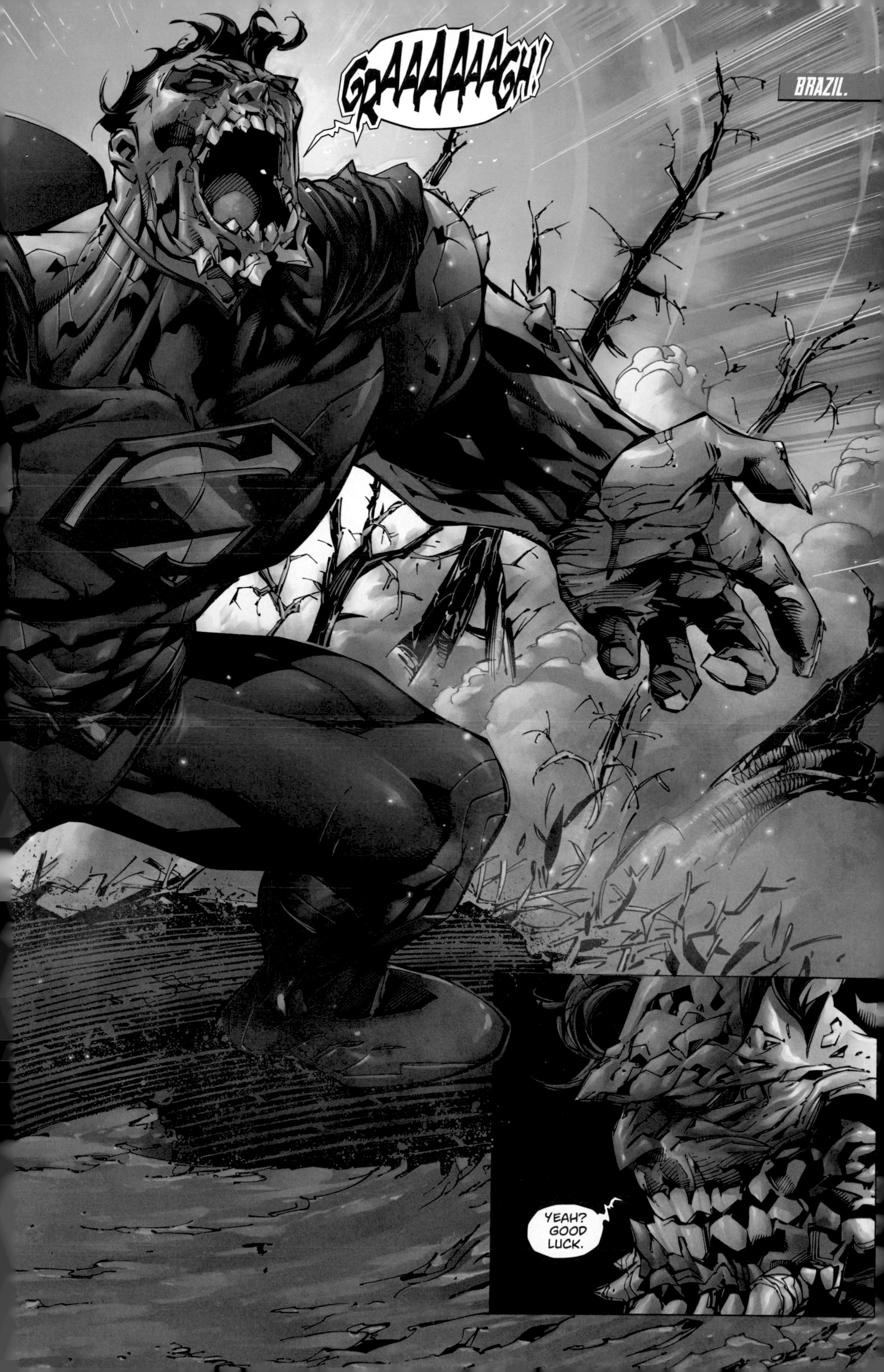
GRAAAAAAGH!
BRAZIL.
YEAH? GOOD LUCK.

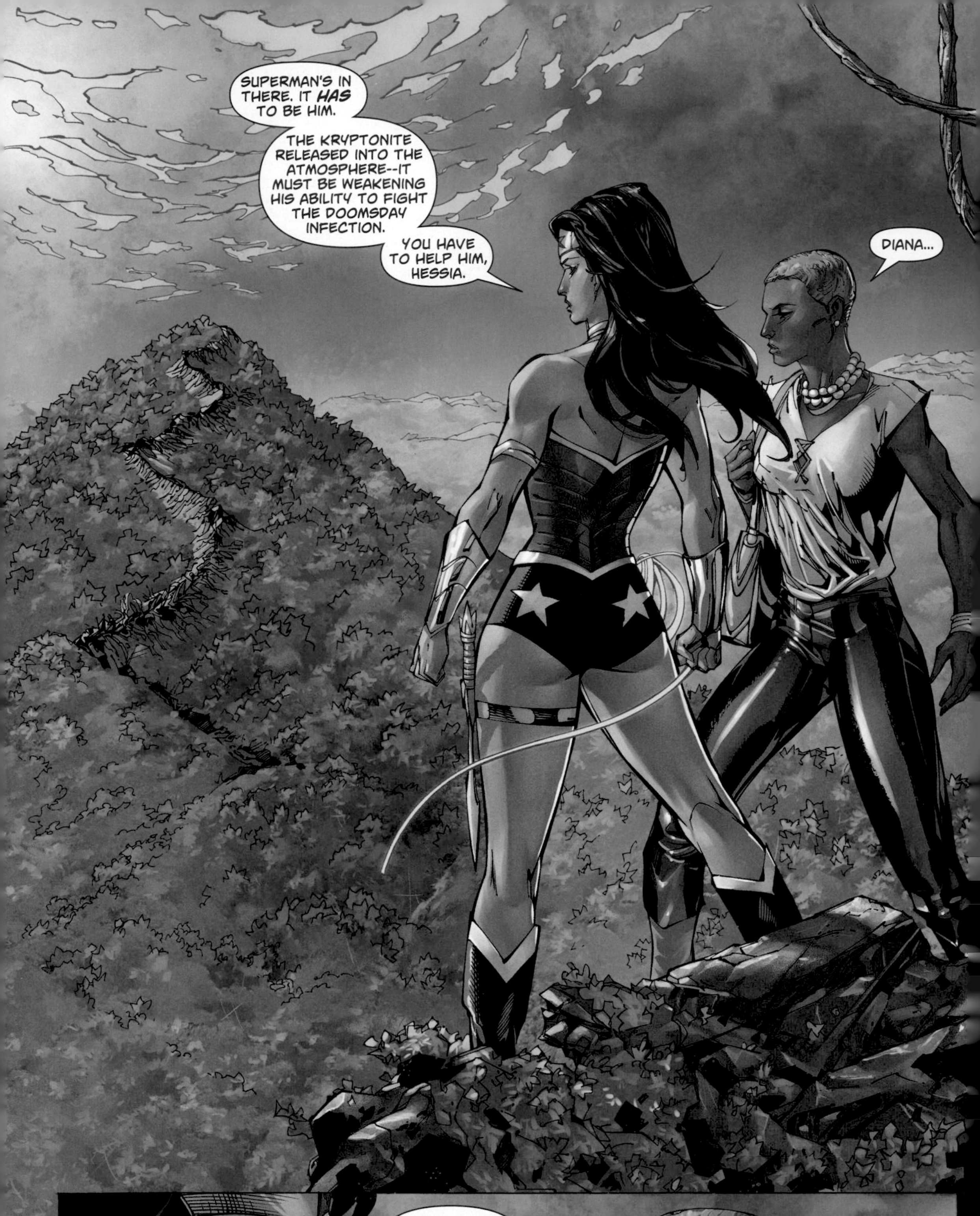
SUPERMAN'S IN THERE. IT **HAS** TO BE HIM.
THE KRYPTONITE RELEASED INTO THE ATMOSPHERE--IT MUST BE WEAKENING HIS ABILITY TO FIGHT THE DOOMSDAY INFECTION.
YOU HAVE TO HELP HIM, HESSIA.
DIANA...

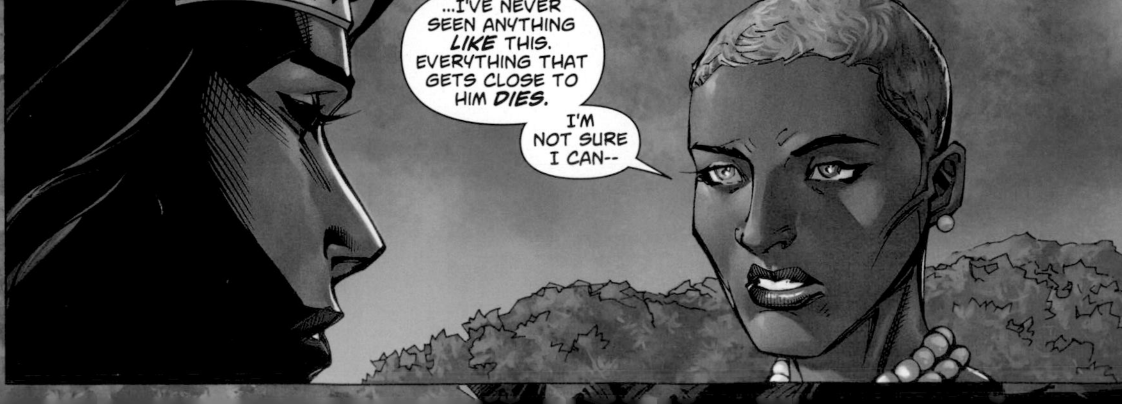
...I'VE NEVER SEEN ANYTHING **LIKE** THIS. EVERYTHING THAT GETS CLOSE TO HIM **DIES**.
I'M NOT SURE I CAN--

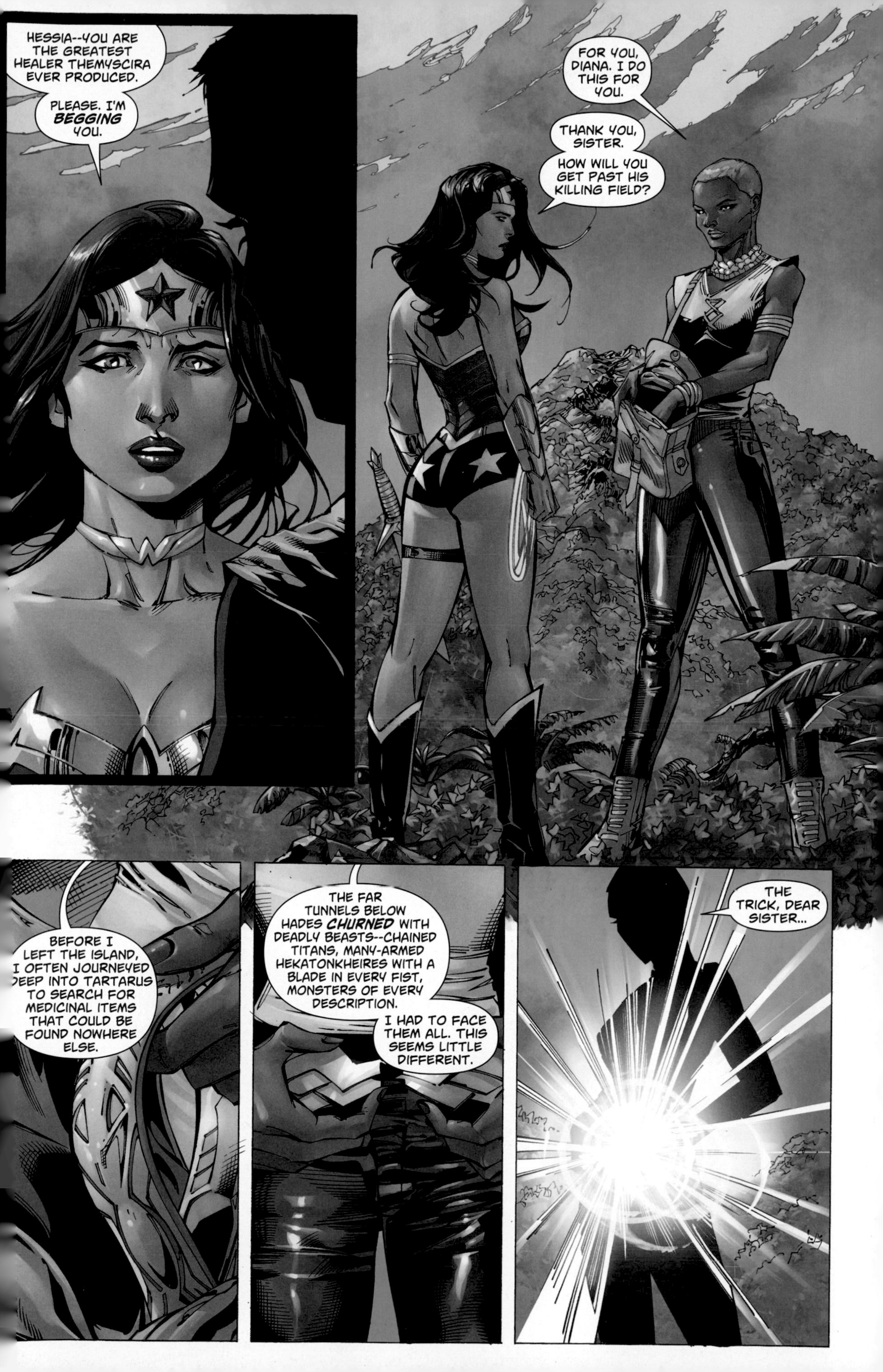
HESSIA--YOU ARE THE GREATEST HEALER THEMYSCIRA EVER PRODUCED.
PLEASE. I'M BEGGING YOU.
FOR YOU, DIANA. I DO THIS FOR YOU.
THANK YOU, SISTER.
HOW WILL YOU GET PAST HIS KILLING FIELD?
BEFORE I LEFT THE ISLAND, I OFTEN JOURNEYED DEEP INTO TARTARUS TO SEARCH FOR MEDICINAL ITEMS THAT COULD BE FOUND NOWHERE ELSE.
THE FAR TUNNELS BELOW HADES CHURNED WITH DEADLY BEASTS--CHAINED TITANS, MANY-ARMED HEKATONKHEIRES WITH A BLADE IN EVERY FIST, MONSTERS OF EVERY DESCRIPTION.
I HAD TO FACE THEM ALL. THIS SEEMS LITTLE DIFFERENT.
THE TRICK, DEAR SISTER...

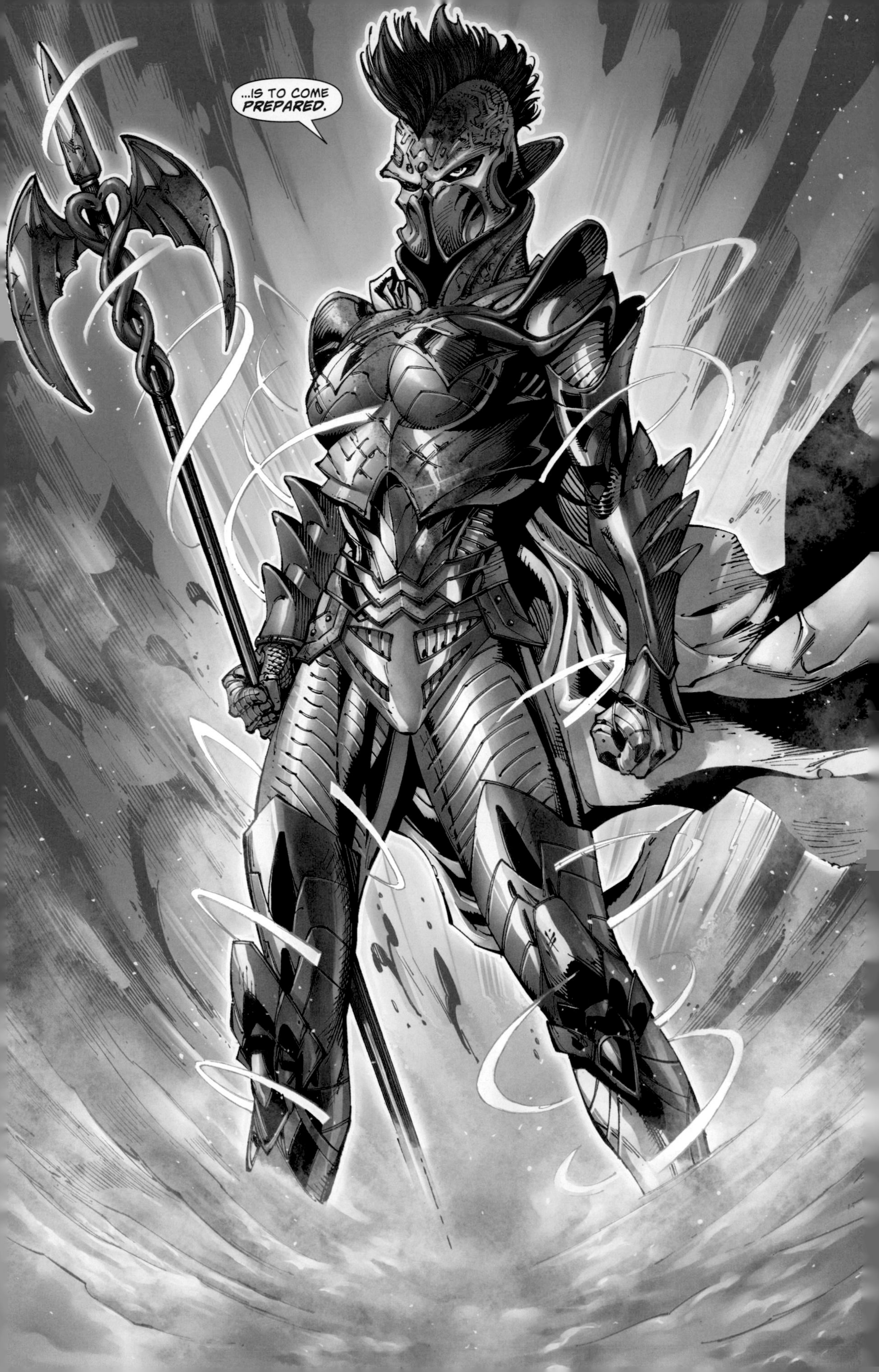
...IS TO COME PREPARED.

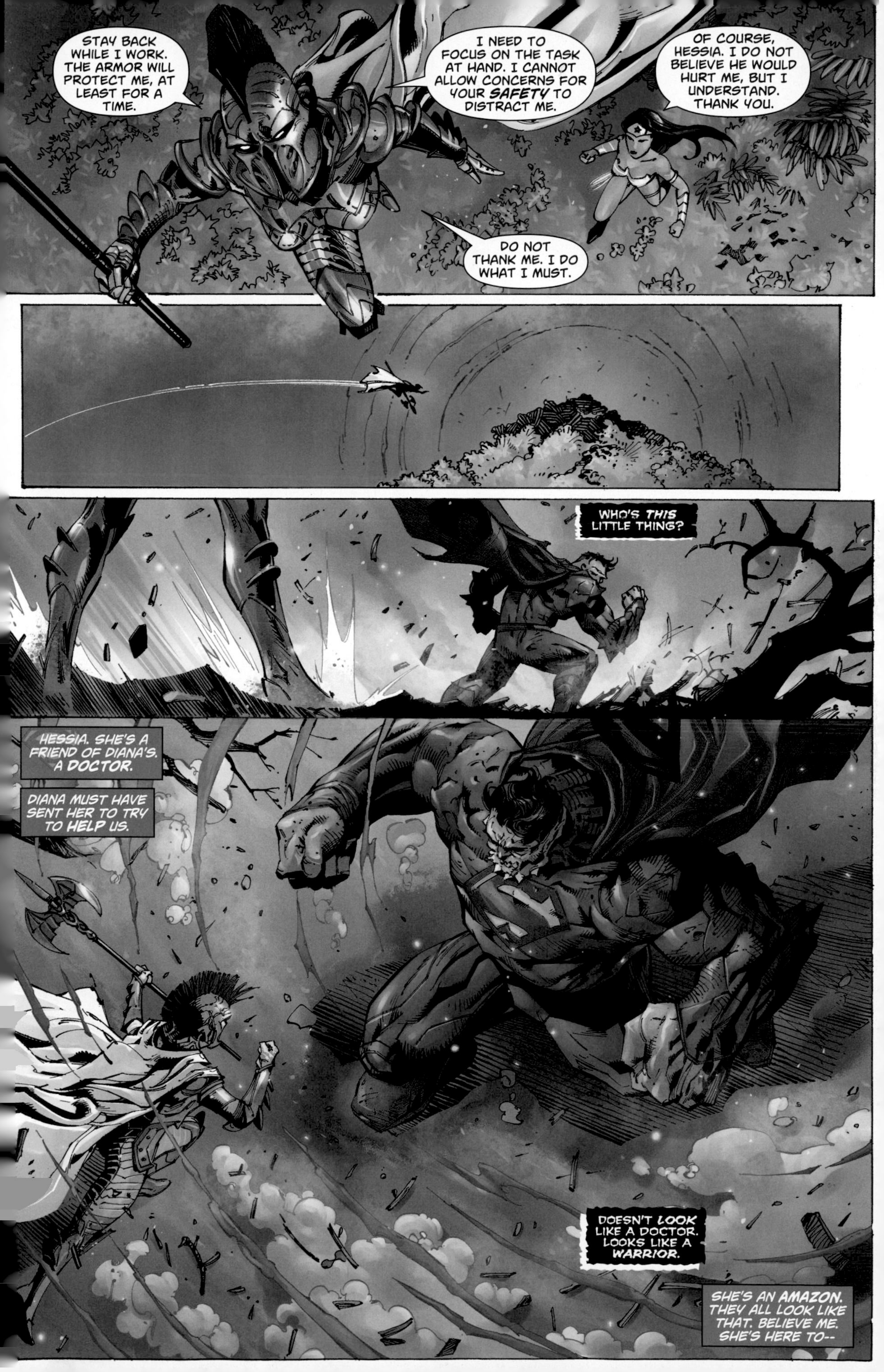
STAY BACK WHILE I WORK. THE ARMOR WILL PROTECT ME, AT LEAST FOR A TIME.
I NEED TO FOCUS ON THE TASK AT HAND. I CANNOT ALLOW CONCERNS FOR YOUR SAFETY TO DISTRACT ME.
OF COURSE, HESSIA. I DO NOT BELIEVE HE WOULD HURT ME, BUT I UNDERSTAND. THANK YOU.
DO NOT THANK ME. I DO WHAT I MUST.
WHO'S THIS LITTLE THING?
HESSIA. SHE'S A FRIEND OF DIANA'S. A DOCTOR.
DIANA MUST HAVE SENT HER TO TRY TO HELP US.
DOESN'T LOOK LIKE A DOCTOR. LOOKS LIKE A WARRIOR.
SHE'S AN AMAZON. THEY ALL LOOK LIKE THAT. BELIEVE ME. SHE'S HERE TO--

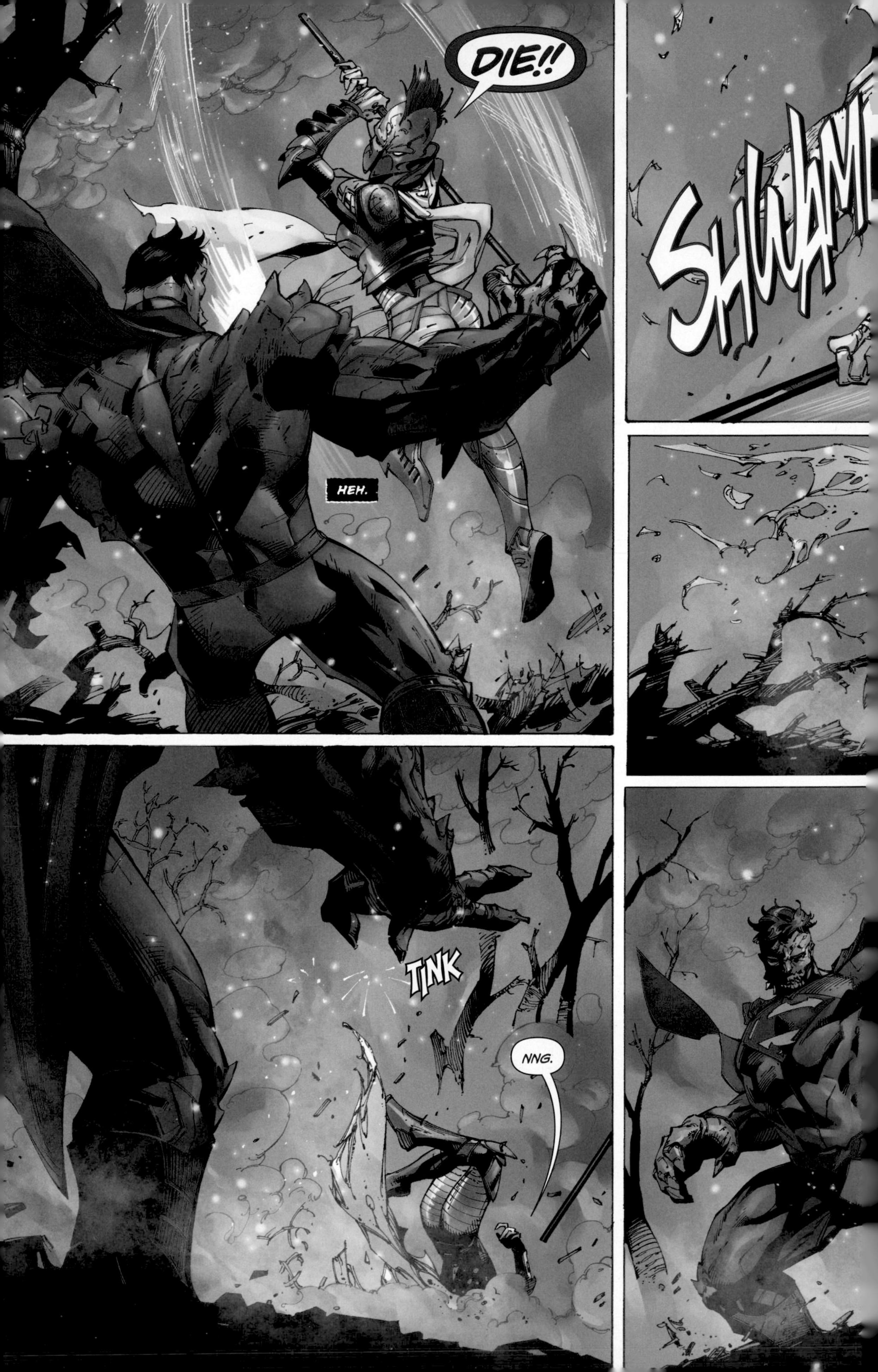
DIE!!
HEH.
SHUUMM
TINK
NNG.

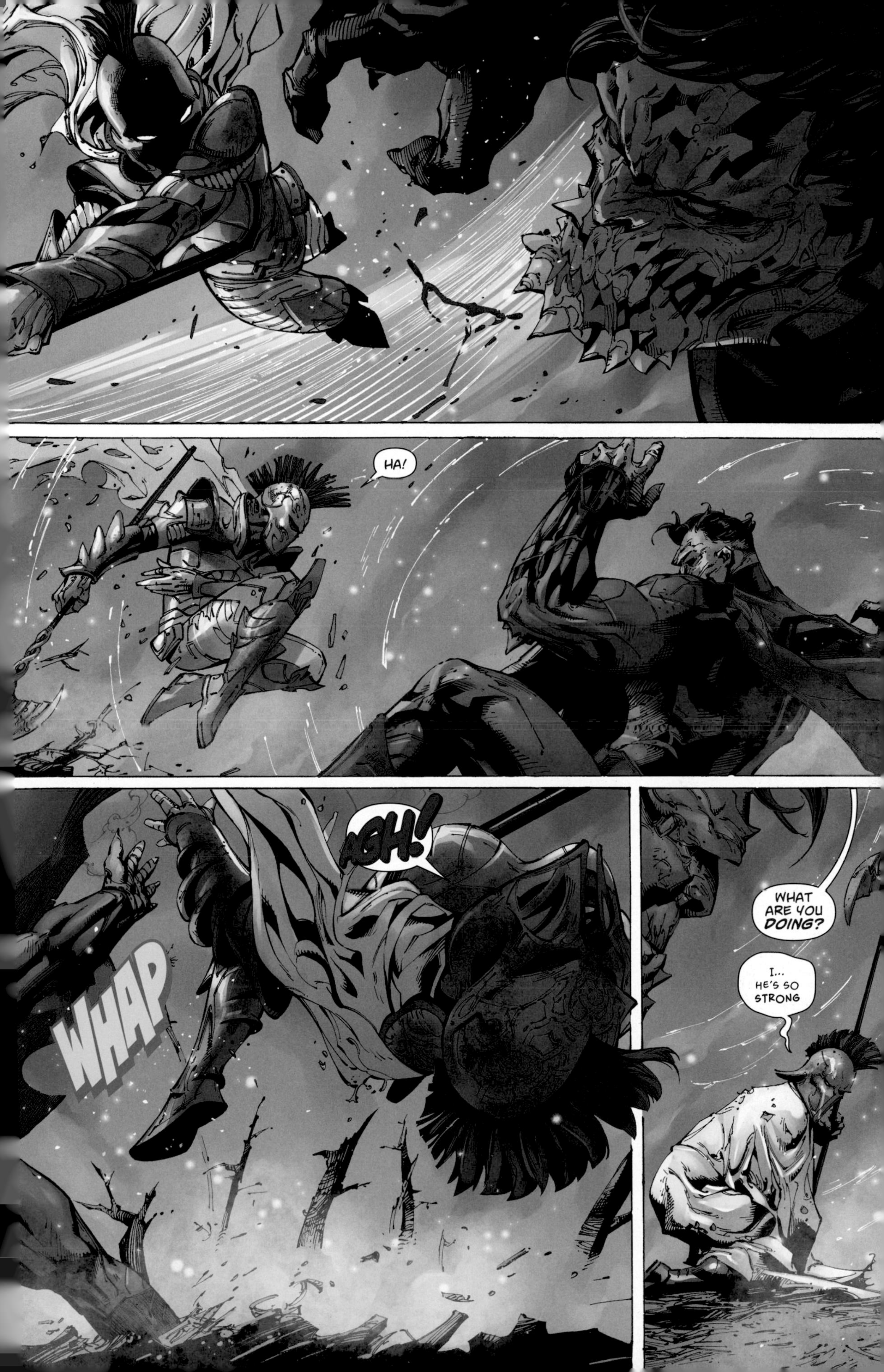
HA!
AGH!
WHAP
WHAT ARE YOU DOING?
I... HE'S SO STRONG

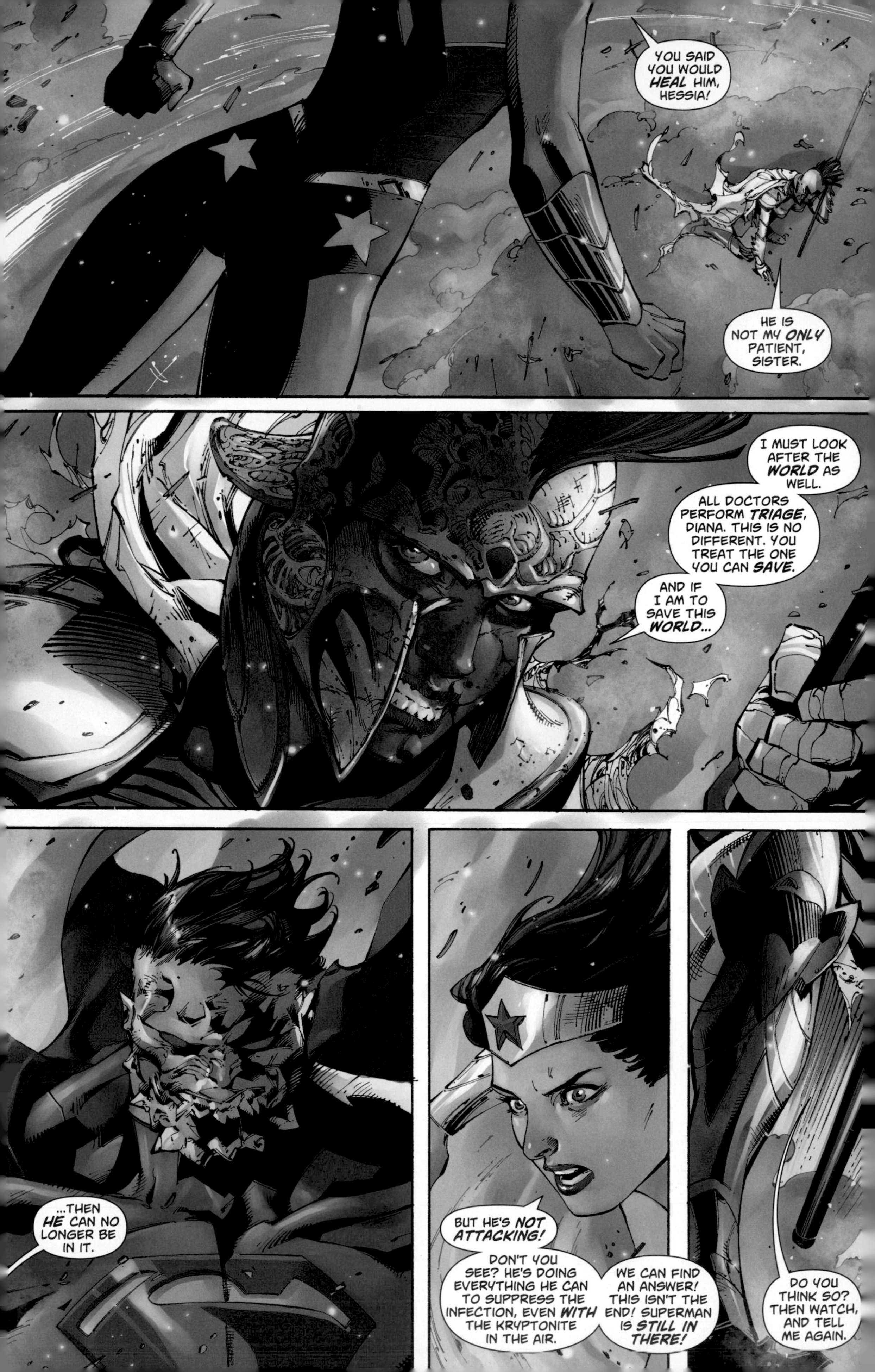
YOU SAID YOU WOULD HEAL HIM, HESSIA!
HE IS NOT MY ONLY PATIENT, SISTER.
I MUST LOOK AFTER THE WORLD AS WELL.
ALL DOCTORS PERFORM TRIAGE, DIANA. THIS IS NO DIFFERENT. YOU TREAT THE ONE YOU CAN SAVE.
AND IF I AM TO SAVE THIS WORLD...
...THEN HE CAN NO LONGER BE IN IT.
BUT HE'S NOT ATTACKING!
DON'T YOU SEE? HE'S DOING EVERYTHING HE CAN TO SUPPRESS THE INFECTION, EVEN WITH THE KRYPTONITE IN THE AIR.
WE CAN FIND AN ANSWER! THIS ISN'T THE END! SUPERMAN IS STILL IN THERE!
DO YOU THINK SO? THEN WATCH, AND TELL ME AGAIN.

HEAR ME!

I REVEALED YOUR RELATIONSHIP WITH WONDER WOMAN TO THE WORLD, SUPERMAN.

I DID IT FOR DIANA --AND FOR *YOU.* IT WAS WHAT YOU *NEEDED.*

I *HATE* THIS. I THOUGHT YOU WERE *GOOD* FOR EACH OTHER.

I WAS *WRONG.*

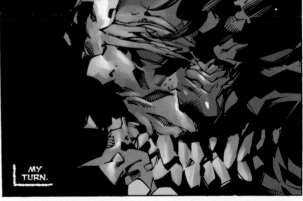

MY TURN.

KRACK

RRRAGGGH!

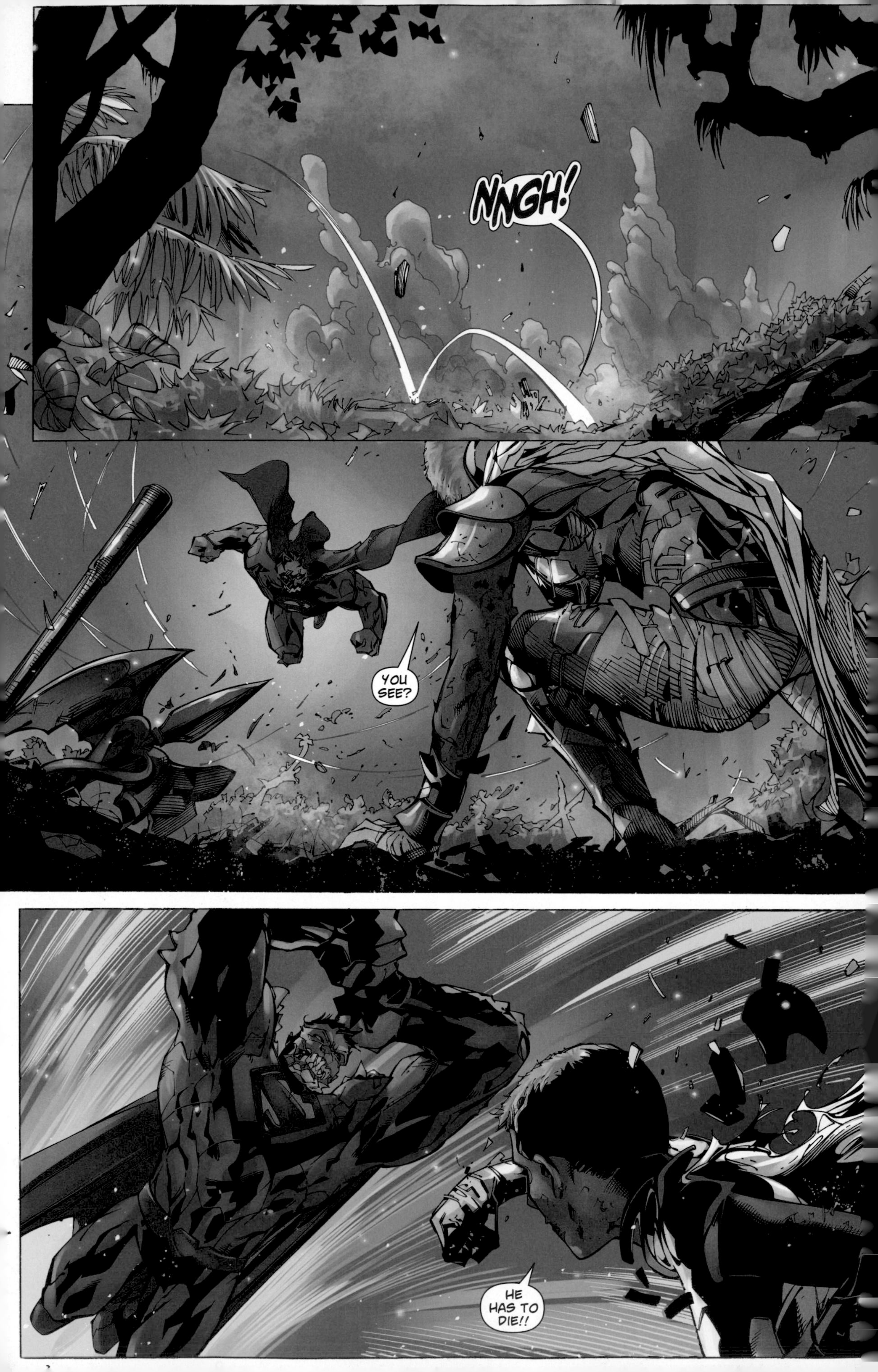
NNGH!
YOU SEE?
HE HAS TO DIE!!

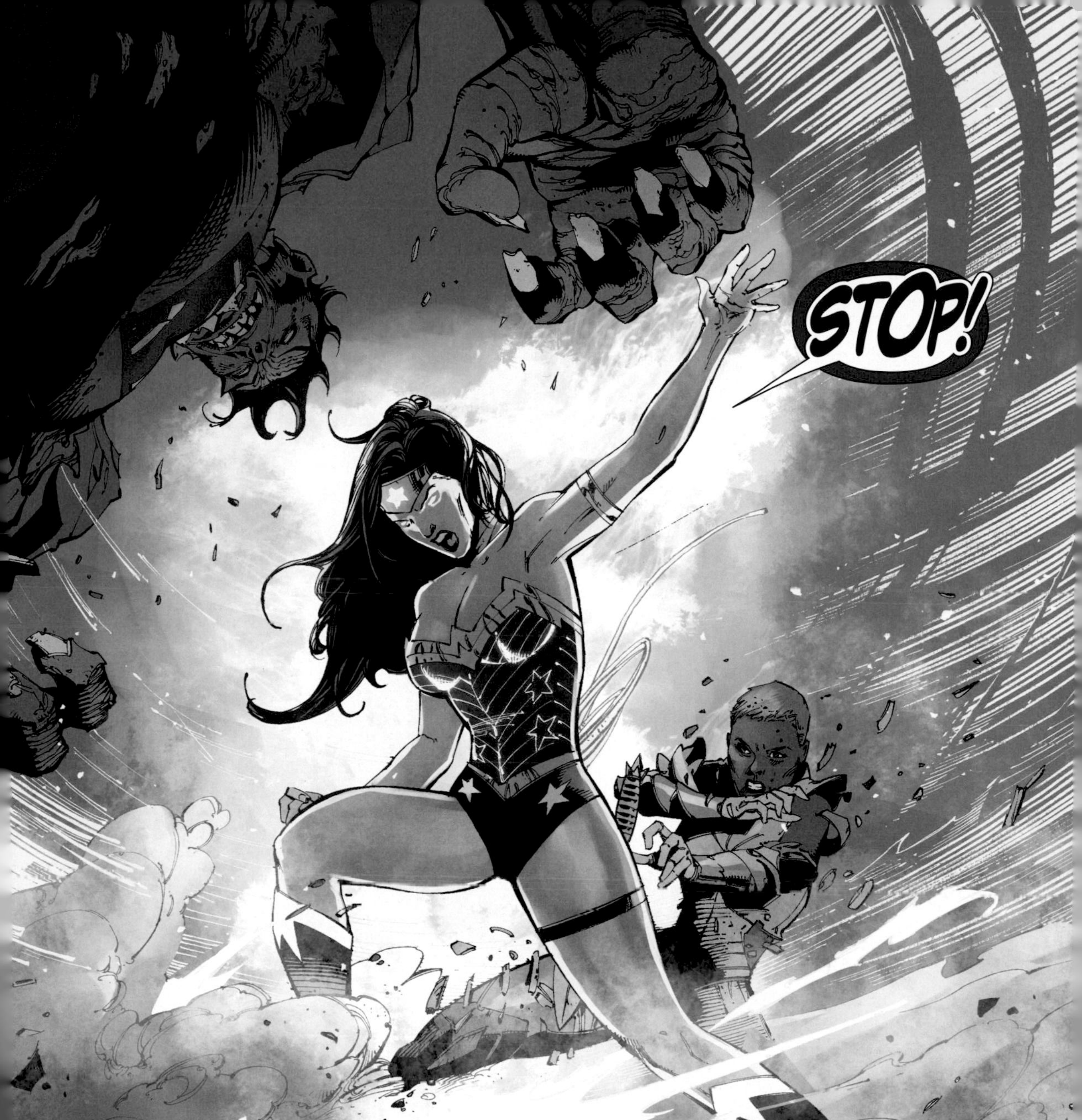
STOP!

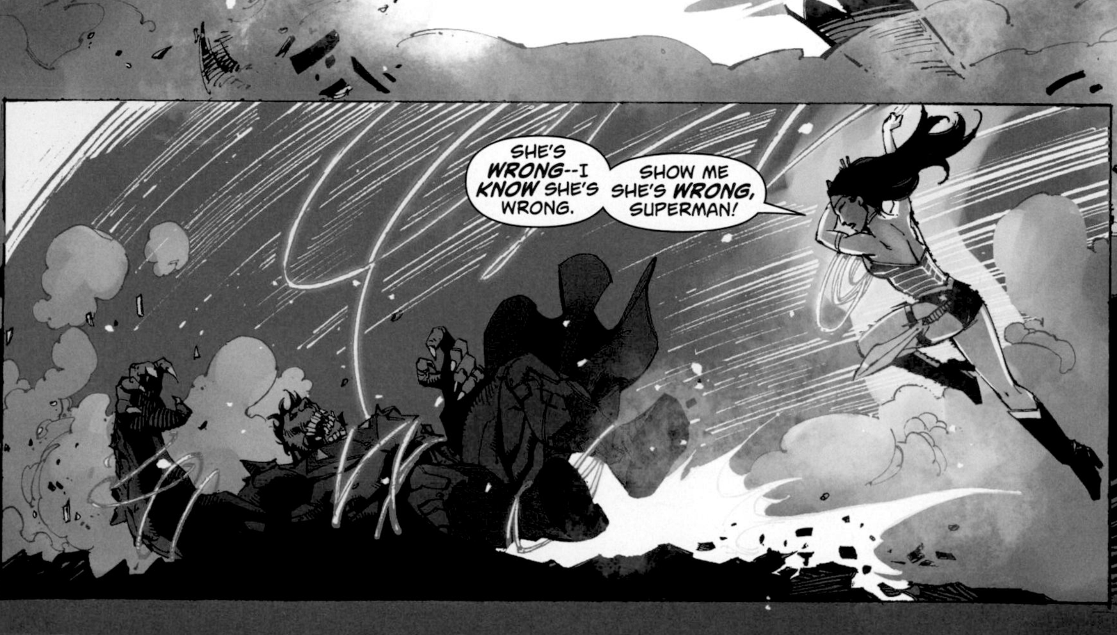
SHE'S WRONG--I KNOW SHE'S WRONG.
SHOW ME SHE'S WRONG, SUPERMAN!

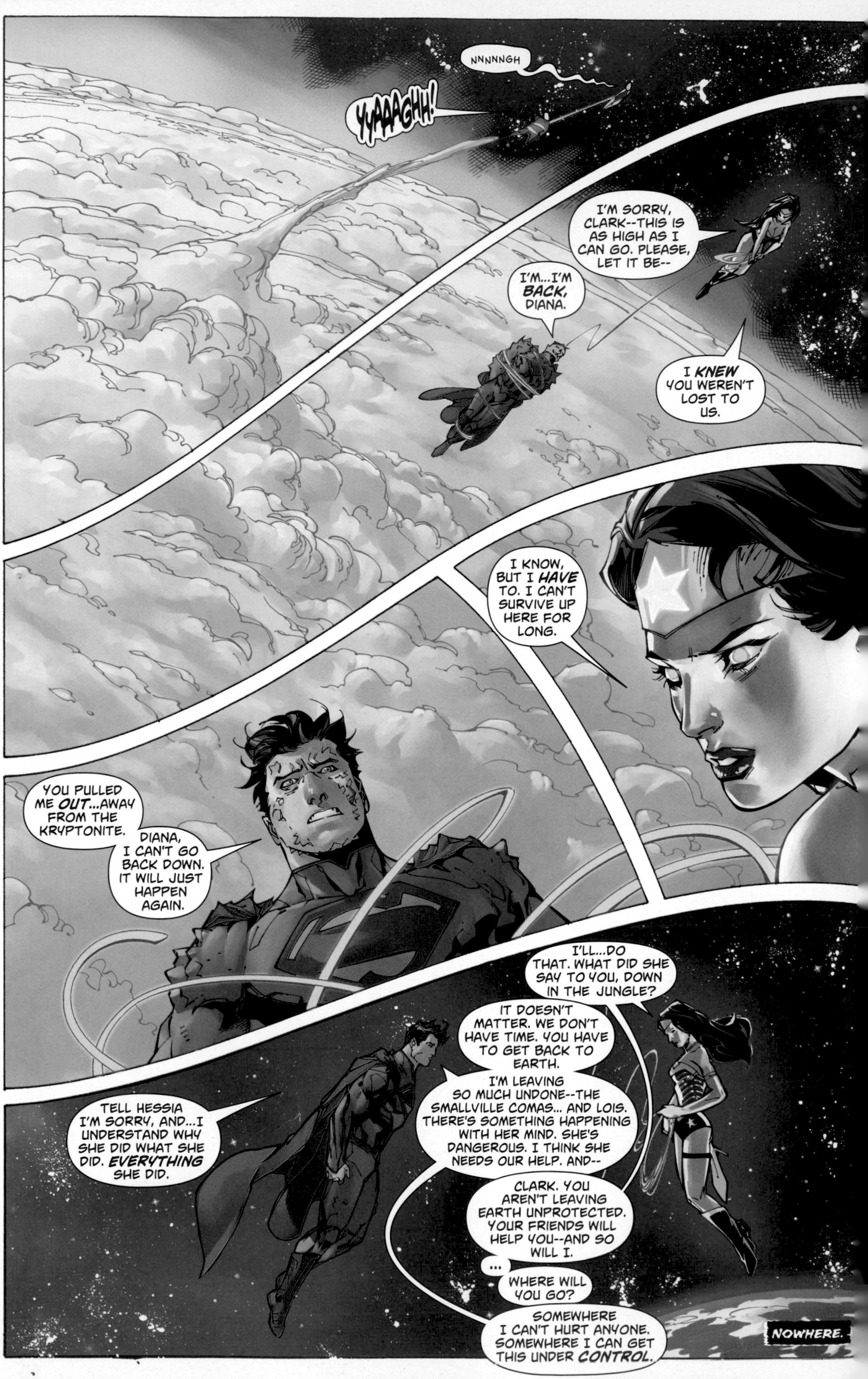

NNNNNGH
YYAAAGHH!
I'M SORRY, CLARK--THIS IS AS HIGH AS I CAN GO. PLEASE, LET IT BE--
I'M...I'M **BACK,** DIANA.
I **KNEW** YOU WEREN'T LOST TO US.
YOU PULLED ME **OUT**...AWAY FROM THE KRYPTONITE.
DIANA, I CAN'T GO BACK DOWN. IT WILL JUST HAPPEN AGAIN.
I KNOW, BUT I **HAVE** TO. I CAN'T SURVIVE UP HERE FOR LONG.
I'LL...DO THAT. WHAT DID SHE SAY TO YOU, DOWN IN THE JUNGLE?
TELL HESSIA I'M SORRY, AND...I UNDERSTAND WHY SHE DID WHAT SHE DID. **EVERYTHING** SHE DID.
IT DOESN'T MATTER. WE DON'T HAVE TIME. YOU HAVE TO GET BACK TO EARTH.
I'M LEAVING SO MUCH UNDONE--THE SMALLVILLE COMAS... AND LOIS. THERE'S SOMETHING HAPPENING WITH HER MIND. SHE'S DANGEROUS. I THINK SHE NEEDS OUR HELP. AND--
CLARK. YOU AREN'T LEAVING EARTH UNPROTECTED. YOUR FRIENDS WILL HELP YOU--AND SO WILL I.
...
WHERE WILL YOU GO?
SOMEWHERE I CAN'T HURT ANYONE. SOMEWHERE I CAN GET THIS UNDER **CONTROL**.
NOWHERE.

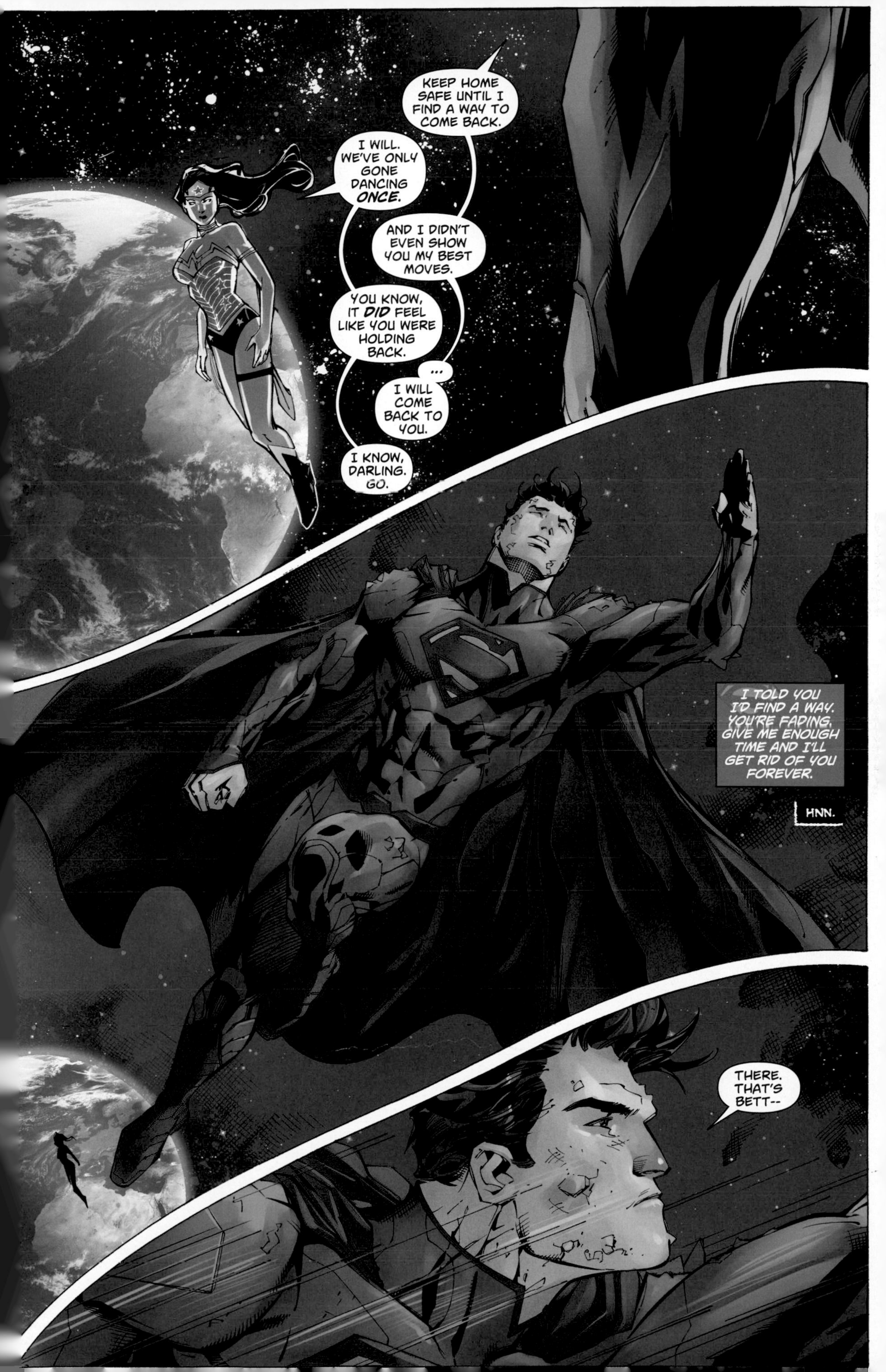
KEEP HOME SAFE UNTIL I FIND A WAY TO COME BACK.
I WILL. WE'VE ONLY GONE DANCING ONCE.
AND I DIDN'T EVEN SHOW YOU MY BEST MOVES.
YOU KNOW, IT DID FEEL LIKE YOU WERE HOLDING BACK.
...
I WILL COME BACK TO YOU.
I KNOW, DARLING. GO.
I TOLD YOU I'D FIND A WAY. YOU'RE FADING. GIVE ME ENOUGH TIME AND I'LL GET RID OF YOU FOREVER.
HNN.
THERE. THAT'S BETT--

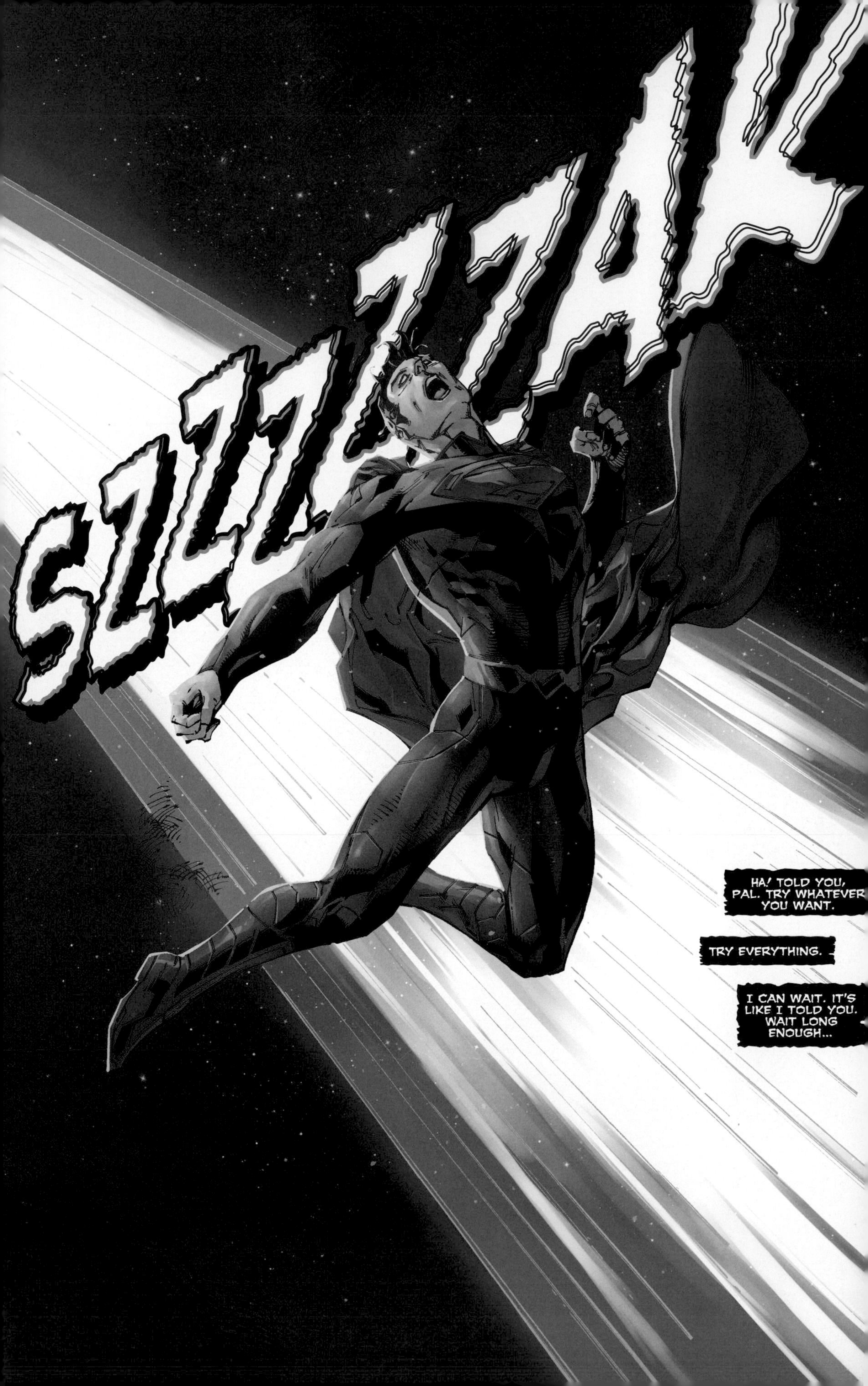
SZZZZZZAK
HA! TOLD YOU, PAL. TRY WHATEVER YOU WANT.
TRY EVERYTHING.
I CAN WAIT. IT'S LIKE I TOLD YOU. WAIT LONG ENOUGH...

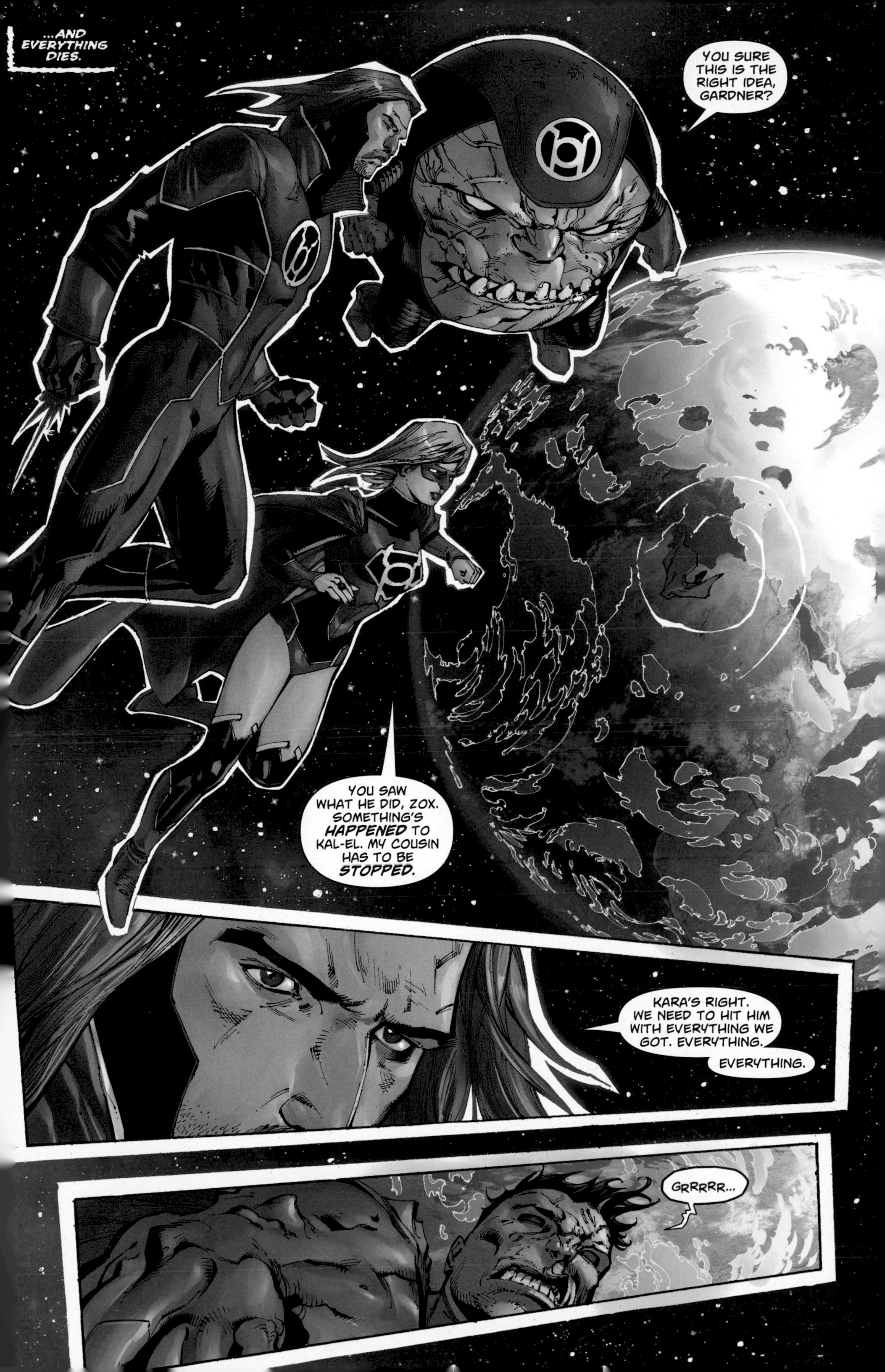
...AND EVERYTHING DIES.
YOU SURE THIS IS THE RIGHT IDEA, GARDNER?
YOU SAW WHAT HE DID, ZOX. SOMETHING'S HAPPENED TO KAL-EL. MY COUSIN HAS TO BE STOPPED.
KARA'S RIGHT. WE NEED TO HIT HIM WITH EVERYTHING WE GOT. EVERYTHING.
EVERYTHING.
GRRRRR...

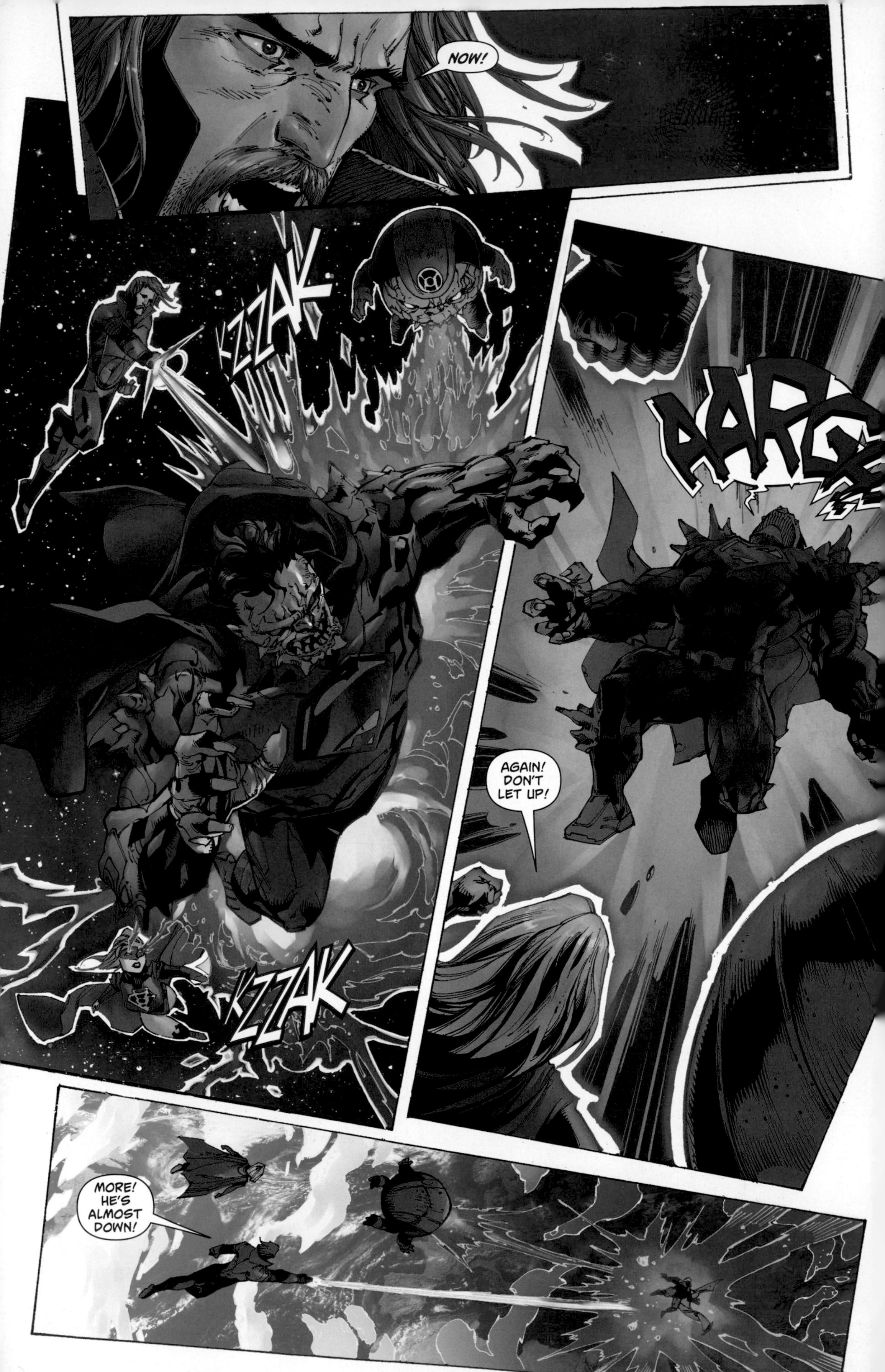
NOW!
K'ZZAK
K'ZZAK
AARGH
AGAIN! DON'T LET UP!
MORE! HE'S ALMOST DOWN!

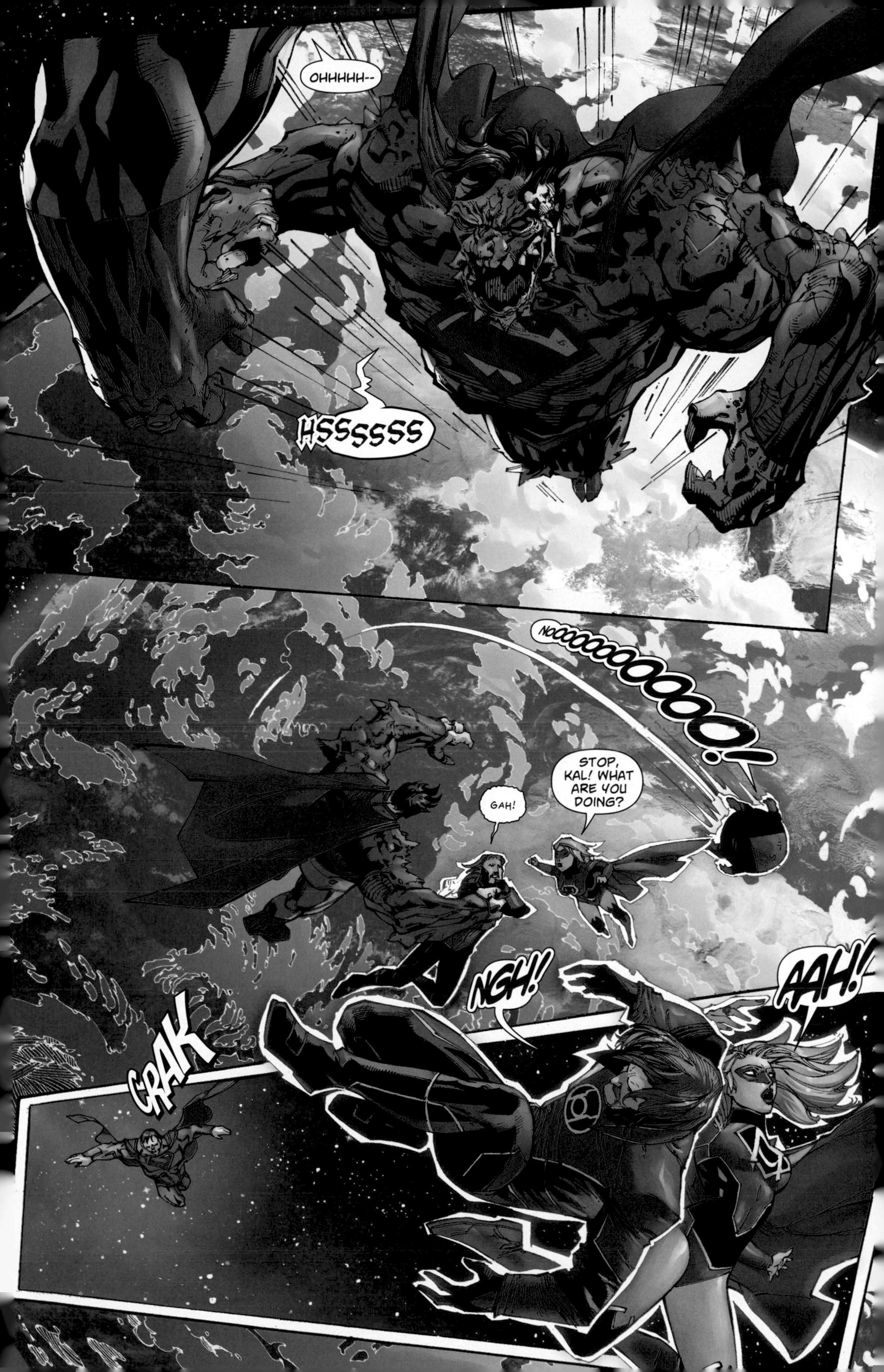
OHHHHH--
HSSSSSS
NOOOOOOOOOOOOO!
STOP, KAL! WHAT ARE YOU DOING?
GAH!
NGH!
AAH!
CRAK

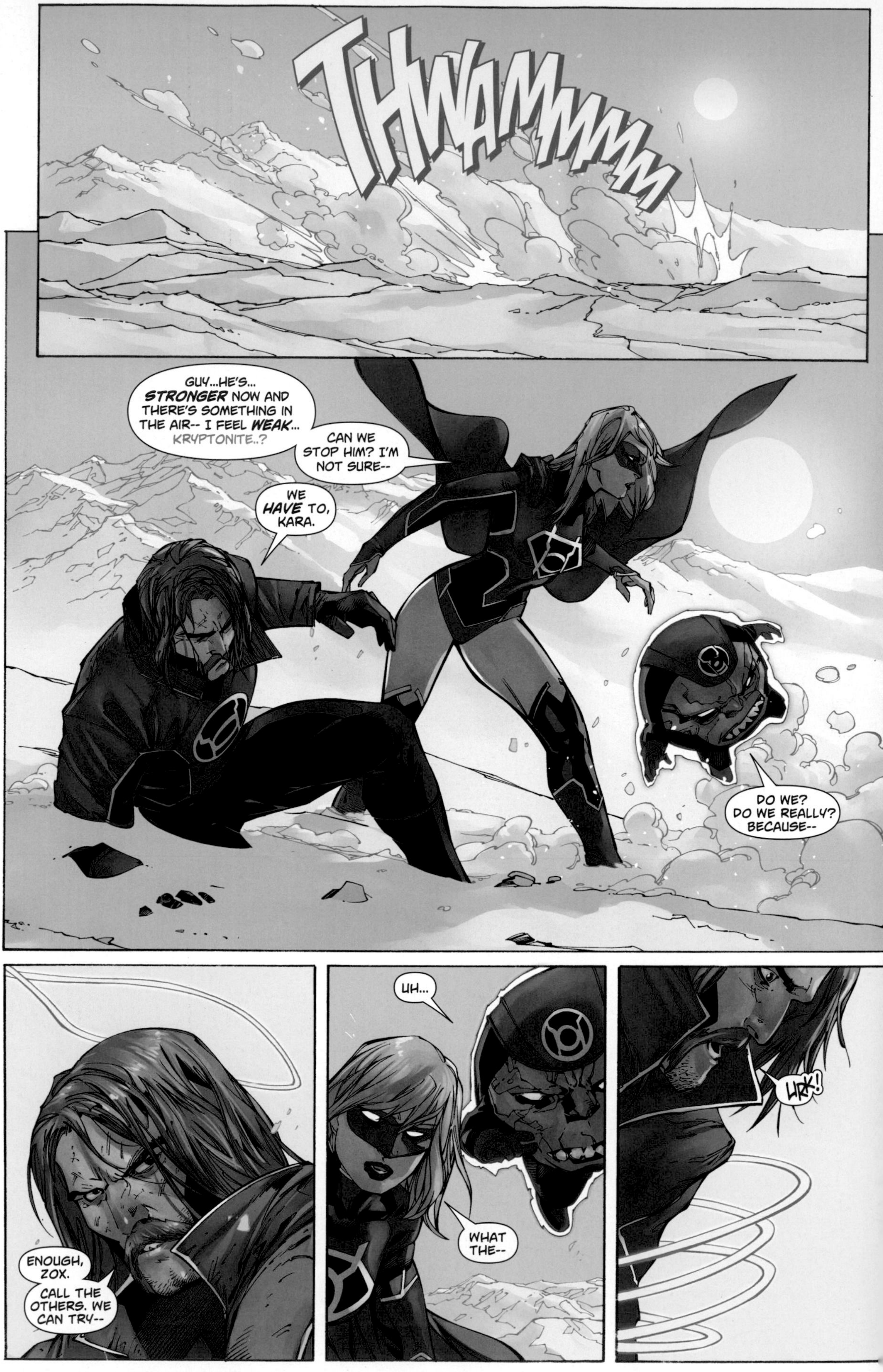
THWAMMMM
GUY...HE'S... STRONGER NOW AND THERE'S SOMETHING IN THE AIR-- I FEEL WEAK... KRYPTONITE..?
CAN WE STOP HIM? I'M NOT SURE--
WE HAVE TO, KARA.
DO WE? DO WE REALLY? BECAUSE--
ENOUGH, ZOX.
CALL THE OTHERS. WE CAN TRY--
UH...
WHAT THE--
URK!

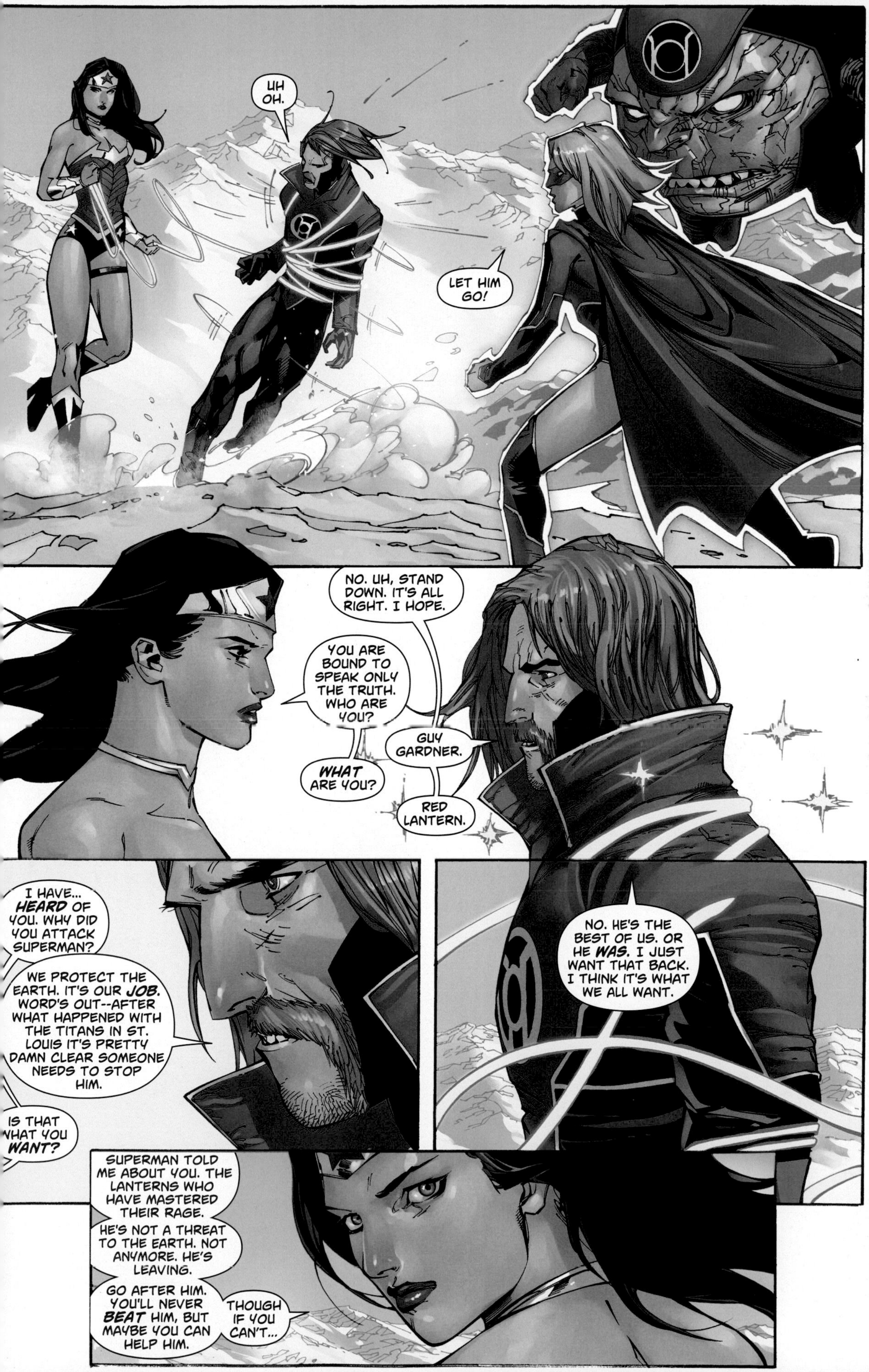
UH OH.
LET HIM GO!
NO. UH, STAND DOWN. IT'S ALL RIGHT. I HOPE.
YOU ARE BOUND TO SPEAK ONLY THE TRUTH. WHO ARE YOU?
GUY GARDNER.
WHAT ARE YOU?
RED LANTERN.
I HAVE... HEARD OF YOU. WHY DID YOU ATTACK SUPERMAN?
WE PROTECT THE EARTH. IT'S OUR JOB. WORD'S OUT--AFTER WHAT HAPPENED WITH THE TITANS IN ST. LOUIS IT'S PRETTY DAMN CLEAR SOMEONE NEEDS TO STOP HIM.
IS THAT WHAT YOU WANT?
NO. HE'S THE BEST OF US. OR HE WAS. I JUST WANT THAT BACK. I THINK IT'S WHAT WE ALL WANT.
SUPERMAN TOLD ME ABOUT YOU. THE LANTERNS WHO HAVE MASTERED THEIR RAGE.
HE'S NOT A THREAT TO THE EARTH. NOT ANYMORE. HE'S LEAVING.
GO AFTER HIM. YOU'LL NEVER BEAT HIM, BUT MAYBE YOU CAN HELP HIM.
THOUGH IF YOU CAN'T...

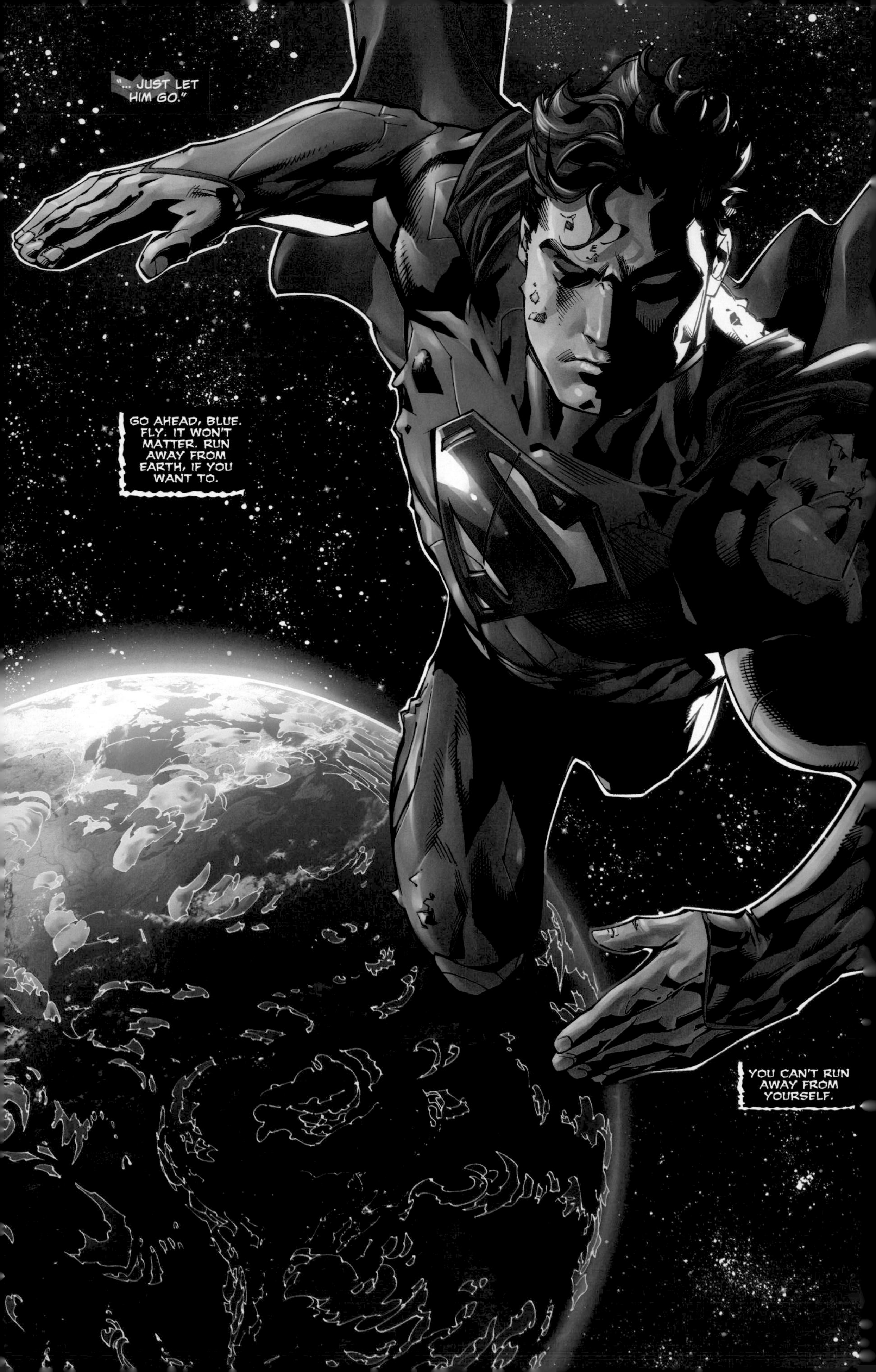
"... JUST LET HIM GO."
GO AHEAD, BLUE. FLY. IT WON'T MATTER. RUN AWAY FROM EARTH, IF YOU WANT TO.
YOU CAN'T RUN AWAY FROM YOURSELF.

DISTANCE

PAULO SIQUEIRA PASCAL ALIXE pencillers **PASCAL ALIXE** inker
cover by **TONY S. DANIEL** & **TOMEU MOREY**

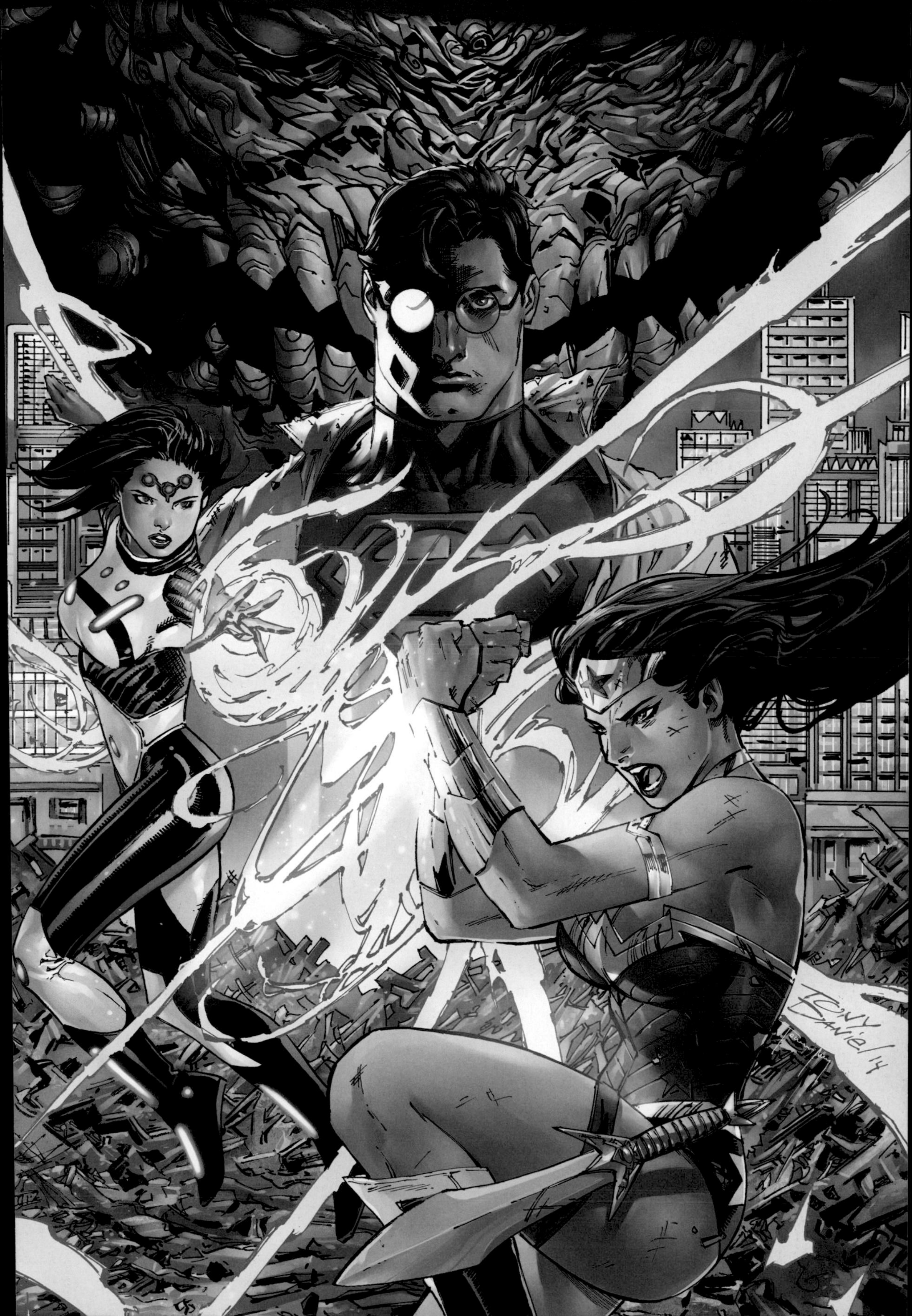
TONY DANIEL '14

WORLD   U.S.   METROPOLIS   BUSINESS   OPINION   SPORTS   ARTS   STYLE   VIDEO

Daily Planet
DAILY PLANET

July 9, 20

CRISIS IN METROPOLIS

Photo by James

By Lois Lane

First let me apologize for editorializing this piece, but it is hard not to when you see the city that you have made your home collapse into utter and complete chaos.

As of 12:00 P.M. this Wednesday, the City of Metropolis fell into a citywide coma. Only the outlying areas of the boroughs of Park Ridge and Bakerline were spared, as everything around them literally fell, resulting in massive accidents throughout involving buses, cars, trains and aircraft in the area losing control. The death toll has not yet been tallied, as the army is not allowing anyone near the city limits. EMS teams

responding to the event suffered the same affliction.

Any information being gathered at this point is being done through satellite and long-range sensors.

As similar events occurred in Smallville, Kansas, just days ago, everyone is conjecturing what the connection is.

"It's obvious, isn't it," commented James Hom, one of the few survivors who happened to be out of town for the week. "Superman tears Doomsday apart in Smallville, which had just suffered the same symptoms, and next thing you know Superman is turning into another Doomsday." He added, "And where do we see

the most sightings of Superman'
Metropolis."

Whether this is all connected to the now Monster of Steel still remains pure conjecture, as no one from the scientific commun or Justice League is available fo quesitons. Eyewitnesses in Braz did claim that a path of death followed Superman as he flew through the Amazon. This was much like the death field gener- ated by the first Doomsday as h walked across India and Africa.

At this point, Superman has le Earth, so is this the last event o will it be repeated and where it will strike next?

How will this all affect Supergirl?
Smallville still under quarantine— no change in victims

What is the Justice League's respon
Weather—Mostly Cloudy Green

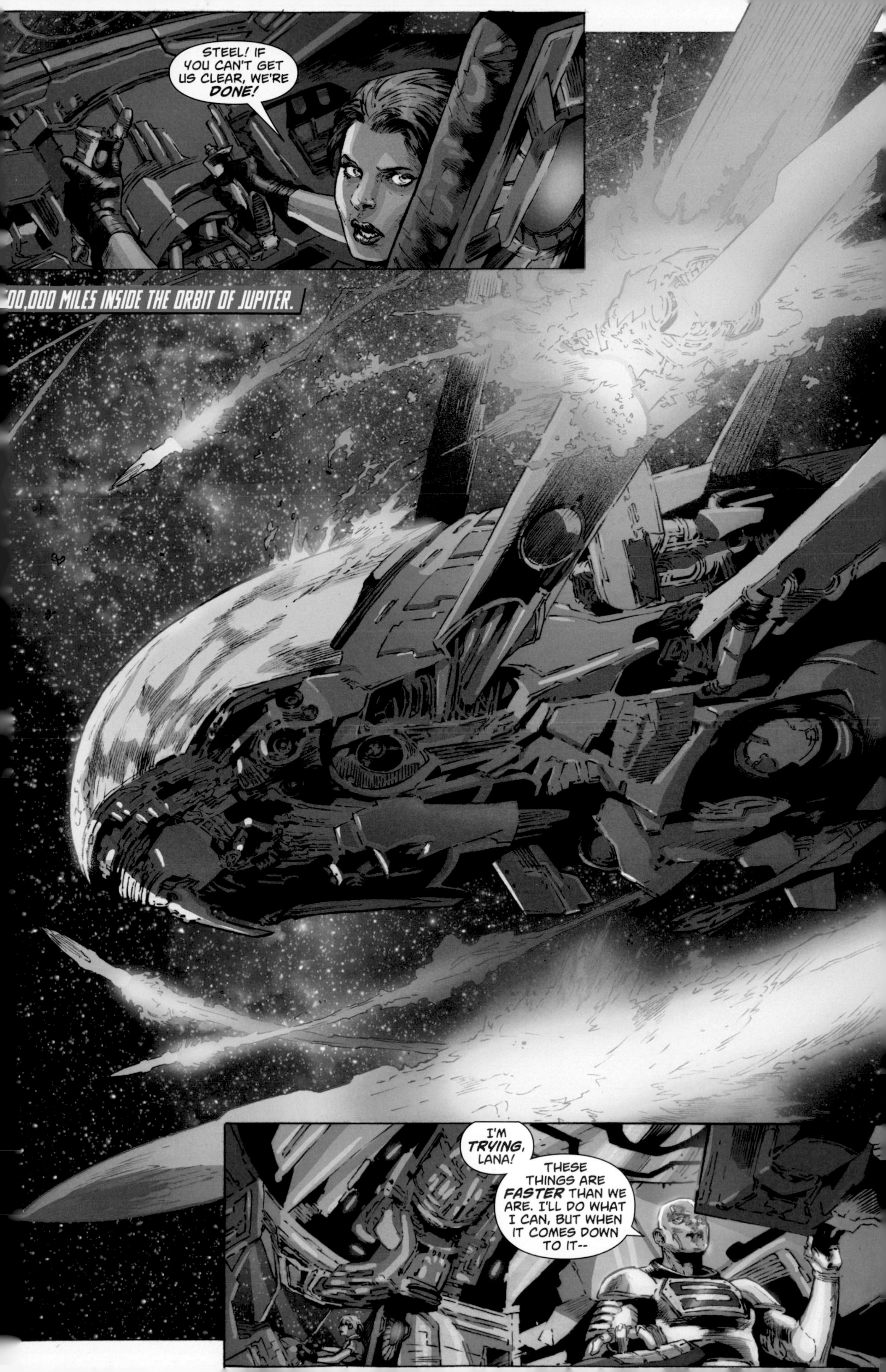
STEEL! IF YOU CAN'T GET US CLEAR, WE'RE DONE!
00,000 MILES INSIDE THE ORBIT OF JUPITER.
I'M TRYING, LANA!
THESE THINGS ARE FASTER THAN WE ARE. I'LL DO WHAT I CAN, BUT WHEN IT COMES DOWN TO IT--

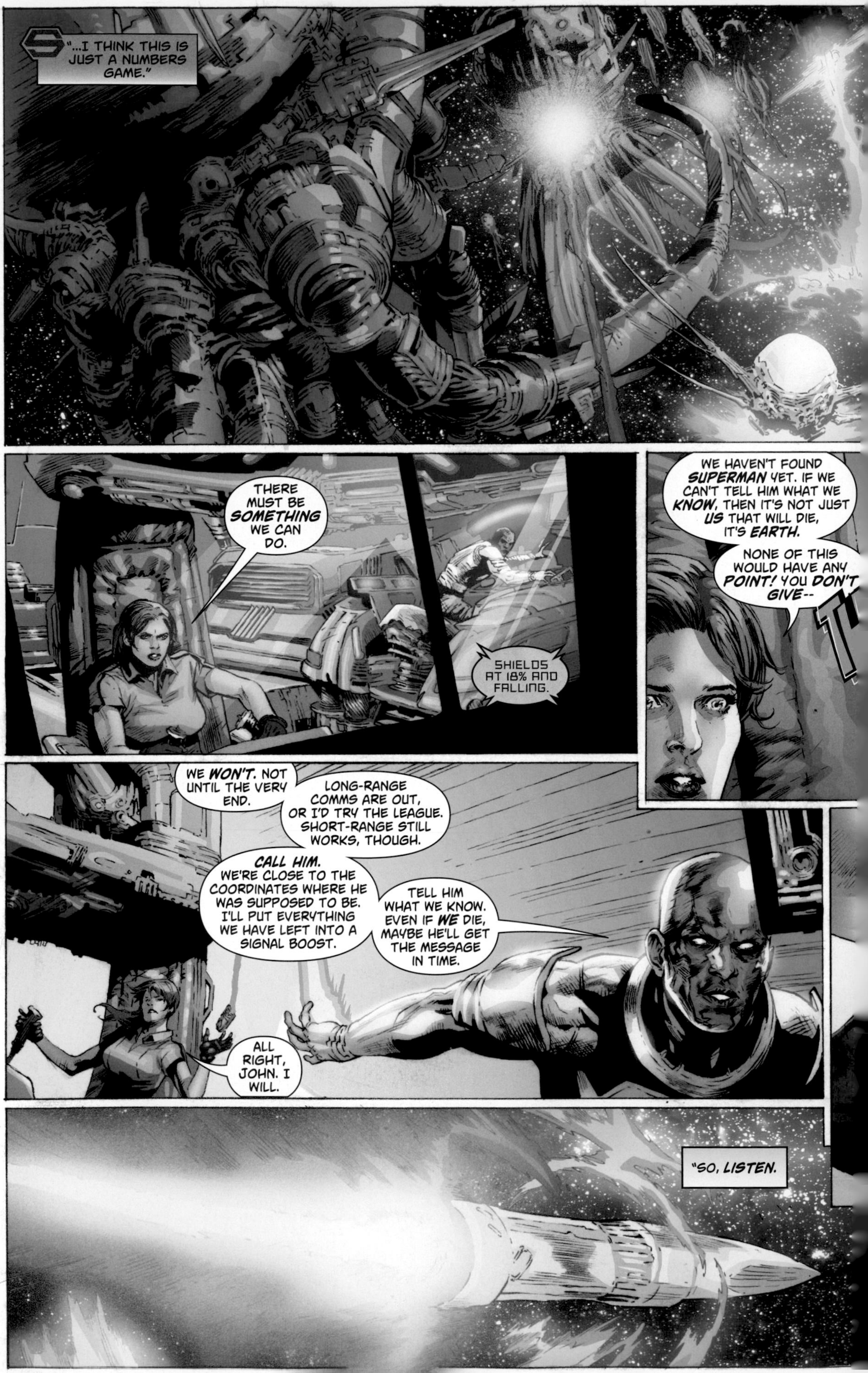
"...I THINK THIS IS JUST A NUMBERS GAME."
THERE MUST BE SOMETHING WE CAN DO.
SHIELDS AT 18% AND FALLING.
WE HAVEN'T FOUND SUPERMAN YET. IF WE CAN'T TELL HIM WHAT WE KNOW, THEN IT'S NOT JUST US THAT WILL DIE, IT'S EARTH.
NONE OF THIS WOULD HAVE ANY POINT! YOU DON'T GIVE--
WE WON'T. NOT UNTIL THE VERY END.
LONG-RANGE COMMS ARE OUT, OR I'D TRY THE LEAGUE. SHORT-RANGE STILL WORKS, THOUGH.
CALL HIM. WE'RE CLOSE TO THE COORDINATES WHERE HE WAS SUPPOSED TO BE. I'LL PUT EVERYTHING WE HAVE LEFT INTO A SIGNAL BOOST.
TELL HIM WHAT WE KNOW. EVEN IF WE DIE, MAYBE HE'LL GET THE MESSAGE IN TIME.
ALL RIGHT, JOHN. I WILL.
"SO, LISTEN.

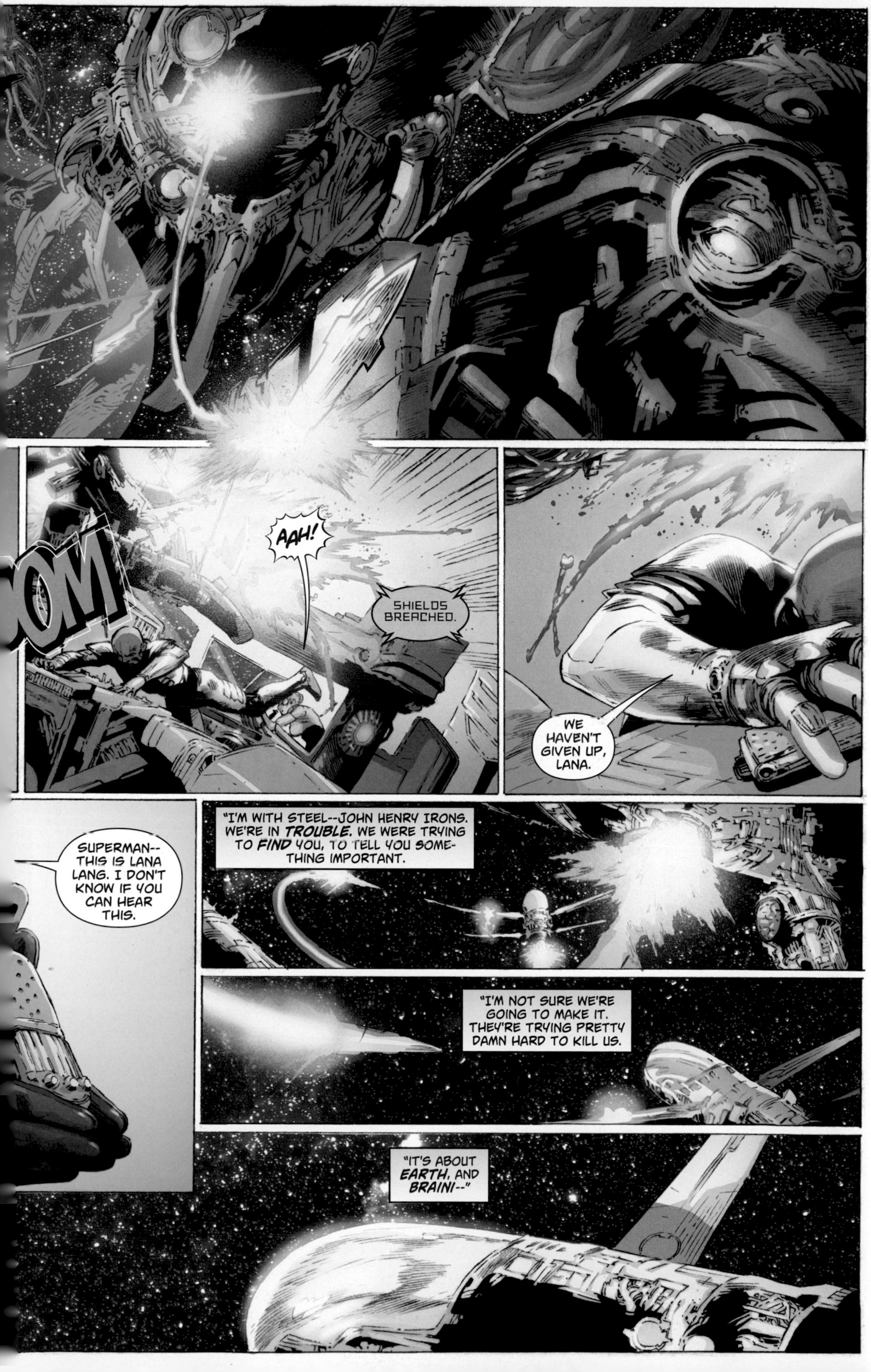

DOOM
AAH!
SHIELDS BREACHED.
WE HAVEN'T GIVEN UP, LANA.
SUPERMAN-- THIS IS LANA LANG. I DON'T KNOW IF YOU CAN HEAR THIS.
"I'M WITH STEEL--JOHN HENRY IRONS. WE'RE IN *TROUBLE.* WE WERE TRYING TO *FIND* YOU, TO TELL YOU SOMETHING IMPORTANT.
"I'M NOT SURE WE'RE GOING TO MAKE IT. THEY'RE TRYING PRETTY DAMN HARD TO KILL US.
"IT'S ABOUT *EARTH*, AND *BRAINI*--"

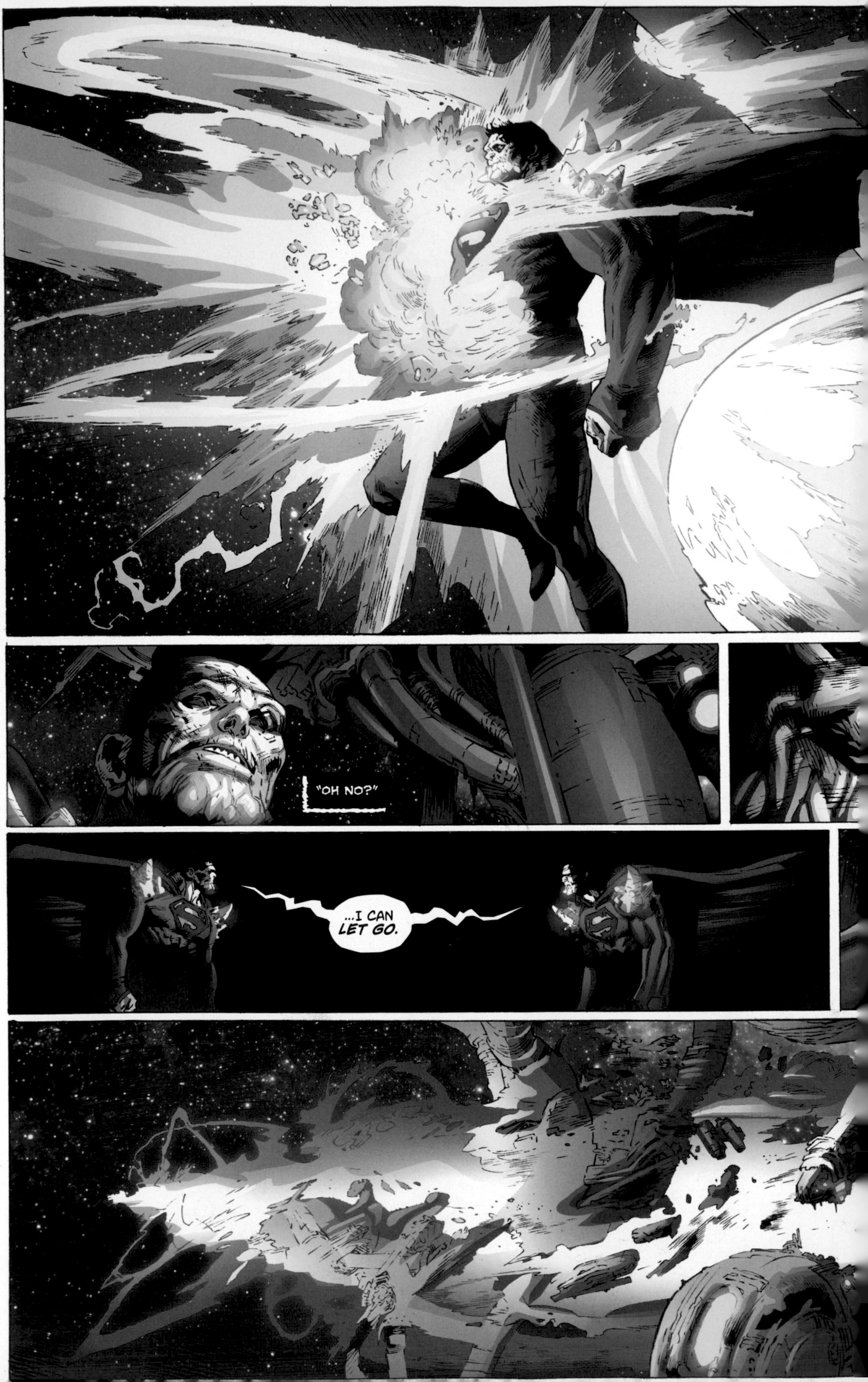
"OH NO?"
...I CAN LET GO.

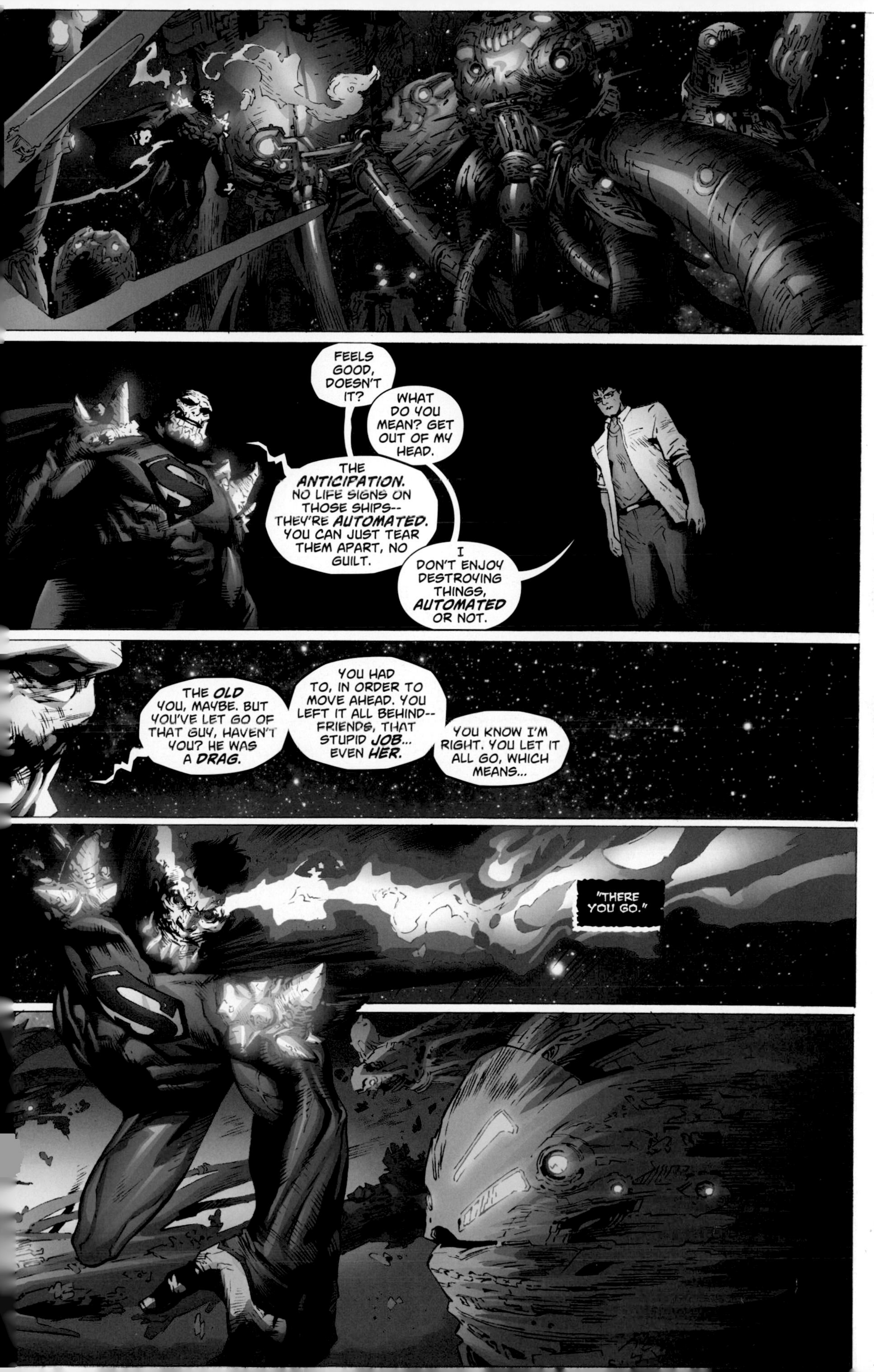
FEELS GOOD, DOESN'T IT?
WHAT DO YOU MEAN? GET OUT OF MY HEAD.
THE ANTICIPATION. NO LIFE SIGNS ON THOSE SHIPS-- THEY'RE AUTOMATED. YOU CAN JUST TEAR THEM APART, NO GUILT.
I DON'T ENJOY DESTROYING THINGS, AUTOMATED OR NOT.
THE OLD YOU, MAYBE. BUT YOU'VE LET GO OF THAT GUY, HAVEN'T YOU? HE WAS A DRAG.
YOU HAD TO, IN ORDER TO MOVE AHEAD. YOU LEFT IT ALL BEHIND-- FRIENDS, THAT STUPID JOB... EVEN HER.
YOU KNOW I'M RIGHT. YOU LET IT ALL GO, WHICH MEANS...
"THERE YOU GO."

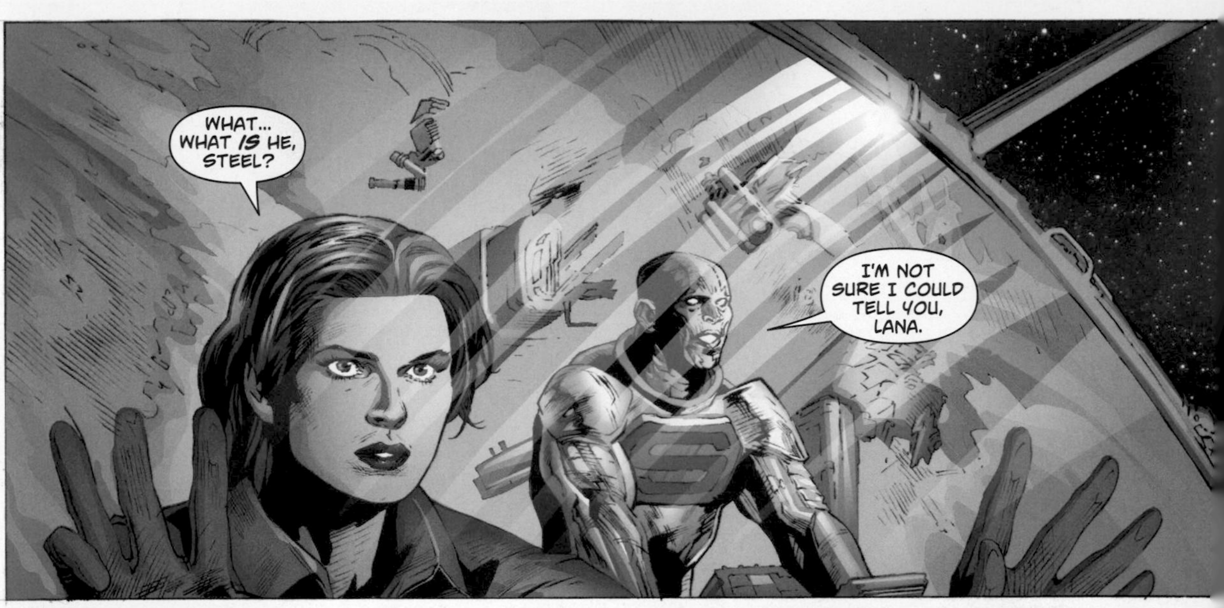
WHAT... WHAT IS HE, STEEL?
I'M NOT SURE I COULD TELL YOU, LANA.
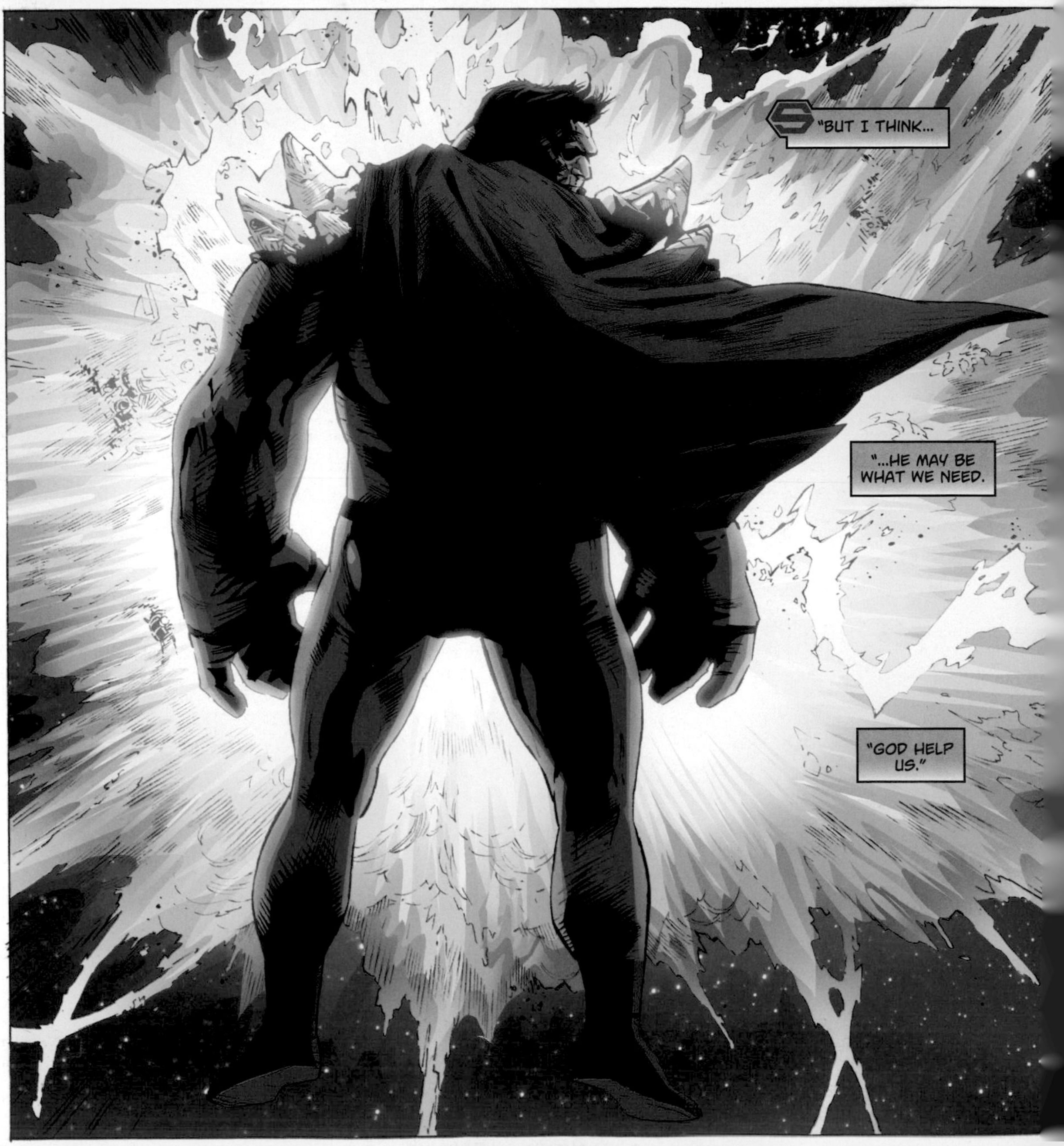
"BUT I THINK...
"...HE MAY BE WHAT WE NEED.
"GOD HELP US."

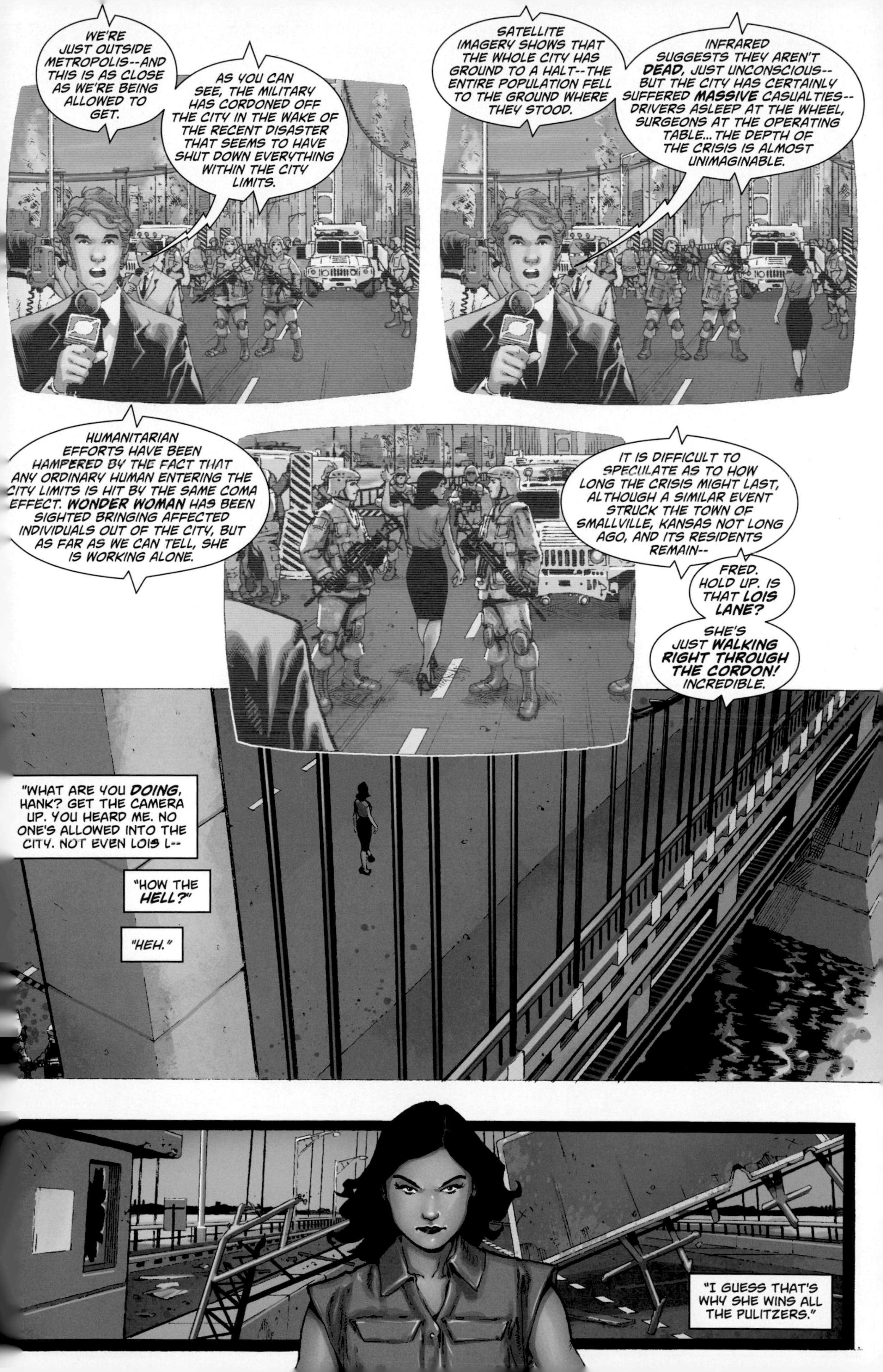
WE'RE JUST OUTSIDE METROPOLIS--AND THIS IS AS CLOSE AS WE'RE BEING ALLOWED TO GET.
AS YOU CAN SEE, THE MILITARY HAS CORDONED OFF THE CITY IN THE WAKE OF THE RECENT DISASTER THAT SEEMS TO HAVE SHUT DOWN EVERYTHING WITHIN THE CITY LIMITS.
SATELLITE IMAGERY SHOWS THAT THE WHOLE CITY HAS GROUND TO A HALT--THE ENTIRE POPULATION FELL TO THE GROUND WHERE THEY STOOD.
INFRARED SUGGESTS THEY AREN'T **DEAD**, JUST UNCONSCIOUS--BUT THE CITY HAS CERTAINLY SUFFERED **MASSIVE** CASUALTIES--DRIVERS ASLEEP AT THE WHEEL, SURGEONS AT THE OPERATING TABLE...THE DEPTH OF THE CRISIS IS ALMOST UNIMAGINABLE.
HUMANITARIAN EFFORTS HAVE BEEN HAMPERED BY THE FACT THAT ANY ORDINARY HUMAN ENTERING THE CITY LIMITS IS HIT BY THE SAME COMA EFFECT. **WONDER WOMAN** HAS BEEN SIGHTED BRINGING AFFECTED INDIVIDUALS OUT OF THE CITY, BUT AS FAR AS WE CAN TELL, SHE IS WORKING ALONE.
IT IS DIFFICULT TO SPECULATE AS TO HOW LONG THE CRISIS MIGHT LAST, ALTHOUGH A SIMILAR EVENT STRUCK THE TOWN OF SMALLVILLE, KANSAS NOT LONG AGO, AND ITS RESIDENTS REMAIN--
FRED. HOLD UP. IS THAT **LOIS LANE?**
SHE'S JUST **WALKING RIGHT THROUGH THE CORDON!** INCREDIBLE.
"WHAT ARE YOU **DOING**, HANK? GET THE CAMERA UP. YOU HEARD ME. NO ONE'S ALLOWED INTO THE CITY. NOT EVEN LOIS L--
"HOW THE **HELL?"**
"HEH."
"I GUESS THAT'S WHY SHE WINS ALL THE PULITZERS."

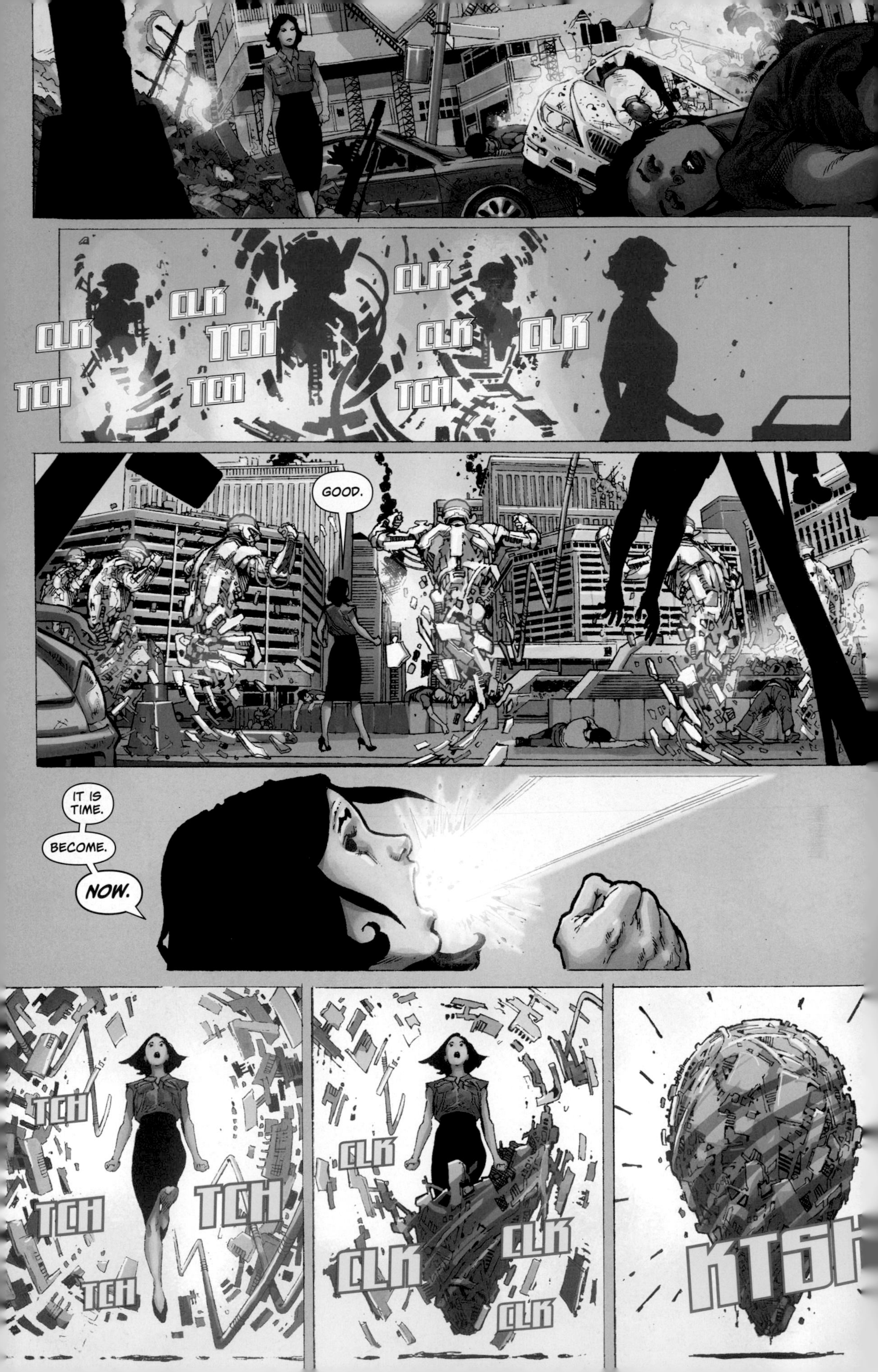
CLK
TCH
CLK
TCH
TCH
CLK
CLK
TCH
CLK
GOOD.
IT IS TIME.
BECOME.
NOW.
TCH
TCH
TCH
TCH
CLK
CLK
CLK
CLK
KTSH

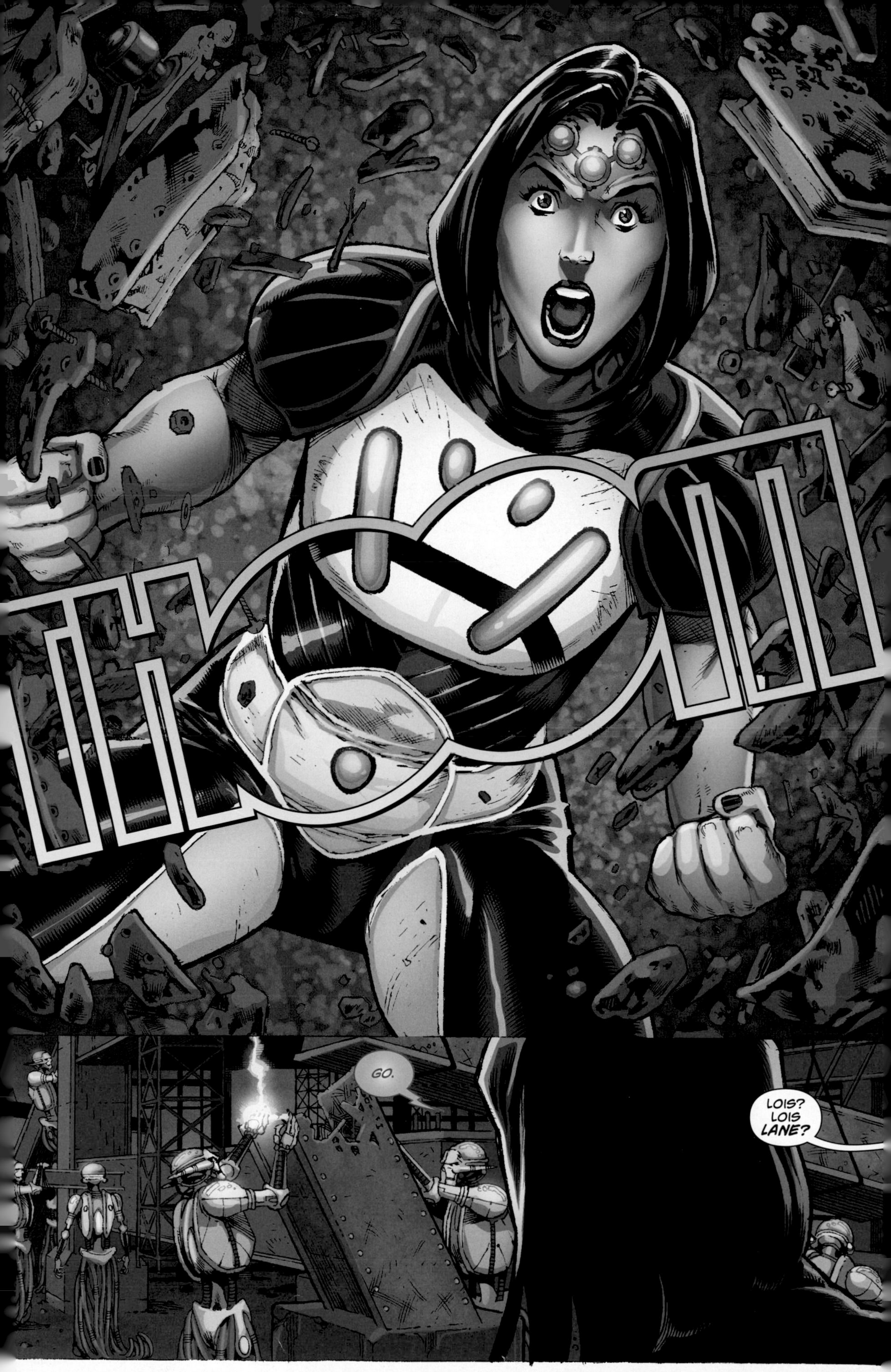
GO.
LOIS? LOIS LANE?

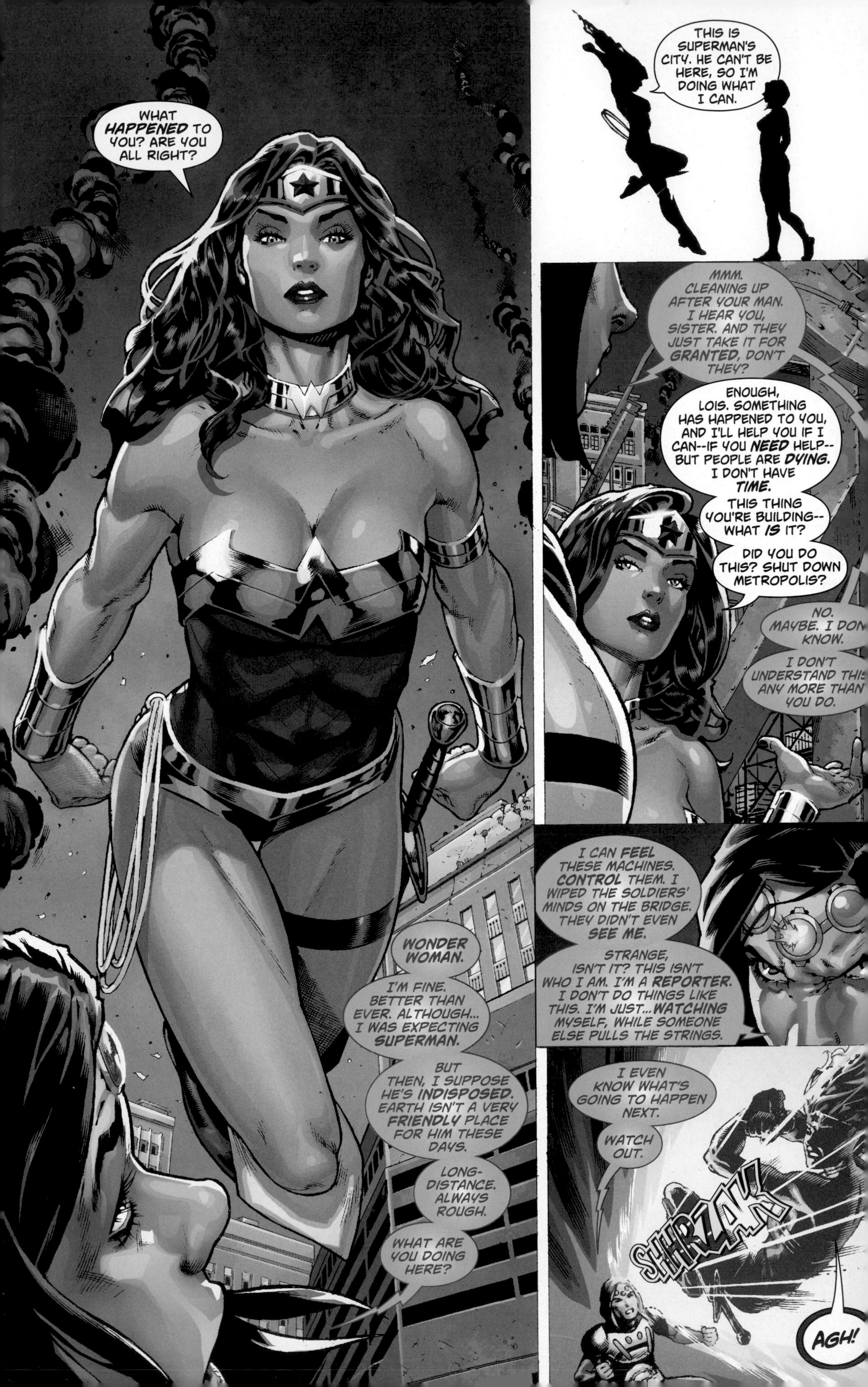
WHAT HAPPENED TO YOU? ARE YOU ALL RIGHT?
WONDER WOMAN.
I'M FINE. BETTER THAN EVER. ALTHOUGH... I WAS EXPECTING SUPERMAN.
BUT THEN, I SUPPOSE HE'S INDISPOSED. EARTH ISN'T A VERY FRIENDLY PLACE FOR HIM THESE DAYS.
LONG-DISTANCE. ALWAYS ROUGH.
WHAT ARE YOU DOING HERE?
THIS IS SUPERMAN'S CITY. HE CAN'T BE HERE, SO I'M DOING WHAT I CAN.
MMM. CLEANING UP AFTER YOUR MAN. I HEAR YOU, SISTER. AND THEY JUST TAKE IT FOR GRANTED, DON'T THEY?
ENOUGH, LOIS. SOMETHING HAS HAPPENED TO YOU, AND I'LL HELP YOU IF I CAN--IF YOU NEED HELP--BUT PEOPLE ARE DYING. I DON'T HAVE TIME.
THIS THING YOU'RE BUILDING--WHAT IS IT?
DID YOU DO THIS? SHUT DOWN METROPOLIS?
NO. MAYBE. I DON KNOW.
I DON'T UNDERSTAND THIS ANY MORE THAN YOU DO.
I CAN FEEL THESE MACHINES. CONTROL THEM. I WIPED THE SOLDIERS' MINDS ON THE BRIDGE. THEY DIDN'T EVEN SEE ME.
STRANGE, ISN'T IT? THIS ISN'T WHO I AM. I'M A REPORTER. I DON'T DO THINGS LIKE THIS. I'M JUST...WATCHING MYSELF, WHILE SOMEONE ELSE PULLS THE STRINGS.
I EVEN KNOW WHAT'S GOING TO HAPPEN NEXT.
WATCH OUT.
SHRZAK
AGH!

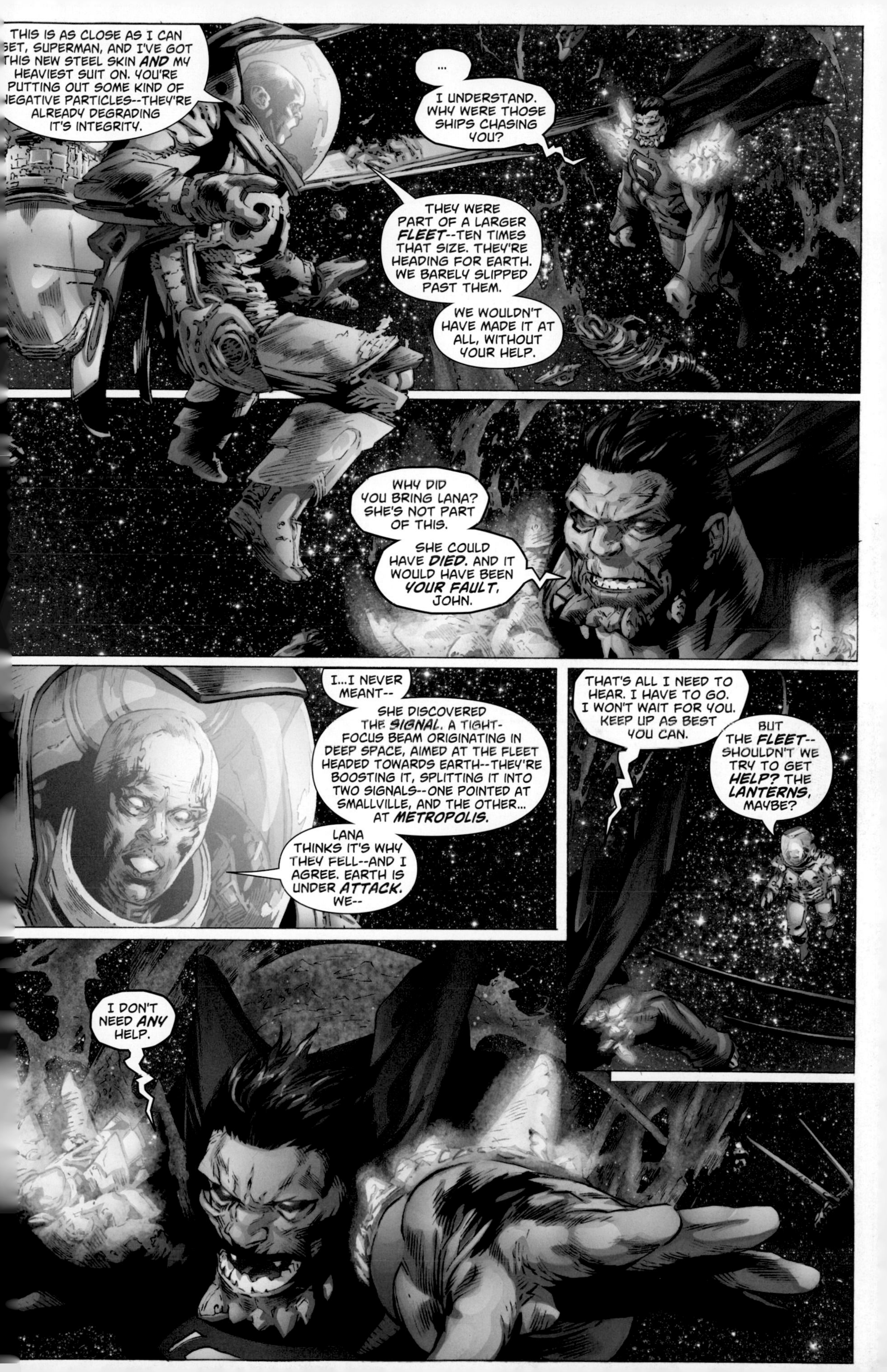
THIS IS AS CLOSE AS I CAN GET, SUPERMAN, AND I'VE GOT THIS NEW STEEL SKIN AND MY HEAVIEST SUIT ON. YOU'RE PUTTING OUT SOME KIND OF NEGATIVE PARTICLES--THEY'RE ALREADY DEGRADING IT'S INTEGRITY.
...
I UNDERSTAND. WHY WERE THOSE SHIPS CHASING YOU?
THEY WERE PART OF A LARGER FLEET--TEN TIMES THAT SIZE. THEY'RE HEADING FOR EARTH. WE BARELY SLIPPED PAST THEM.
WE WOULDN'T HAVE MADE IT AT ALL, WITHOUT YOUR HELP.
WHY DID YOU BRING LANA? SHE'S NOT PART OF THIS.
SHE COULD HAVE DIED. AND IT WOULD HAVE BEEN YOUR FAULT, JOHN.
I...I NEVER MEANT--
SHE DISCOVERED THE SIGNAL. A TIGHT-FOCUS BEAM ORIGINATING IN DEEP SPACE, AIMED AT THE FLEET HEADED TOWARDS EARTH--THEY'RE BOOSTING IT, SPLITTING IT INTO TWO SIGNALS--ONE POINTED AT SMALLVILLE, AND THE OTHER... AT METROPOLIS.
LANA THINKS IT'S WHY THEY FELL--AND I AGREE. EARTH IS UNDER ATTACK. WE--
THAT'S ALL I NEED TO HEAR. I HAVE TO GO. I WON'T WAIT FOR YOU. KEEP UP AS BEST YOU CAN.
BUT THE FLEET--SHOULDN'T WE TRY TO GET HELP? THE LANTERNS, MAYBE?
I DON'T NEED ANY HELP.

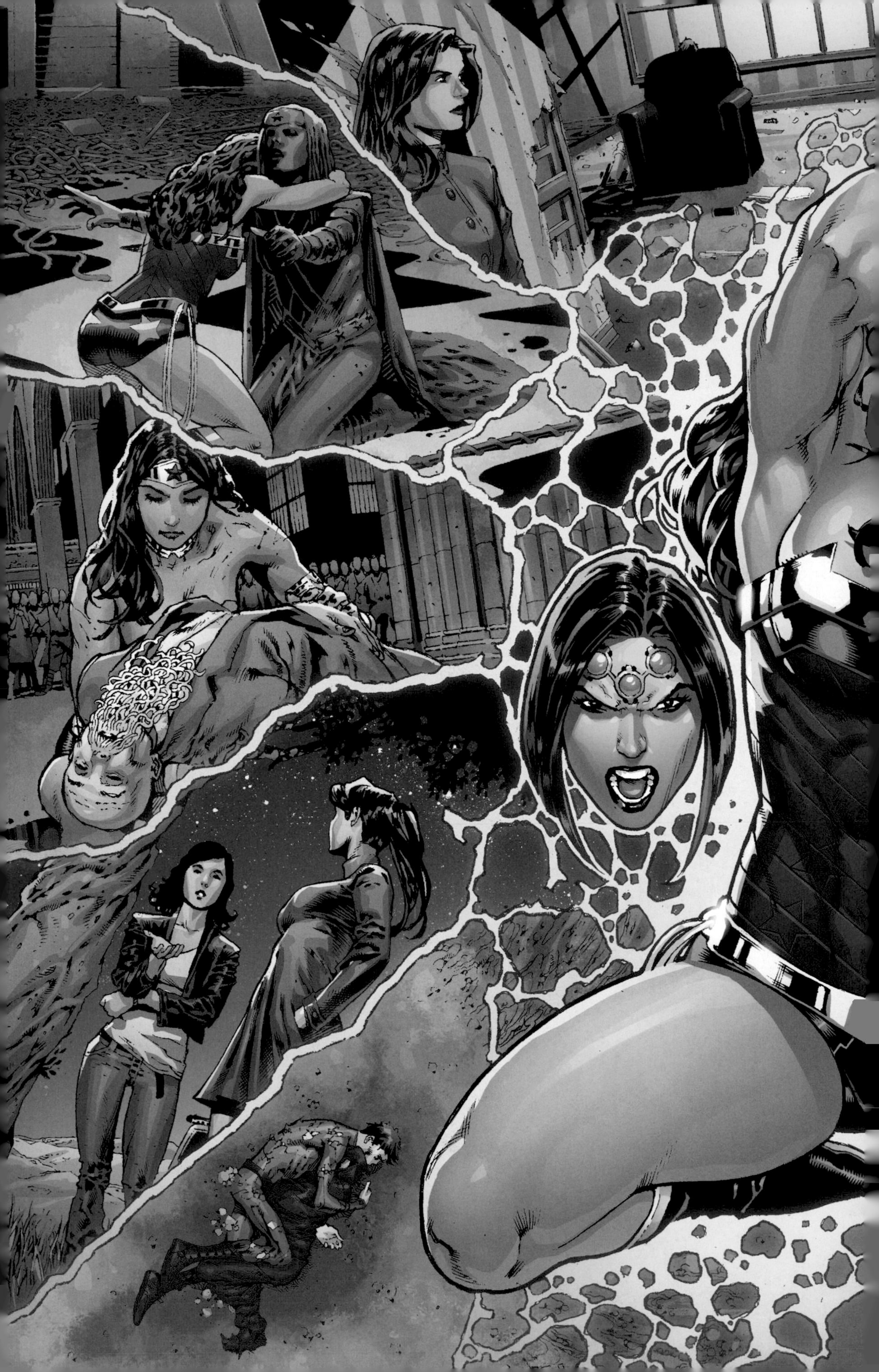

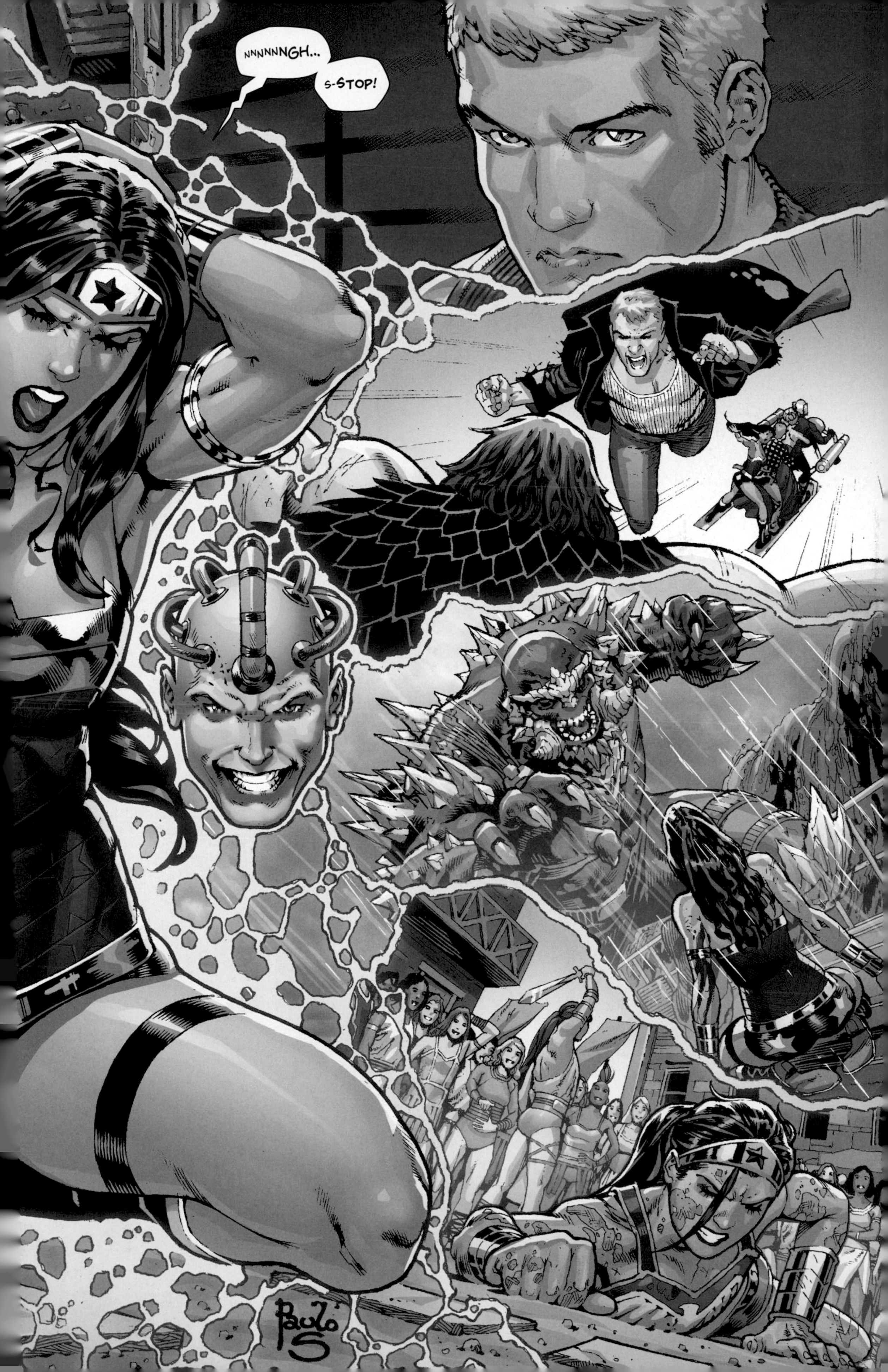
NNNNNNGH...
S-STOP!
Paulo S

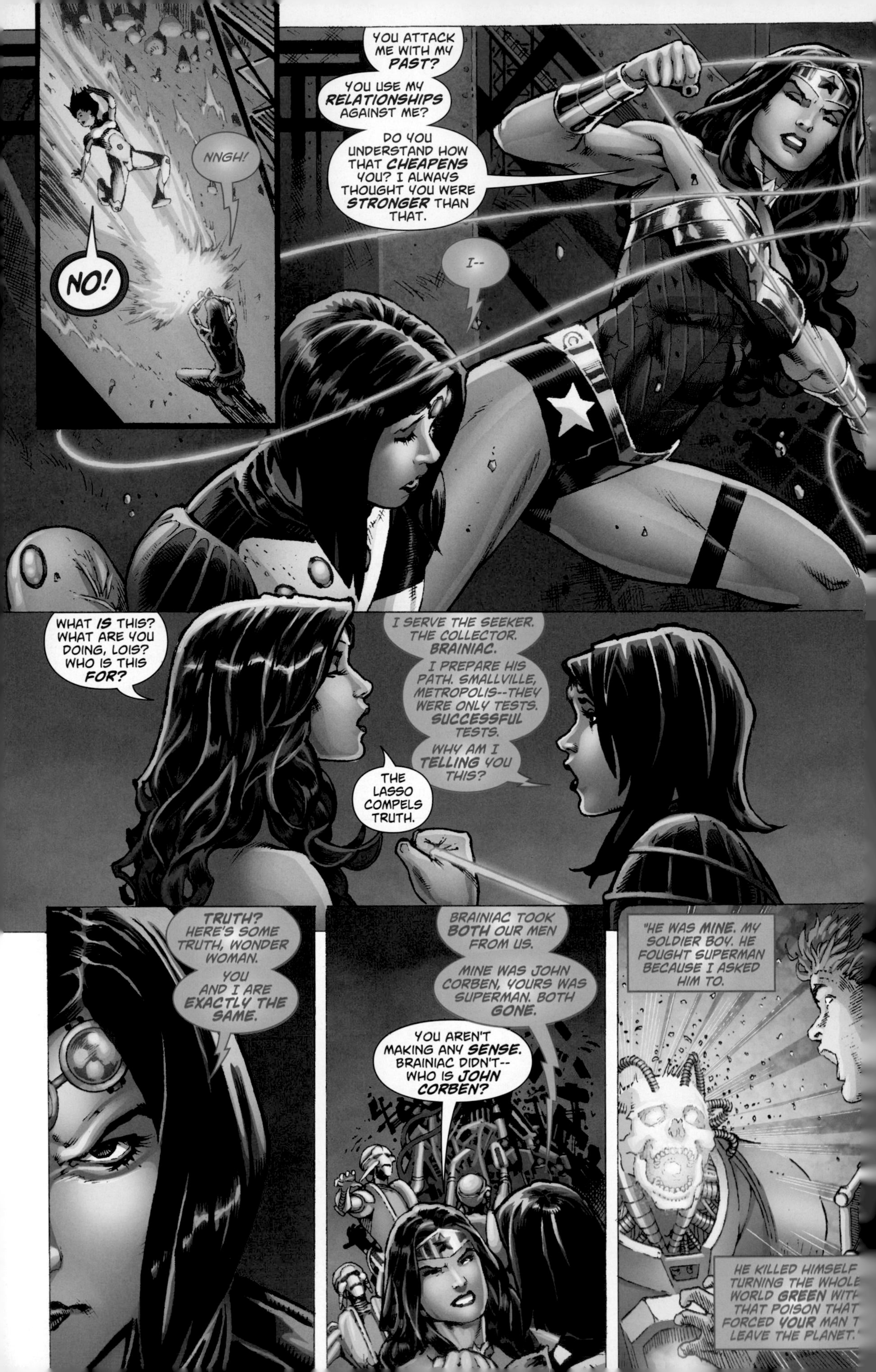
NNGH!
NO!
YOU ATTACK ME WITH MY PAST?
YOU USE MY RELATIONSHIPS AGAINST ME?
DO YOU UNDERSTAND HOW THAT CHEAPENS YOU? I ALWAYS THOUGHT YOU WERE STRONGER THAN THAT.
I--
WHAT IS THIS? WHAT ARE YOU DOING, LOIS? WHO IS THIS FOR?
I SERVE THE SEEKER. THE COLLECTOR. BRAINIAC.
I PREPARE HIS PATH. SMALLVILLE, METROPOLIS--THEY WERE ONLY TESTS. SUCCESSFUL TESTS.
WHY AM I TELLING YOU THIS?
THE LASSO COMPELS TRUTH.
TRUTH? HERE'S SOME TRUTH, WONDER WOMAN.
YOU AND I ARE EXACTLY THE SAME.
BRAINIAC TOOK BOTH OUR MEN FROM US.
MINE WAS JOHN CORBEN, YOURS WAS SUPERMAN. BOTH GONE.
YOU AREN'T MAKING ANY SENSE. BRAINIAC DIDN'T-- WHO IS JOHN CORBEN?
"HE WAS MINE. MY SOLDIER BOY. HE FOUGHT SUPERMAN BECAUSE I ASKED HIM TO.
HE KILLED HIMSELF TURNING THE WHOLE WORLD GREEN WITH THAT POISON THAT FORCED YOUR MAN TO LEAVE THE PLANET."

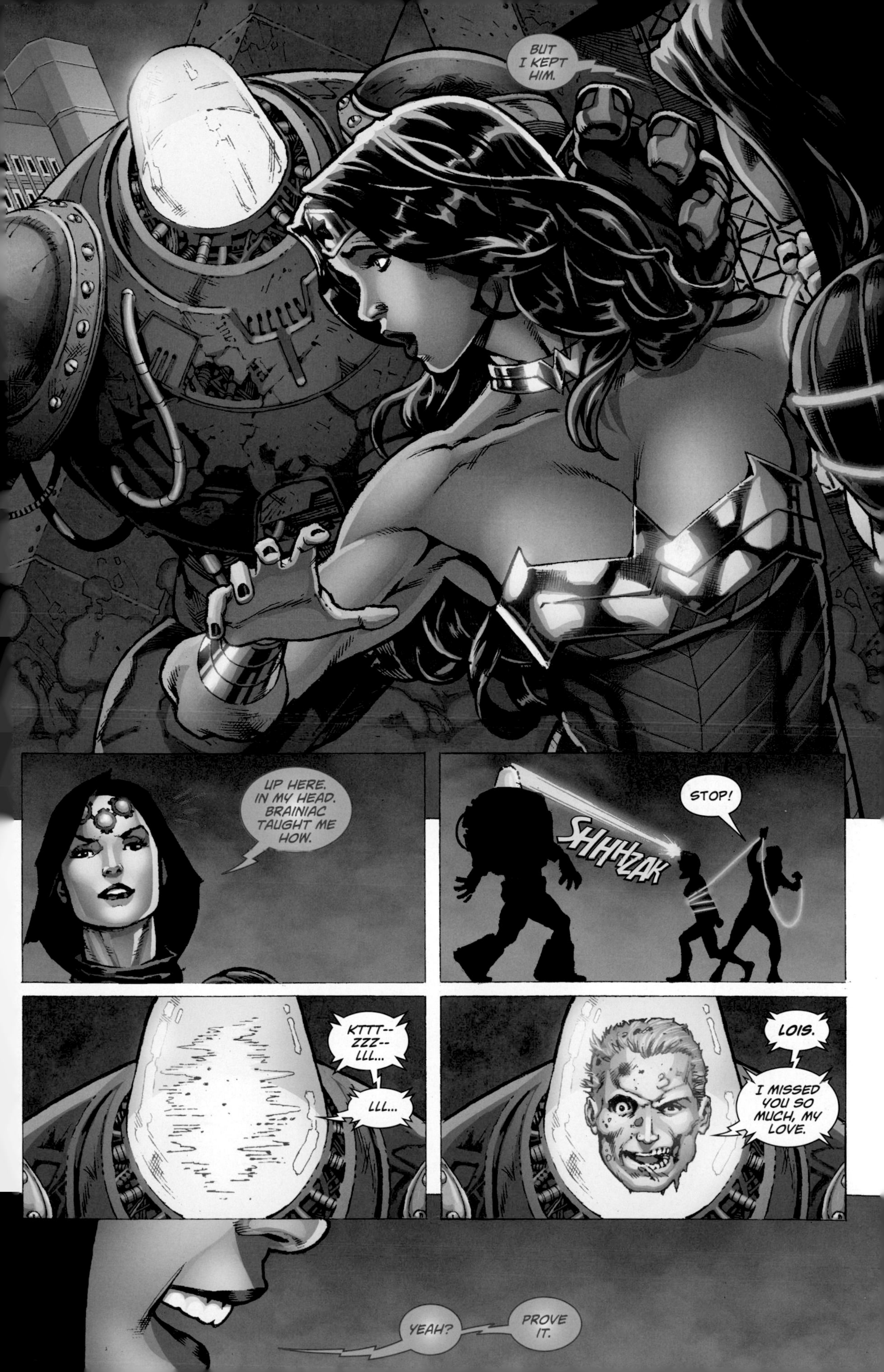
BUT I KEPT HIM.
UP HERE. IN MY HEAD. BRAINIAC TAUGHT ME HOW.
SHHHZAK
STOP!
KTTT-- ZZZ-- LLL...
LLL...
LOIS.
I MISSED YOU SO MUCH, MY LOVE.
YEAH?
PROVE IT.

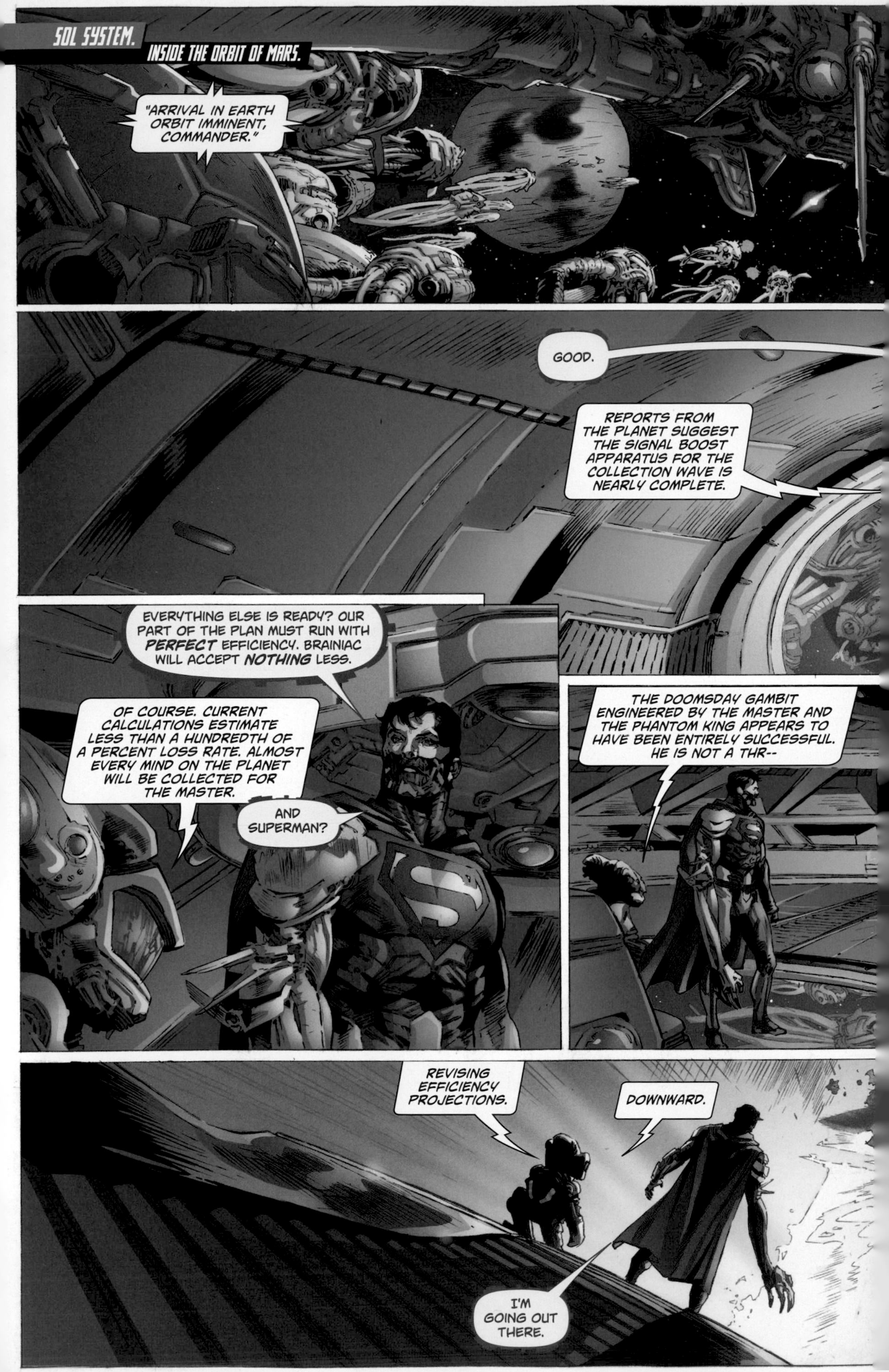
SOL SYSTEM.
INSIDE THE ORBIT OF MARS.
"ARRIVAL IN EARTH ORBIT IMMINENT, COMMANDER."
GOOD.
REPORTS FROM THE PLANET SUGGEST THE SIGNAL BOOST APPARATUS FOR THE COLLECTION WAVE IS NEARLY COMPLETE.
EVERYTHING ELSE IS READY? OUR PART OF THE PLAN MUST RUN WITH PERFECT EFFICIENCY. BRAINIAC WILL ACCEPT NOTHING LESS.
OF COURSE. CURRENT CALCULATIONS ESTIMATE LESS THAN A HUNDREDTH OF A PERCENT LOSS RATE. ALMOST EVERY MIND ON THE PLANET WILL BE COLLECTED FOR THE MASTER.
AND SUPERMAN?
THE DOOMSDAY GAMBIT ENGINEERED BY THE MASTER AND THE PHANTOM KING APPEARS TO HAVE BEEN ENTIRELY SUCCESSFUL. HE IS NOT A THR--
REVISING EFFICIENCY PROJECTIONS.
DOWNWARD.
I'M GOING OUT THERE.

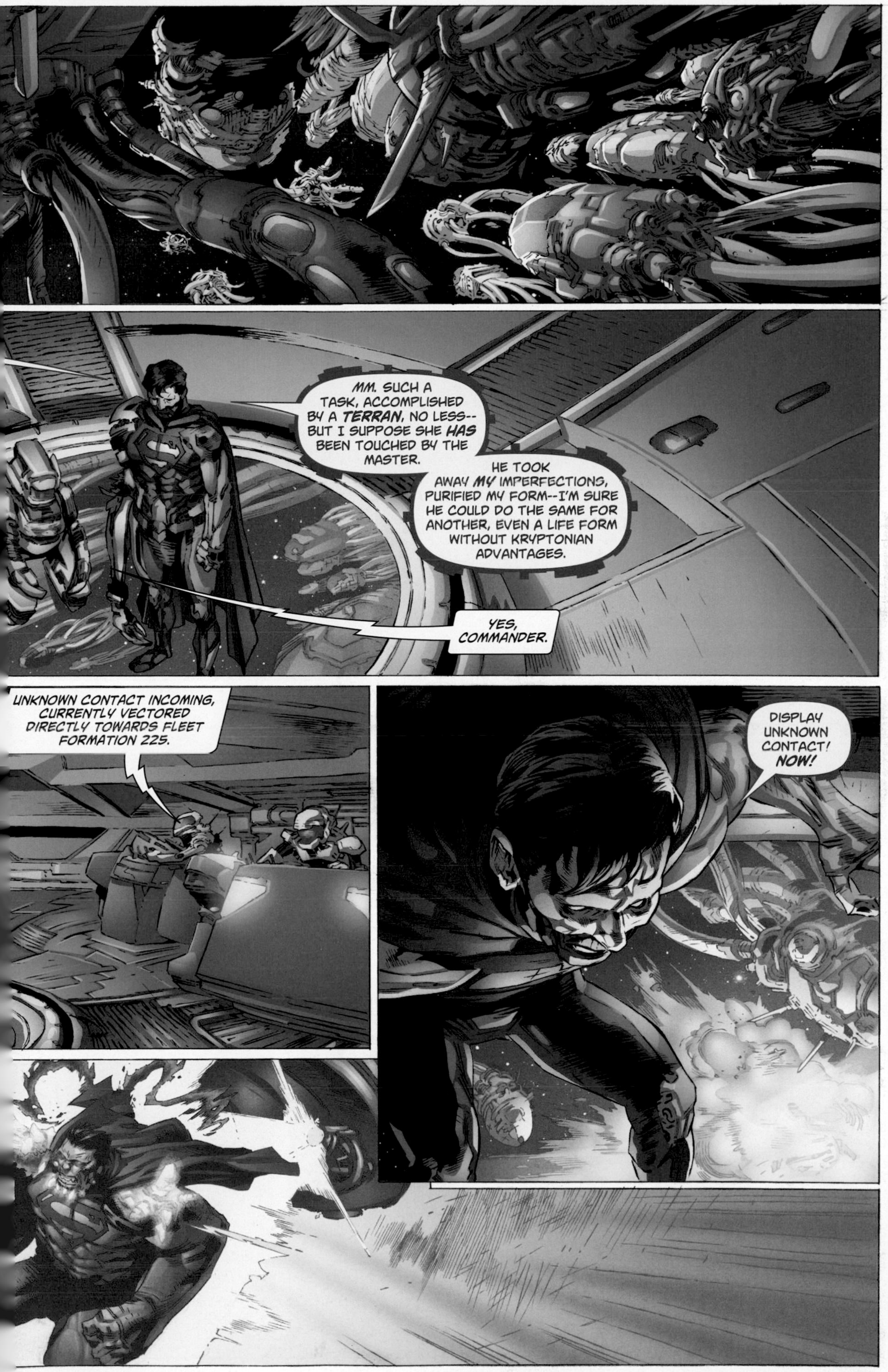
MM. SUCH A TASK, ACCOMPLISHED BY A TERRAN, NO LESS--BUT I SUPPOSE SHE HAS BEEN TOUCHED BY THE MASTER.
HE TOOK AWAY MY IMPERFECTIONS, PURIFIED MY FORM--I'M SURE HE COULD DO THE SAME FOR ANOTHER, EVEN A LIFE FORM WITHOUT KRYPTONIAN ADVANTAGES.
YES, COMMANDER.
UNKNOWN CONTACT INCOMING, CURRENTLY VECTORED DIRECTLY TOWARDS FLEET FORMATION 225.
DISPLAY UNKNOWN CONTACT! NOW!

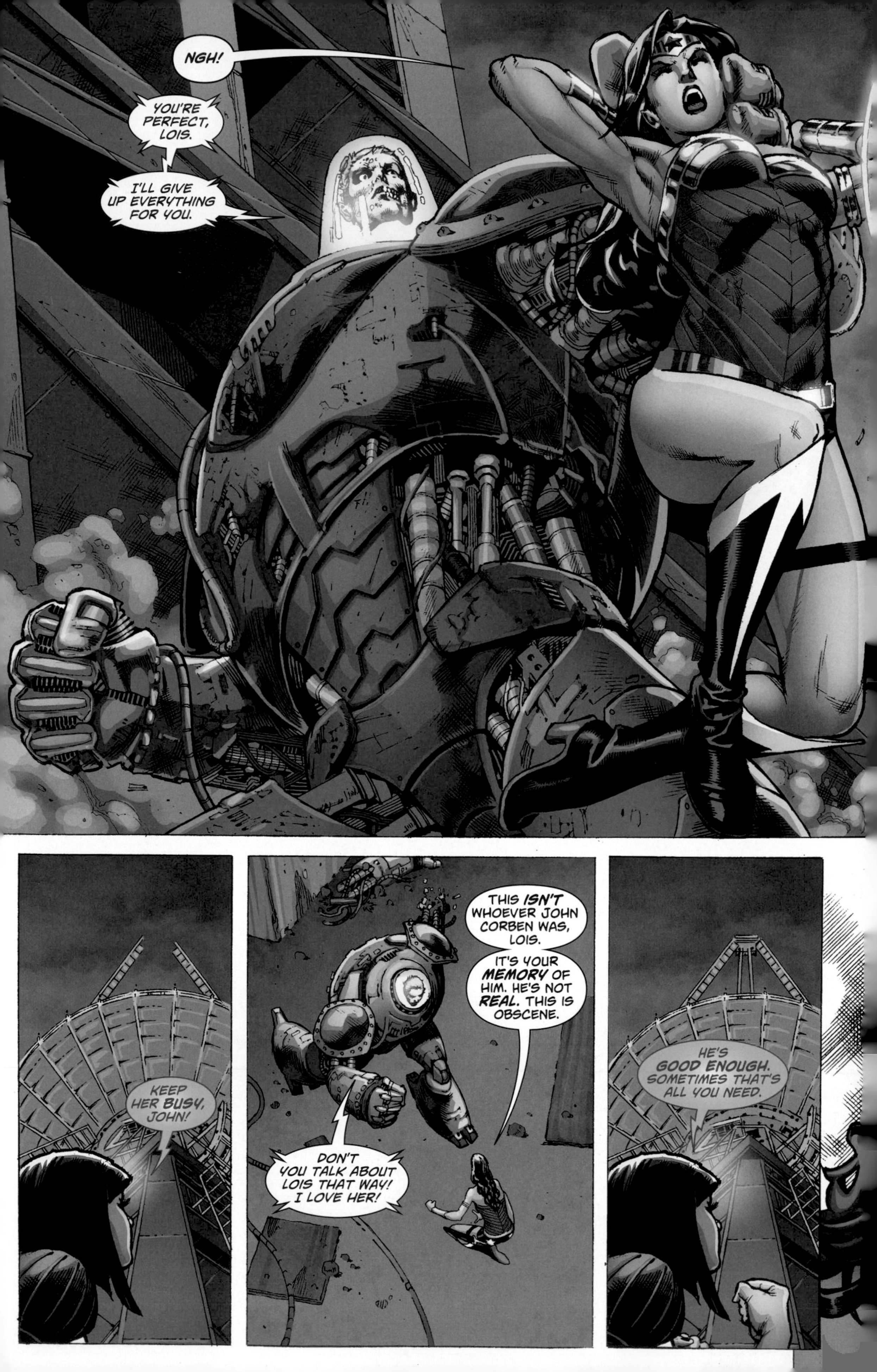
NGH!
YOU'RE PERFECT, LOIS.
I'LL GIVE UP EVERYTHING FOR YOU.
KEEP HER BUSY, JOHN!
THIS ISN'T WHOEVER JOHN CORBEN WAS, LOIS.
IT'S YOUR MEMORY OF HIM. HE'S NOT REAL. THIS IS OBSCENE.
DON'T YOU TALK ABOUT LOIS THAT WAY! I LOVE HER!
HE'S GOOD ENOUGH. SOMETIMES THAT'S ALL YOU NEED.

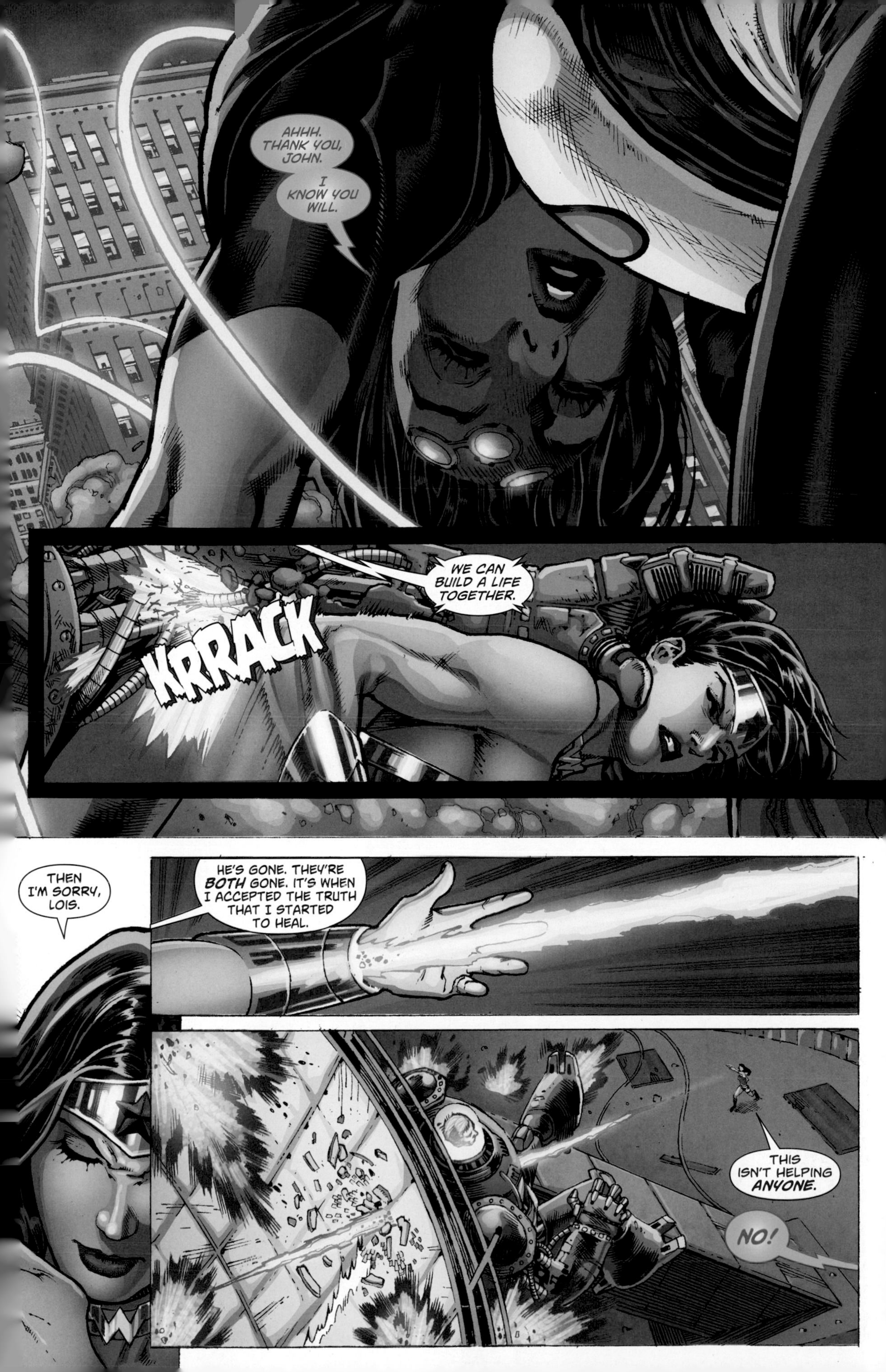
AHHH. THANK YOU, JOHN.
I KNOW YOU WILL.
WE CAN BUILD A LIFE TOGETHER.
KRRACK
THEN I'M SORRY, LOIS.
HE'S GONE. THEY'RE BOTH GONE. IT'S WHEN I ACCEPTED THE TRUTH THAT I STARTED TO HEAL.
THIS ISN'T HELPING ANYONE.
NO!

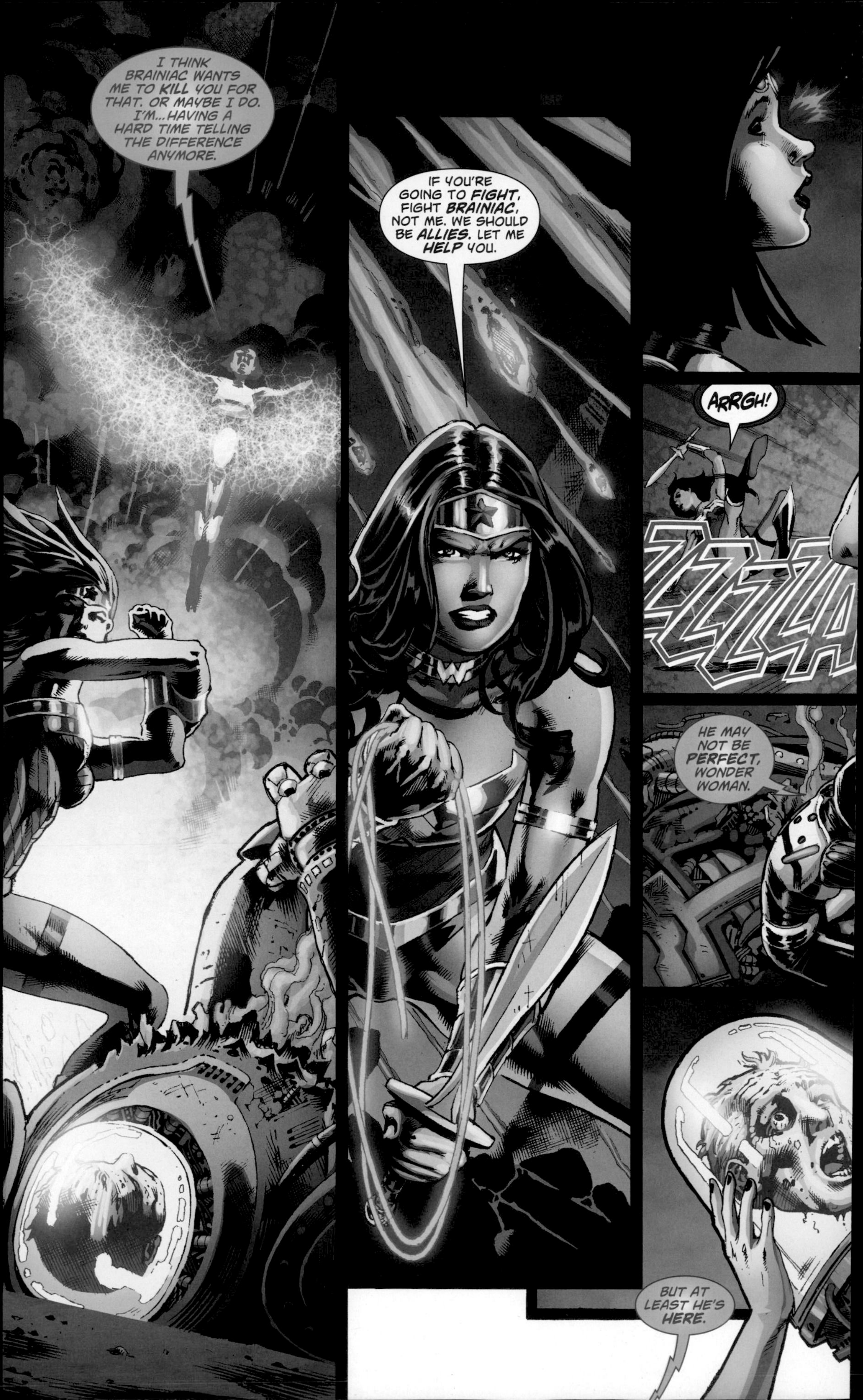
I THINK BRAINIAC WANTS ME TO KILL YOU FOR THAT. OR MAYBE I DO. I'M...HAVING A HARD TIME TELLING THE DIFFERENCE ANYMORE.
IF YOU'RE GOING TO FIGHT, FIGHT BRAINIAC, NOT ME. WE SHOULD BE ALLIES. LET ME HELP YOU.
ARRGH!
HE MAY NOT BE PERFECT, WONDER WOMAN.
BUT AT LEAST HE'S HERE.

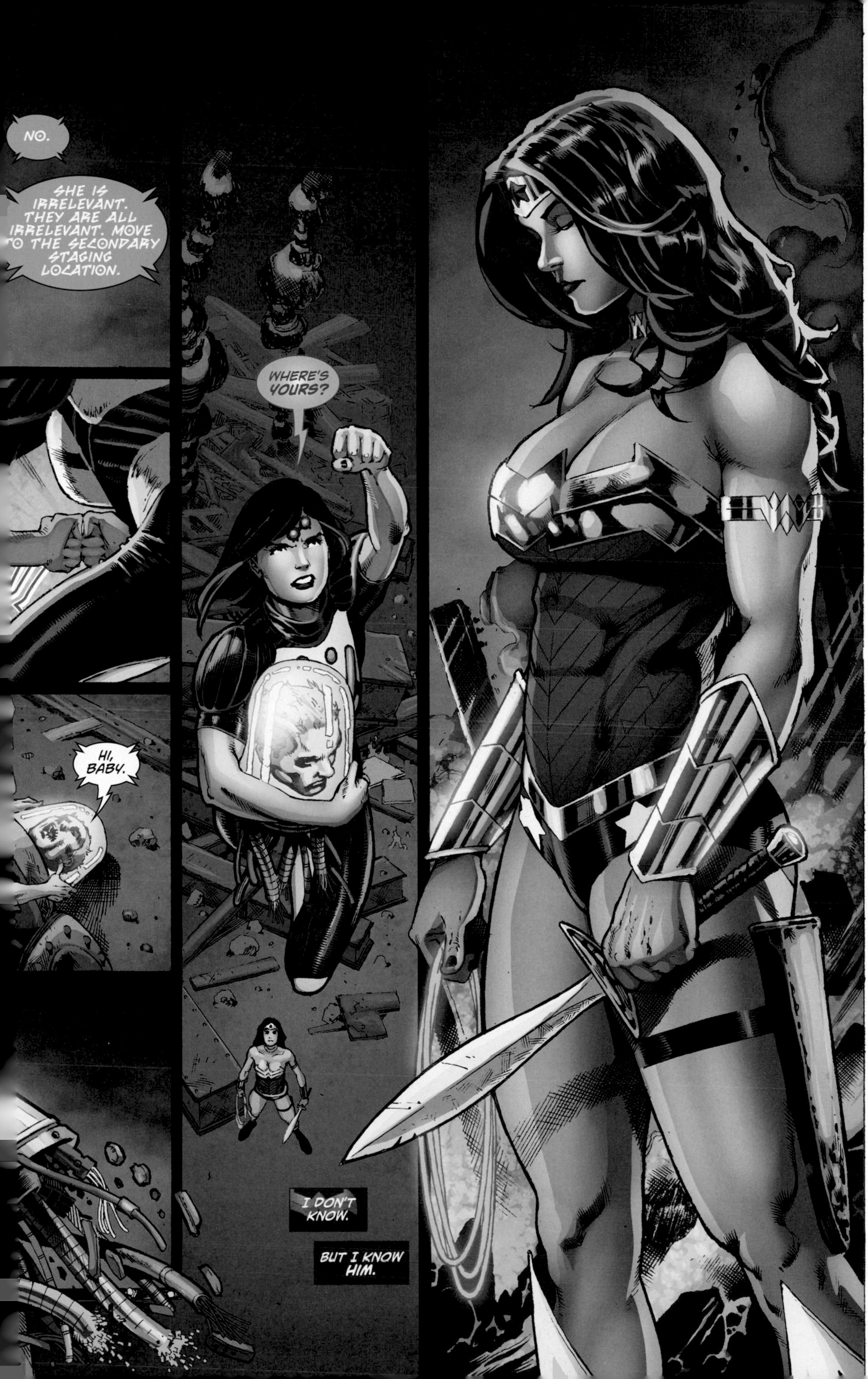
NO.
SHE IS IRRELEVANT. THEY ARE ALL IRRELEVANT. MOVE TO THE SECONDARY STAGING LOCATION.
HI, BABY.
WHERE'S YOURS?
I DON'T KNOW.
BUT I KNOW HIM.

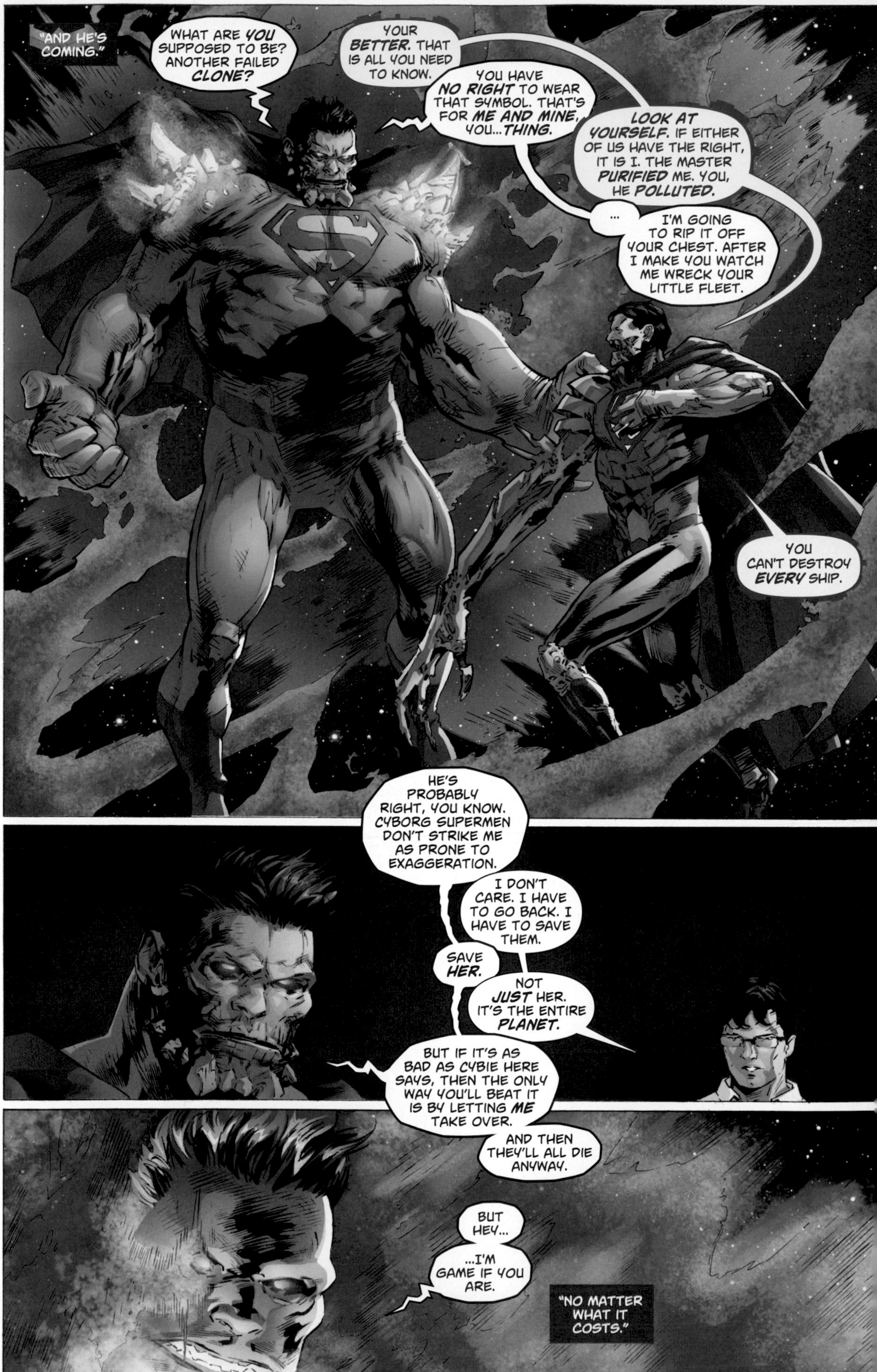
"AND HE'S COMING."
WHAT ARE YOU SUPPOSED TO BE? ANOTHER FAILED CLONE?
YOUR BETTER. THAT IS ALL YOU NEED TO KNOW.
YOU HAVE NO RIGHT TO WEAR THAT SYMBOL. THAT'S FOR ME AND MINE, YOU...THING.
LOOK AT YOURSELF. IF EITHER OF US HAVE THE RIGHT, IT IS I. THE MASTER PURIFIED ME. YOU, HE POLLUTED.
...
I'M GOING TO RIP IT OFF YOUR CHEST. AFTER I MAKE YOU WATCH ME WRECK YOUR LITTLE FLEET.
YOU CAN'T DESTROY EVERY SHIP.
HE'S PROBABLY RIGHT, YOU KNOW. CYBORG SUPERMEN DON'T STRIKE ME AS PRONE TO EXAGGERATION.
I DON'T CARE. I HAVE TO GO BACK. I HAVE TO SAVE THEM.
SAVE HER.
NOT JUST HER. IT'S THE ENTIRE PLANET.
BUT IF IT'S AS BAD AS CYBIE HERE SAYS, THEN THE ONLY WAY YOU'LL BEAT IT IS BY LETTING ME TAKE OVER.
AND THEN THEY'LL ALL DIE ANYWAY.
BUT HEY...
...I'M GAME IF YOU ARE.
"NO MATTER WHAT IT COSTS."

THE PROMISE

ED BENES TONY S. DANIEL PASCAL ALIXE CLIFF RICHARDS JACK HERBERT pencillers
JAIME MENDOZA MATT BANNING VICENTE CIFUENTES PASCAL ALIXE CLIFF RICHARDS inkers
cover by TONY S. DANIEL & TOMEU MOREY

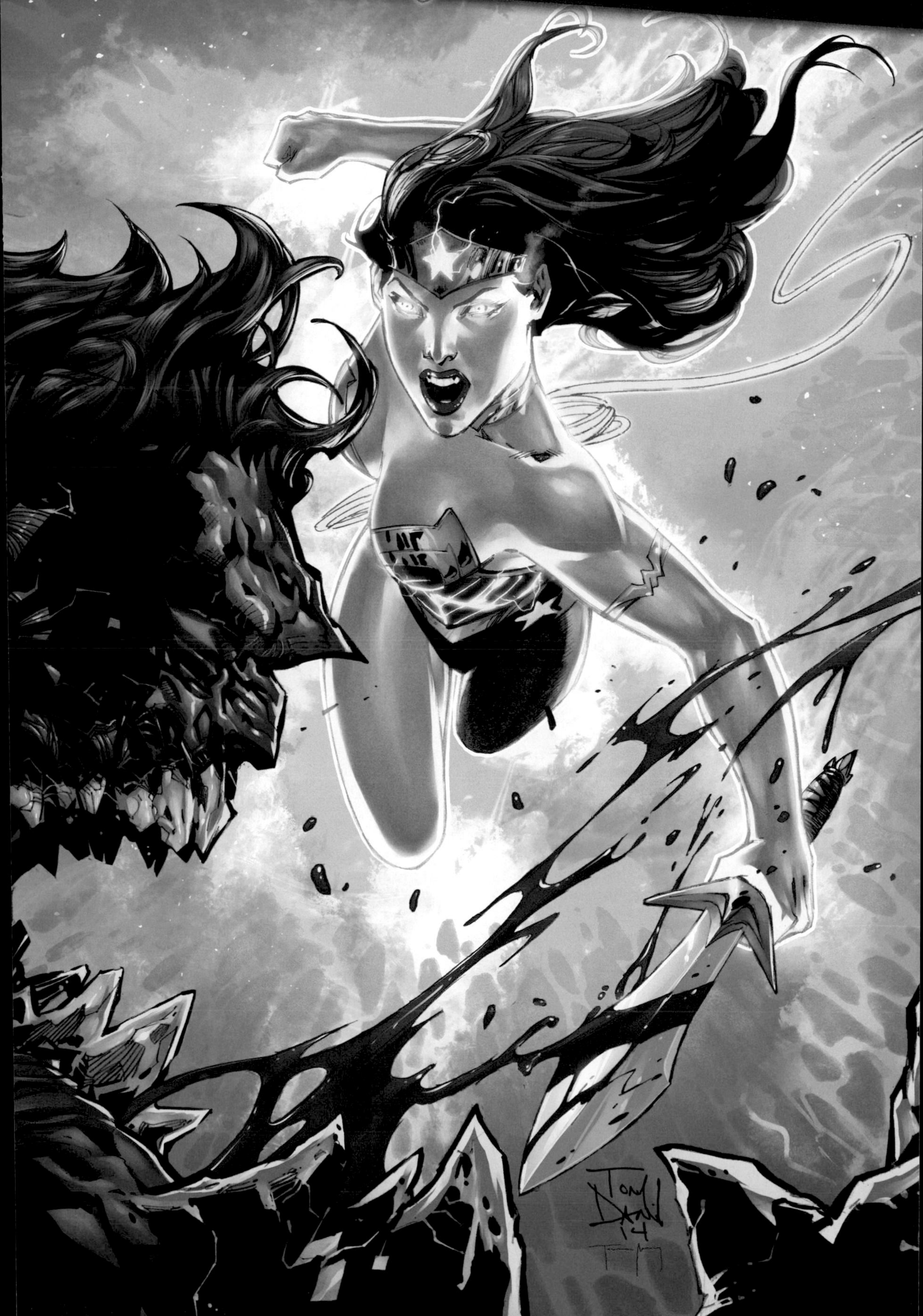

WORLD   U.S.   METROPOLIS   BUSINESS   OPINION   SPORTS   ARTS   STYLE   VIDEO

July 30, 2014

Daily Planet

WORLD WITHOUT
S U P E R M A N

JL Satellite Images

By Lois Lane

Five years ago, a strange visitor from another planet insinuated his presence on Metropolis by seemingly saving us from another alien that we started to call Brainiac. Metropolis had been shrunk and stolen by Brainiac and this Superman went out and defeated him leading to the restoration of the city.

At least that is the story that was printed then.

Looking at the events that have occurred in the past few days—the entire populations of Smallville, Kansas, and Metropolis having all fallen into inexplicable comas in places the Kryptonian has centered his activities on—we have to ask who is the true villain?

Another pretense at heroism by the Kryptonian came with his destruction of the creature dubbed Doomsday. But this has only led to Kal-El's transformation into

something even deadlier, perhaps his true form? Was Brainiac, in fact, trying to spare us from the fate that Superman's existence would have us suffer? Was there a reason an entire Planet like Krypton was destroyed because o creatures like him?

With a nimbus of death that marks his every step, perhaps we should rethink our opinion of Brainiac and open our minds to th possibility that his return could be our only hope against SuperDoon

404 Error   404 Error
404 Error

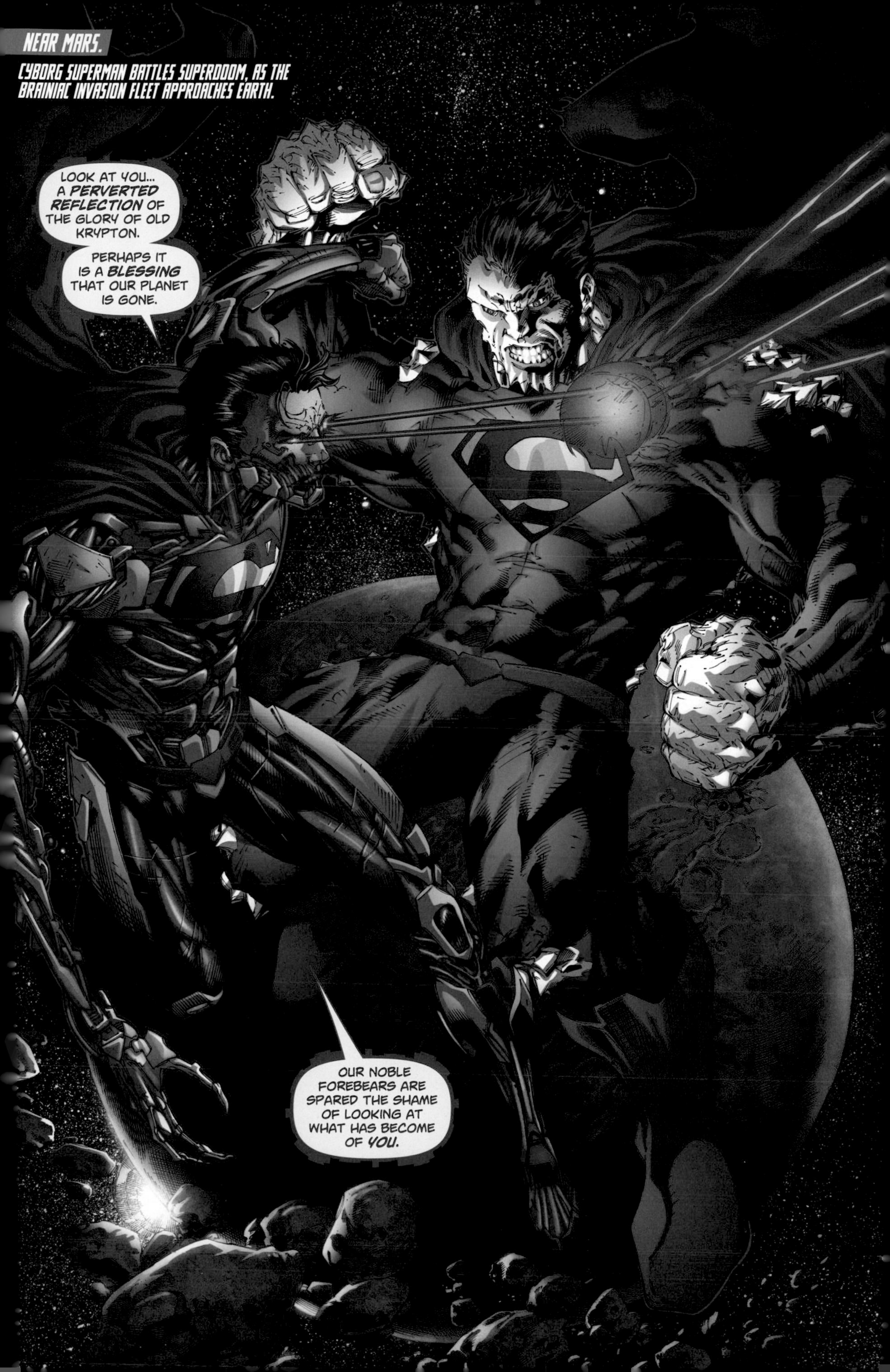
NEAR MARS.
CYBORG SUPERMAN BATTLES SUPERDOOM, AS THE BRAINIAC INVASION FLEET APPROACHES EARTH.
LOOK AT YOU... A PERVERTED REFLECTION OF THE GLORY OF OLD KRYPTON.
PERHAPS IT IS A BLESSING THAT OUR PLANET IS GONE.
OUR NOBLE FOREBEARS ARE SPARED THE SHAME OF LOOKING AT WHAT HAS BECOME OF YOU.

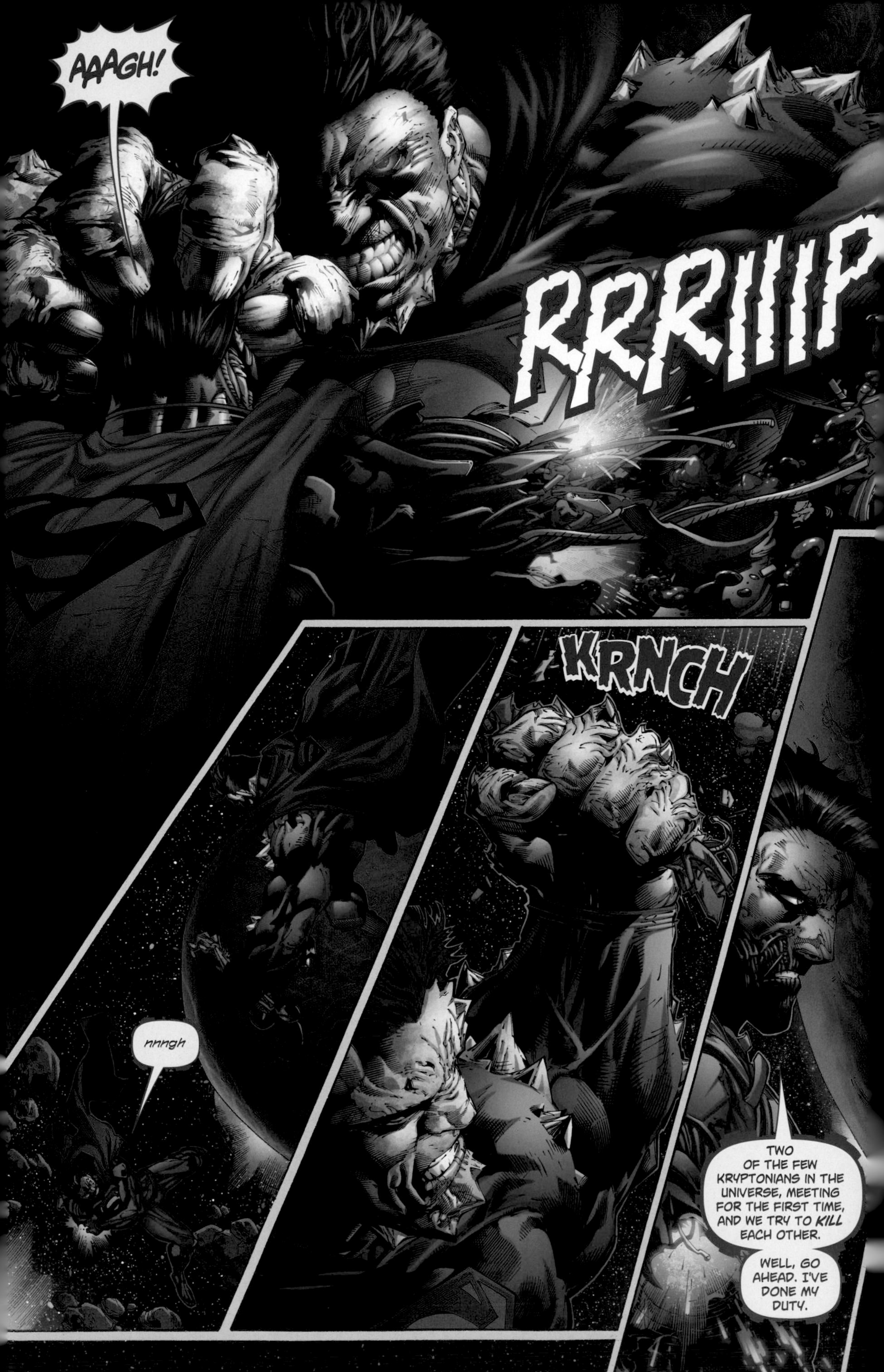
AAAGH!
RRRIIIP
KRNCH
nnngh
TWO OF THE FEW KRYPTONIANS IN THE UNIVERSE, MEETING FOR THE FIRST TIME, AND WE TRY TO KILL EACH OTHER.
WELL, GO AHEAD. I'VE DONE MY DUTY.

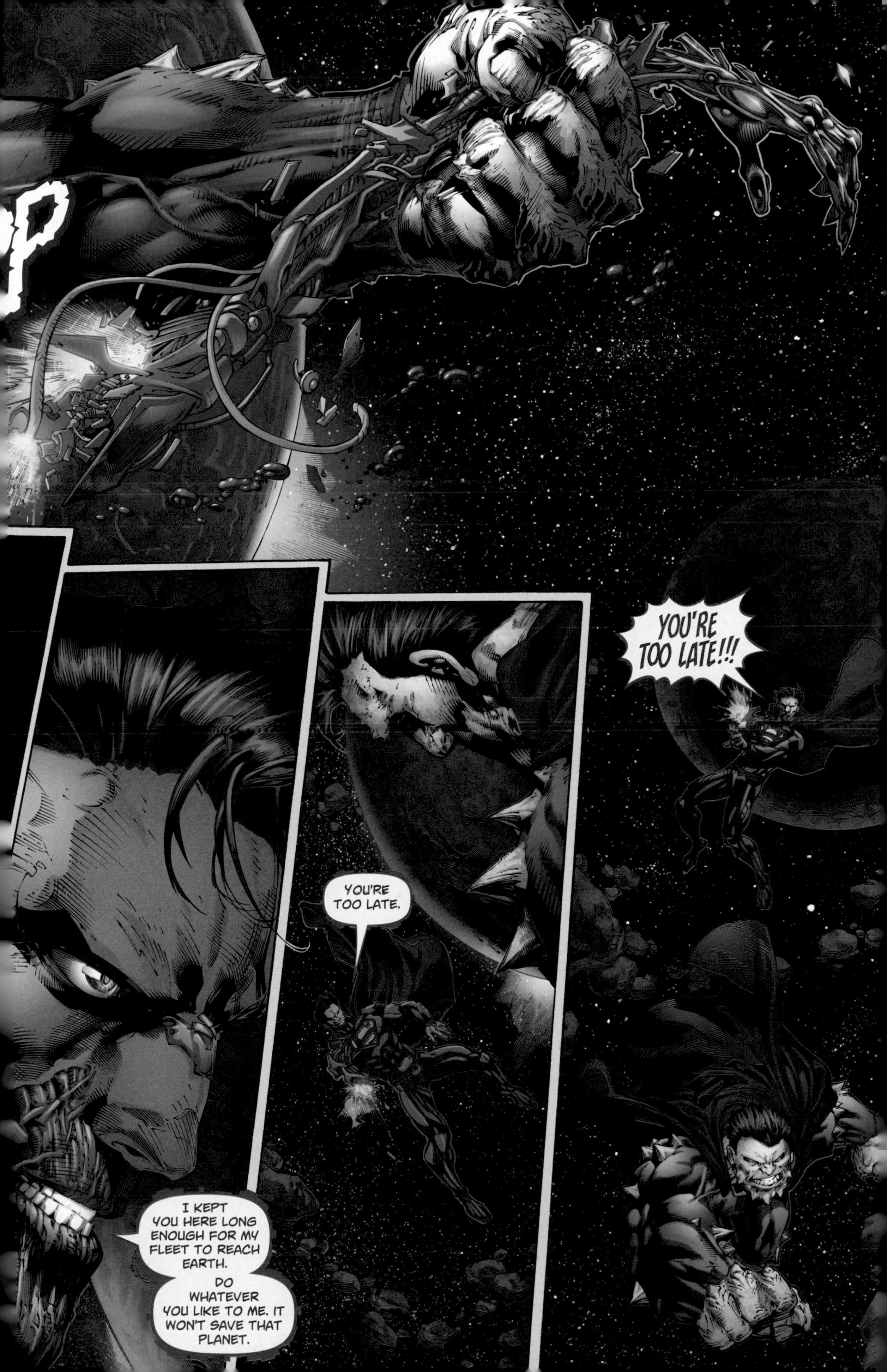
YOU'RE TOO LATE.
YOU'RE TOO LATE!!!
I KEPT YOU HERE LONG ENOUGH FOR MY FLEET TO REACH EARTH.
DO WHATEVER YOU LIKE TO ME. IT WON'T SAVE THAT PLANET.

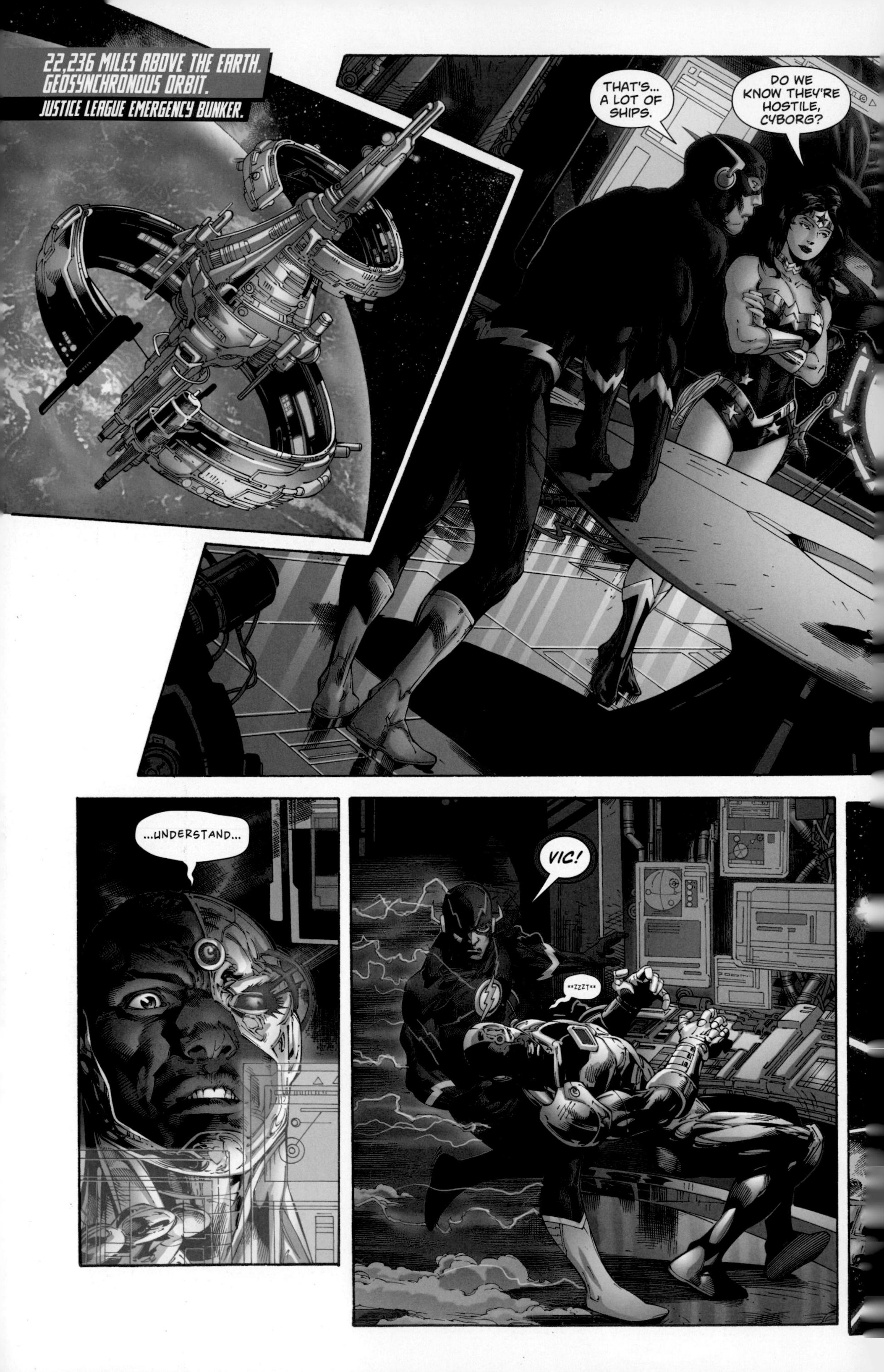
22,236 MILES ABOVE THE EARTH. GEOSYNCHRONOUS ORBIT.
JUSTICE LEAGUE EMERGENCY BUNKER.
THAT'S... A LOT OF SHIPS.
DO WE KNOW THEY'RE HOSTILE, CYBORG?
...UNDERSTAND...
VIC!
ZZZT

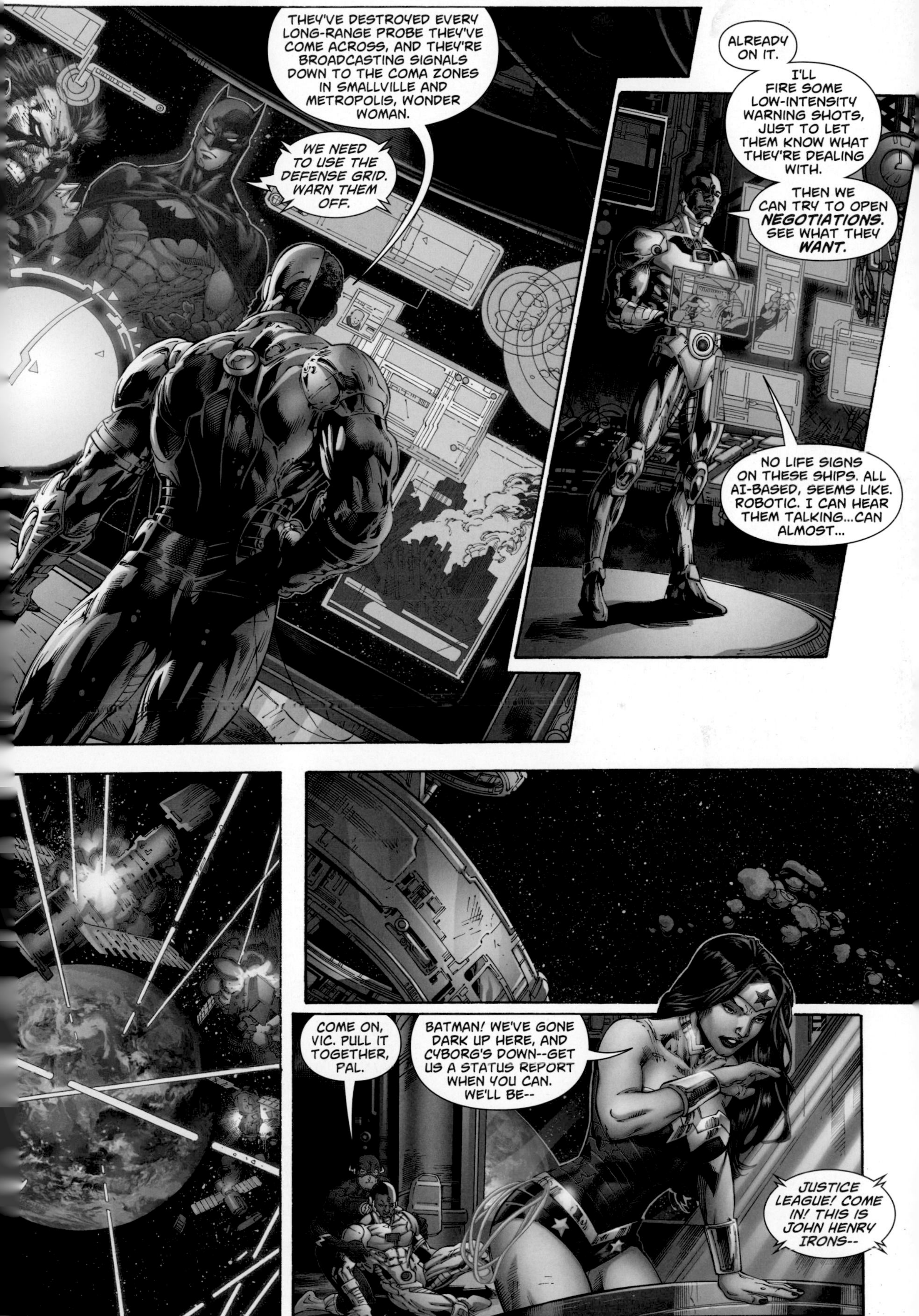
THEY'VE DESTROYED EVERY LONG-RANGE PROBE THEY'VE COME ACROSS, AND THEY'RE BROADCASTING SIGNALS DOWN TO THE COMA ZONES IN SMALLVILLE AND METROPOLIS, WONDER WOMAN.
WE NEED TO USE THE DEFENSE GRID. WARN THEM OFF.
ALREADY ON IT.
I'LL FIRE SOME LOW-INTENSITY WARNING SHOTS, JUST TO LET THEM KNOW WHAT THEY'RE DEALING WITH.
THEN WE CAN TRY TO OPEN NEGOTIATIONS. SEE WHAT THEY WANT.
NO LIFE SIGNS ON THESE SHIPS. ALL AI-BASED, SEEMS LIKE. ROBOTIC. I CAN HEAR THEM TALKING...CAN ALMOST...
COME ON, VIC. PULL IT TOGETHER, PAL.
BATMAN! WE'VE GONE DARK UP HERE, AND CYBORG'S DOWN--GET US A STATUS REPORT WHEN YOU CAN. WE'LL BE--
JUSTICE LEAGUE! COME IN! THIS IS JOHN HENRY IRONS--

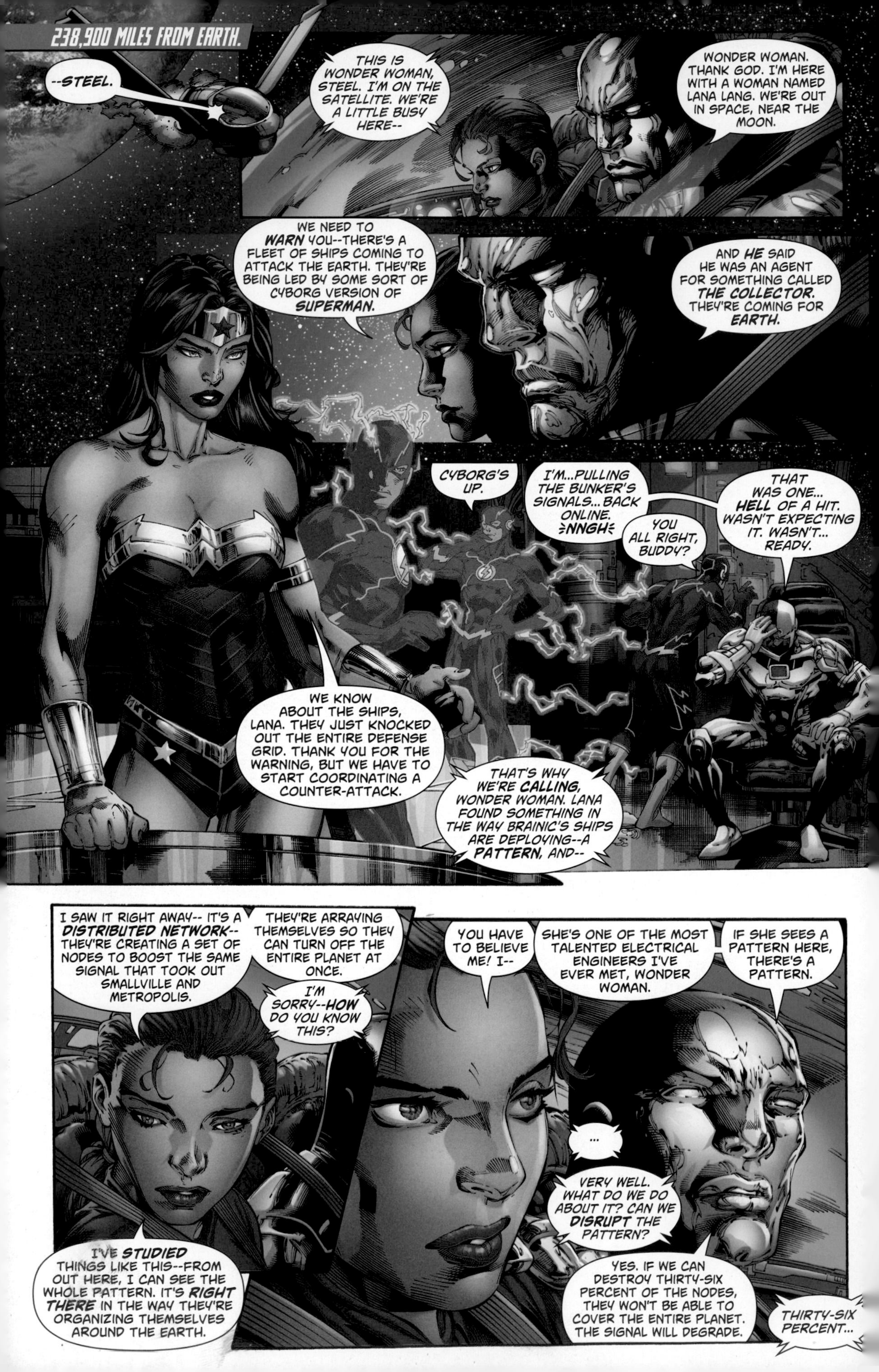
238,900 MILES FROM EARTH.
--STEEL.
THIS IS WONDER WOMAN, STEEL. I'M ON THE SATELLITE. WE'RE A LITTLE BUSY HERE--
WONDER WOMAN. THANK GOD. I'M HERE WITH A WOMAN NAMED LANA LANG. WE'RE OUT IN SPACE, NEAR THE MOON.
WE NEED TO WARN YOU--THERE'S A FLEET OF SHIPS COMING TO ATTACK THE EARTH. THEY'RE BEING LED BY SOME SORT OF CYBORG VERSION OF SUPERMAN.
AND HE SAID HE WAS AN AGENT FOR SOMETHING CALLED THE COLLECTOR. THEY'RE COMING FOR EARTH.
CYBORG'S UP.
I'M...PULLING THE BUNKER'S SIGNALS...BACK ONLINE. NNGH
YOU ALL RIGHT, BUDDY?
THAT WAS ONE... HELL OF A HIT. WASN'T EXPECTING IT. WASN'T... READY.
WE KNOW ABOUT THE SHIPS, LANA. THEY JUST KNOCKED OUT THE ENTIRE DEFENSE GRID. THANK YOU FOR THE WARNING, BUT WE HAVE TO START COORDINATING A COUNTER-ATTACK.
THAT'S WHY WE'RE CALLING, WONDER WOMAN. LANA FOUND SOMETHING IN THE WAY BRAINIC'S SHIPS ARE DEPLOYING--A PATTERN, AND--
I SAW IT RIGHT AWAY-- IT'S A DISTRIBUTED NETWORK-- THEY'RE CREATING A SET OF NODES TO BOOST THE SAME SIGNAL THAT TOOK OUT SMALLVILLE AND METROPOLIS.
THEY'RE ARRAYING THEMSELVES SO THEY CAN TURN OFF THE ENTIRE PLANET AT ONCE.
I'M SORRY--HOW DO YOU KNOW THIS?
I'VE STUDIED THINGS LIKE THIS--FROM OUT HERE, I CAN SEE THE WHOLE PATTERN. IT'S RIGHT THERE IN THE WAY THEY'RE ORGANIZING THEMSELVES AROUND THE EARTH.
YOU HAVE TO BELIEVE ME! I--
SHE'S ONE OF THE MOST TALENTED ELECTRICAL ENGINEERS I'VE EVER MET, WONDER WOMAN.
IF SHE SEES A PATTERN HERE, THERE'S A PATTERN.
...
VERY WELL. WHAT DO WE DO ABOUT IT? CAN WE DISRUPT THE PATTERN?
YES. IF WE CAN DESTROY THIRTY-SIX PERCENT OF THE NODES, THEY WON'T BE ABLE TO COVER THE ENTIRE PLANET. THE SIGNAL WILL DEGRADE.
THIRTY-SIX PERCENT...

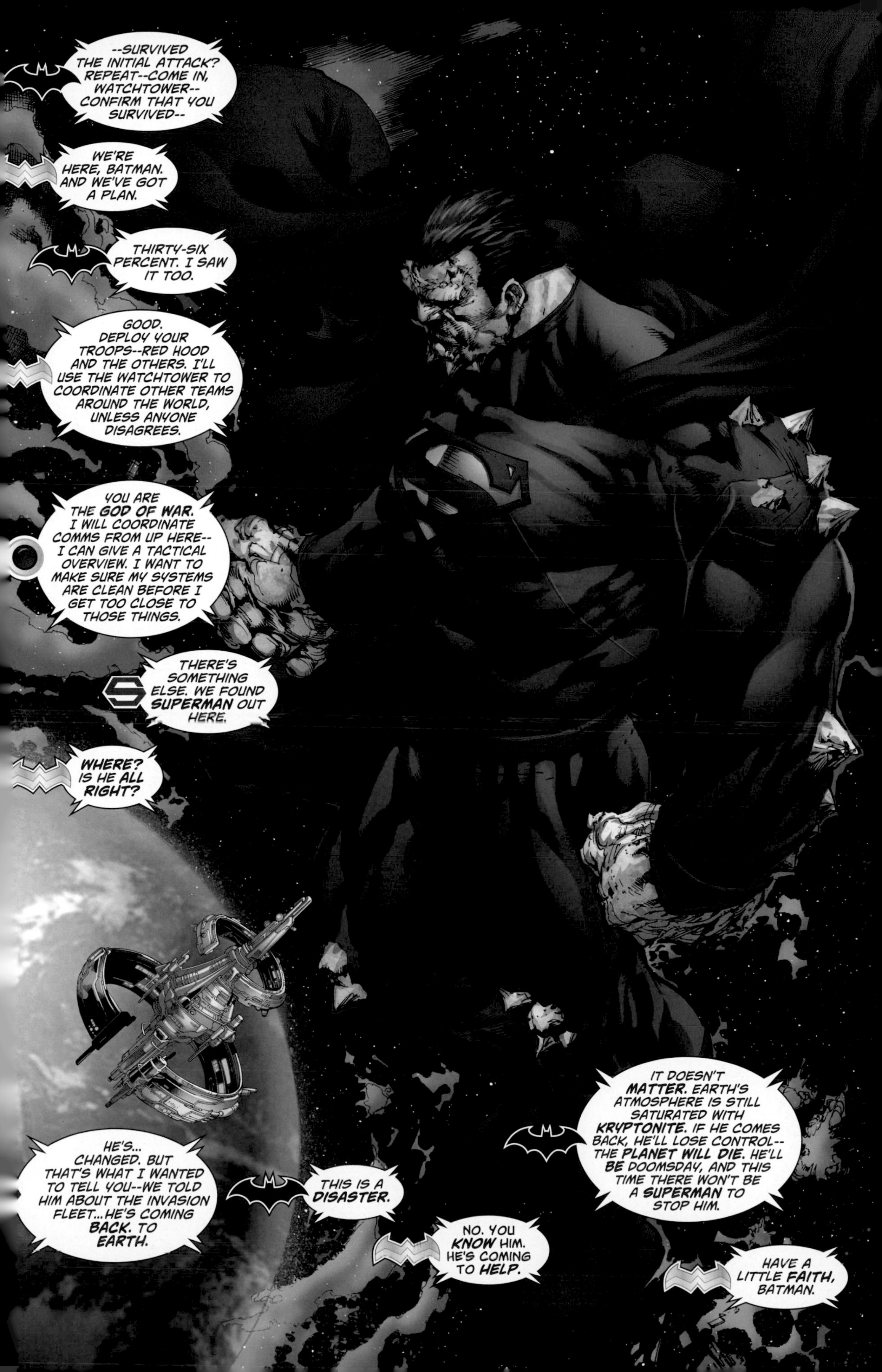
--SURVIVED THE INITIAL ATTACK? REPEAT--COME IN, WATCHTOWER--CONFIRM THAT YOU SURVIVED--
WE'RE HERE, BATMAN. AND WE'VE GOT A PLAN.
THIRTY-SIX PERCENT. I SAW IT TOO.
GOOD. DEPLOY YOUR TROOPS--RED HOOD AND THE OTHERS. I'LL USE THE WATCHTOWER TO COORDINATE OTHER TEAMS AROUND THE WORLD, UNLESS ANYONE DISAGREES.
YOU ARE THE GOD OF WAR. I WILL COORDINATE COMMS FROM UP HERE--I CAN GIVE A TACTICAL OVERVIEW. I WANT TO MAKE SURE MY SYSTEMS ARE CLEAN BEFORE I GET TOO CLOSE TO THOSE THINGS.
THERE'S SOMETHING ELSE. WE FOUND SUPERMAN OUT HERE.
WHERE? IS HE ALL RIGHT?
HE'S... CHANGED. BUT THAT'S WHAT I WANTED TO TELL YOU--WE TOLD HIM ABOUT THE INVASION FLEET...HE'S COMING BACK. TO EARTH.
THIS IS A DISASTER.
IT DOESN'T MATTER. EARTH'S ATMOSPHERE IS STILL SATURATED WITH KRYPTONITE. IF HE COMES BACK, HE'LL LOSE CONTROL--THE PLANET WILL DIE. HE'LL BE DOOMSDAY, AND THIS TIME THERE WON'T BE A SUPERMAN TO STOP HIM.
NO. YOU KNOW HIM. HE'S COMING TO HELP.
HAVE A LITTLE FAITH, BATMAN.

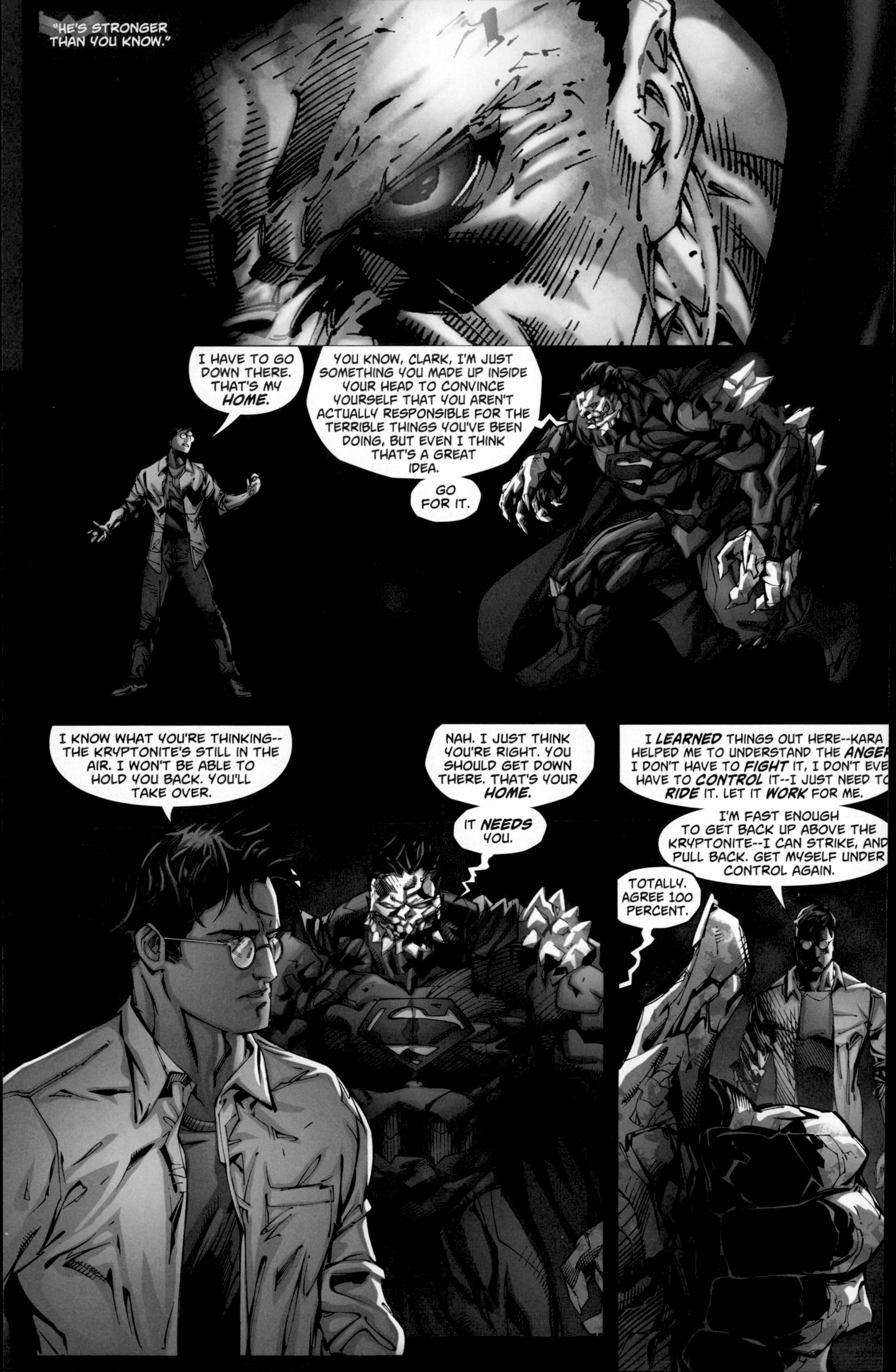
"HE'S STRONGER THAN YOU KNOW."
I HAVE TO GO DOWN THERE. THAT'S MY HOME.
YOU KNOW, CLARK, I'M JUST SOMETHING YOU MADE UP INSIDE YOUR HEAD TO CONVINCE YOURSELF THAT YOU AREN'T ACTUALLY RESPONSIBLE FOR THE TERRIBLE THINGS YOU'VE BEEN DOING, BUT EVEN I THINK THAT'S A GREAT IDEA.
GO FOR IT.
I KNOW WHAT YOU'RE THINKING--THE KRYPTONITE'S STILL IN THE AIR. I WON'T BE ABLE TO HOLD YOU BACK. YOU'LL TAKE OVER.
NAH. I JUST THINK YOU'RE RIGHT. YOU SHOULD GET DOWN THERE. THAT'S YOUR HOME.
IT NEEDS YOU.
I LEARNED THINGS OUT HERE--KARA HELPED ME TO UNDERSTAND THE ANGER. I DON'T HAVE TO FIGHT IT, I DON'T EVEN HAVE TO CONTROL IT--I JUST NEED TO RIDE IT. LET IT WORK FOR ME.
I'M FAST ENOUGH TO GET BACK UP ABOVE THE KRYPTONITE--I CAN STRIKE, AND PULL BACK. GET MYSELF UNDER CONTROL AGAIN.
TOTALLY. AGREE 100 PERCENT.

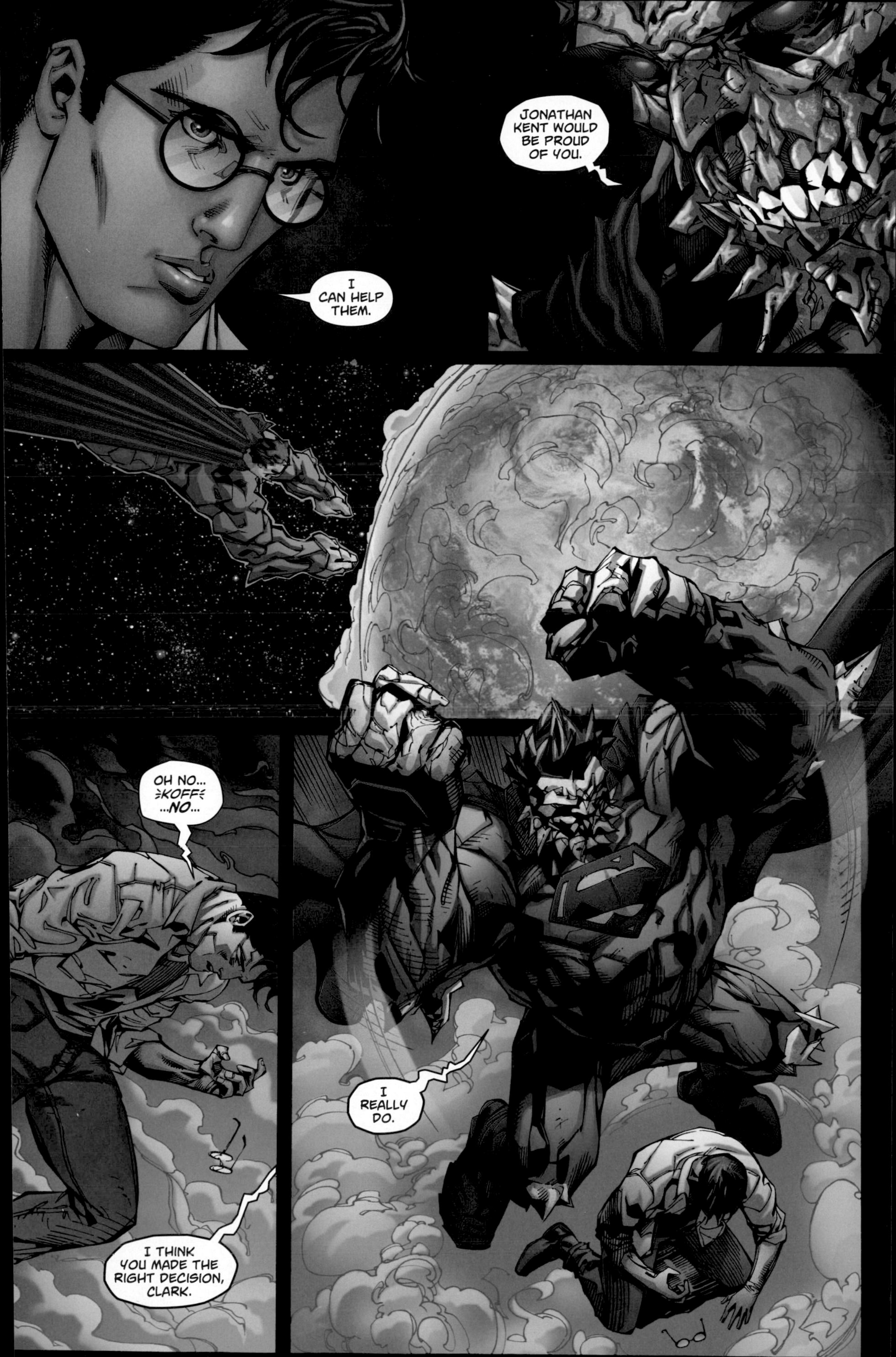

I CAN HELP THEM.
JONATHAN KENT WOULD BE PROUD OF YOU.
OH NO... ≶KOFF≶ ...NO...
I THINK YOU MADE THE RIGHT DECISION, CLARK.
I REALLY DO.

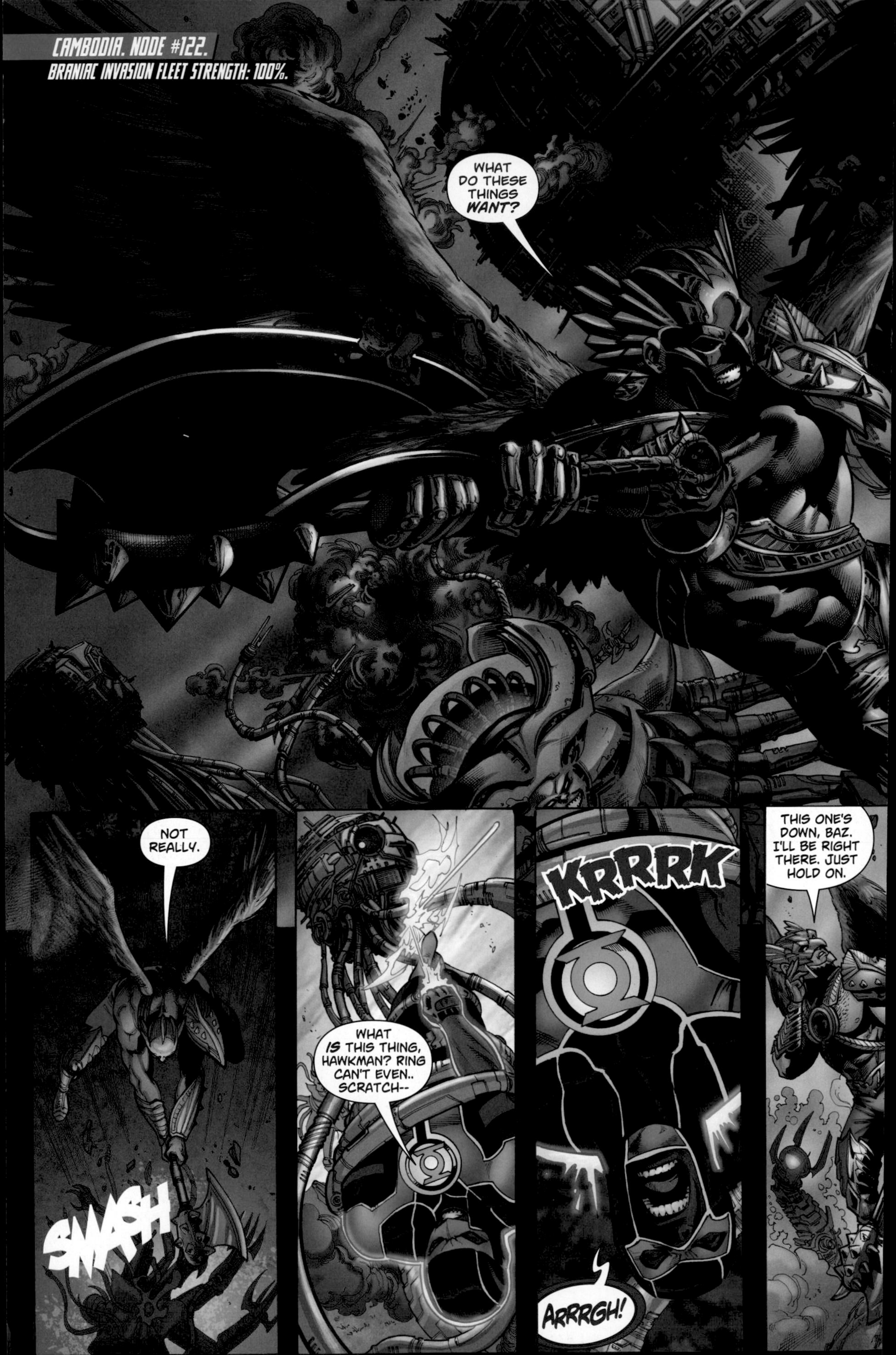
CAMBODIA. NODE #122.
BRANIAC INVASION FLEET STRENGTH: 100%.
WHAT DO THESE THINGS WANT?
NOT REALLY.
SMASH
WHAT IS THIS THING, HAWKMAN? RING CAN'T EVEN.. SCRATCH--
KRRRK
ARRRGH!
THIS ONE'S DOWN, BAZ. I'LL BE RIGHT THERE. JUST HOLD ON.

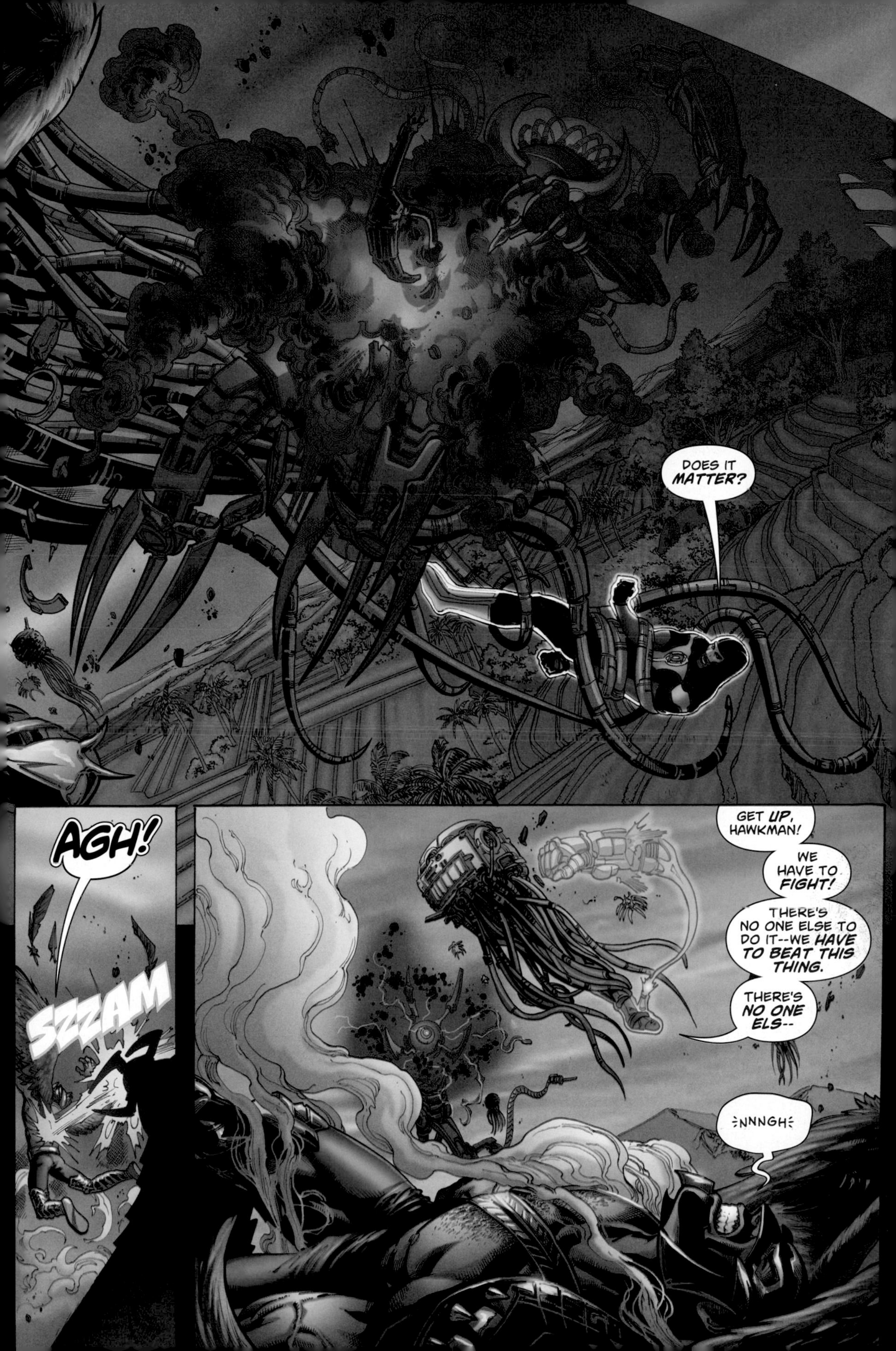
DOES IT MATTER?
AGH!
SZZAM
GET UP, HAWKMAN!
WE HAVE TO FIGHT!
THERE'S NO ONE ELSE TO DO IT--WE HAVE TO BEAT THIS THING.
THERE'S NO ONE ELS--
NNNGH

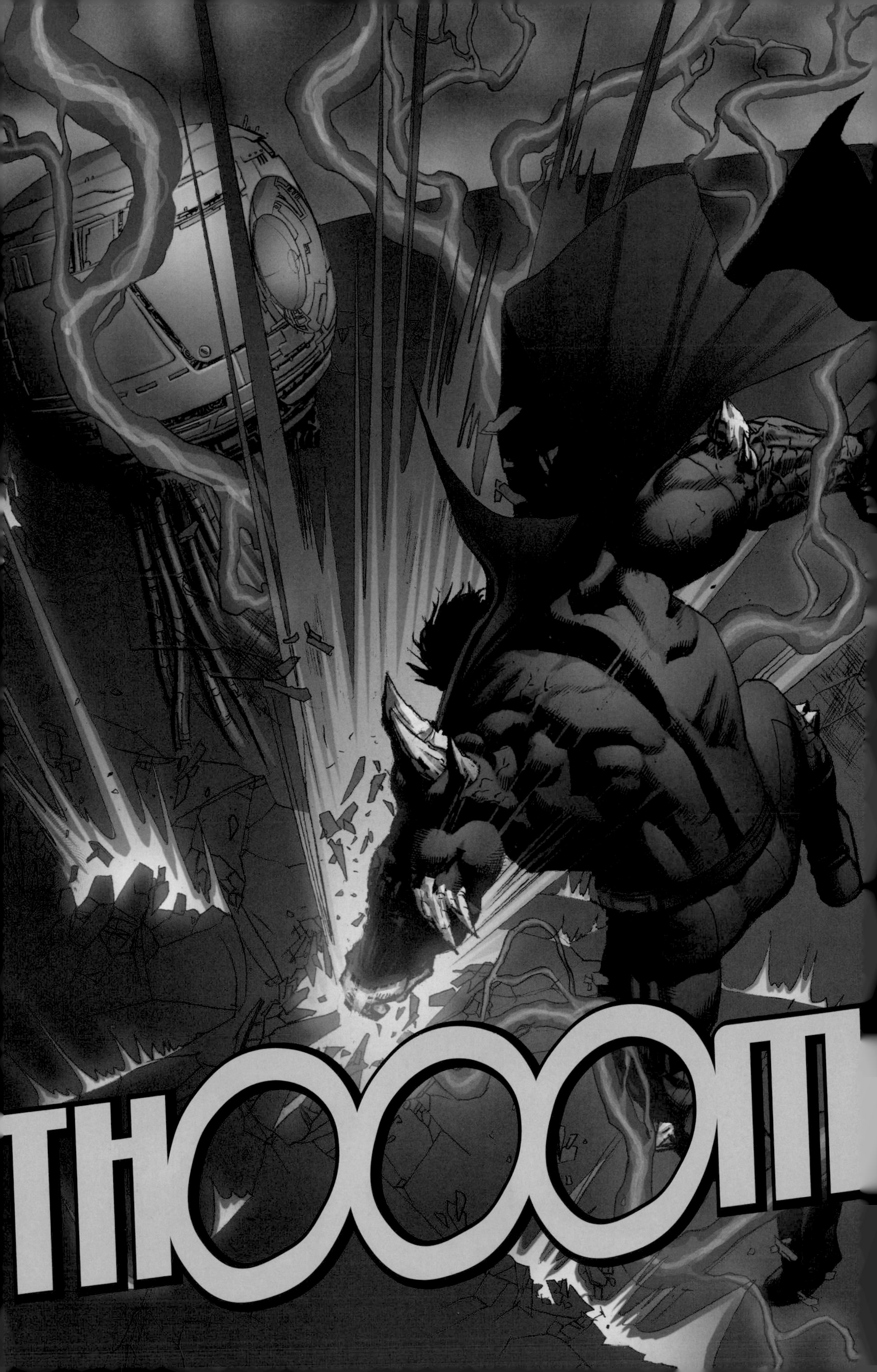
THOOOM

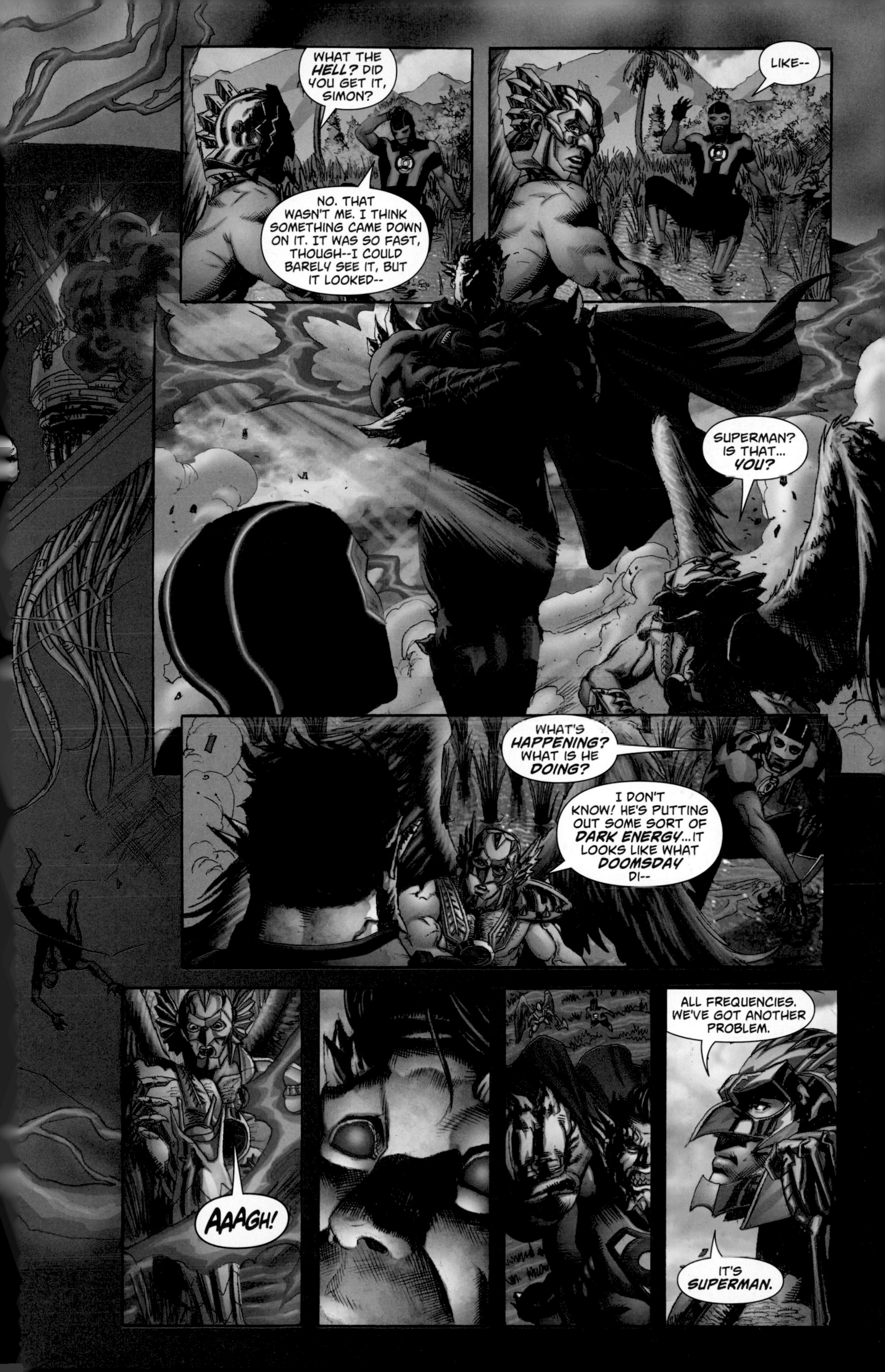
WHAT THE HELL? DID YOU GET IT, SIMON?
NO. THAT WASN'T ME. I THINK SOMETHING CAME DOWN ON IT. IT WAS SO FAST, THOUGH--I COULD BARELY SEE IT, BUT IT LOOKED--
LIKE--
SUPERMAN? IS THAT... YOU?
WHAT'S HAPPENING? WHAT IS HE DOING?
I DON'T KNOW! HE'S PUTTING OUT SOME SORT OF DARK ENERGY...IT LOOKS LIKE WHAT DOOMSDAY DI--
AAAGH!
ALL FREQUENCIES. WE'VE GOT ANOTHER PROBLEM.
IT'S SUPERMAN.

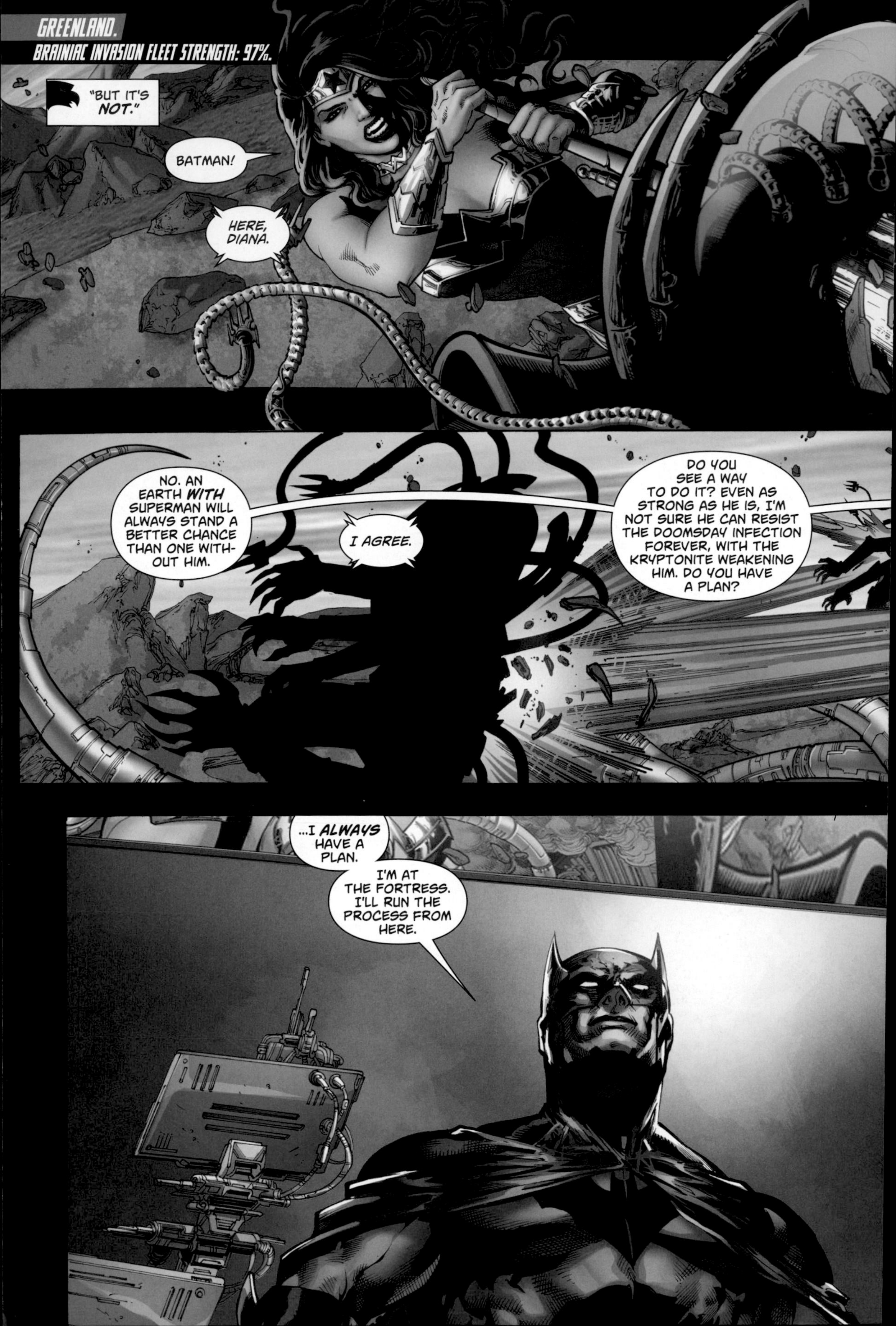

GREENLAND.
BRAINIAC INVASION FLEET STRENGTH: 97%.
"BUT IT'S NOT."
BATMAN!
HERE, DIANA.
NO. AN EARTH WITH SUPERMAN WILL ALWAYS STAND A BETTER CHANCE THAN ONE WITH-OUT HIM.
I AGREE.
DO YOU SEE A WAY TO DO IT? EVEN AS STRONG AS HE IS, I'M NOT SURE HE CAN RESIST THE DOOMSDAY INFECTION FOREVER, WITH THE KRYPTONITE WEAKENING HIM. DO YOU HAVE A PLAN?
...I ALWAYS HAVE A PLAN.
I'M AT THE FORTRESS. I'LL RUN THE PROCESS FROM HERE.

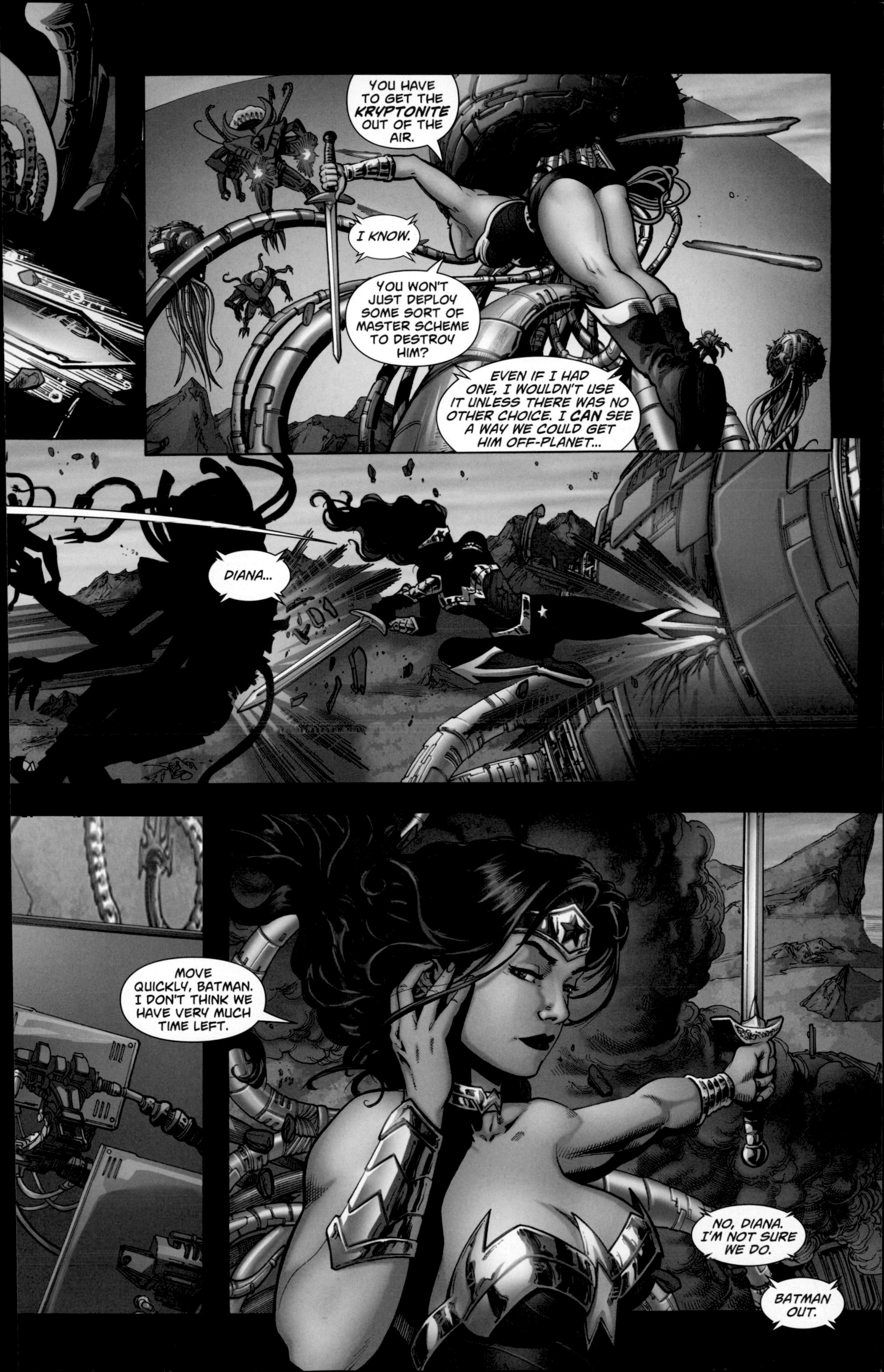
YOU HAVE TO GET THE KRYPTONITE OUT OF THE AIR.
I KNOW.
YOU WON'T JUST DEPLOY SOME SORT OF MASTER SCHEME TO DESTROY HIM?
EVEN IF I HAD ONE, I WOULDN'T USE IT UNLESS THERE WAS NO OTHER CHOICE. I CAN SEE A WAY WE COULD GET HIM OFF-PLANET...
DIANA...
MOVE QUICKLY, BATMAN. I DON'T THINK WE HAVE VERY MUCH TIME LEFT.
NO, DIANA. I'M NOT SURE WE DO.
BATMAN OUT.

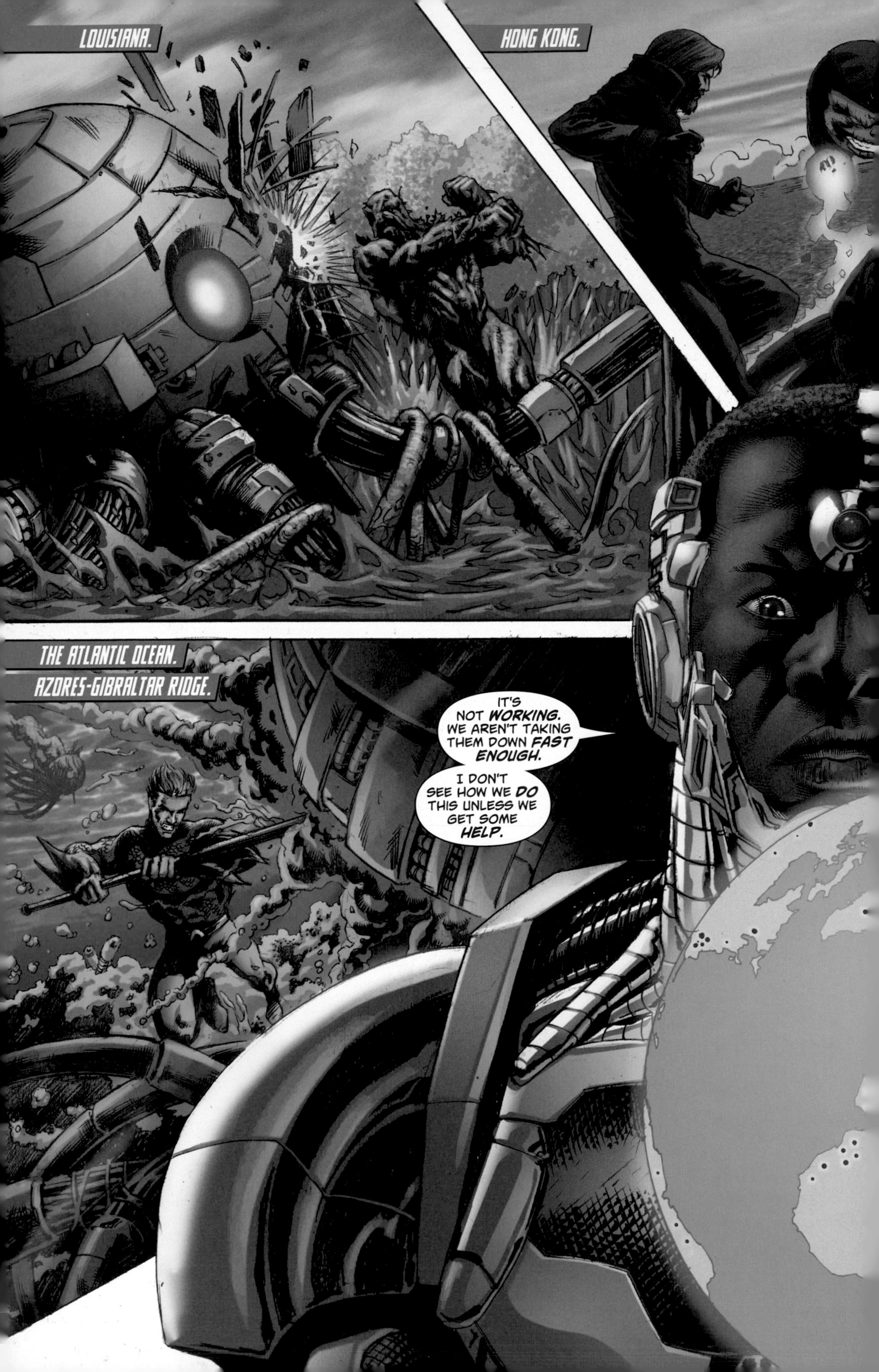
LOUISIANA.
HONG KONG.
THE ATLANTIC OCEAN.
AZORES-GIBRALTAR RIDGE.
IT'S NOT WORKING. WE AREN'T TAKING THEM DOWN FAST ENOUGH.
I DON'T SEE HOW WE DO THIS UNLESS WE GET SOME HELP.

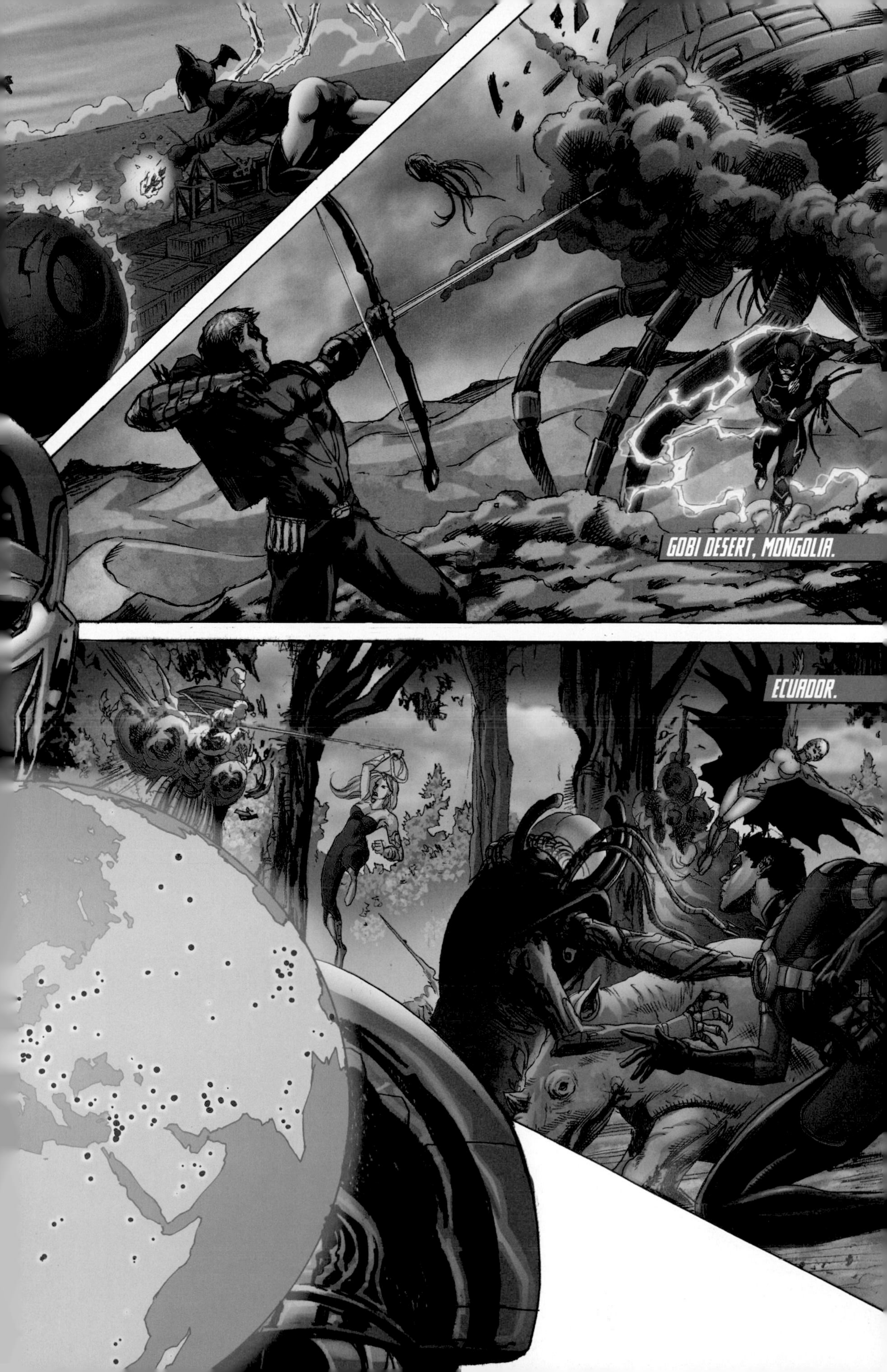
GOBI DESERT, MONGOLIA.
ECUADOR.

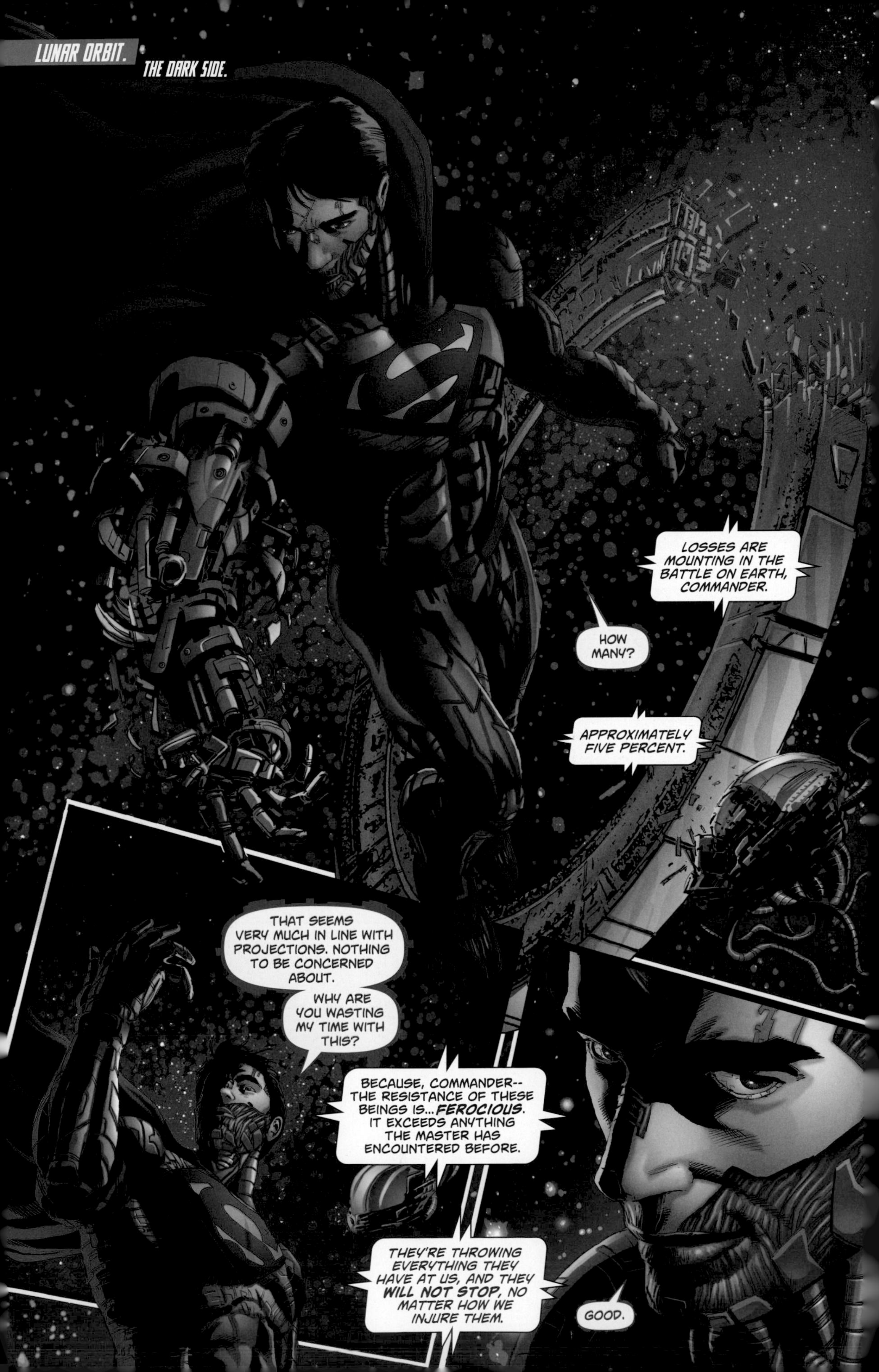
LUNAR ORBIT.
THE DARK SIDE.
LOSSES ARE MOUNTING IN THE BATTLE ON EARTH, COMMANDER.
HOW MANY?
APPROXIMATELY FIVE PERCENT.
THAT SEEMS VERY MUCH IN LINE WITH PROJECTIONS. NOTHING TO BE CONCERNED ABOUT.
WHY ARE YOU WASTING MY TIME WITH THIS?
BECAUSE, COMMANDER-- THE RESISTANCE OF THESE BEINGS IS...FEROCIOUS. IT EXCEEDS ANYTHING THE MASTER HAS ENCOUNTERED BEFORE.
THEY'RE THROWING EVERYTHING THEY HAVE AT US, AND THEY WILL NOT STOP, NO MATTER HOW WE INJURE THEM.
GOOD.

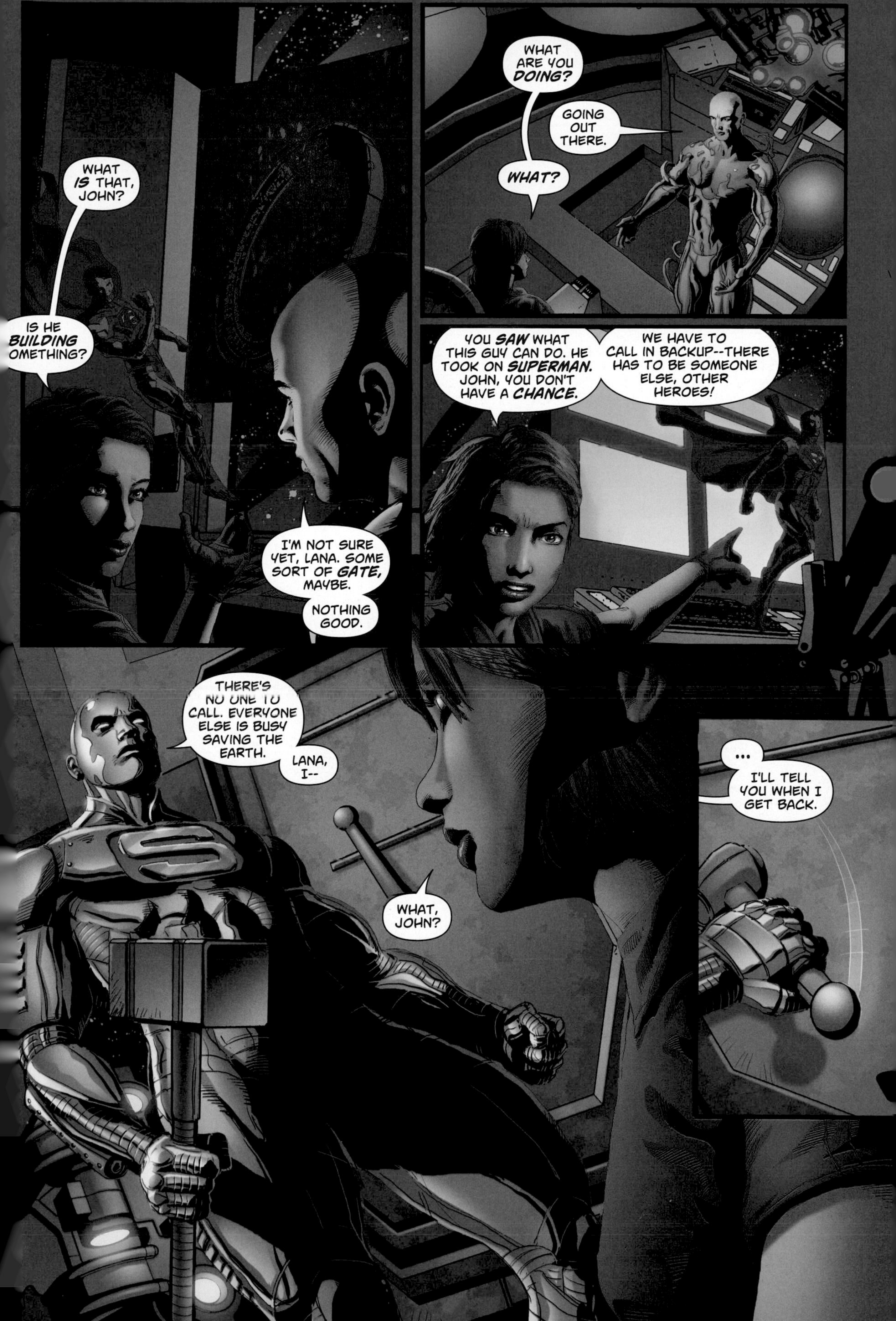
WHAT IS THAT, JOHN?
IS HE BUILDING OMETHING?
I'M NOT SURE YET, LANA. SOME SORT OF GATE, MAYBE.
NOTHING GOOD.
WHAT ARE YOU DOING?
GOING OUT THERE.
WHAT?
YOU SAW WHAT THIS GUY CAN DO. HE TOOK ON SUPERMAN. JOHN, YOU DON'T HAVE A CHANCE.
WE HAVE TO CALL IN BACKUP--THERE HAS TO BE SOMEONE ELSE, OTHER HEROES!
THERE'S NO ONE TO CALL. EVERYONE ELSE IS BUSY SAVING THE EARTH.
LANA, I--
WHAT, JOHN?
...
I'LL TELL YOU WHEN I GET BACK.

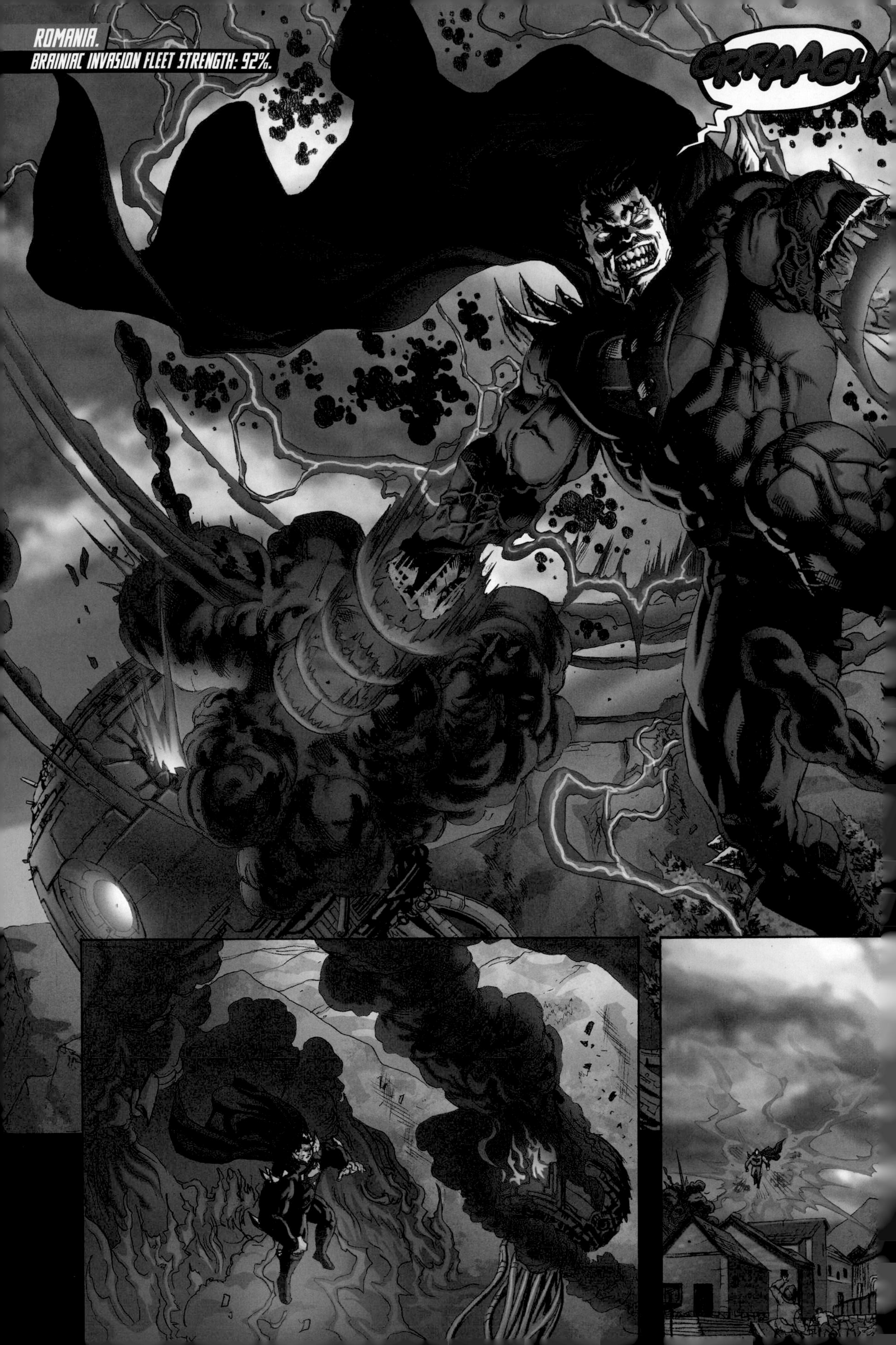
ROMANIA.
BRAINIAC INVASION FLEET STRENGTH: 92%.
GRRAAGH!

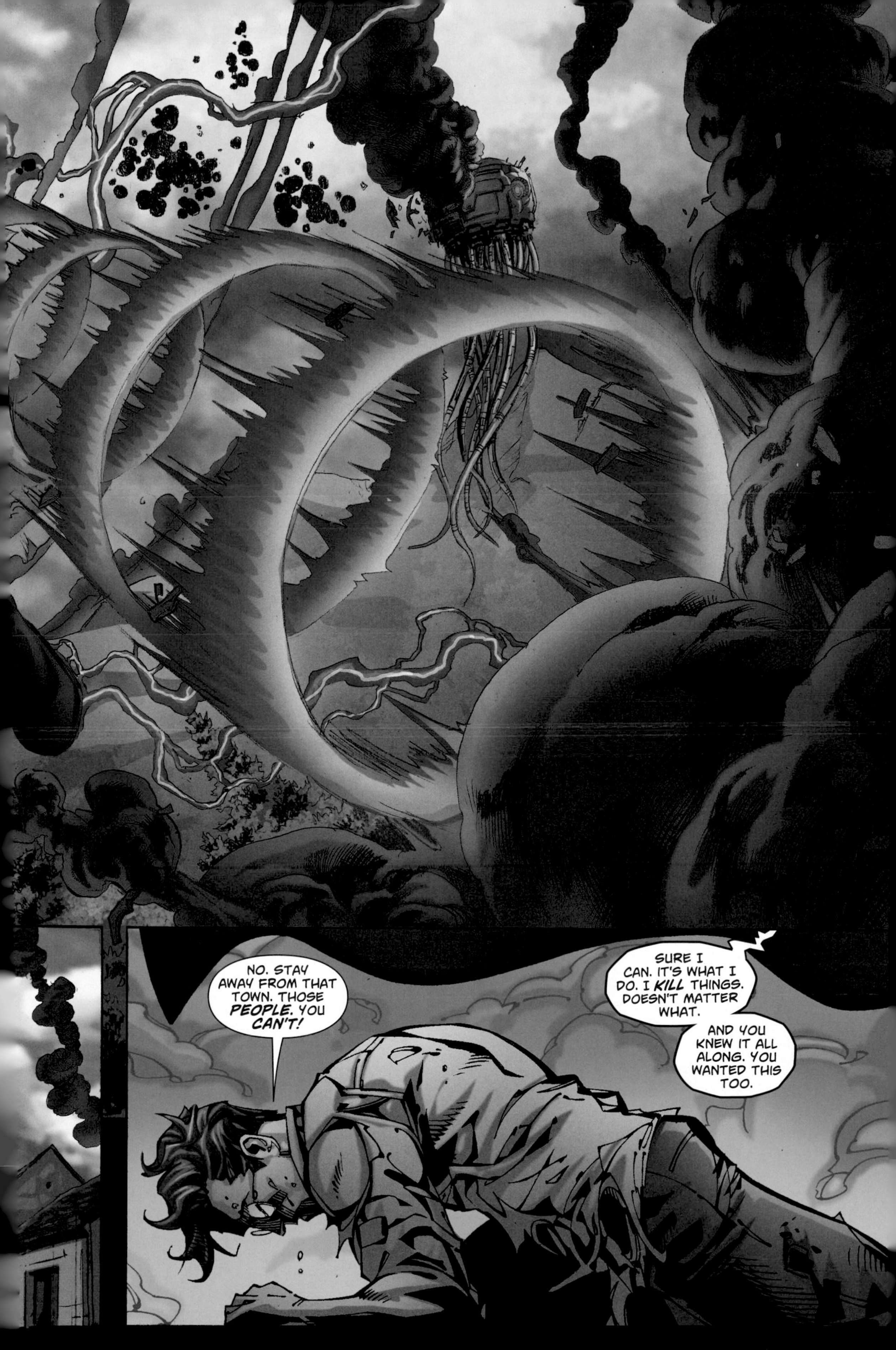
NO. STAY AWAY FROM THAT TOWN. THOSE PEOPLE. YOU CAN'T!
SURE I CAN. IT'S WHAT I DO. I KILL THINGS. DOESN'T MATTER WHAT.
AND YOU KNEW IT ALL ALONG. YOU WANTED THIS TOO.

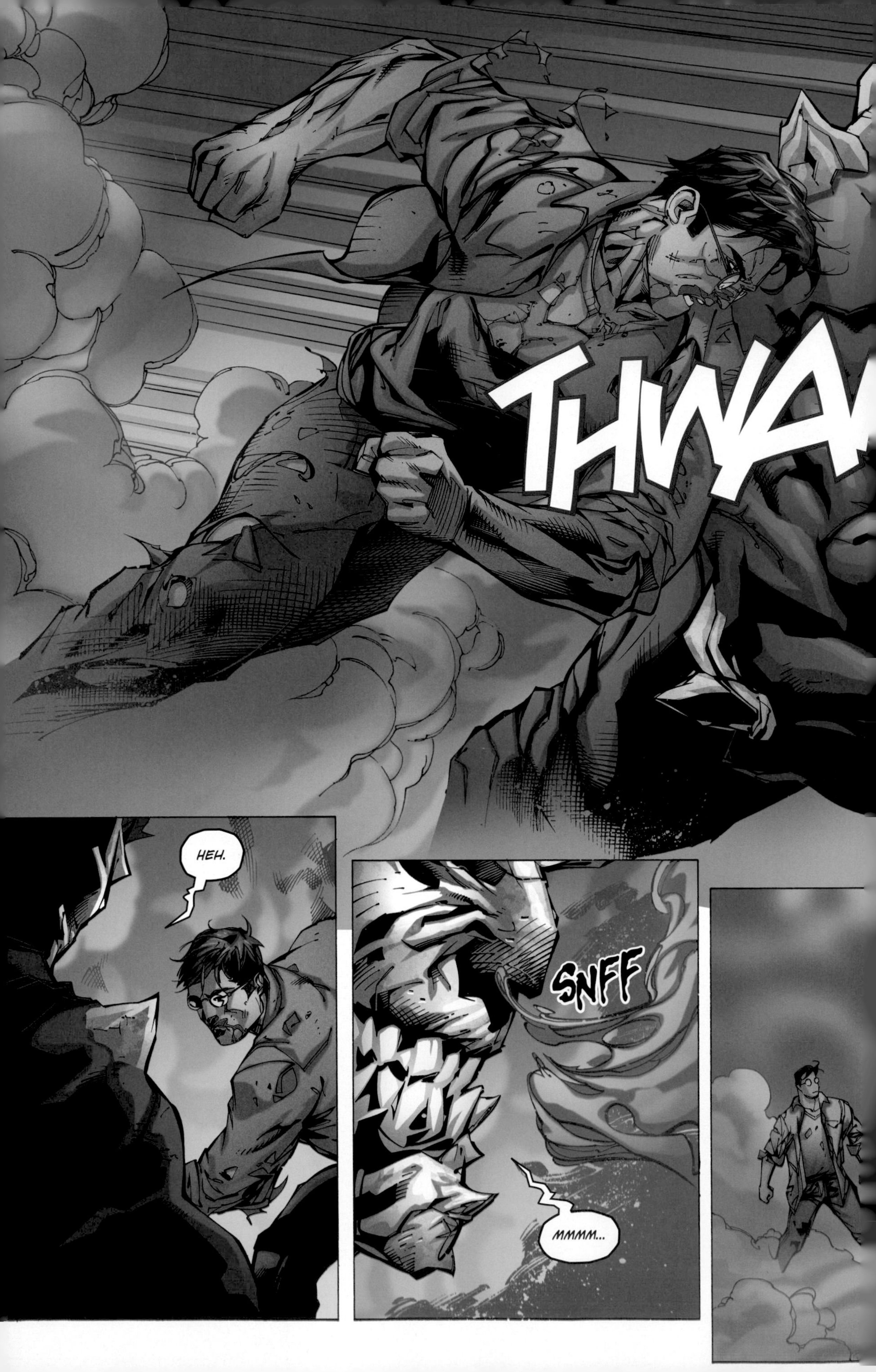
THWA
HEH.
SNFF
MMMM...

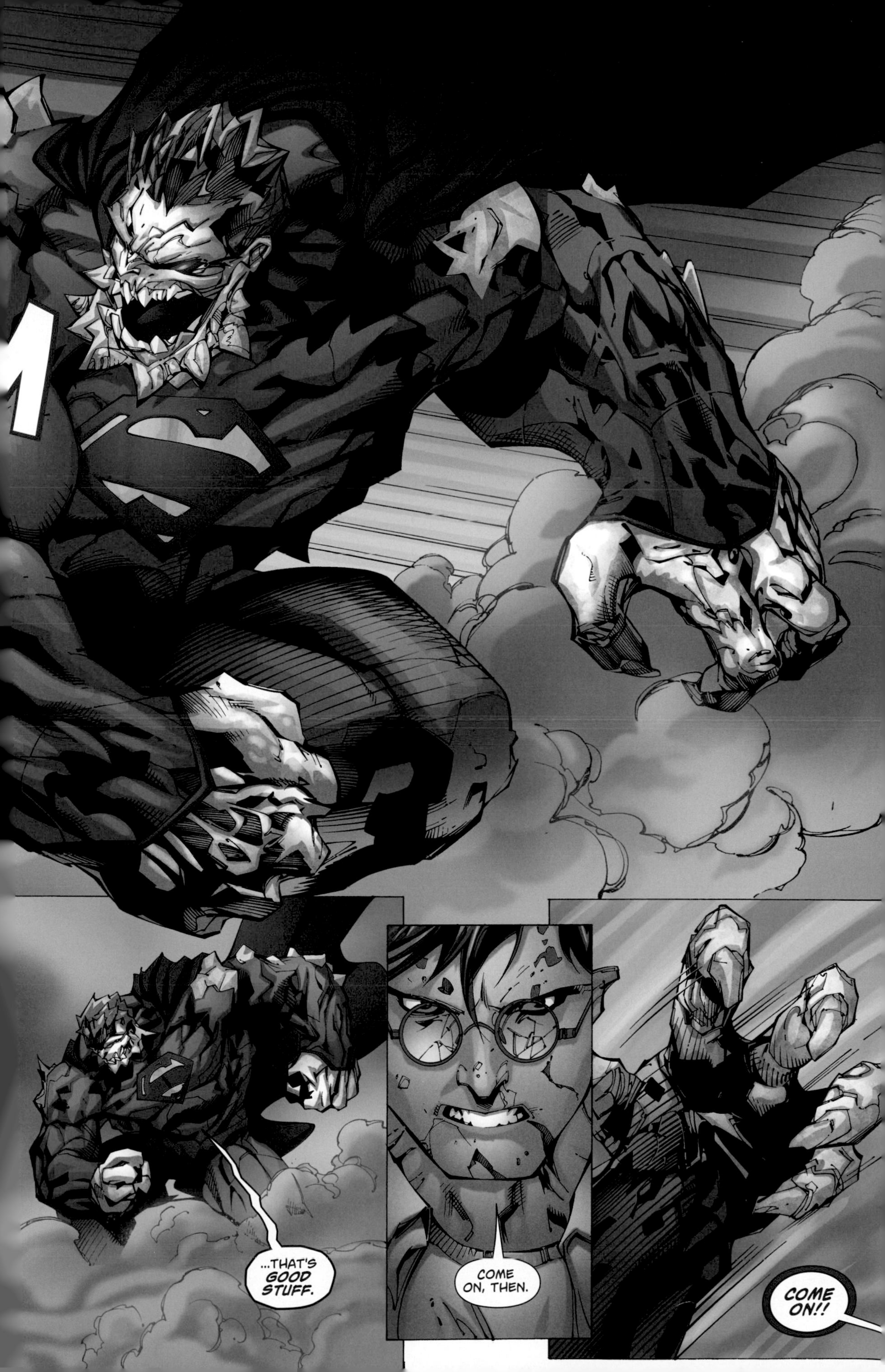
...THAT'S GOOD STUFF.
COME ON, THEN.
COME ON!!

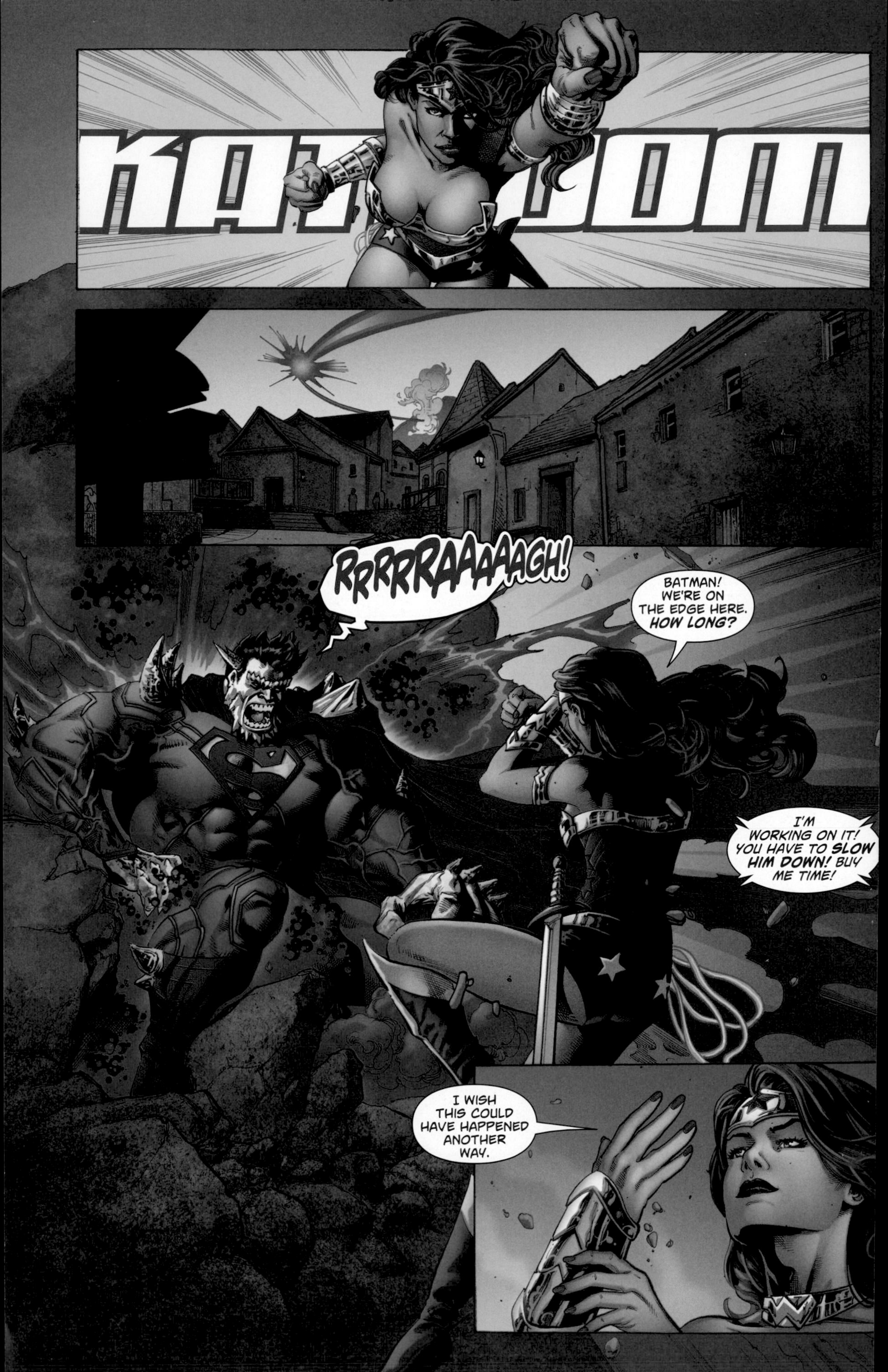
RRRRRAAAAAGH!
BATMAN! WE'RE ON THE EDGE HERE. HOW LONG?
I'M WORKING ON IT! YOU HAVE TO SLOW HIM DOWN! BUY ME TIME!
I WISH THIS COULD HAVE HAPPENED ANOTHER WAY.

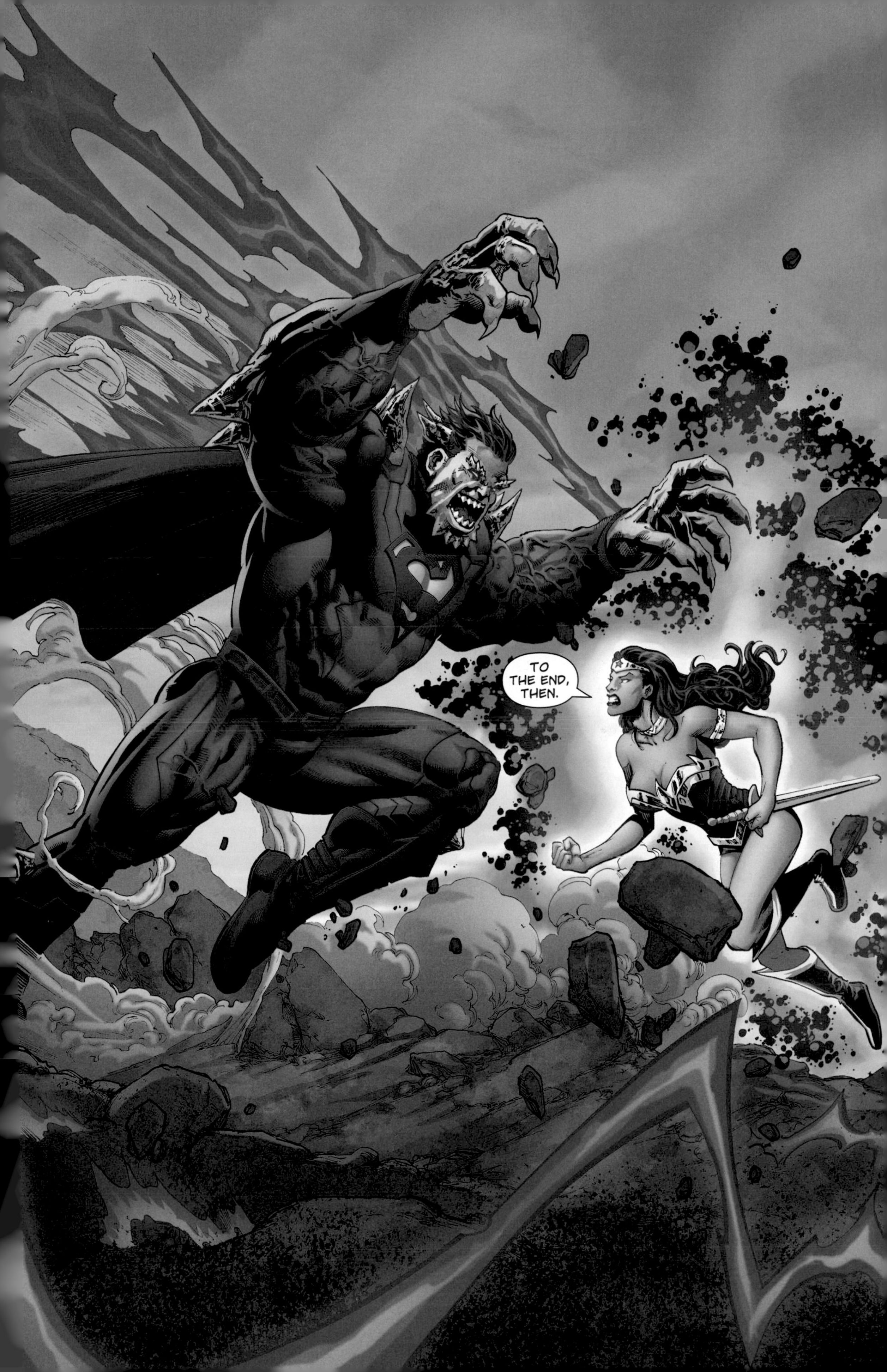
TO THE END, THEN.

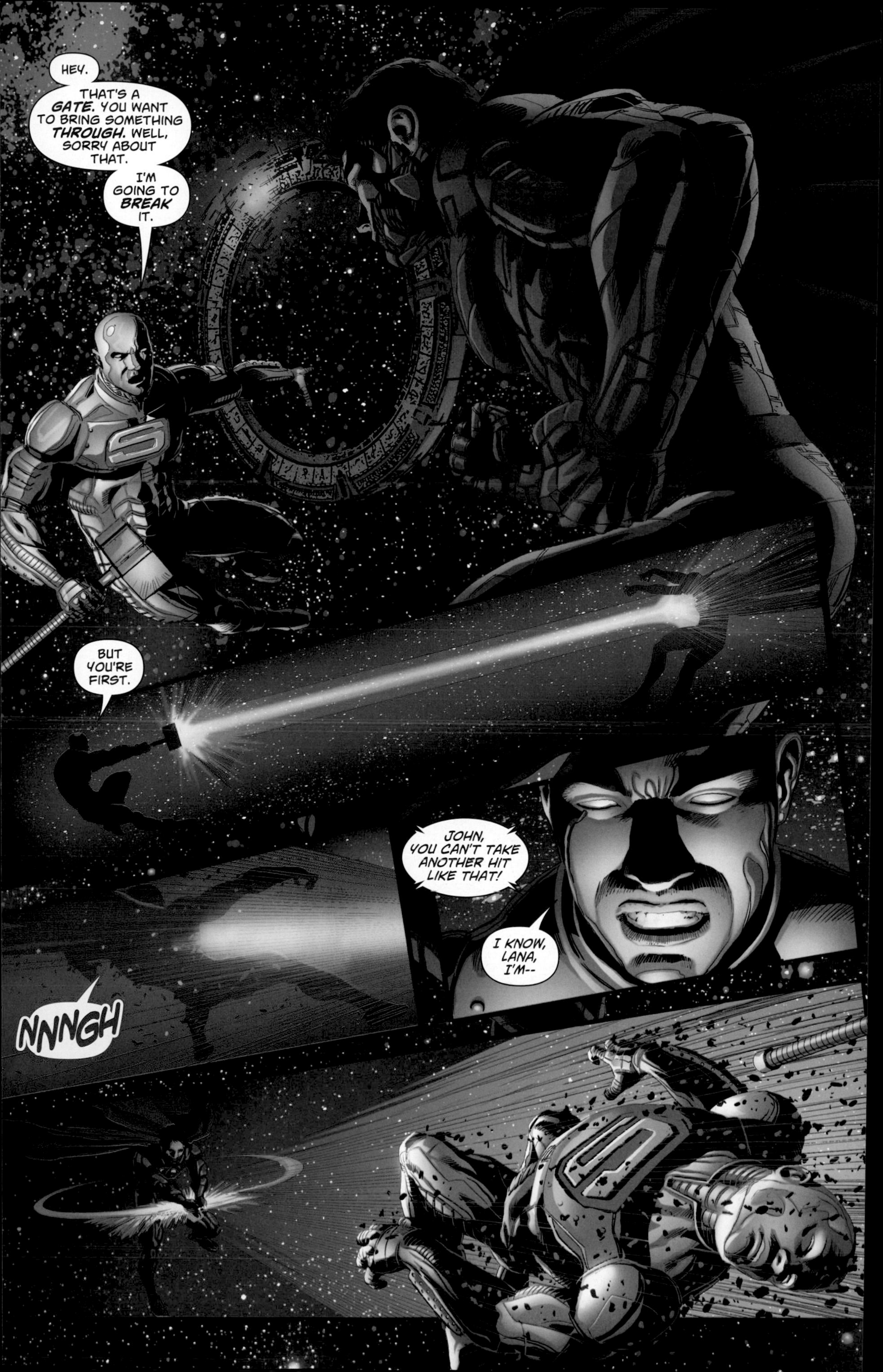
HEY.
THAT'S A GATE. YOU WANT TO BRING SOMETHING THROUGH. WELL, SORRY ABOUT THAT.
I'M GOING TO BREAK IT.
BUT YOU'RE FIRST.
JOHN, YOU CAN'T TAKE ANOTHER HIT LIKE THAT!
I KNOW, LANA, I'M--
NNNGH

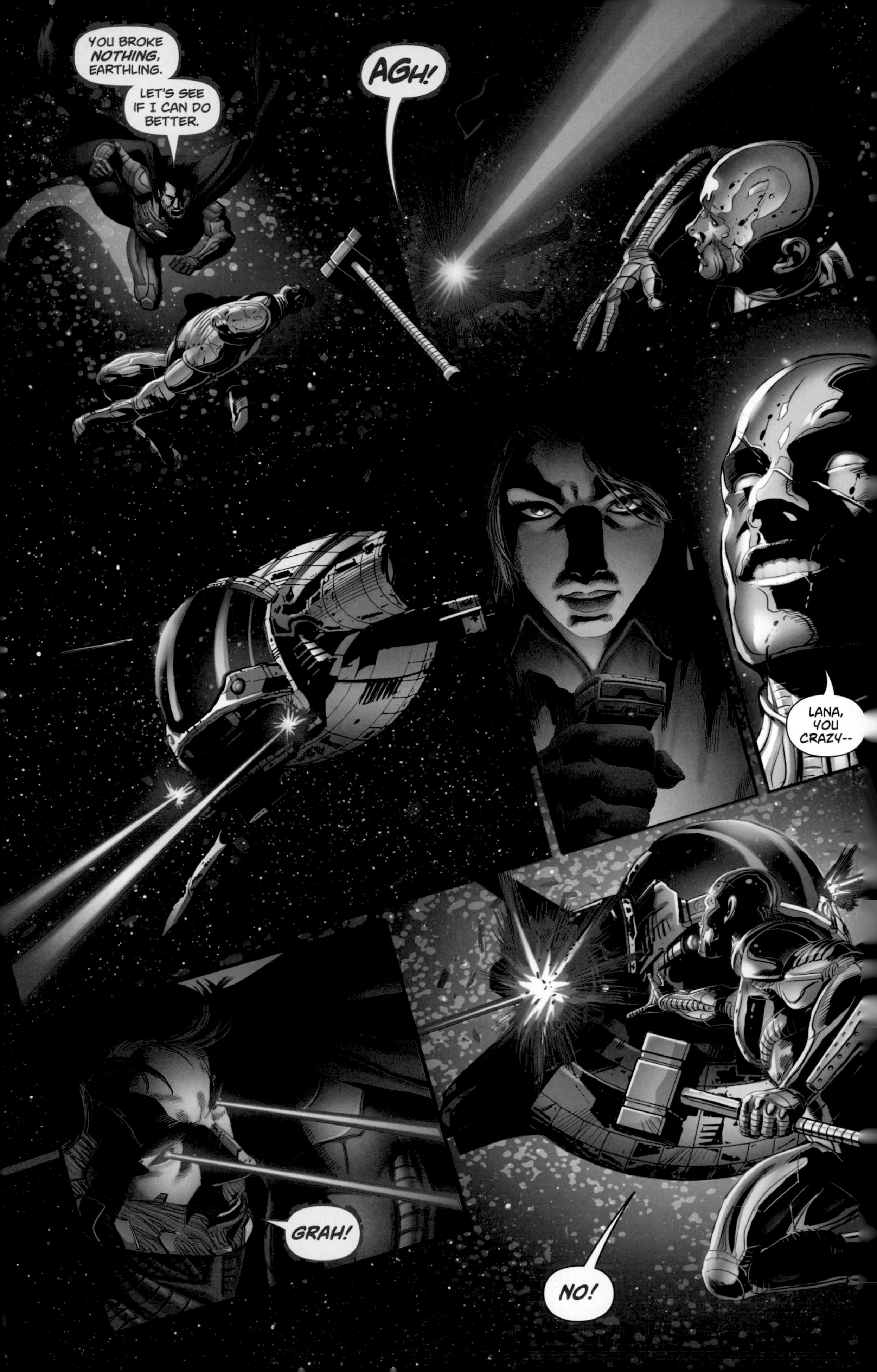
YOU BROKE NOTHING, EARTHLING.
LET'S SEE IF I CAN DO BETTER.
AGH!
LANA, YOU CRAZY--
GRAH!
NO!

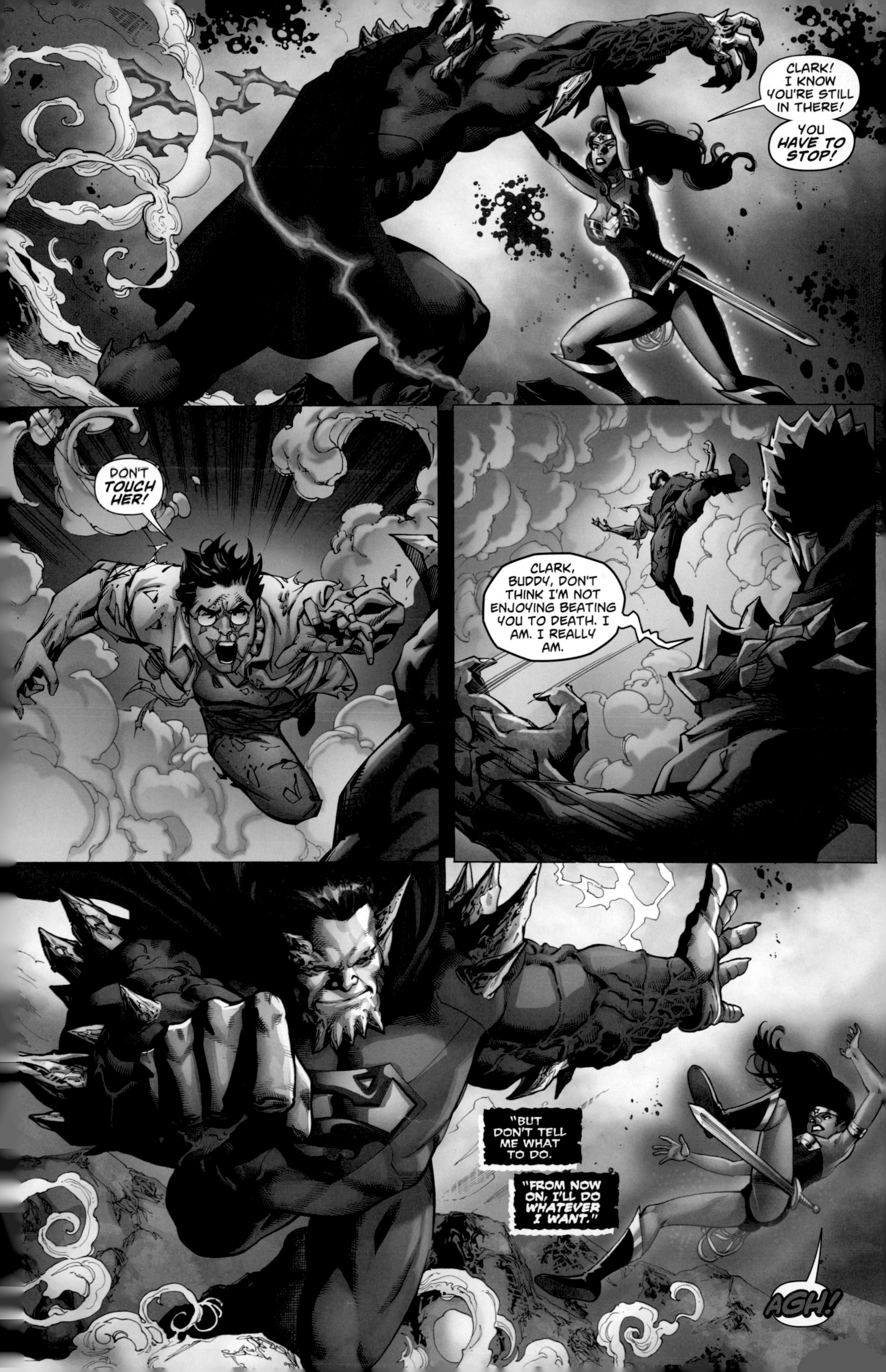
CLARK! I KNOW YOU'RE STILL IN THERE!
YOU HAVE TO STOP!
DON'T TOUCH HER!
CLARK, BUDDY, DON'T THINK I'M NOT ENJOYING BEATING YOU TO DEATH. I AM. I REALLY AM.
"BUT DON'T TELL ME WHAT TO DO.
"FROM NOW ON, I'LL DO WHATEVER I WANT."
AGH!

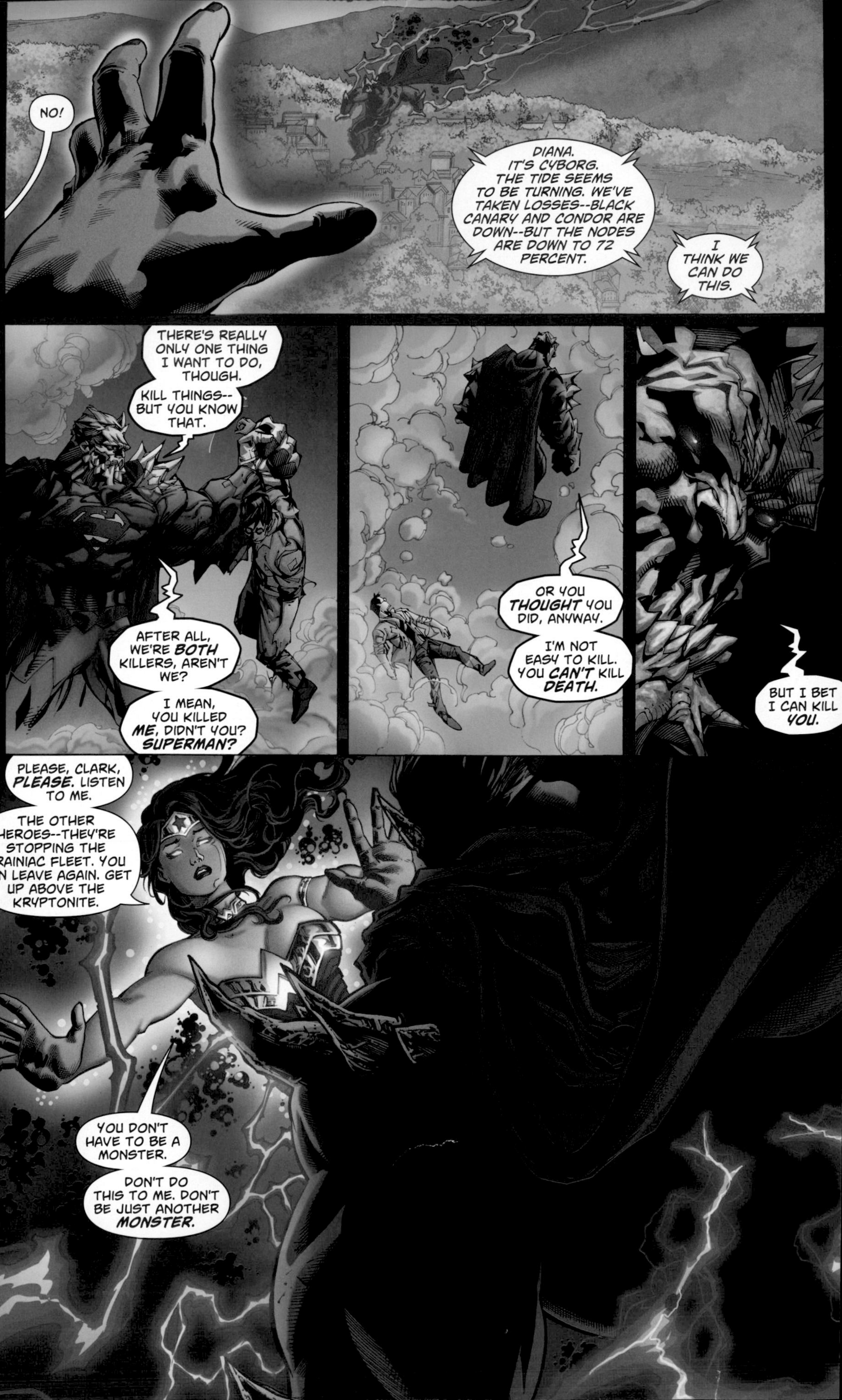
NO!
DIANA. IT'S CYBORG. THE TIDE SEEMS TO BE TURNING. WE'VE TAKEN LOSSES--BLACK CANARY AND CONDOR ARE DOWN--BUT THE NODES ARE DOWN TO 72 PERCENT.
I THINK WE CAN DO THIS.
THERE'S REALLY ONLY ONE THING I WANT TO DO, THOUGH.
KILL THINGS-- BUT YOU KNOW THAT.
AFTER ALL, WE'RE BOTH KILLERS, AREN'T WE?
I MEAN, YOU KILLED ME, DIDN'T YOU? SUPERMAN?
OR YOU THOUGHT YOU DID, ANYWAY.
I'M NOT EASY TO KILL. YOU CAN'T KILL DEATH.
BUT I BET I CAN KILL YOU.
PLEASE, CLARK, PLEASE. LISTEN TO ME.
THE OTHER HEROES--THEY'RE STOPPING THE BRAINIAC FLEET. YOU CAN LEAVE AGAIN. GET UP ABOVE THE KRYPTONITE.
YOU DON'T HAVE TO BE A MONSTER.
DON'T DO THIS TO ME. DON'T BE JUST ANOTHER MONSTER.

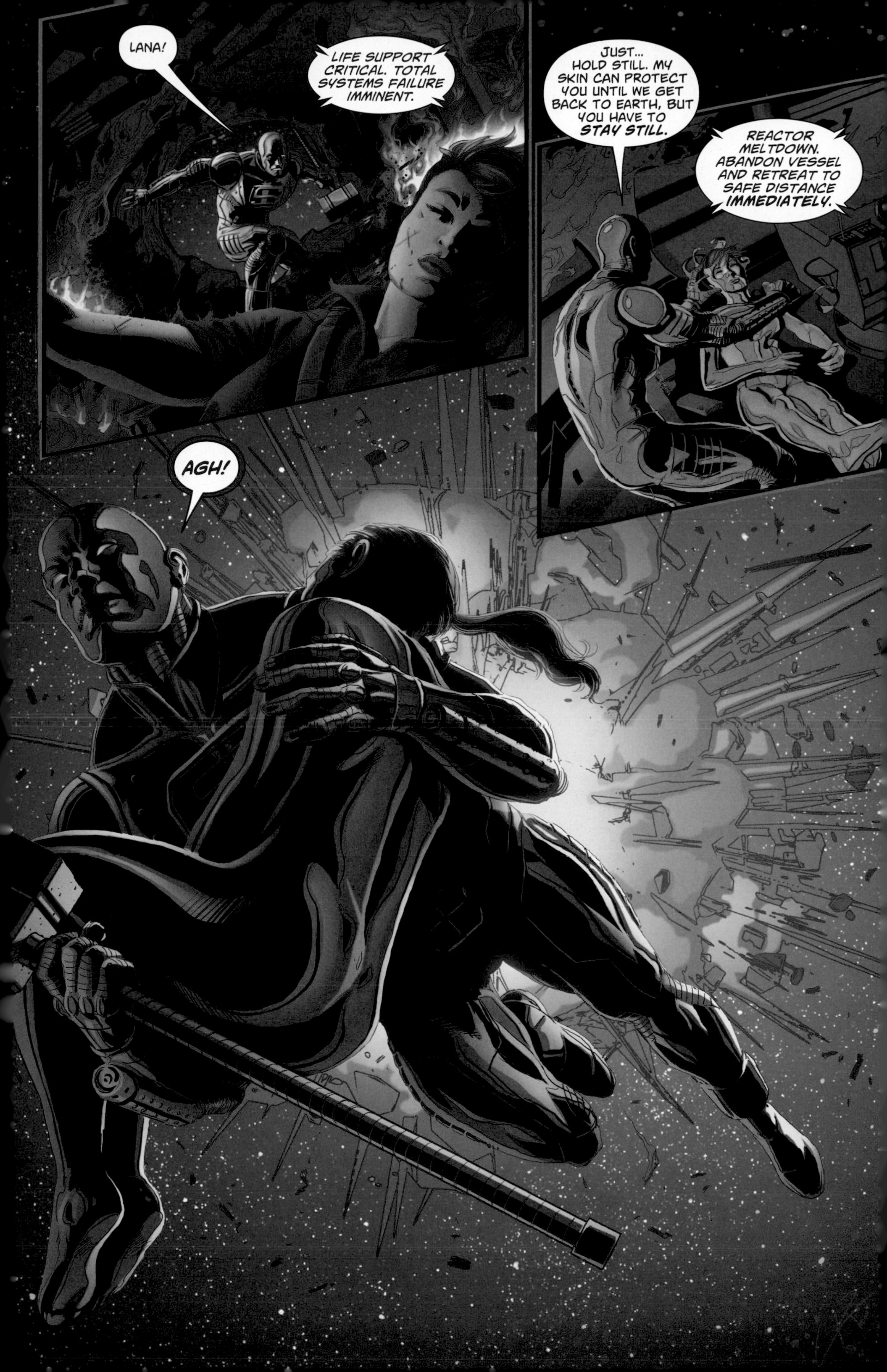
LANA!
LIFE SUPPORT CRITICAL. TOTAL SYSTEMS FAILURE IMMINENT.
JUST... HOLD STILL. MY SKIN CAN PROTECT YOU UNTIL WE GET BACK TO EARTH, BUT YOU HAVE TO **STAY STILL.**
REACTOR MELTDOWN. ABANDON VESSEL AND RETREAT TO SAFE DISTANCE **IMMEDIATELY.**
AGH!

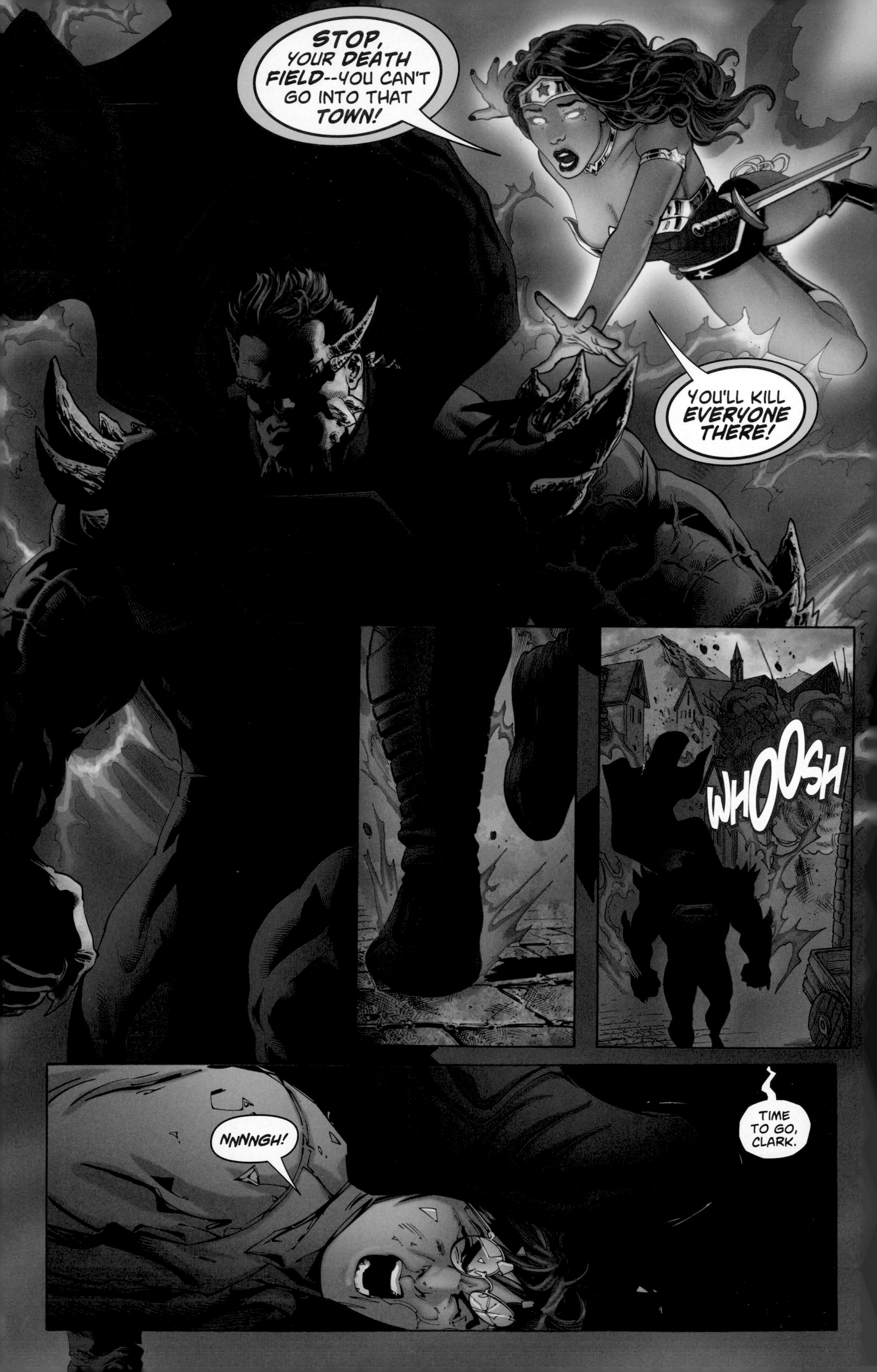
STOP, YOUR DEATH FIELD--YOU CAN'T GO INTO THAT TOWN!
YOU'LL KILL EVERYONE THERE!
WHOOSH
NNNNGH!
TIME TO GO, CLARK.

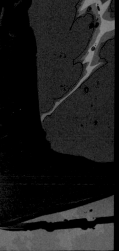

THANK GOD.

BATMAN TO WONDER WOMAN. WE DID IT--WE WERE ABLE TO PULL THE KRYPTONITE FROM THE ATMOSPHERE.

YOU MADE ME PROMISE, CLARK. IF WE EVER GOT TO THIS POINT, I'D DO WHAT I HAD TO DO!

YOU MADE ME *PROMISE!*

SUPERMAN SHOULD FEEL THE EFFECTS BY NOW.

"IT'S TOO LATE, BRUCE."

IT'S TOO LATE.

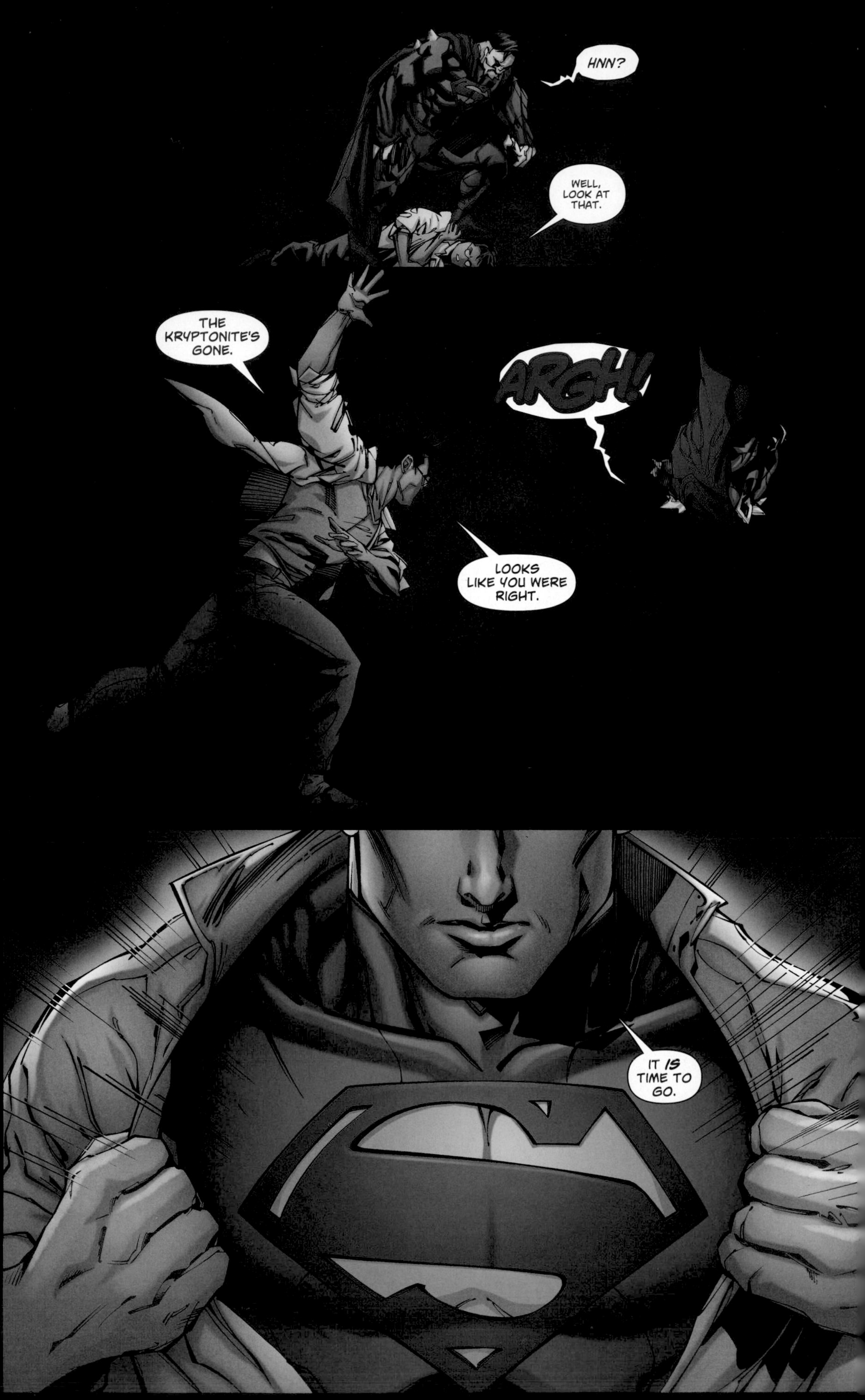
HNN?
WELL, LOOK AT THAT.
THE KRYPTONITE'S GONE.
ARGH!
LOOKS LIKE YOU WERE RIGHT.
IT *IS* TIME TO GO.

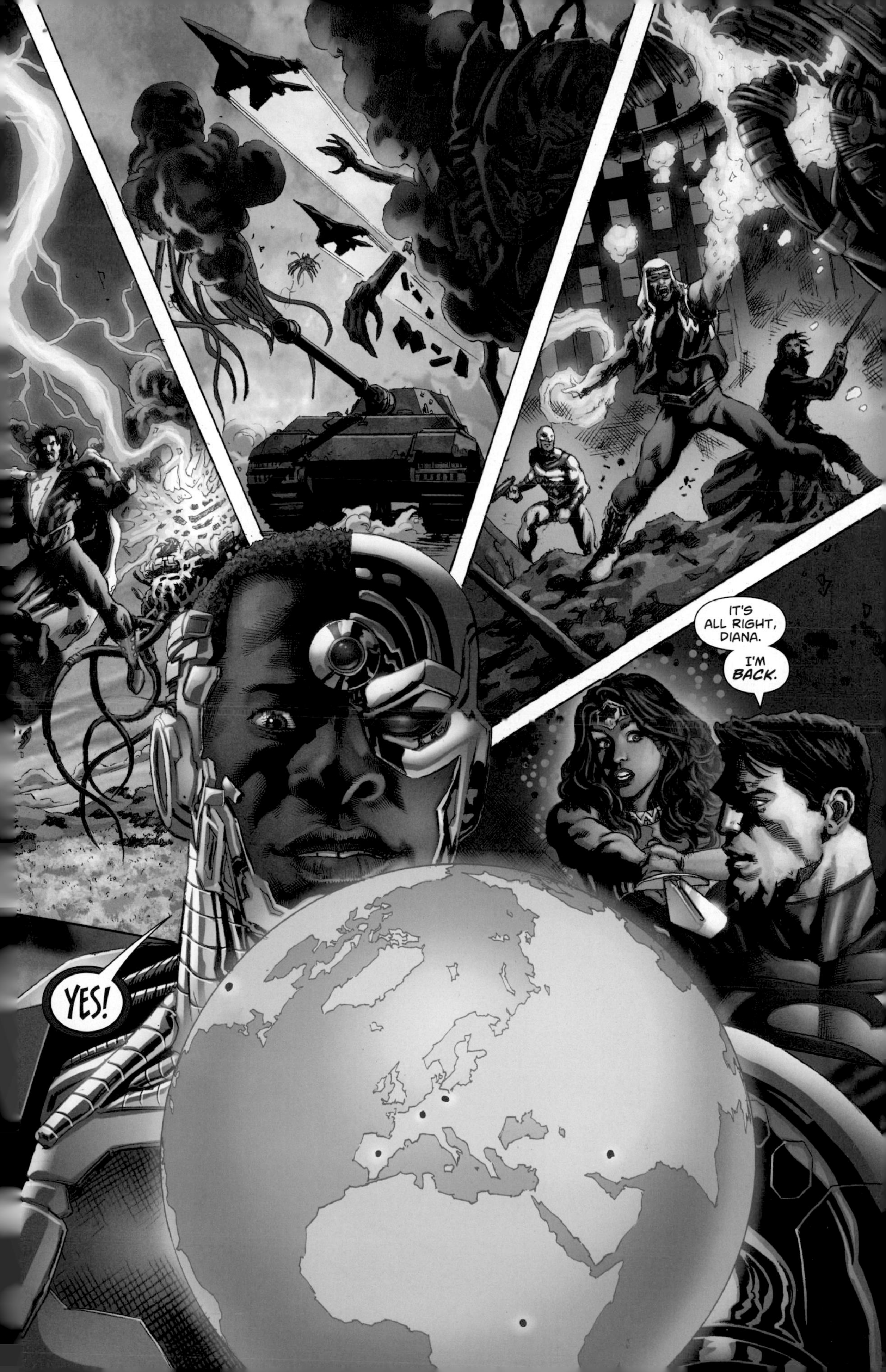
IT'S ALL RIGHT, DIANA.
I'M BACK.
YES!

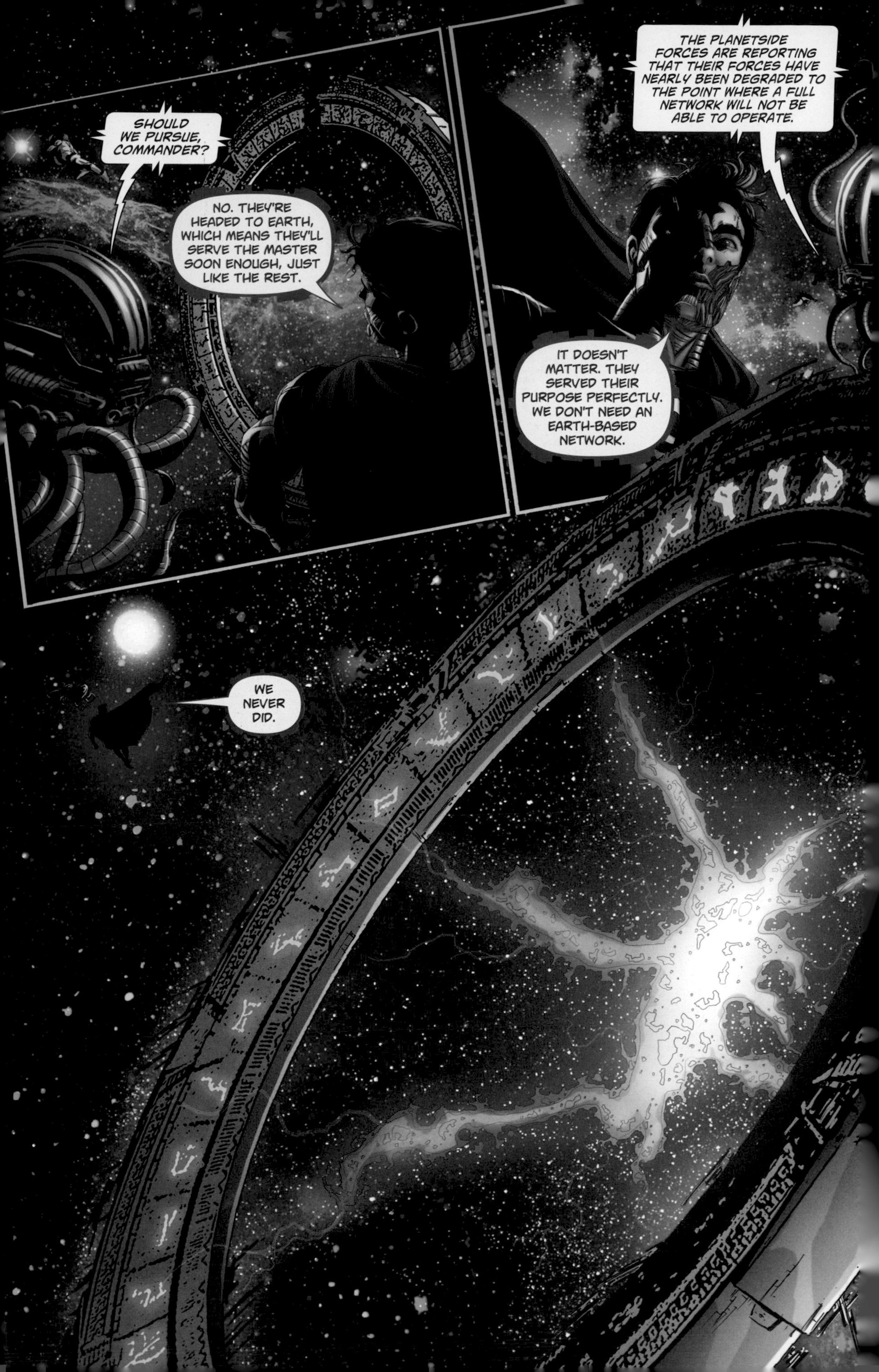
SHOULD WE PURSUE, COMMANDER?
NO. THEY'RE HEADED TO EARTH, WHICH MEANS THEY'LL SERVE THE MASTER SOON ENOUGH, JUST LIKE THE REST.
THE PLANETSIDE FORCES ARE REPORTING THAT THEIR FORCES HAVE NEARLY BEEN DEGRADED TO THE POINT WHERE A FULL NETWORK WILL NOT BE ABLE TO OPERATE.
IT DOESN'T MATTER. THEY SERVED THEIR PURPOSE PERFECTLY. WE DON'T NEED AN EARTH-BASED NETWORK.
WE NEVER DID.

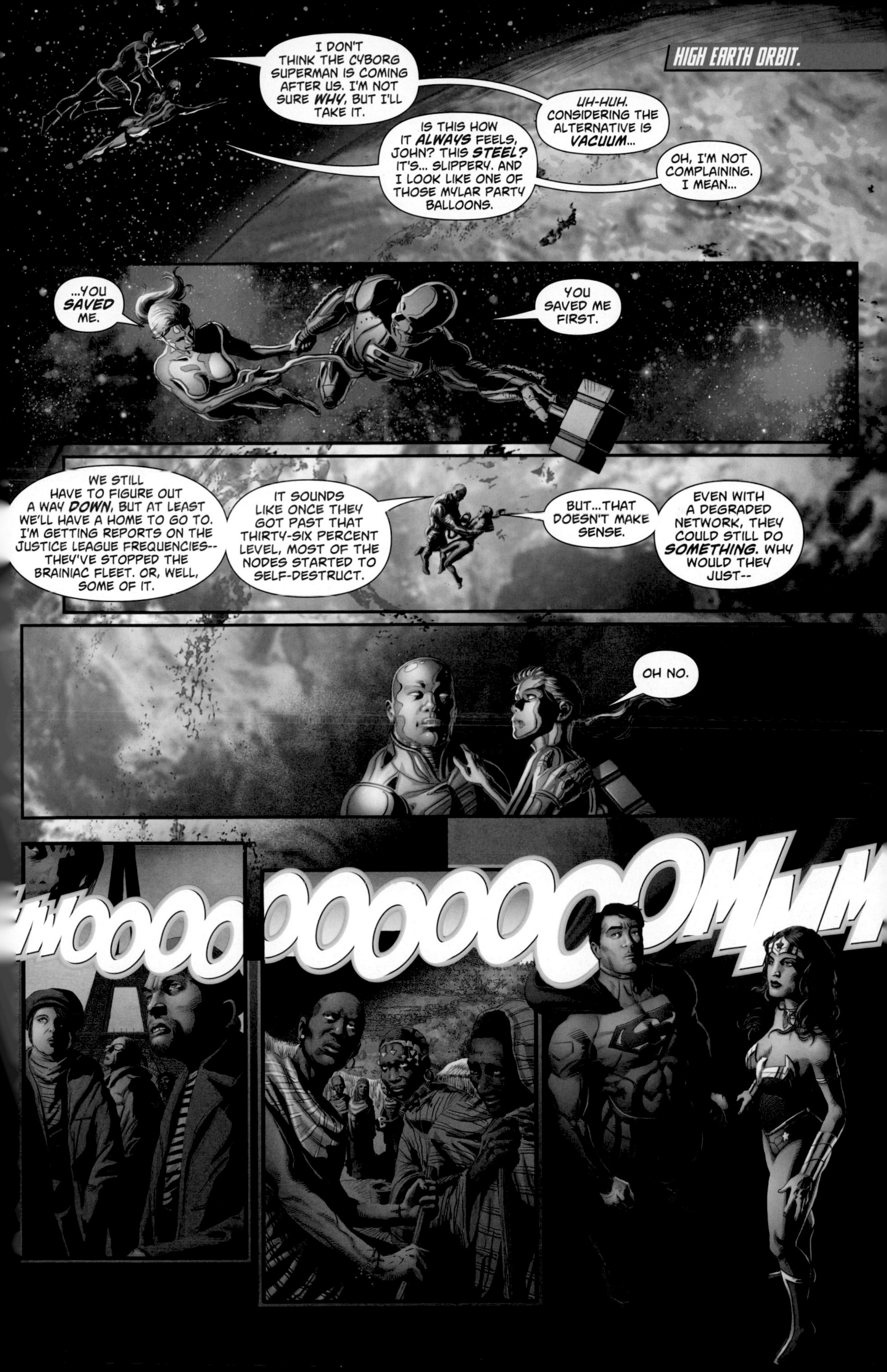
HIGH EARTH ORBIT.
I DON'T THINK THE CYBORG SUPERMAN IS COMING AFTER US. I'M NOT SURE WHY, BUT I'LL TAKE IT.
UH-HUH. CONSIDERING THE ALTERNATIVE IS VACUUM...
IS THIS HOW IT ALWAYS FEELS, JOHN? THIS STEEL? IT'S... SLIPPERY. AND I LOOK LIKE ONE OF THOSE MYLAR PARTY BALLOONS.
OH, I'M NOT COMPLAINING. I MEAN...
...YOU SAVED ME.
YOU SAVED ME FIRST.
WE STILL HAVE TO FIGURE OUT A WAY DOWN, BUT AT LEAST WE'LL HAVE A HOME TO GO TO. I'M GETTING REPORTS ON THE JUSTICE LEAGUE FREQUENCIES-- THEY'VE STOPPED THE BRAINIAC FLEET. OR, WELL, SOME OF IT.
IT SOUNDS LIKE ONCE THEY GOT PAST THAT THIRTY-SIX PERCENT LEVEL, MOST OF THE NODES STARTED TO SELF-DESTRUCT.
BUT...THAT DOESN'T MAKE SENSE.
EVEN WITH A DEGRADED NETWORK, THEY COULD STILL DO SOMETHING. WHY WOULD THEY JUST--
OH NO.
WOOOOOOOOOOOOOMMM

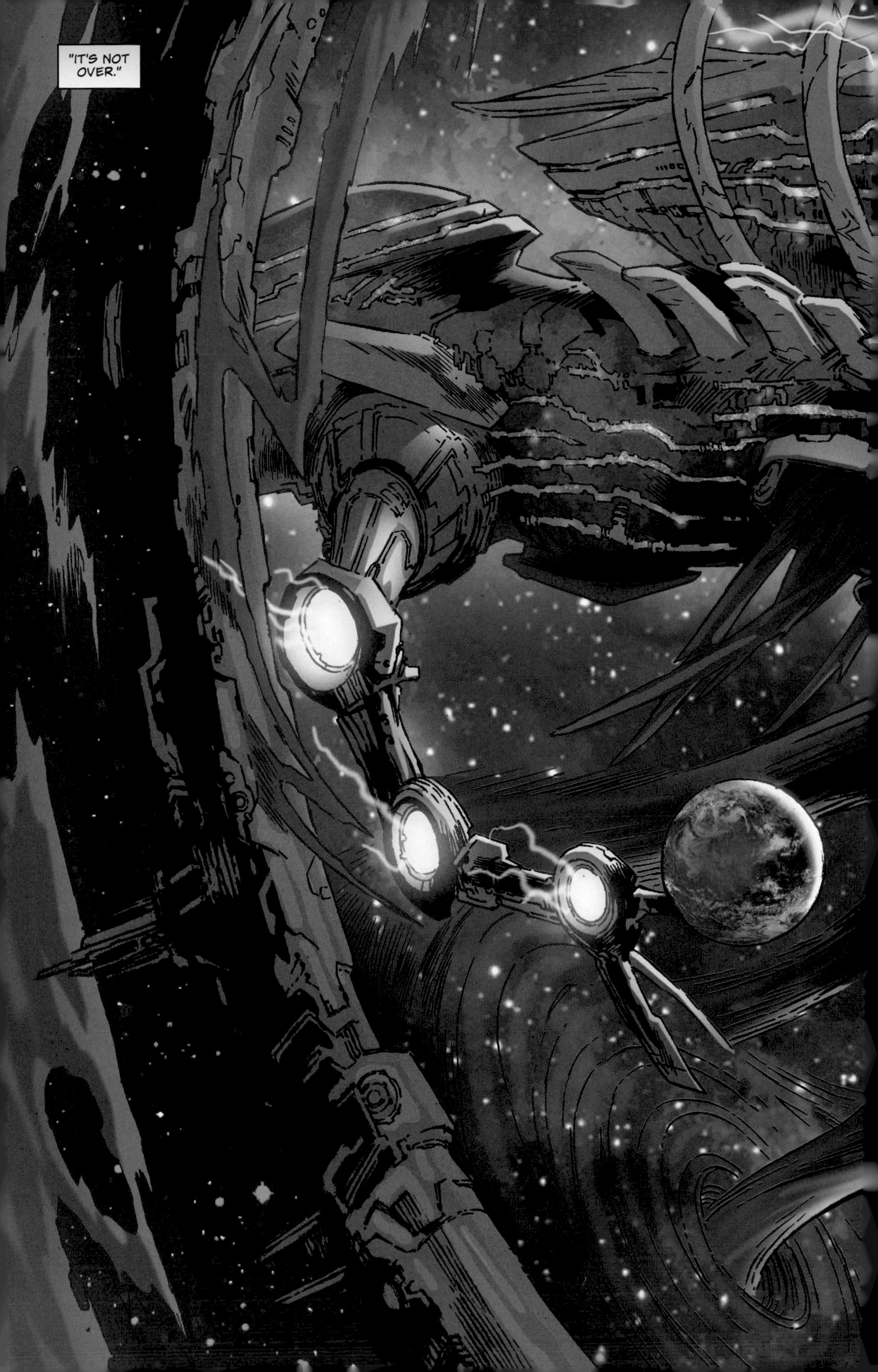
"IT'S NOT OVER."

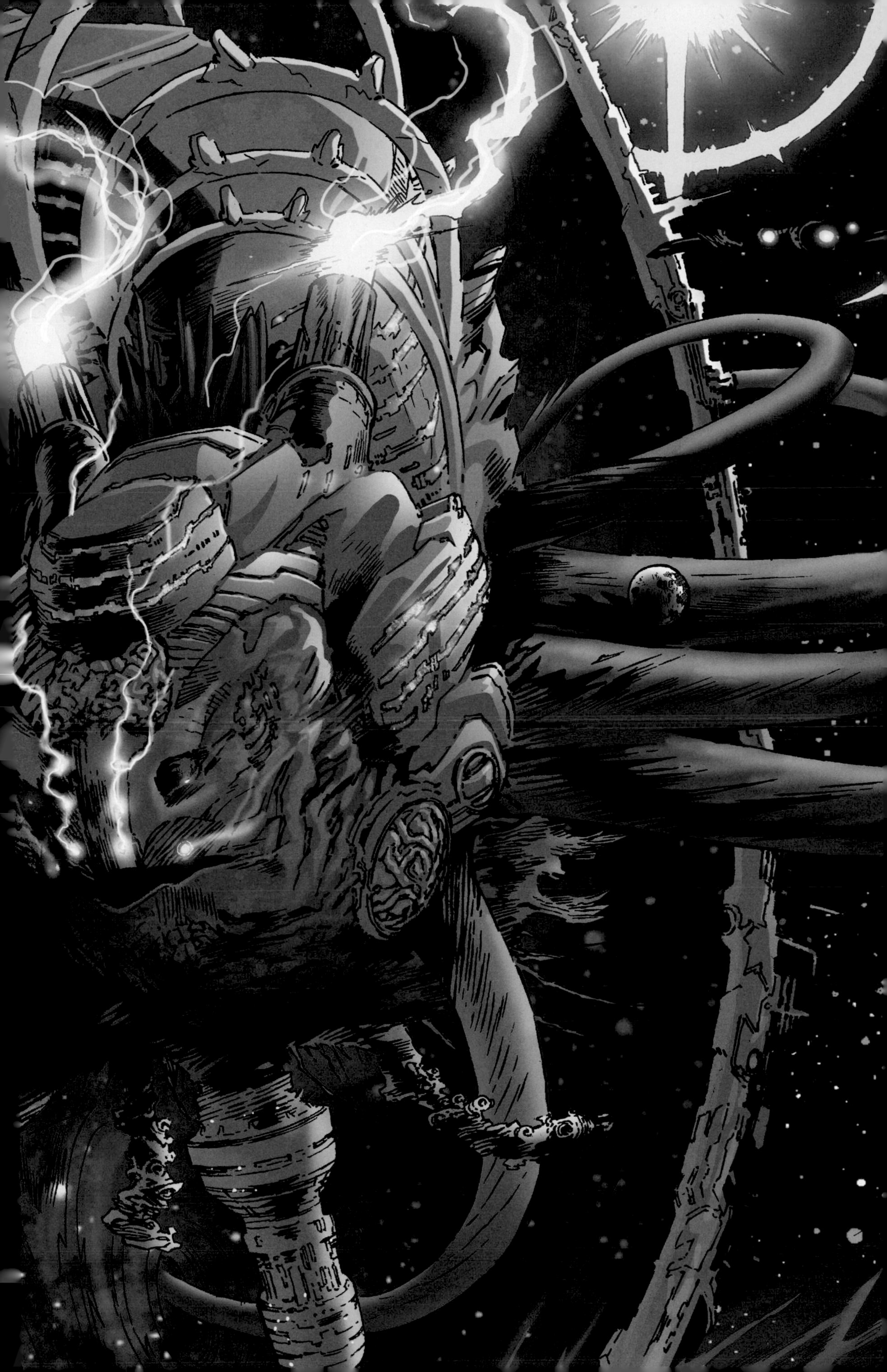

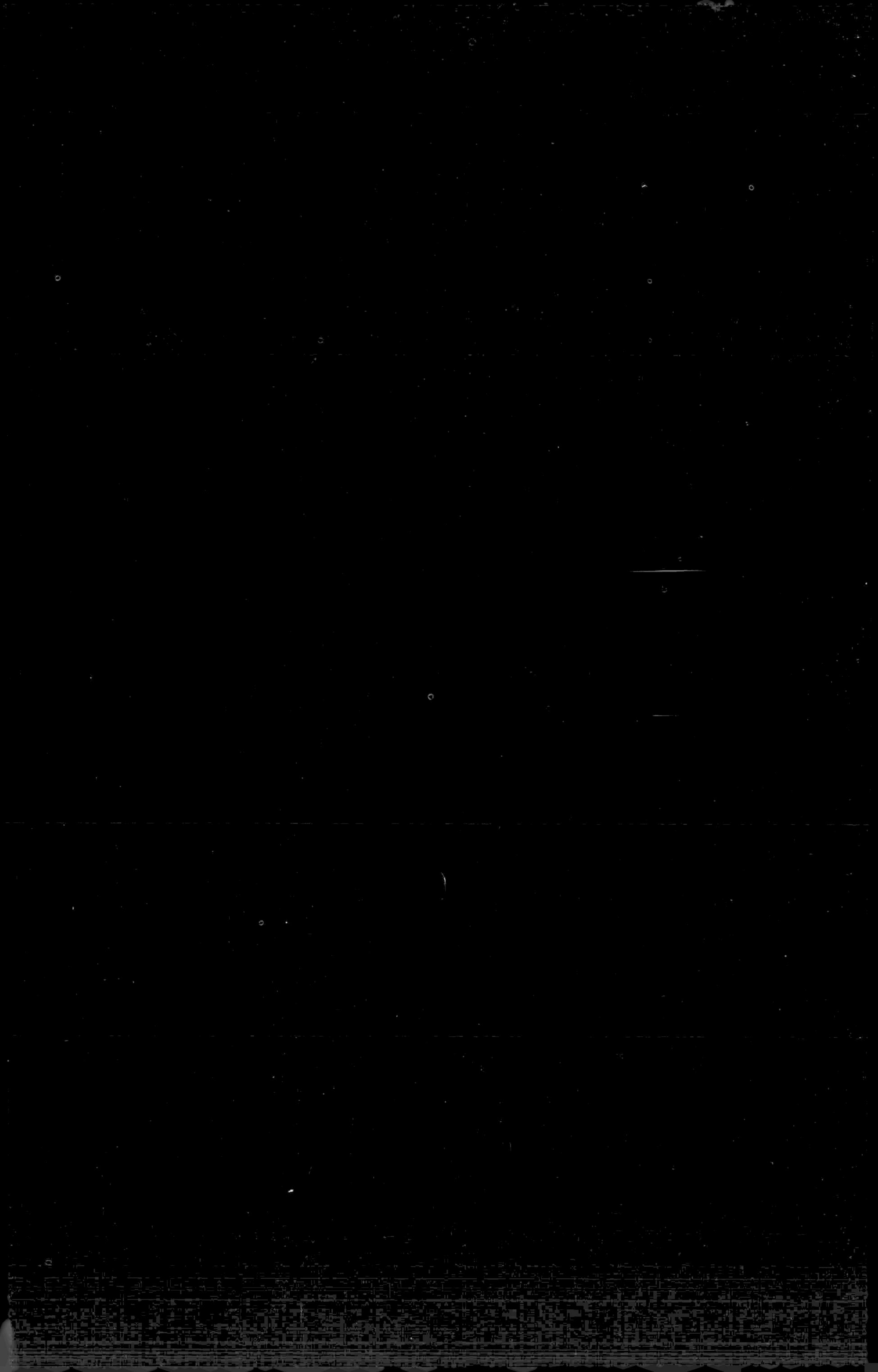

ASSIMILATION

THONY SILAS artist

cover by ED BENES & ALEX SINCLAIR

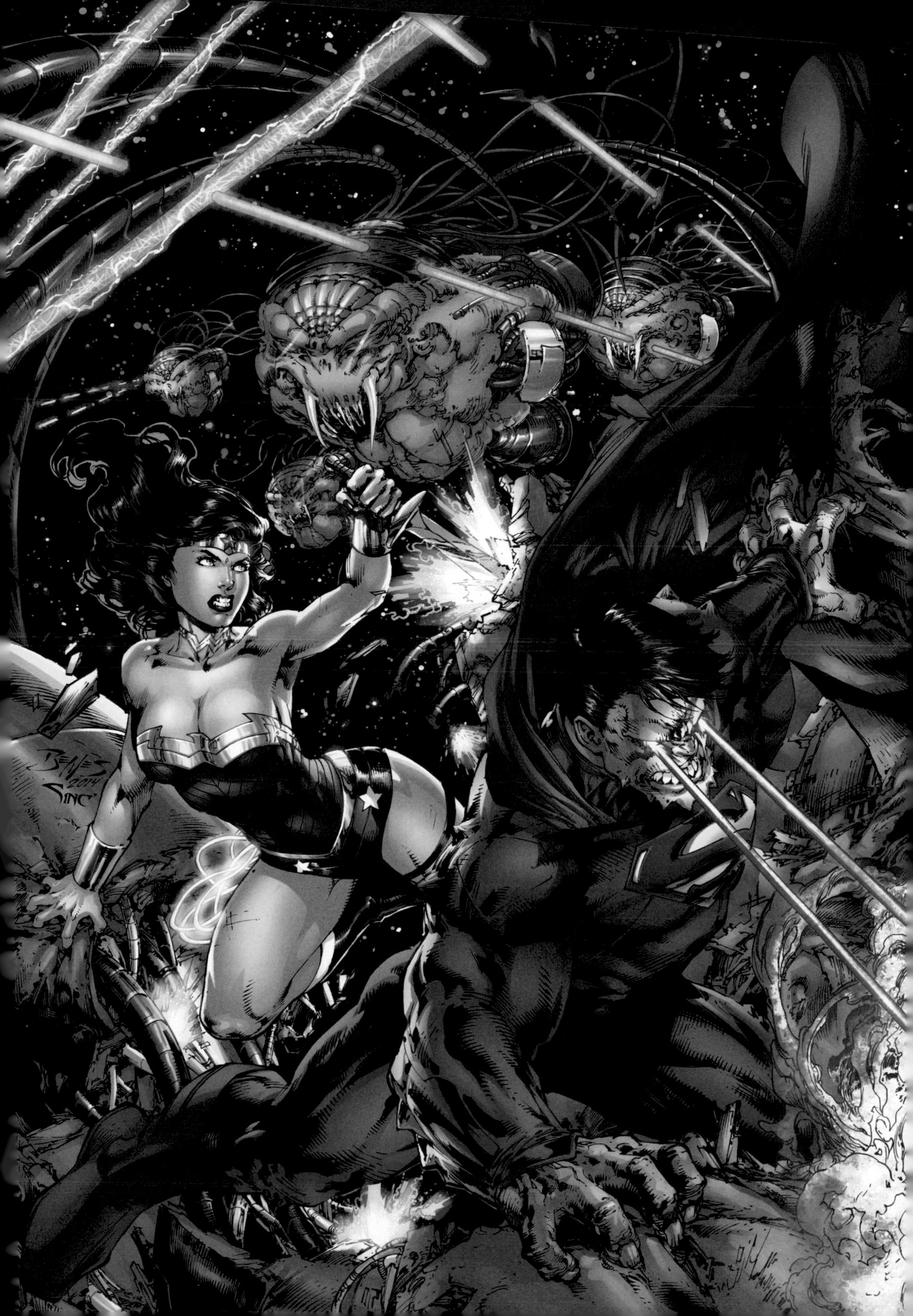

WORLD   U.S.   METROPOLIS   BUSINESS   OPINION   SPORTS   ARTS   STYLE   VIDEO

August 13, 2014

Daily Planet

STAY WHERE YOU ARE!

Fortress: Imagi

By Lois Lane

If you are reading this, stay where you are, stay underground, stay in whatever place is keeping you safe from the mind sucking ravages of Brainiac's World Ship.

A horde of ships led by what can only be described as a Cyborg Superman has decimated our planet's defenses. I am sorry to say, I was also a pawn in this and helped in allowing this first strike to happen. This is all part of an elaborate and calculated plan by the creature we have come to call Brainiac, which began with placing both Smallville and Metropolis' populace in coma states and escalated from there, including infecting Superman with the Doomsday virus that had him leaving Earth.

But Superman is back leading the heroes that remain—Batman, Martian Manhunter, Steel and Wonder Woman in a battle for ou planet.

We will continue the fight!

We will not go quietly into the night!

X	Slideshow - Superdoom's Path of Destruction	404 Error
		404 Error
		404 Error

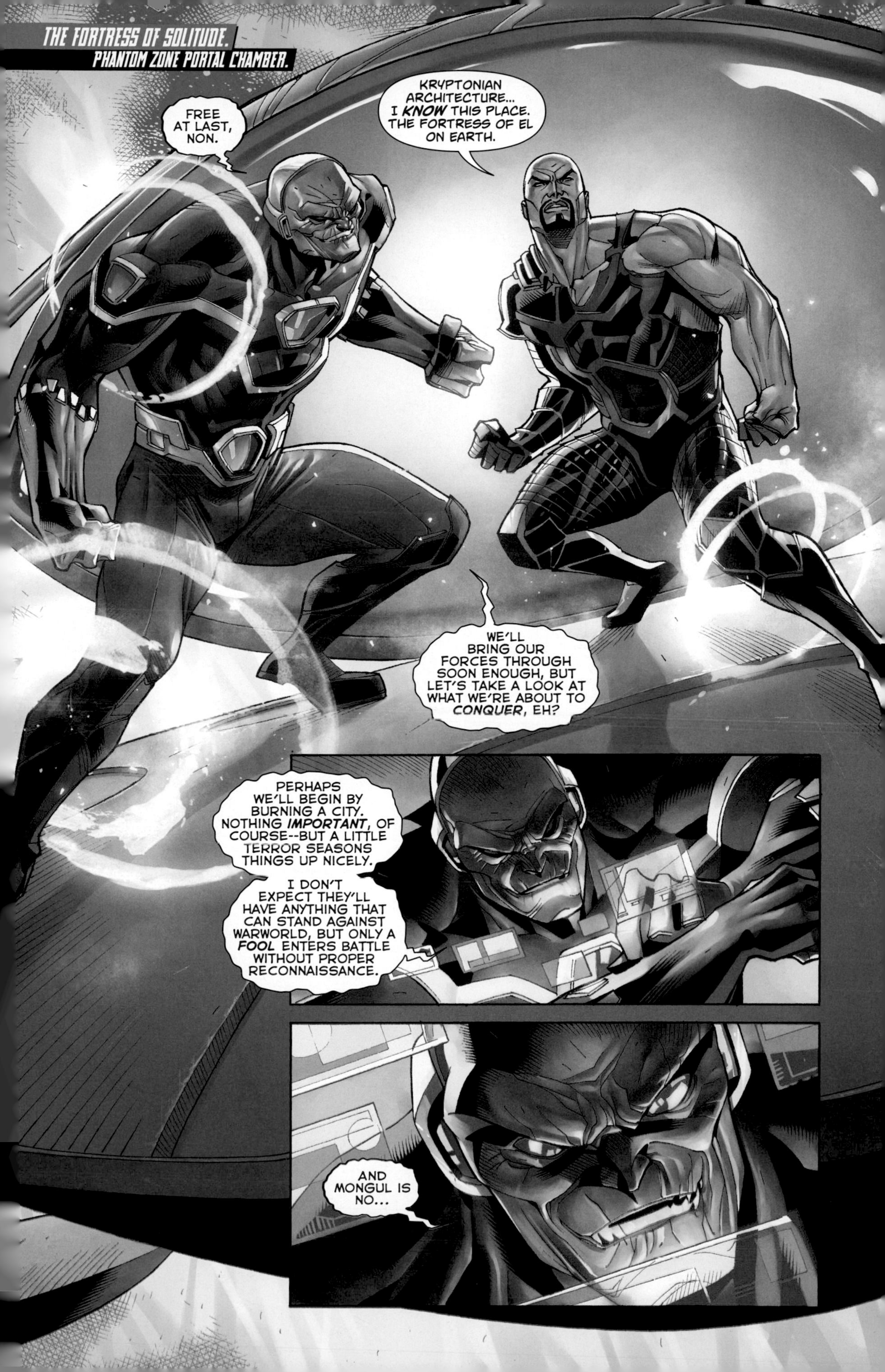
THE FORTRESS OF SOLITUDE.
PHANTOM ZONE PORTAL CHAMBER.
FREE AT LAST, NON.
KRYPTONIAN ARCHITECTURE... I KNOW THIS PLACE. THE FORTRESS OF EL ON EARTH.
WE'LL BRING OUR FORCES THROUGH SOON ENOUGH, BUT LET'S TAKE A LOOK AT WHAT WE'RE ABOUT TO CONQUER, EH?
PERHAPS WE'LL BEGIN BY BURNING A CITY. NOTHING IMPORTANT, OF COURSE--BUT A LITTLE TERROR SEASONS THINGS UP NICELY.
I DON'T EXPECT THEY'LL HAVE ANYTHING THAT CAN STAND AGAINST WARWORLD, BUT ONLY A FOOL ENTERS BATTLE WITHOUT PROPER RECONNAISSANCE.
AND MONGUL IS NO...

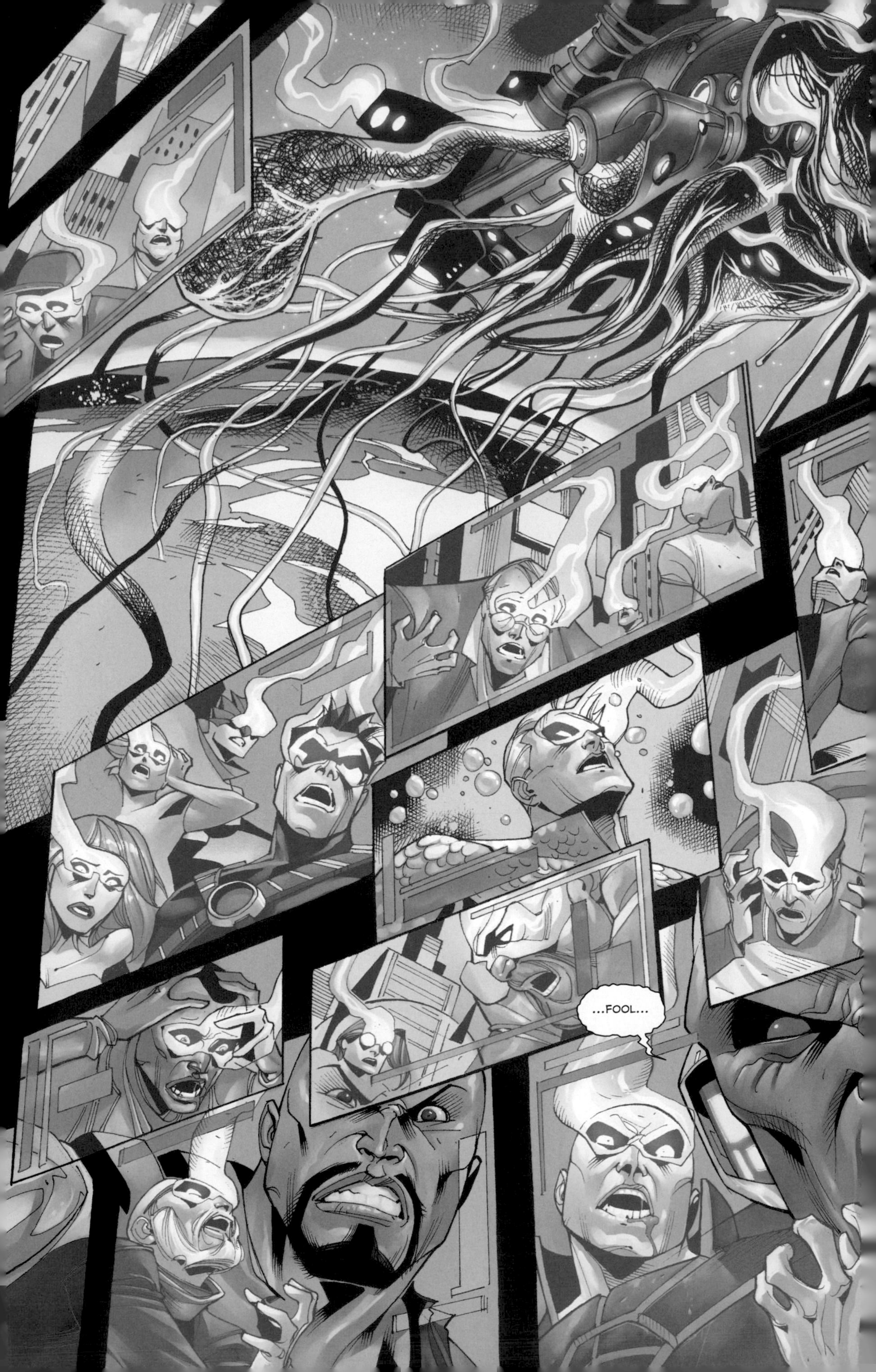
...FOOL...

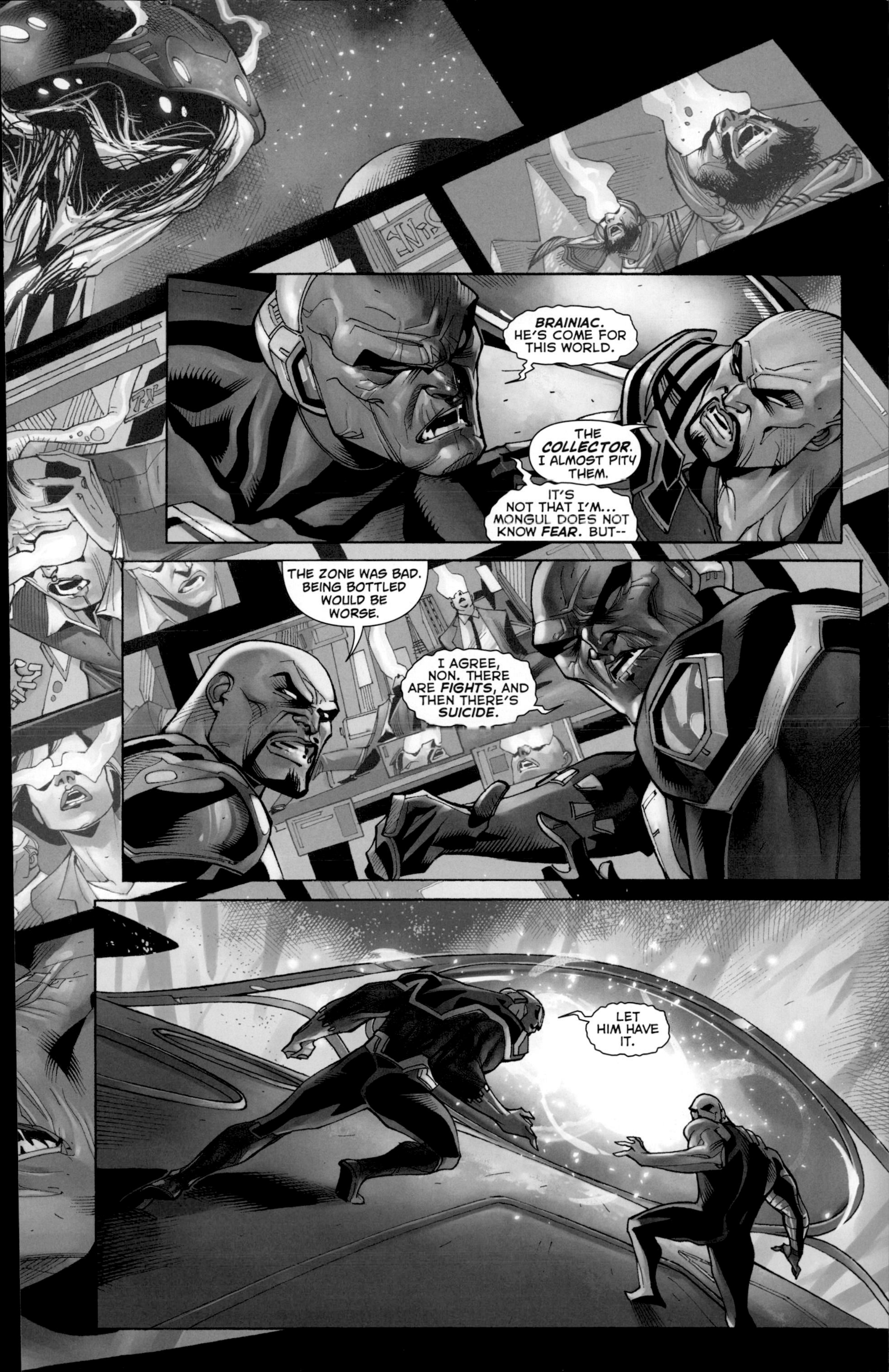
BRAINIAC. HE'S COME FOR THIS WORLD.
THE COLLECTOR. I ALMOST PITY THEM.
IT'S NOT THAT I'M... MONGUL DOES NOT KNOW FEAR. BUT--
THE ZONE WAS BAD. BEING BOTTLED WOULD BE WORSE.
I AGREE, NON. THERE ARE FIGHTS, AND THEN THERE'S SUICIDE.
LET HIM HAVE IT.

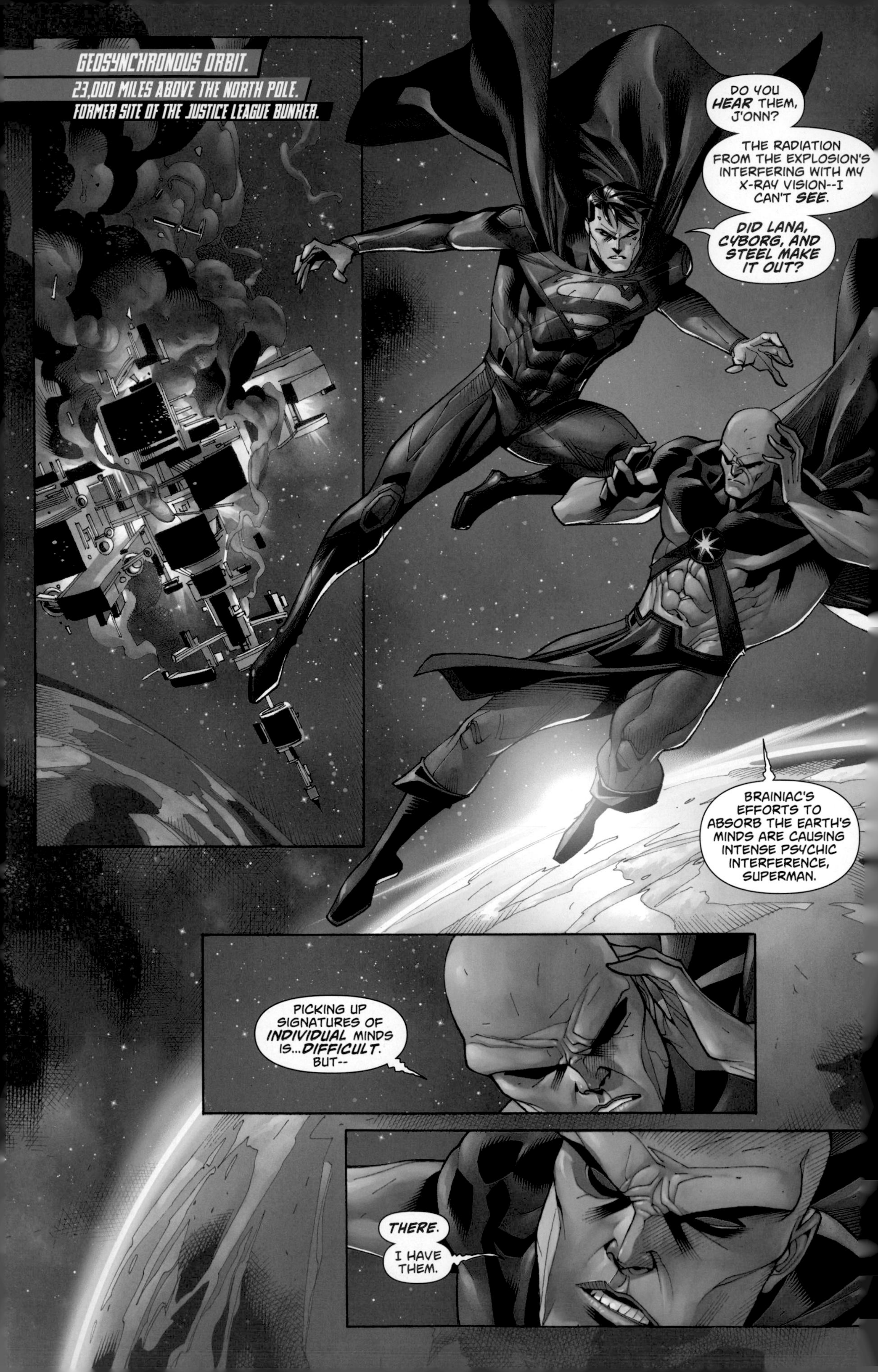
GEOSYNCHRONOUS ORBIT.
23,000 MILES ABOVE THE NORTH POLE.
FORMER SITE OF THE JUSTICE LEAGUE BUNKER.
DO YOU HEAR THEM, J'ONN?
THE RADIATION FROM THE EXPLOSION'S INTERFERING WITH MY X-RAY VISION--I CAN'T SEE.
DID LANA, CYBORG, AND STEEL MAKE IT OUT?
BRAINIAC'S EFFORTS TO ABSORB THE EARTH'S MINDS ARE CAUSING INTENSE PSYCHIC INTERFERENCE, SUPERMAN.
PICKING UP SIGNATURES OF INDIVIDUAL MINDS IS...DIFFICULT. BUT--
THERE.
I HAVE THEM.

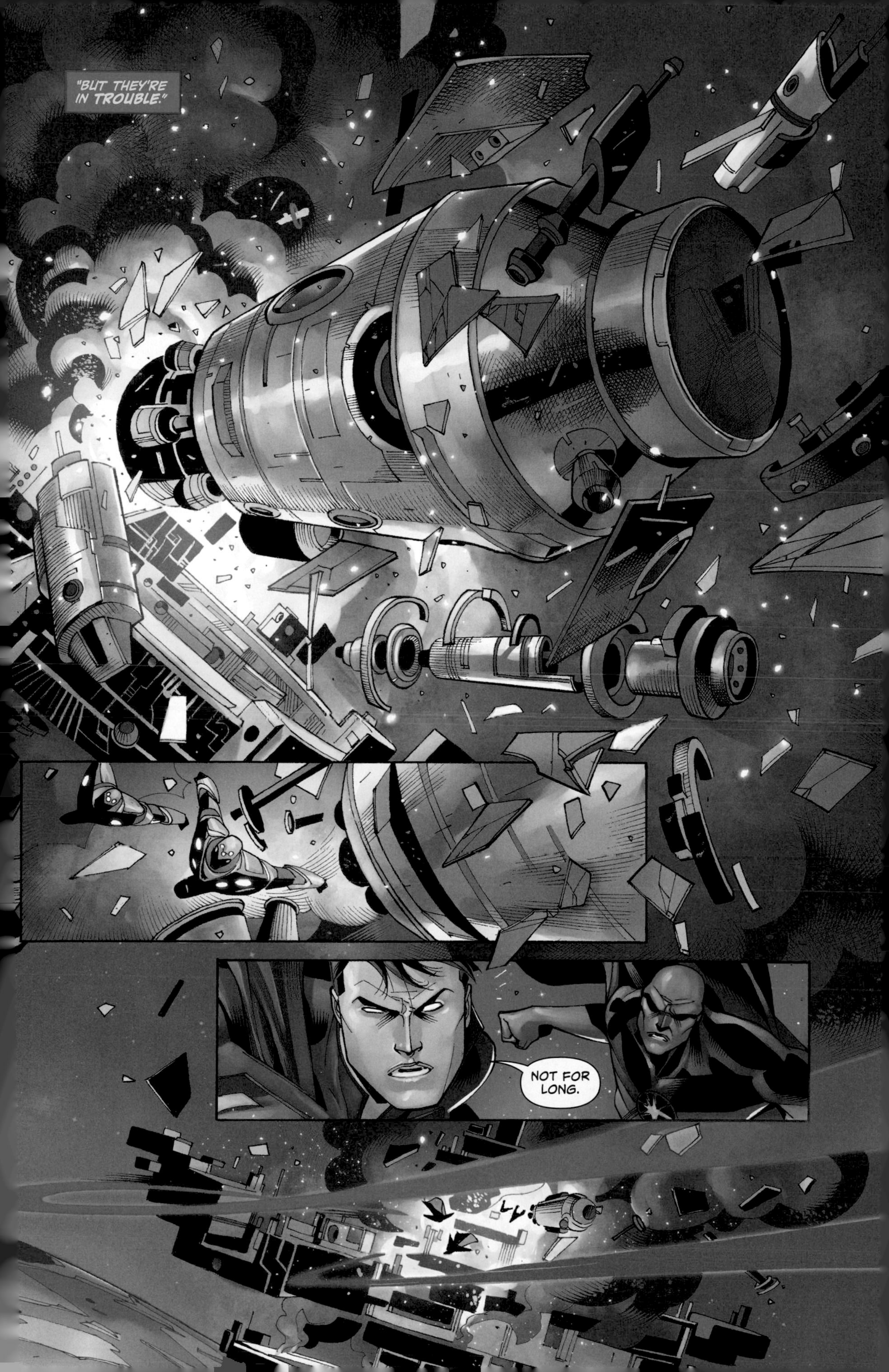
"BUT THEY'RE IN TROUBLE."
NOT FOR LONG.

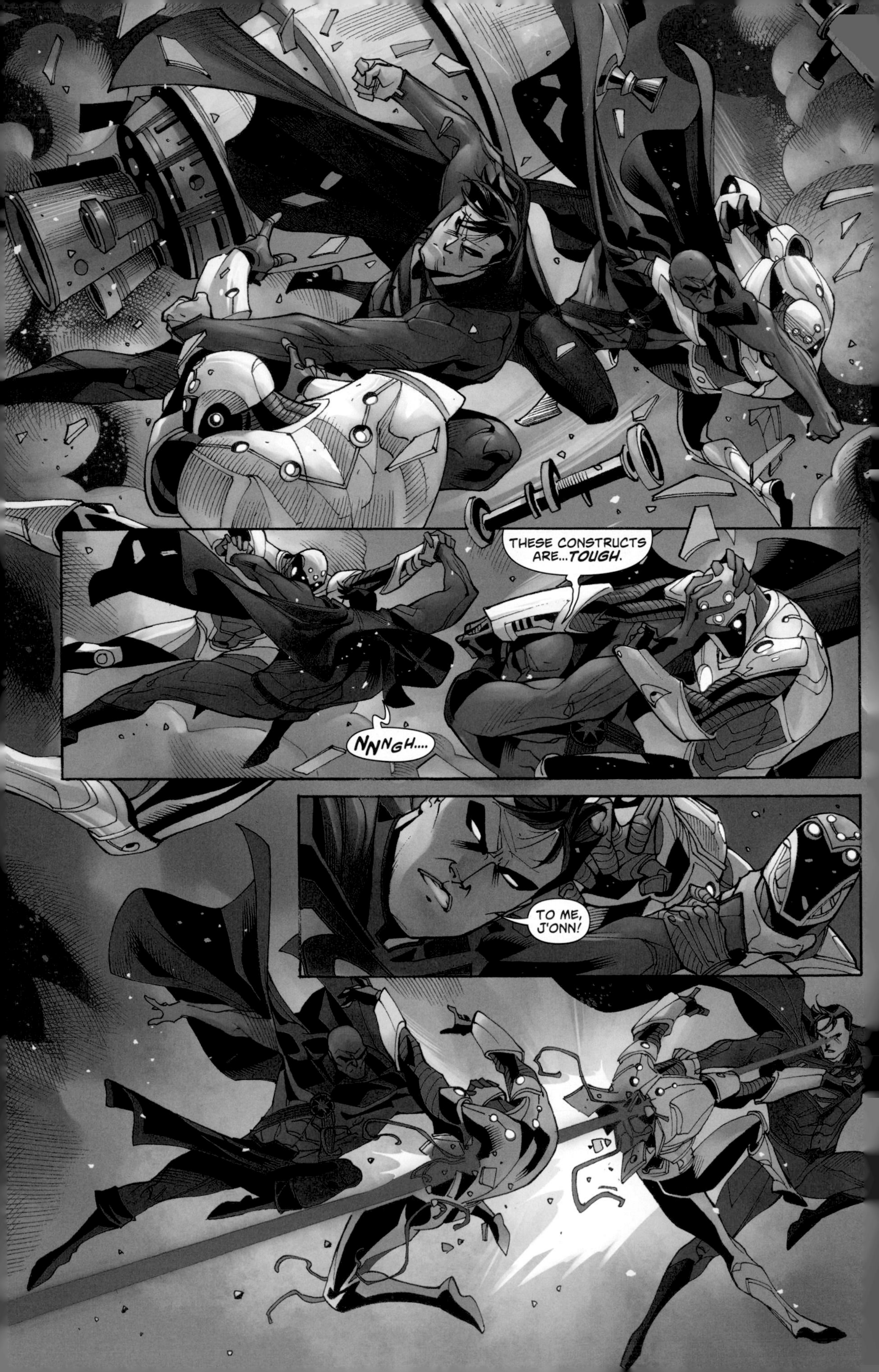
THESE CONSTRUCTS ARE...TOUGH.
NNNGH....
TO ME, J'ONN!

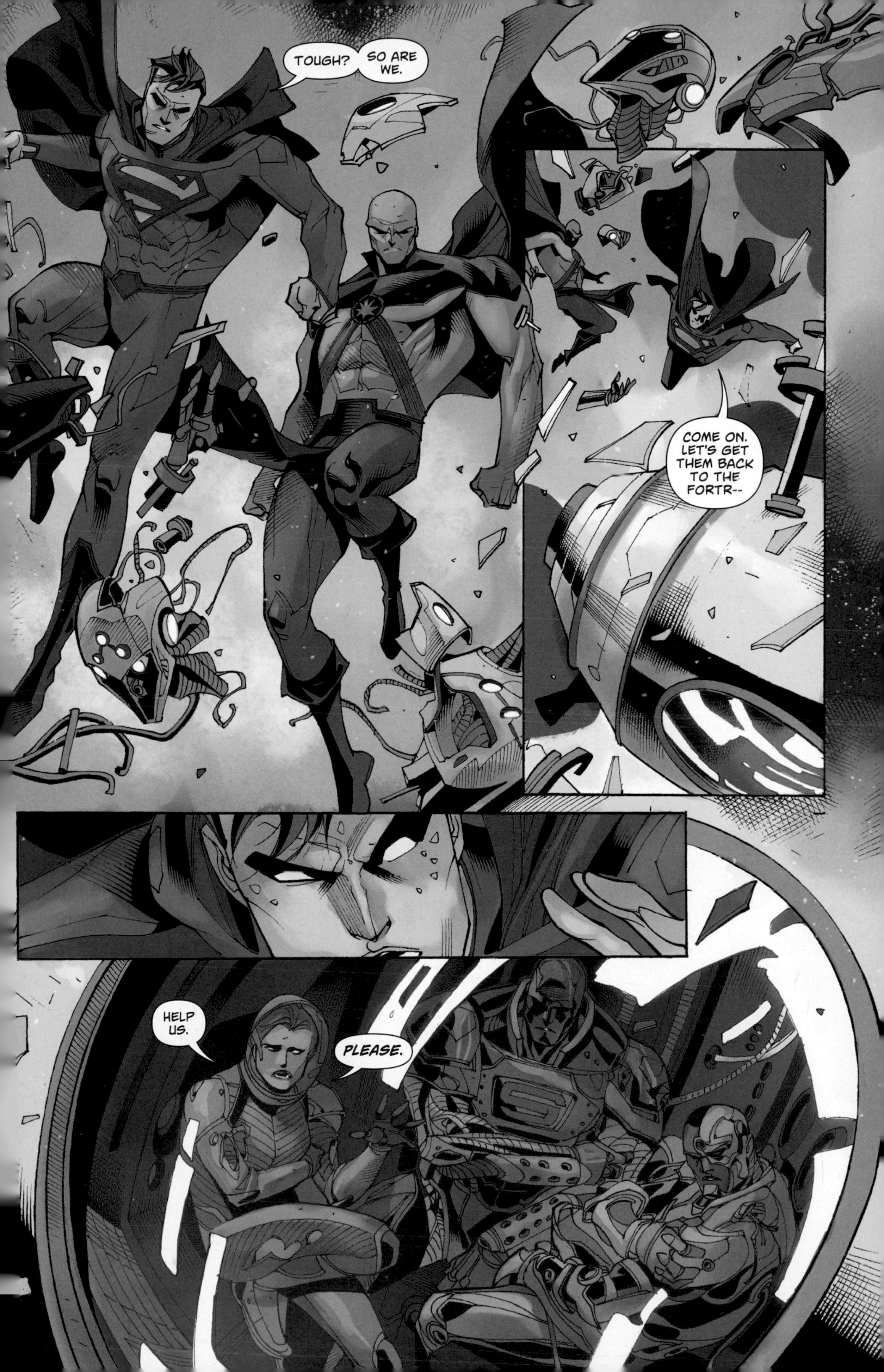
TOUGH?
SO ARE WE.
COME ON. LET'S GET THEM BACK TO THE FORTR--
HELP US.
PLEASE.

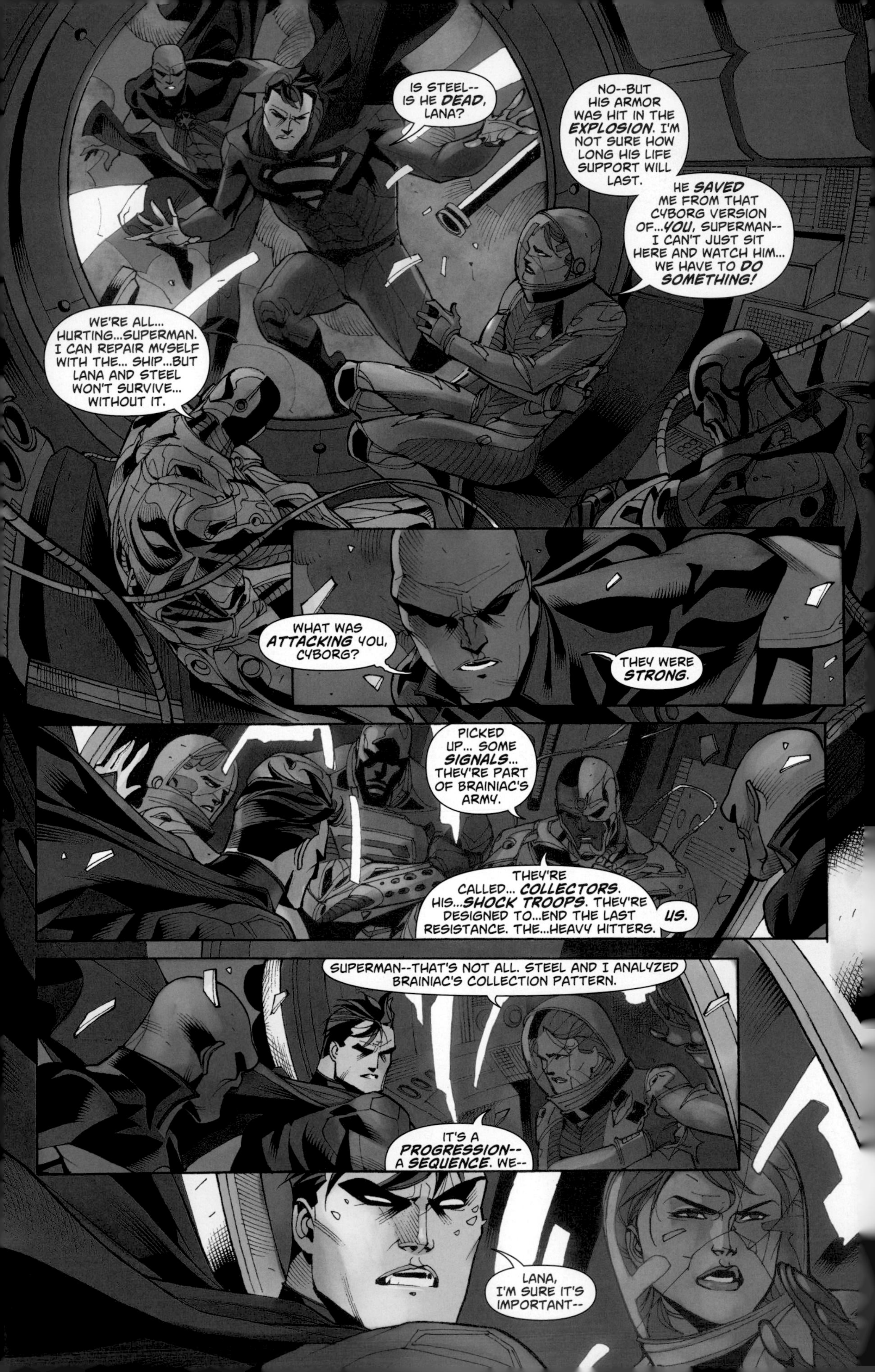
IS STEEL-- IS HE DEAD, LANA?
NO--BUT HIS ARMOR WAS HIT IN THE EXPLOSION. I'M NOT SURE HOW LONG HIS LIFE SUPPORT WILL LAST.
HE SAVED ME FROM THAT CYBORG VERSION OF...YOU, SUPERMAN-- I CAN'T JUST SIT HERE AND WATCH HIM... WE HAVE TO DO SOMETHING!
WE'RE ALL... HURTING...SUPERMAN. I CAN REPAIR MYSELF WITH THE... SHIP...BUT LANA AND STEEL WON'T SURVIVE... WITHOUT IT.
WHAT WAS ATTACKING YOU, CYBORG?
THEY WERE STRONG.
PICKED UP... SOME SIGNALS... THEY'RE PART OF BRAINIAC'S ARMY.
THEY'RE CALLED... COLLECTORS. HIS...SHOCK TROOPS. THEY'RE DESIGNED TO...END THE LAST RESISTANCE. THE...HEAVY HITTERS.
US.
SUPERMAN--THAT'S NOT ALL. STEEL AND I ANALYZED BRAINIAC'S COLLECTION PATTERN.
IT'S A PROGRESSION-- A SEQUENCE. WE--
LANA, I'M SURE IT'S IMPORTANT--

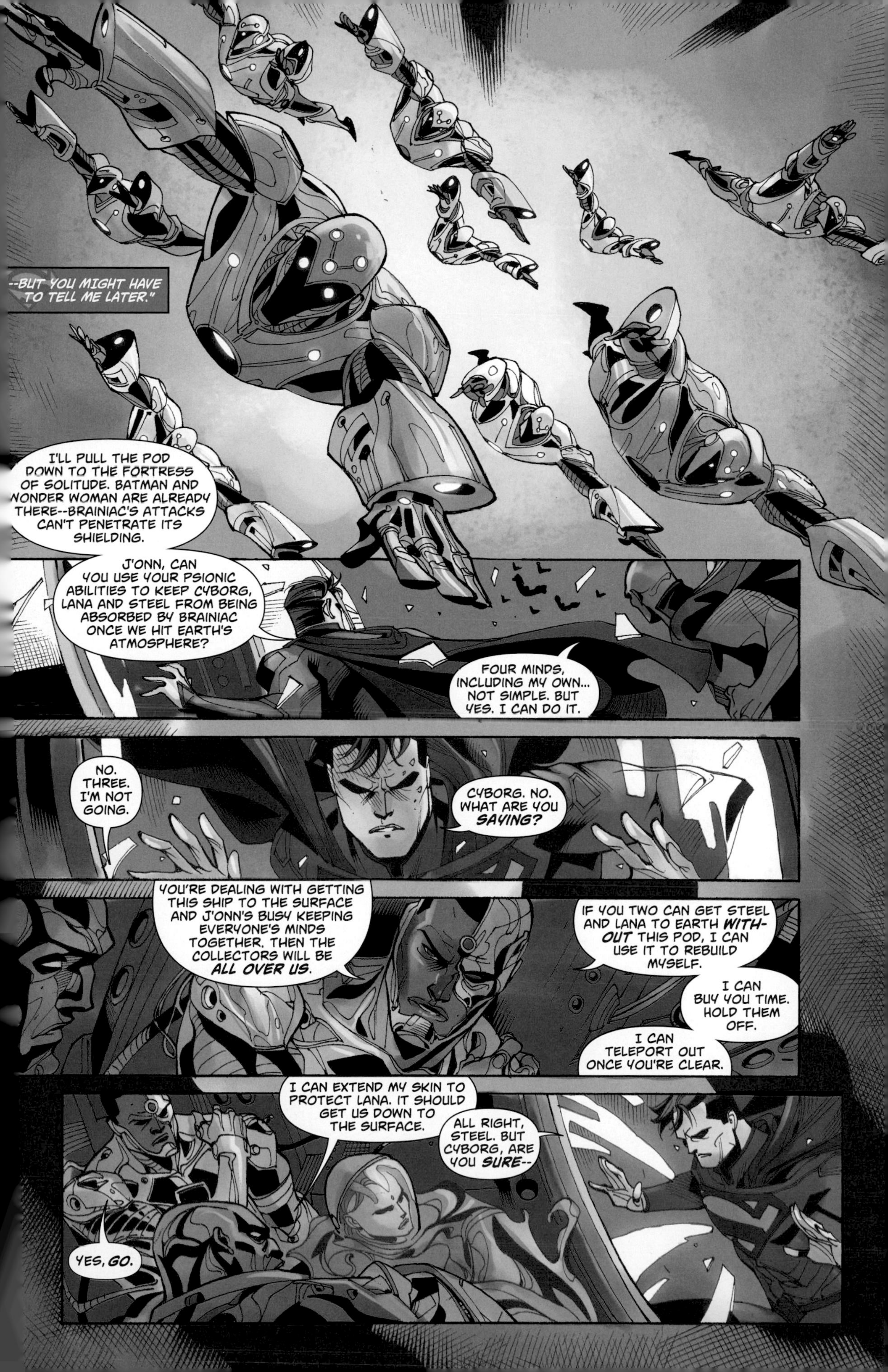

--BUT YOU MIGHT HAVE TO TELL ME LATER."
I'LL PULL THE POD DOWN TO THE FORTRESS OF SOLITUDE. BATMAN AND WONDER WOMAN ARE ALREADY THERE--BRAINIAC'S ATTACKS CAN'T PENETRATE ITS SHIELDING.
J'ONN, CAN YOU USE YOUR PSIONIC ABILITIES TO KEEP CYBORG, LANA AND STEEL FROM BEING ABSORBED BY BRAINIAC ONCE WE HIT EARTH'S ATMOSPHERE?
FOUR MINDS, INCLUDING MY OWN... NOT SIMPLE. BUT YES. I CAN DO IT.
NO. THREE. I'M NOT GOING.
CYBORG. NO. WHAT ARE YOU *SAYING?*
YOU'RE DEALING WITH GETTING THIS SHIP TO THE SURFACE AND J'ONN'S BUSY KEEPING EVERYONE'S MINDS TOGETHER. THEN THE COLLECTORS WILL BE *ALL OVER US*.
IF YOU TWO CAN GET STEEL AND LANA TO EARTH *WITH-OUT* THIS POD, I CAN USE IT TO REBUILD MYSELF.
I CAN BUY YOU TIME. HOLD THEM OFF.
I CAN TELEPORT OUT ONCE YOU'RE CLEAR.
I CAN EXTEND MY SKIN TO PROTECT LANA. IT SHOULD GET US DOWN TO THE SURFACE.
ALL RIGHT, STEEL. BUT CYBORG, ARE YOU *SURE*--
YES, *GO*.

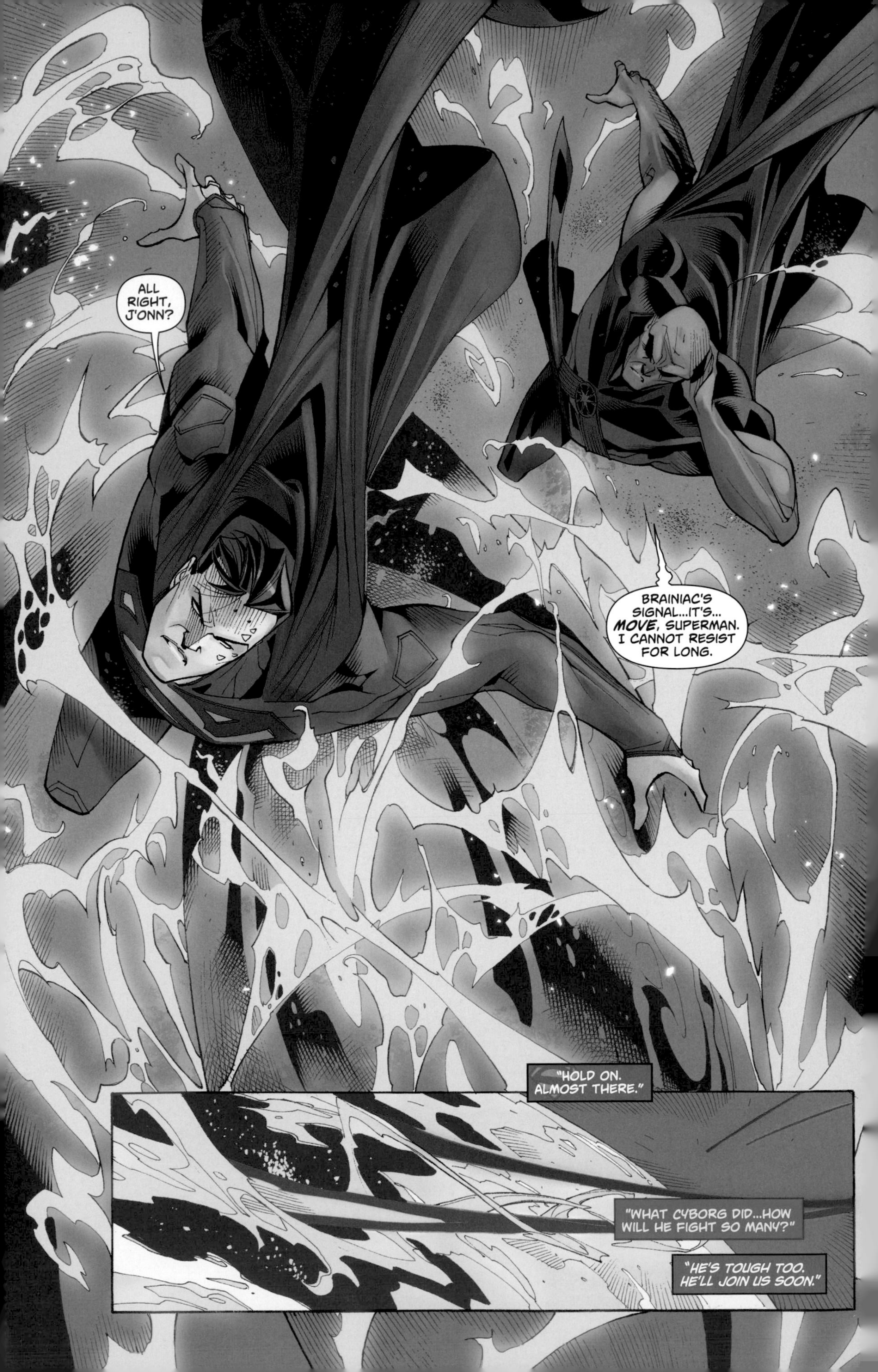
ALL RIGHT, J'ONN?
BRAINIAC'S SIGNAL...IT'S... MOVE, SUPERMAN. I CANNOT RESIST FOR LONG.
"HOLD ON. ALMOST THERE."
"WHAT CYBORG DID...HOW WILL HE FIGHT SO MANY?"
"HE'S TOUGH TOO. HE'LL JOIN US SOON."

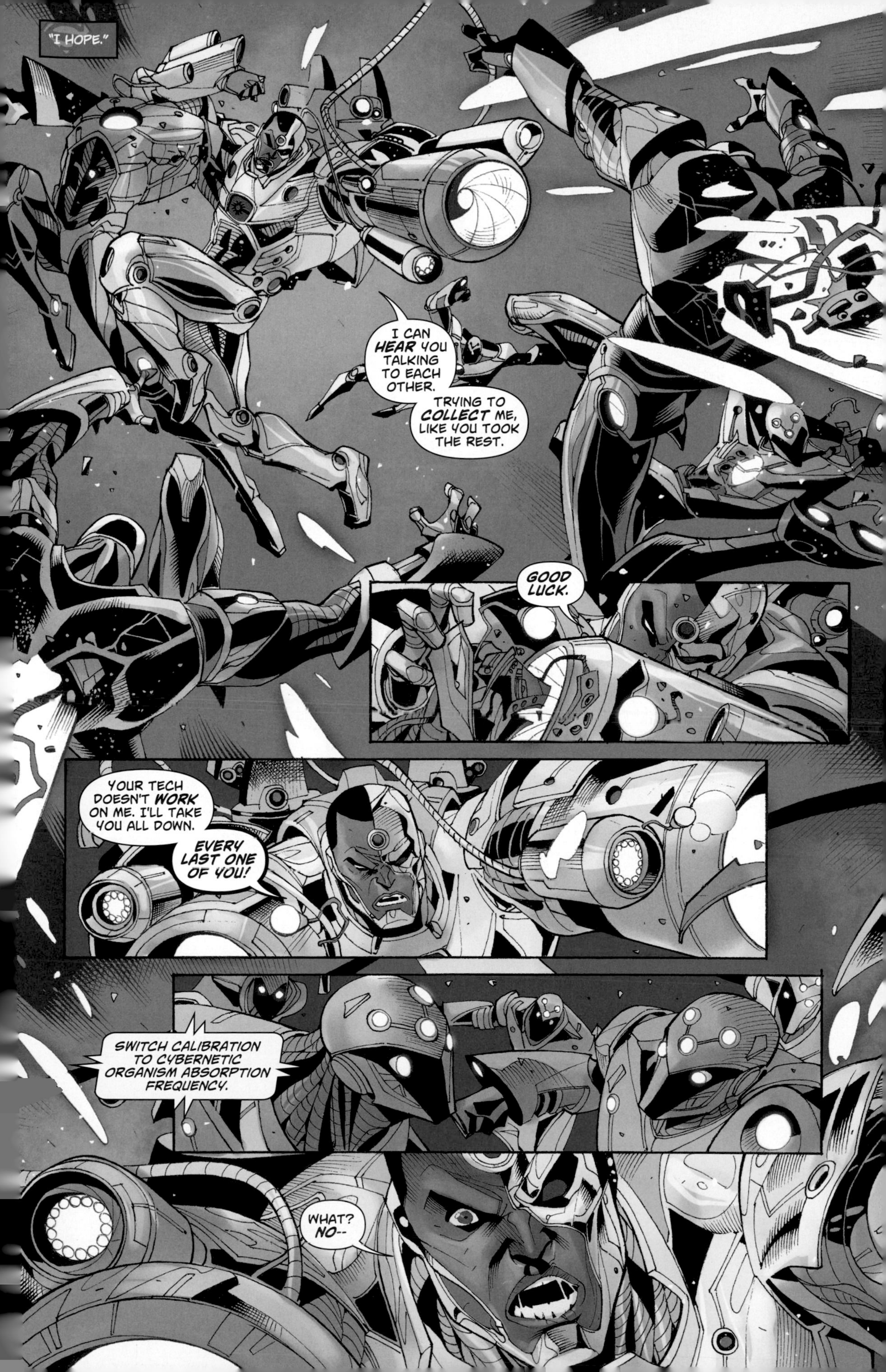

"I HOPE."
I CAN HEAR YOU TALKING TO EACH OTHER.
TRYING TO COLLECT ME, LIKE YOU TOOK THE REST.
GOOD LUCK.
YOUR TECH DOESN'T WORK ON ME. I'LL TAKE YOU ALL DOWN.
EVERY LAST ONE OF YOU!
SWITCH CALIBRATION TO CYBERNETIC ORGANISM ABSORPTION FREQUENCY.
WHAT? NO--

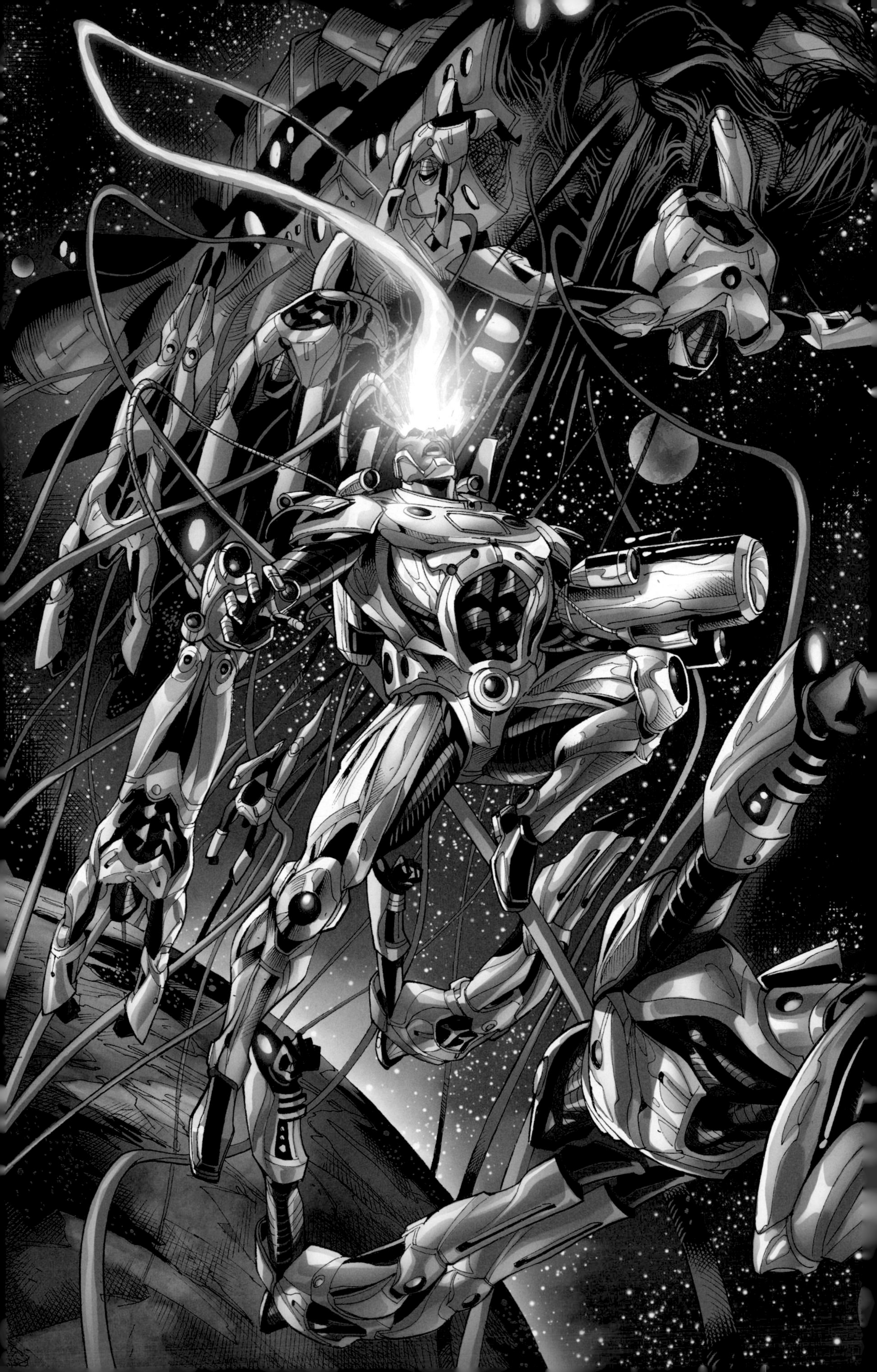

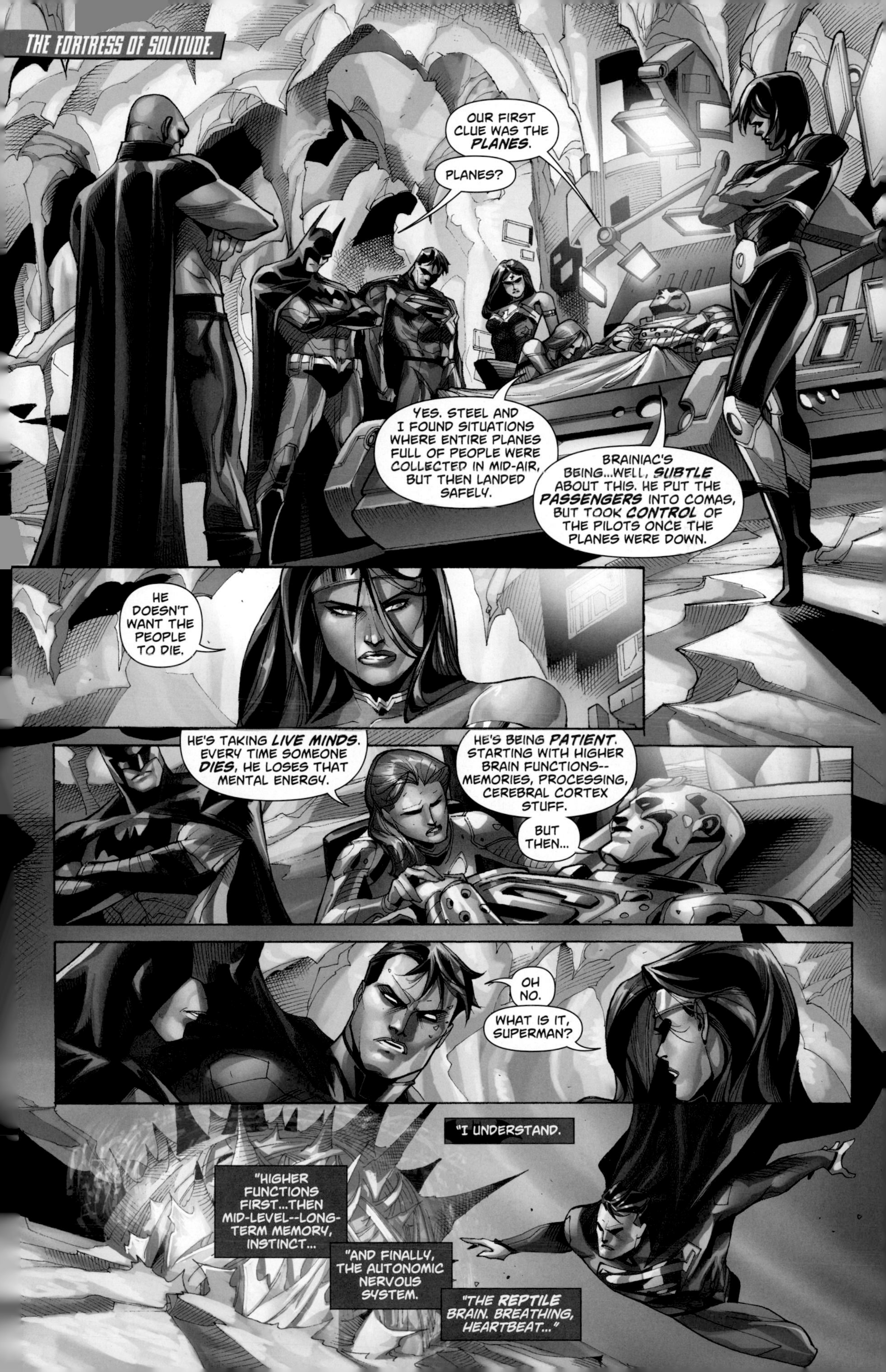
THE FORTRESS OF SOLITUDE.
OUR FIRST CLUE WAS THE PLANES.
PLANES?
YES. STEEL AND I FOUND SITUATIONS WHERE ENTIRE PLANES FULL OF PEOPLE WERE COLLECTED IN MID-AIR, BUT THEN LANDED SAFELY.
BRAINIAC'S BEING...WELL, SUBTLE ABOUT THIS. HE PUT THE PASSENGERS INTO COMAS, BUT TOOK CONTROL OF THE PILOTS ONCE THE PLANES WERE DOWN.
HE DOESN'T WANT THE PEOPLE TO DIE.
HE'S TAKING LIVE MINDS. EVERY TIME SOMEONE DIES, HE LOSES THAT MENTAL ENERGY.
HE'S BEING PATIENT. STARTING WITH HIGHER BRAIN FUNCTIONS--MEMORIES, PROCESSING, CEREBRAL CORTEX STUFF.
BUT THEN...
OH NO.
WHAT IS IT, SUPERMAN?
"I UNDERSTAND.
"HIGHER FUNCTIONS FIRST...THEN MID-LEVEL--LONG-TERM MEMORY, INSTINCT...
"AND FINALLY, THE AUTONOMIC NERVOUS SYSTEM.
"THE REPTILE BRAIN. BREATHING, HEARTBEAT..."

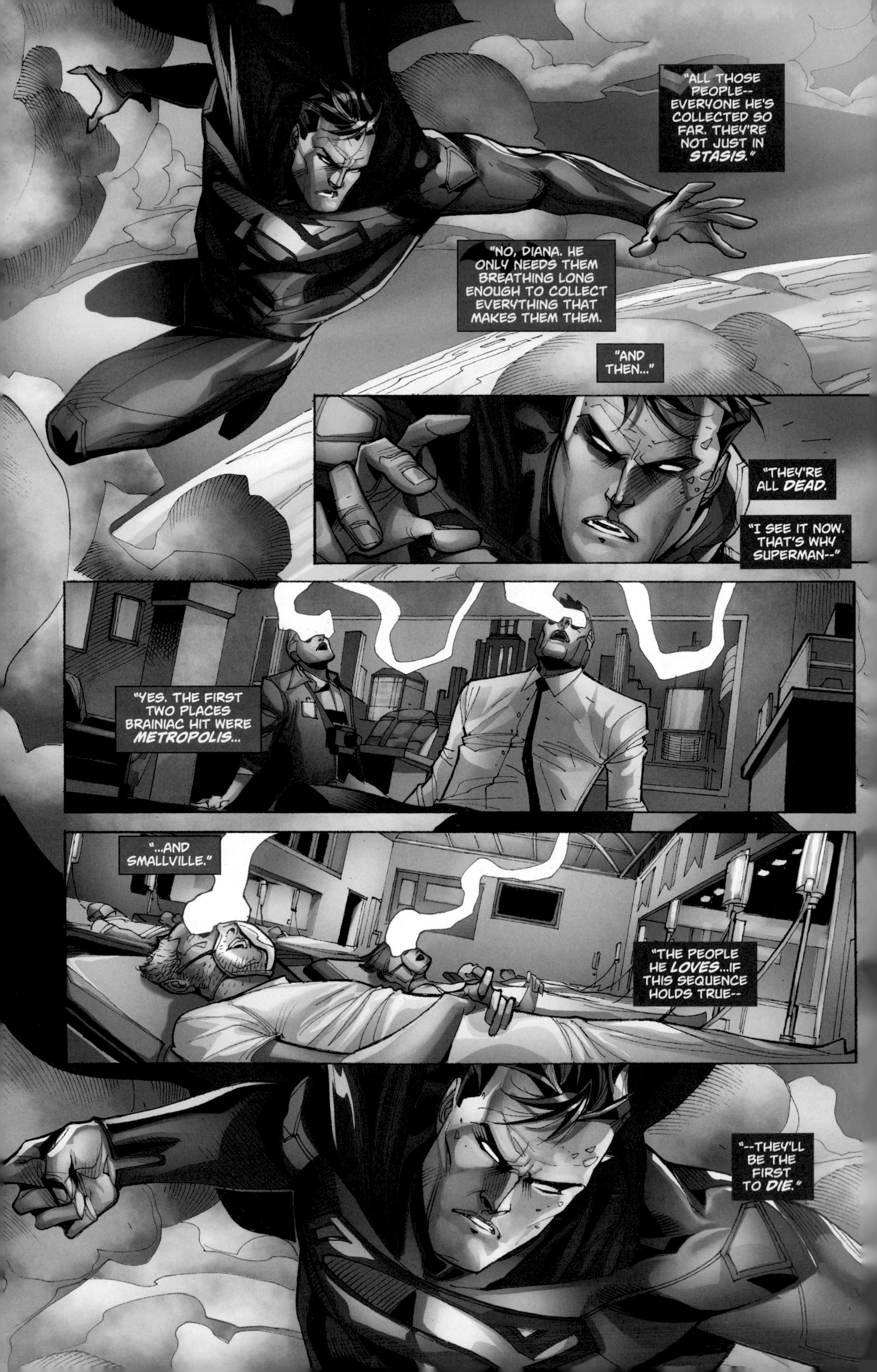
"ALL THOSE PEOPLE-- EVERYONE HE'S COLLECTED SO FAR. THEY'RE NOT JUST IN STASIS."
"NO, DIANA. HE ONLY NEEDS THEM BREATHING LONG ENOUGH TO COLLECT EVERYTHING THAT MAKES THEM THEM.
"AND THEN..."
"THEY'RE ALL DEAD.
"I SEE IT NOW. THAT'S WHY SUPERMAN--"
"YES. THE FIRST TWO PLACES BRAINIAC HIT WERE METROPOLIS...
"...AND SMALLVILLE."
"THE PEOPLE HE LOVES...IF THIS SEQUENCE HOLDS TRUE--
"--THEY'LL BE THE FIRST TO DIE."

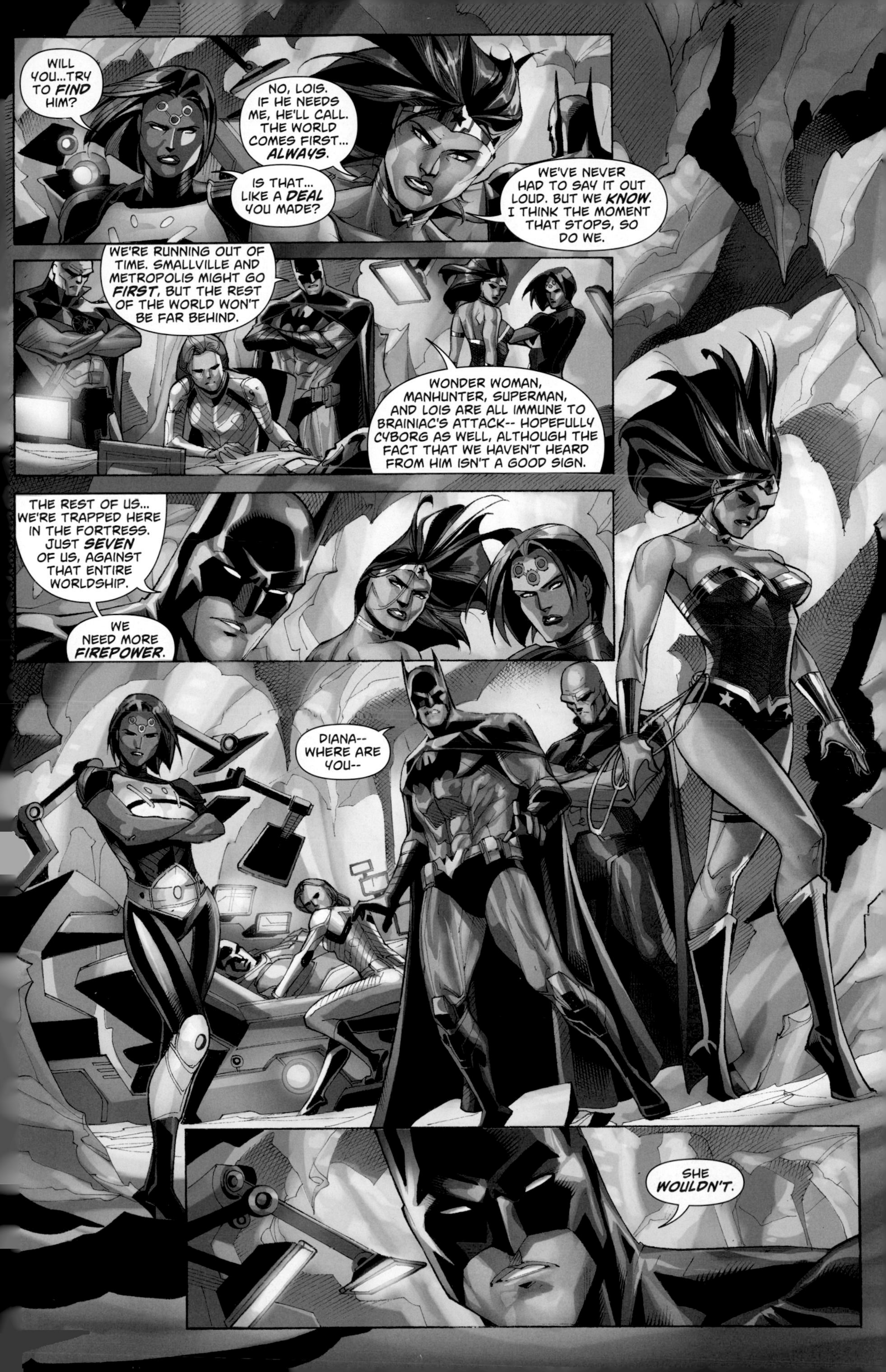
WILL YOU...TRY TO *FIND* HIM?
NO, LOIS. IF HE NEEDS ME, HE'LL CALL. THE WORLD COMES FIRST... *ALWAYS*.
IS THAT... LIKE A *DEAL* YOU MADE?
WE'VE NEVER HAD TO SAY IT OUT LOUD. BUT WE *KNOW*. I THINK THE MOMENT THAT STOPS, SO DO WE.
WE'RE RUNNING OUT OF TIME. SMALLVILLE AND METROPOLIS MIGHT GO *FIRST*, BUT THE REST OF THE WORLD WON'T BE FAR BEHIND.
WONDER WOMAN, MANHUNTER, SUPERMAN, AND LOIS ARE ALL IMMUNE TO BRAINIAC'S ATTACK-- HOPEFULLY CYBORG AS WELL, ALTHOUGH THE FACT THAT WE HAVEN'T HEARD FROM HIM ISN'T A GOOD SIGN.
THE REST OF US... WE'RE TRAPPED HERE IN THE FORTRESS. JUST *SEVEN* OF US, AGAINST THAT ENTIRE WORLDSHIP.
WE NEED MORE *FIREPOWER*.
DIANA-- WHERE ARE YOU--
SHE *WOULDN'T*.

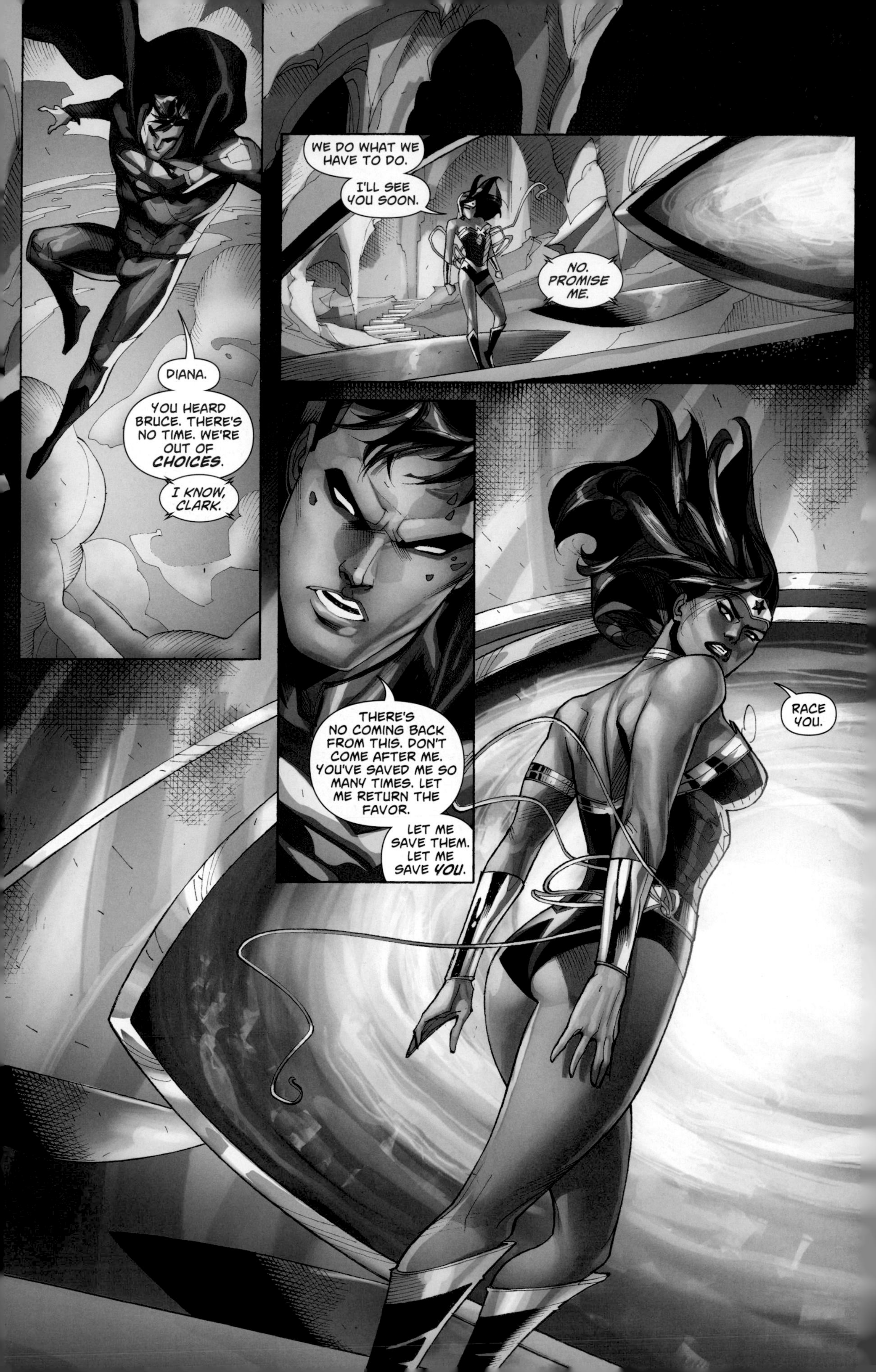
WE DO WHAT WE HAVE TO DO.
I'LL SEE YOU SOON.
NO. PROMISE ME.
DIANA.
YOU HEARD BRUCE. THERE'S NO TIME. WE'RE OUT OF CHOICES.
I KNOW, CLARK.
THERE'S NO COMING BACK FROM THIS. DON'T COME AFTER ME. YOU'VE SAVED ME SO MANY TIMES. LET ME RETURN THE FAVOR.
LET ME SAVE THEM. LET ME SAVE YOU.
RACE YOU.

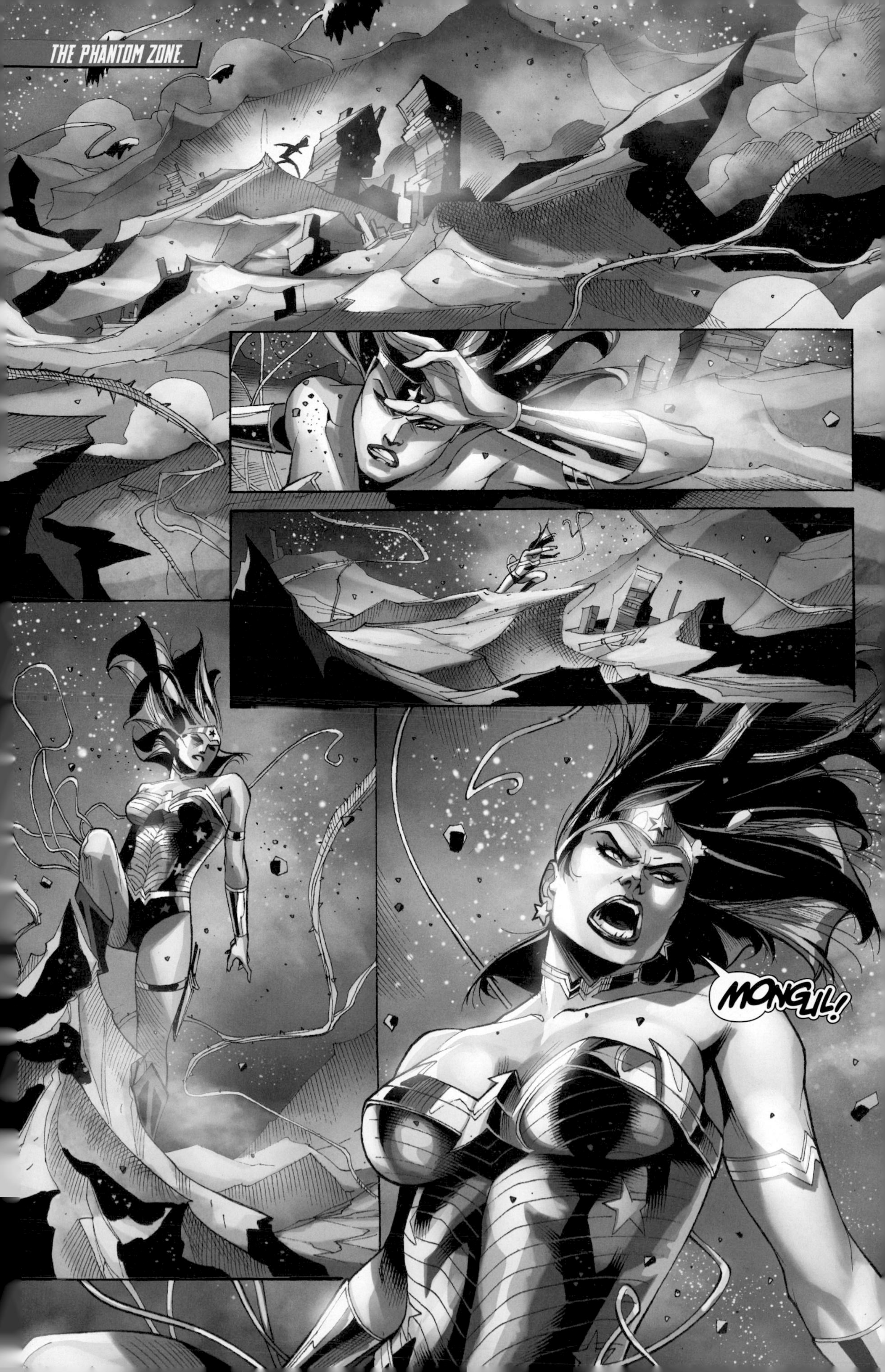
THE PHANTOM ZONE.
MONGUL!

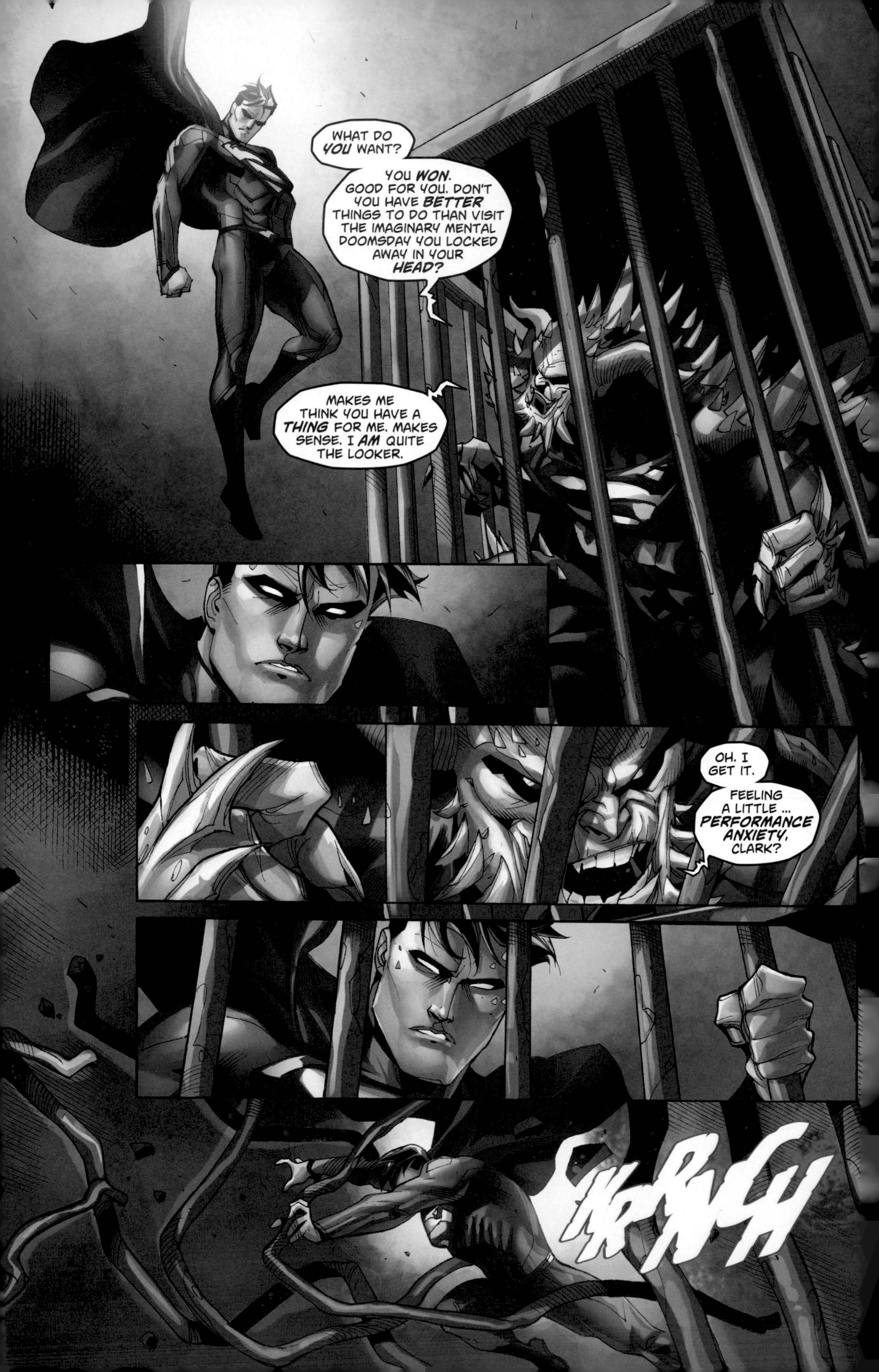
WHAT DO YOU WANT?
YOU WON. GOOD FOR YOU. DON'T YOU HAVE BETTER THINGS TO DO THAN VISIT THE IMAGINARY MENTAL DOOMSDAY YOU LOCKED AWAY IN YOUR HEAD?
MAKES ME THINK YOU HAVE A THING FOR ME. MAKES SENSE. I AM QUITE THE LOOKER.
OH. I GET IT.
FEELING A LITTLE ... PERFORMANCE ANXIETY, CLARK?
SKRANCH

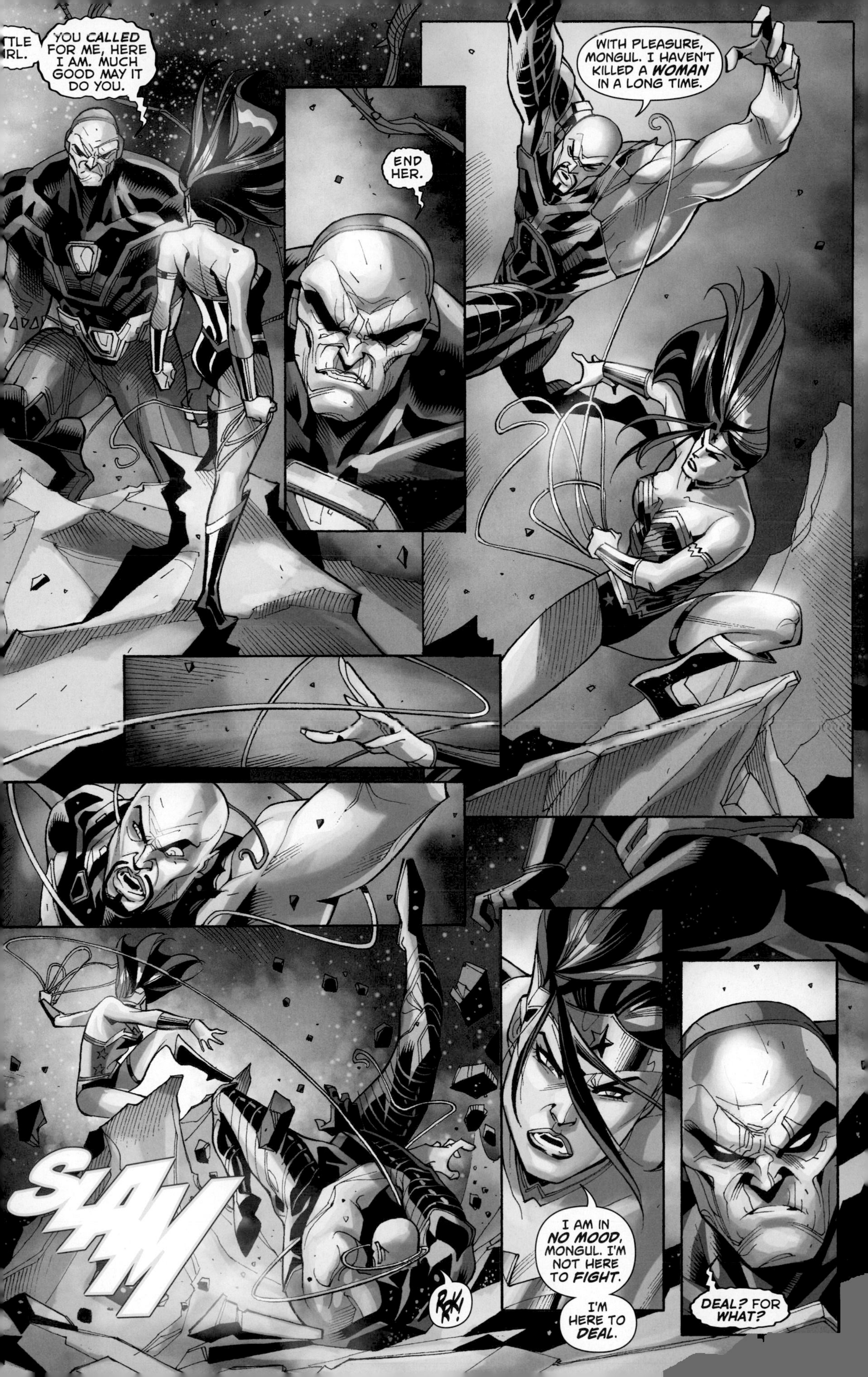

TTLE
RL.
YOU CALLED FOR ME, HERE I AM. MUCH GOOD MAY IT DO YOU.
END HER.
WITH PLEASURE, MONGUL. I HAVEN'T KILLED A WOMAN IN A LONG TIME.
SLAM
RAK!
I AM IN NO MOOD, MONGUL. I'M NOT HERE TO FIGHT.
I'M HERE TO DEAL.
DEAL? FOR WHAT?

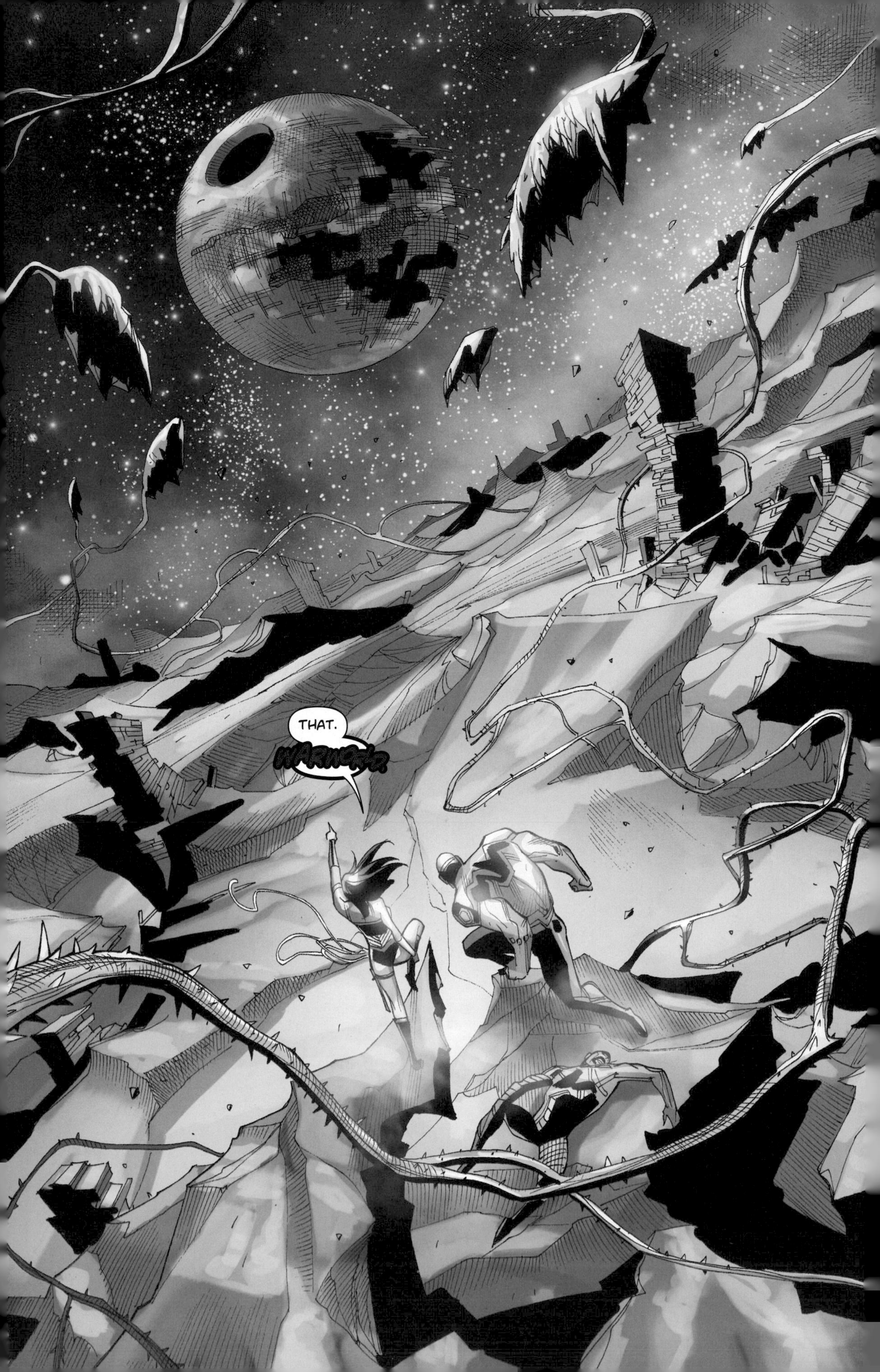
THAT.
WARWORLD.

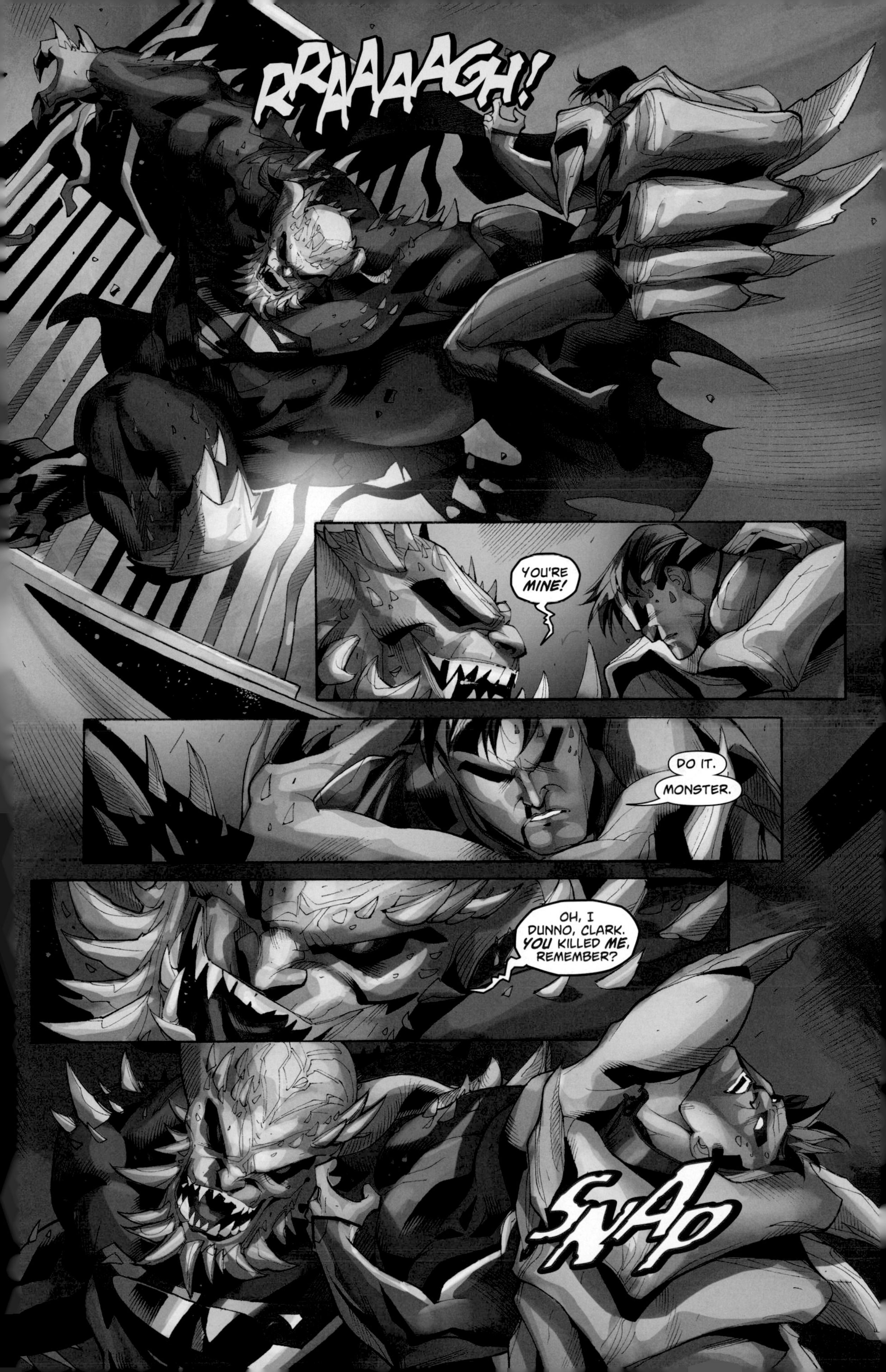
RRAAAAGH!
YOU'RE MINE!
DO IT.
MONSTER.
OH, I DUNNO, CLARK. YOU KILLED ME, REMEMBER?
SNAP

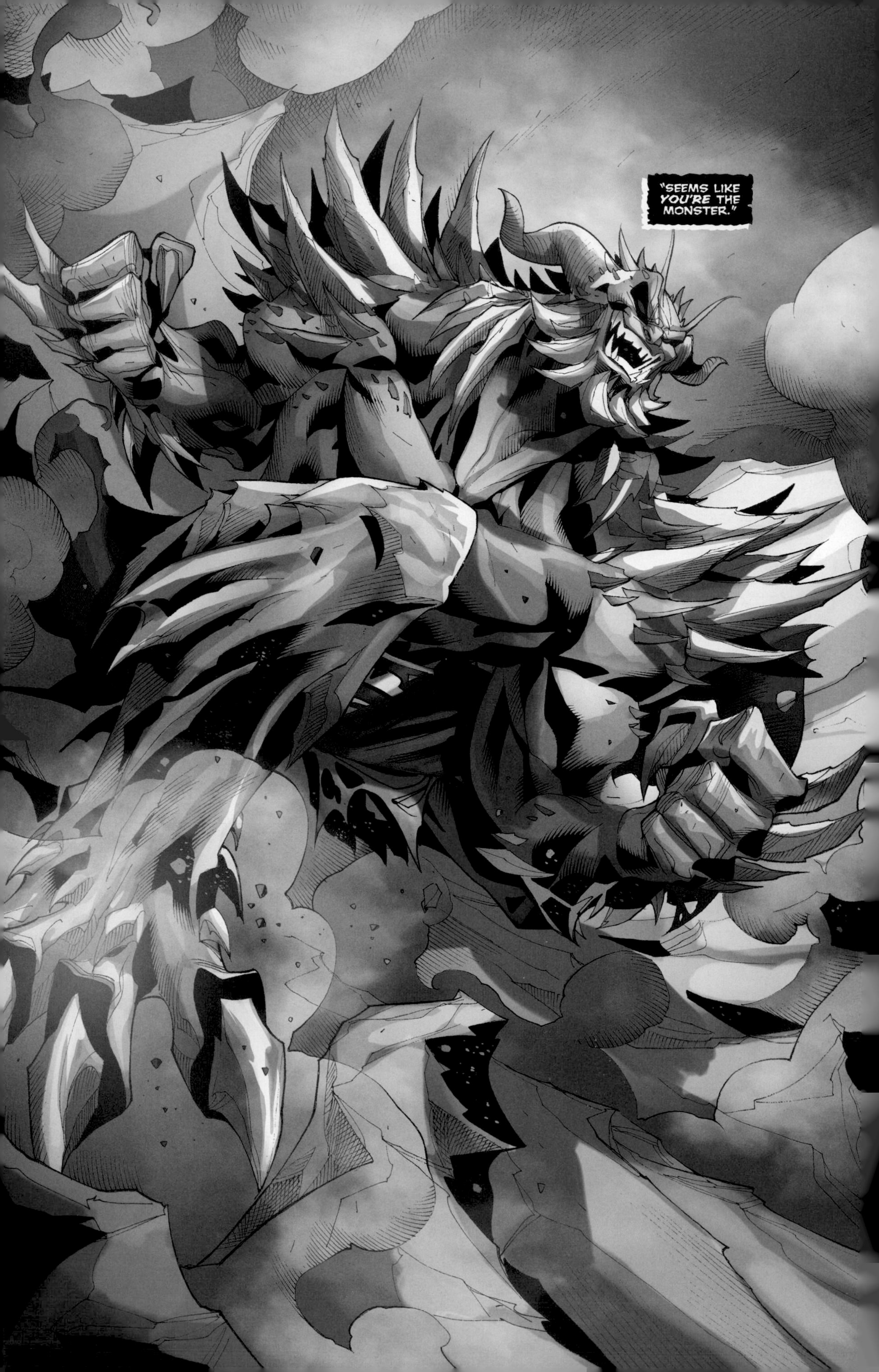
"SEEMS LIKE *YOU'RE* THE MONSTER."

METAPHORMORPHOSIS

JACK HERBERT WALDEN WONG CLIFF RICHARDS artists
cover by TONY S. DANIEL & TOMEU MOREY

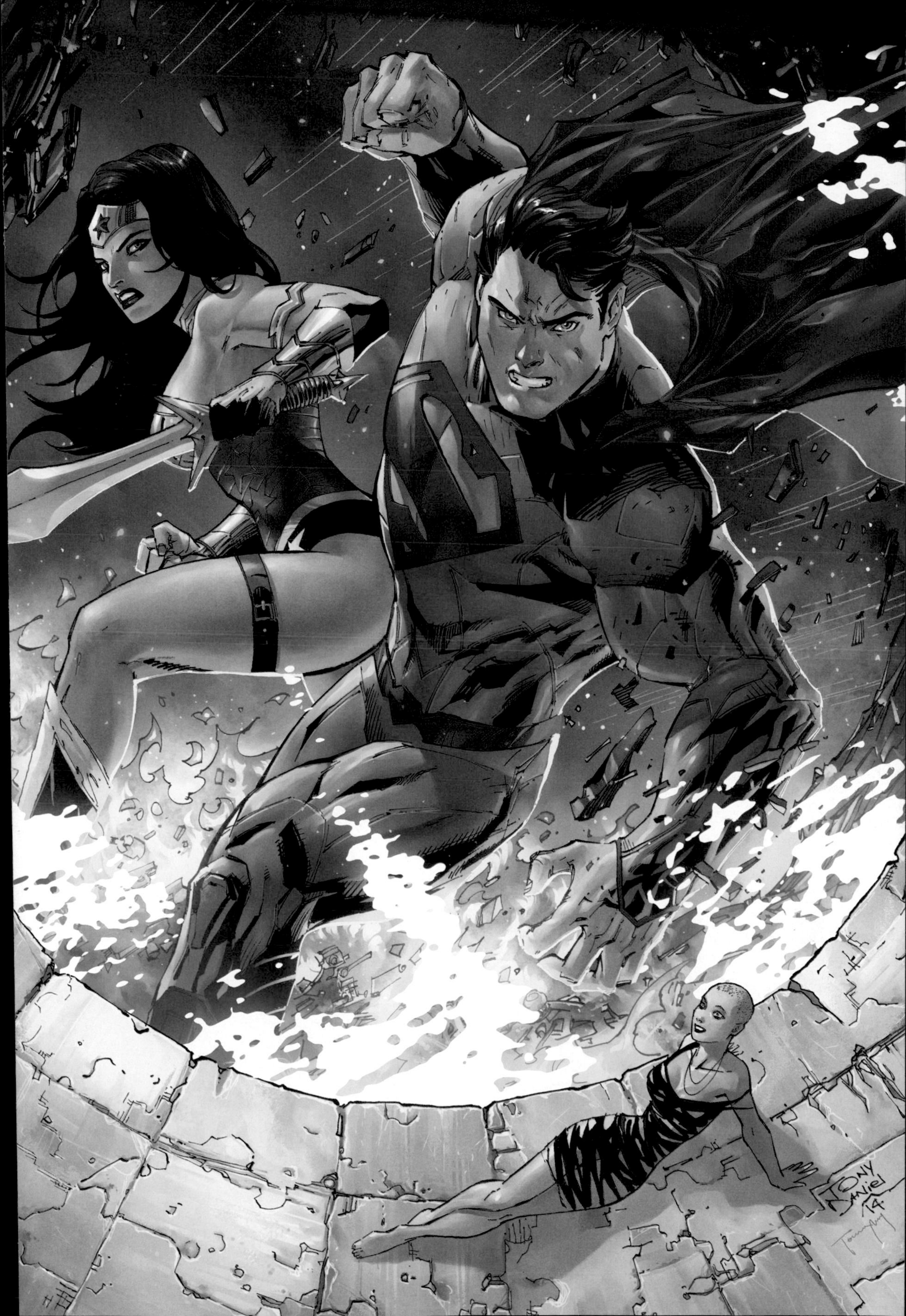
TONY DANIEL '14

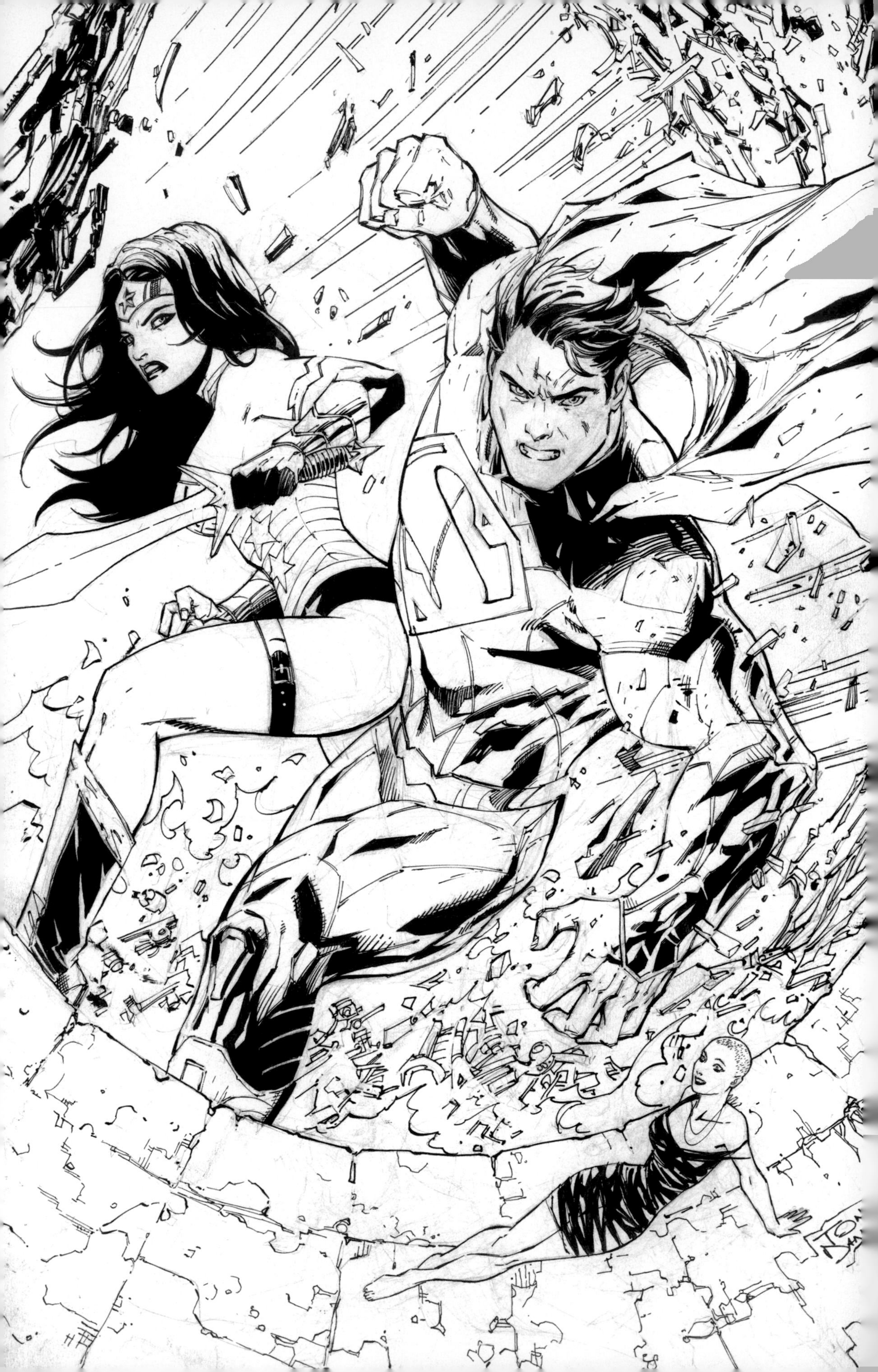

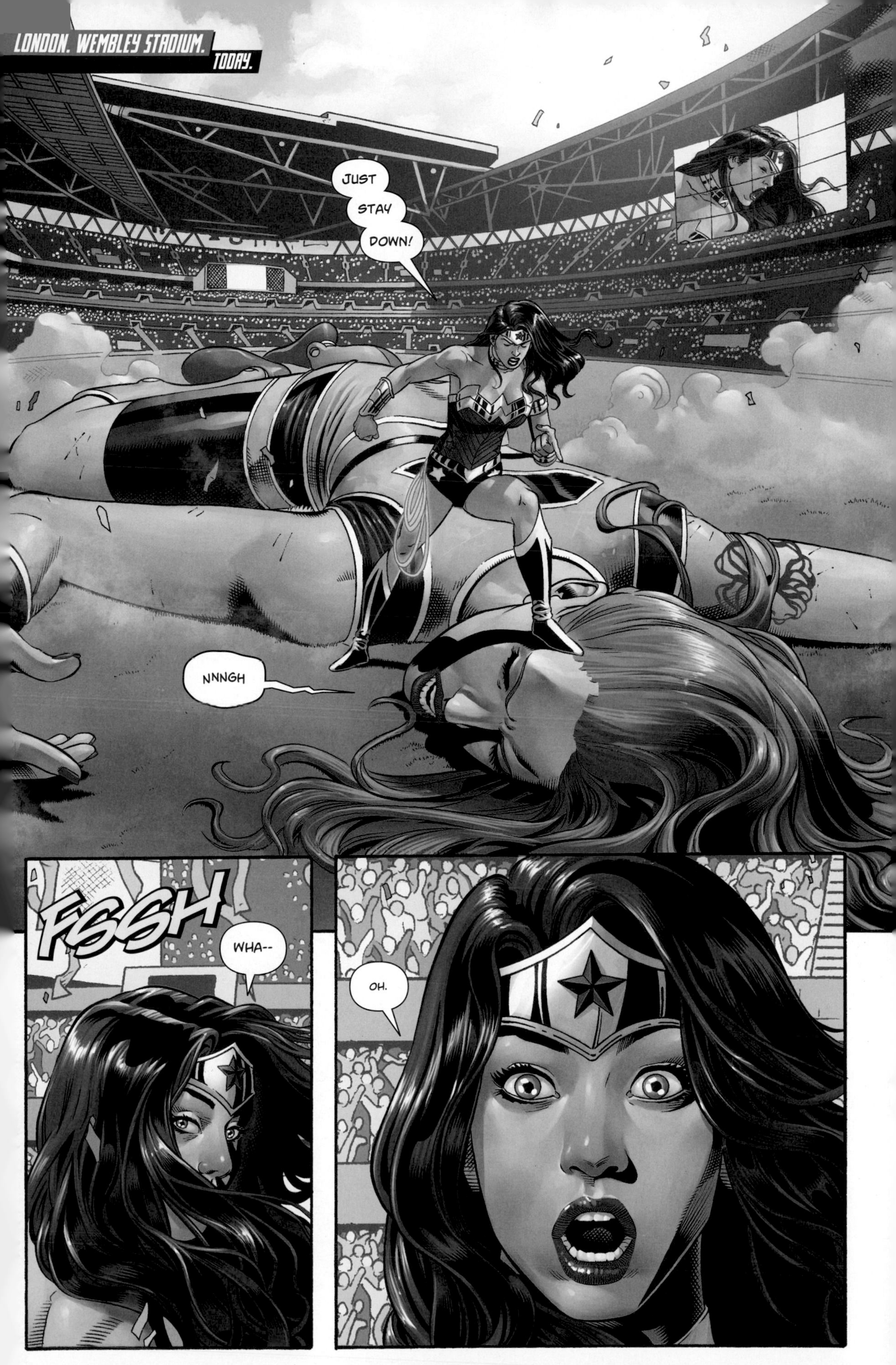
LONDON. WEMBLEY STADIUM.
TODAY.
JUST STAY DOWN!
NNNGH
FSSH
WHA--
OH.

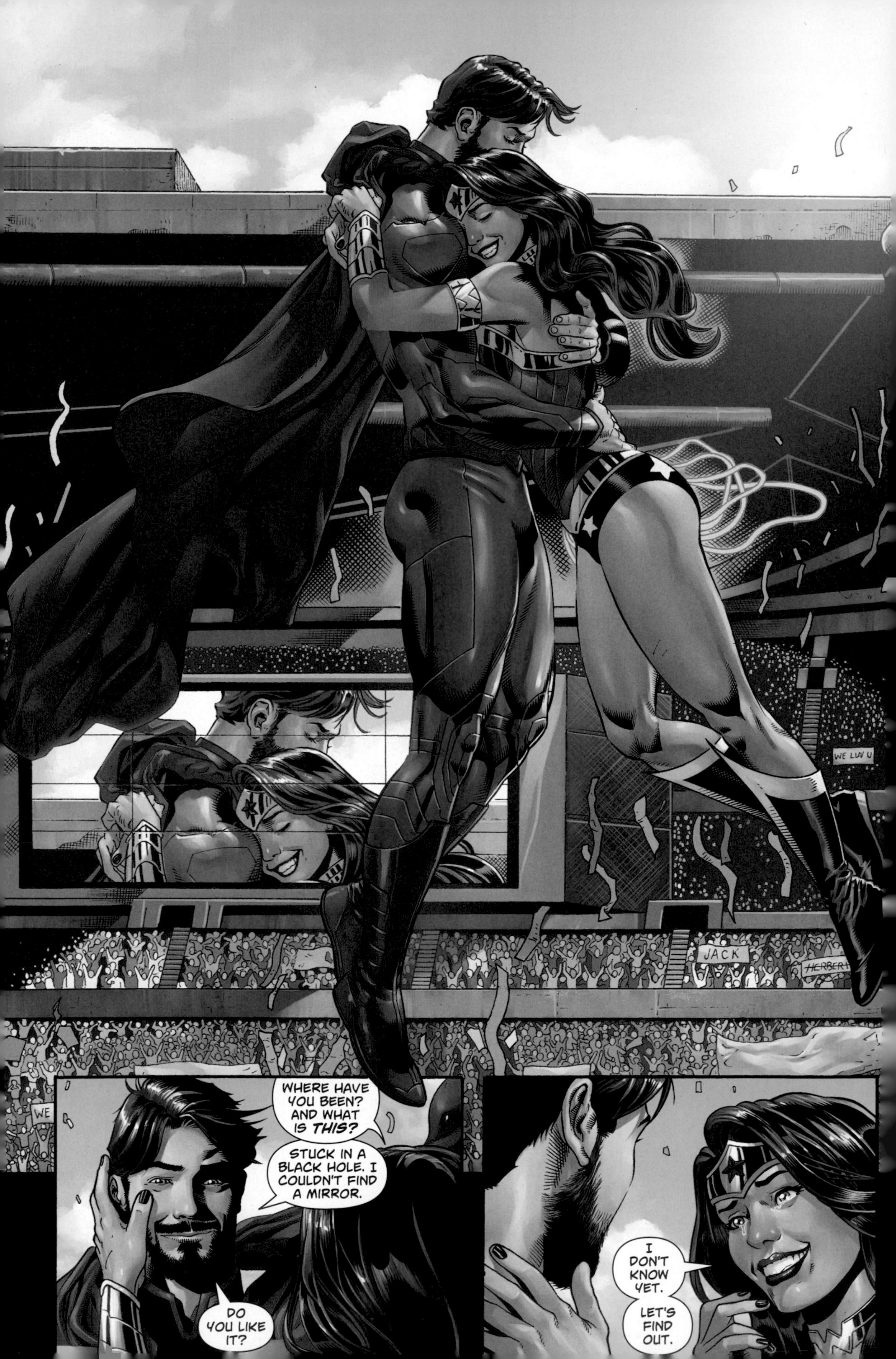

WE LUV U
JACK
HERBERT
WE
WHERE HAVE YOU BEEN? AND WHAT IS *THIS?*
STUCK IN A BLACK HOLE. I COULDN'T FIND A MIRROR.
DO YOU LIKE IT?
I DON'T KNOW YET.
LET'S FIND OUT.

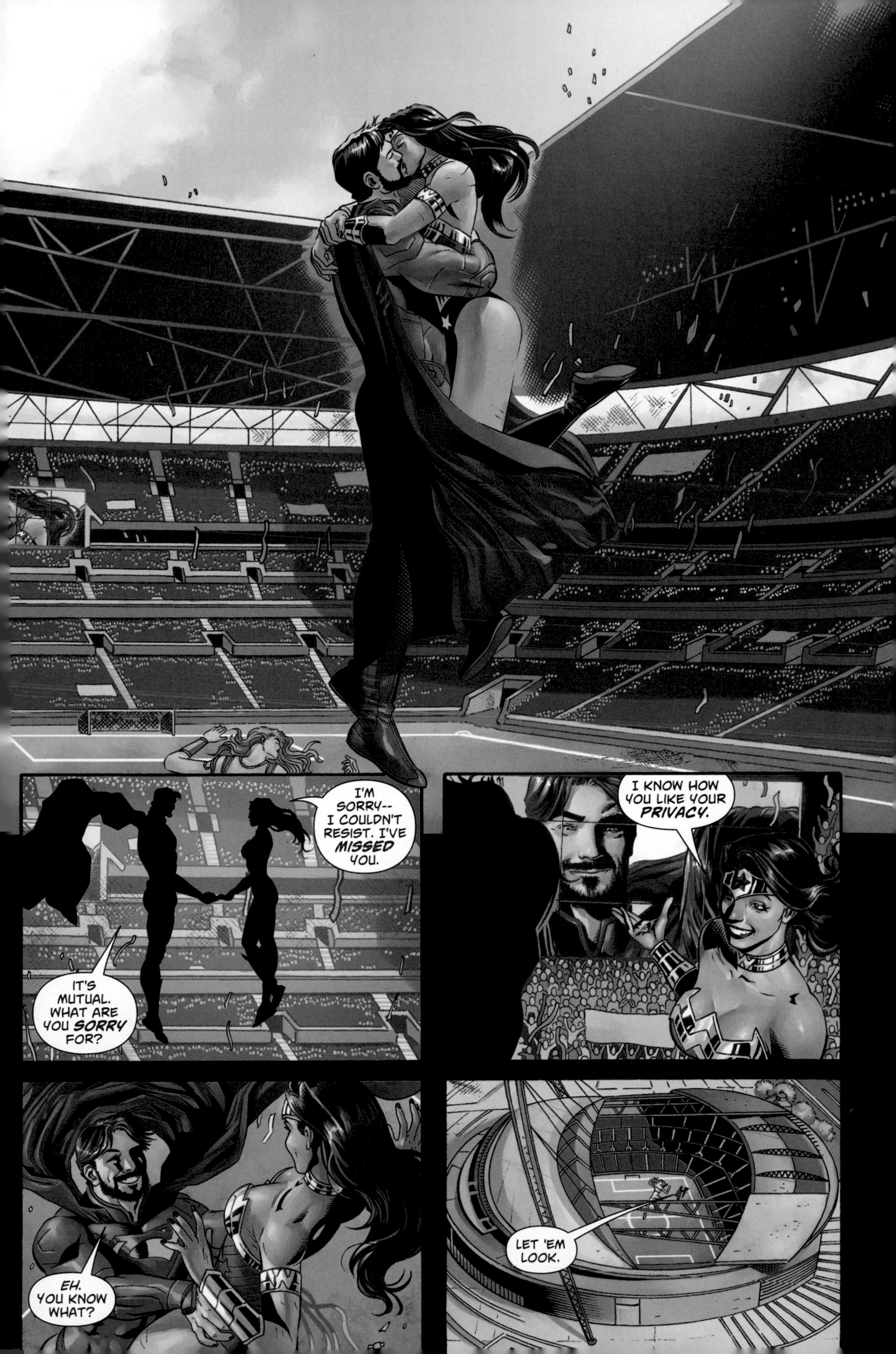
I'M SORRY-- I COULDN'T RESIST. I'VE MISSED YOU.
IT'S MUTUAL. WHAT ARE YOU SORRY FOR?
I KNOW HOW YOU LIKE YOUR PRIVACY.
EH. YOU KNOW WHAT?
LET 'EM LOOK.

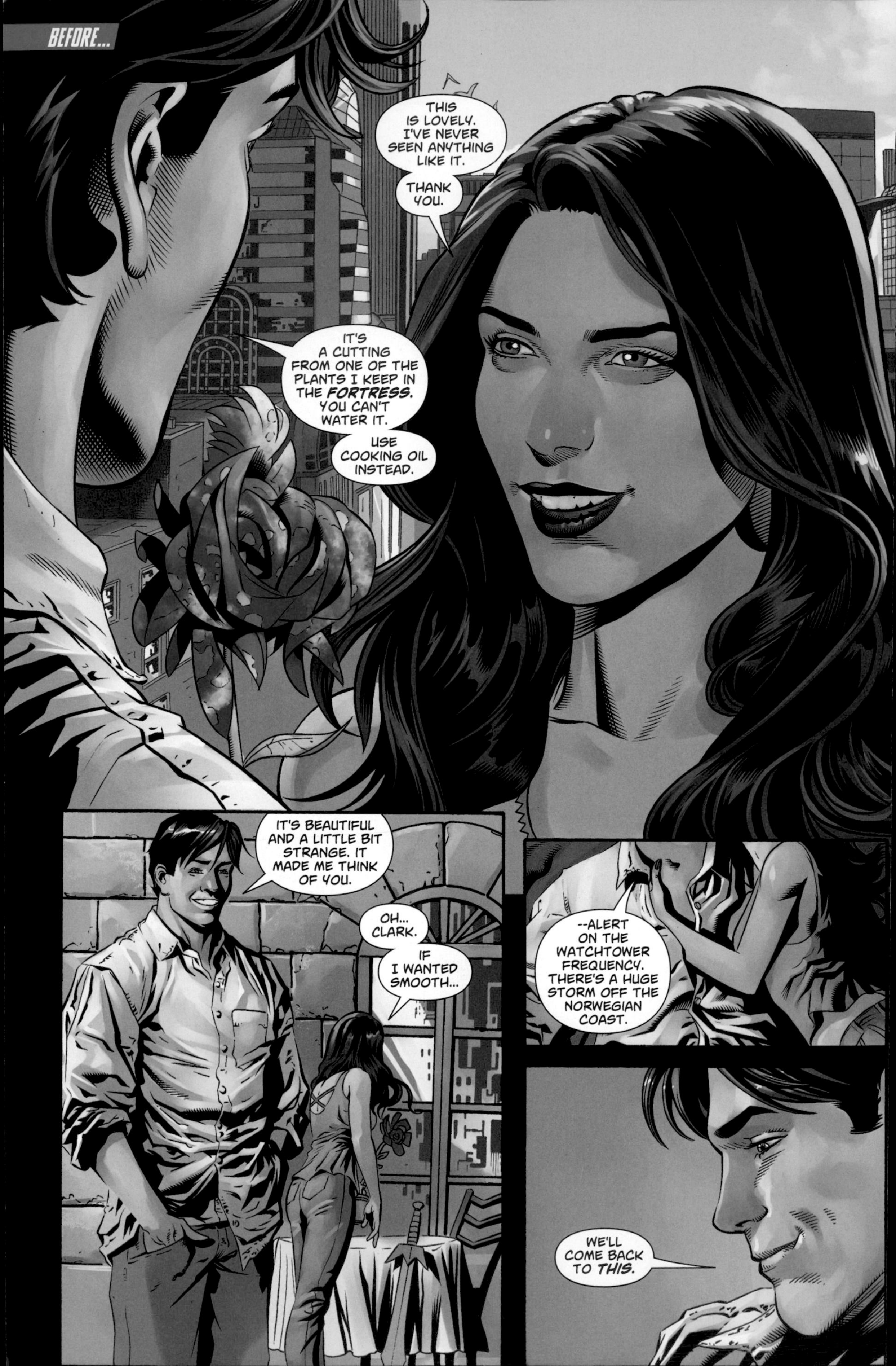
BEFORE...
THIS IS LOVELY. I'VE NEVER SEEN ANYTHING LIKE IT.
THANK YOU.
IT'S A CUTTING FROM ONE OF THE PLANTS I KEEP IN THE FORTRESS. YOU CAN'T WATER IT.
USE COOKING OIL INSTEAD.
IT'S BEAUTIFUL AND A LITTLE BIT STRANGE. IT MADE ME THINK OF YOU.
OH... CLARK.
IF I WANTED SMOOTH...
--ALERT ON THE WATCHTOWER FREQUENCY. THERE'S A HUGE STORM OFF THE NORWEGIAN COAST.
WE'LL COME BACK TO THIS.

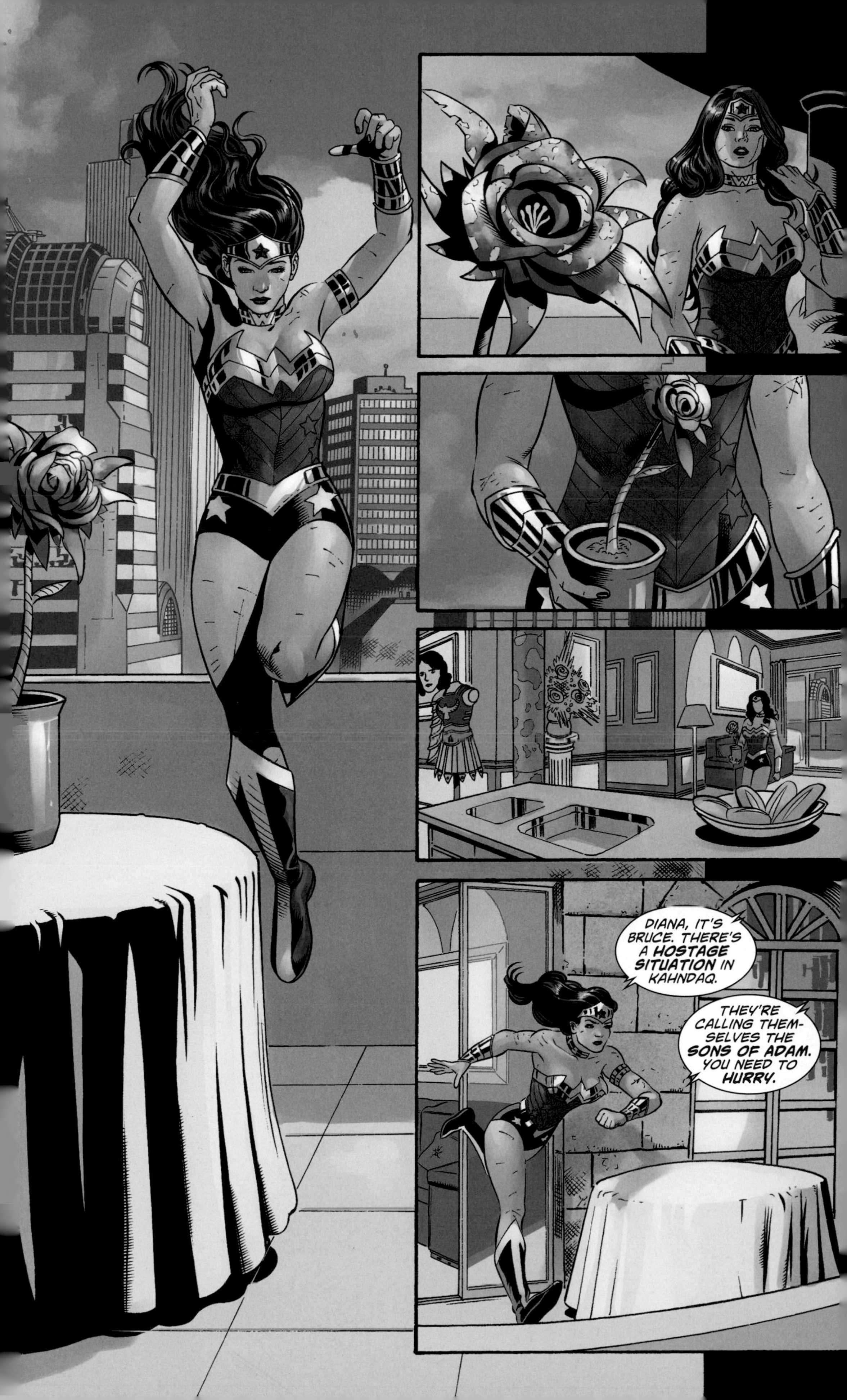
DIANA, IT'S BRUCE. THERE'S A HOSTAGE SITUATION IN KAHNDAQ.
THEY'RE CALLING THEMSELVES THE SONS OF ADAM. YOU NEED TO HURRY.

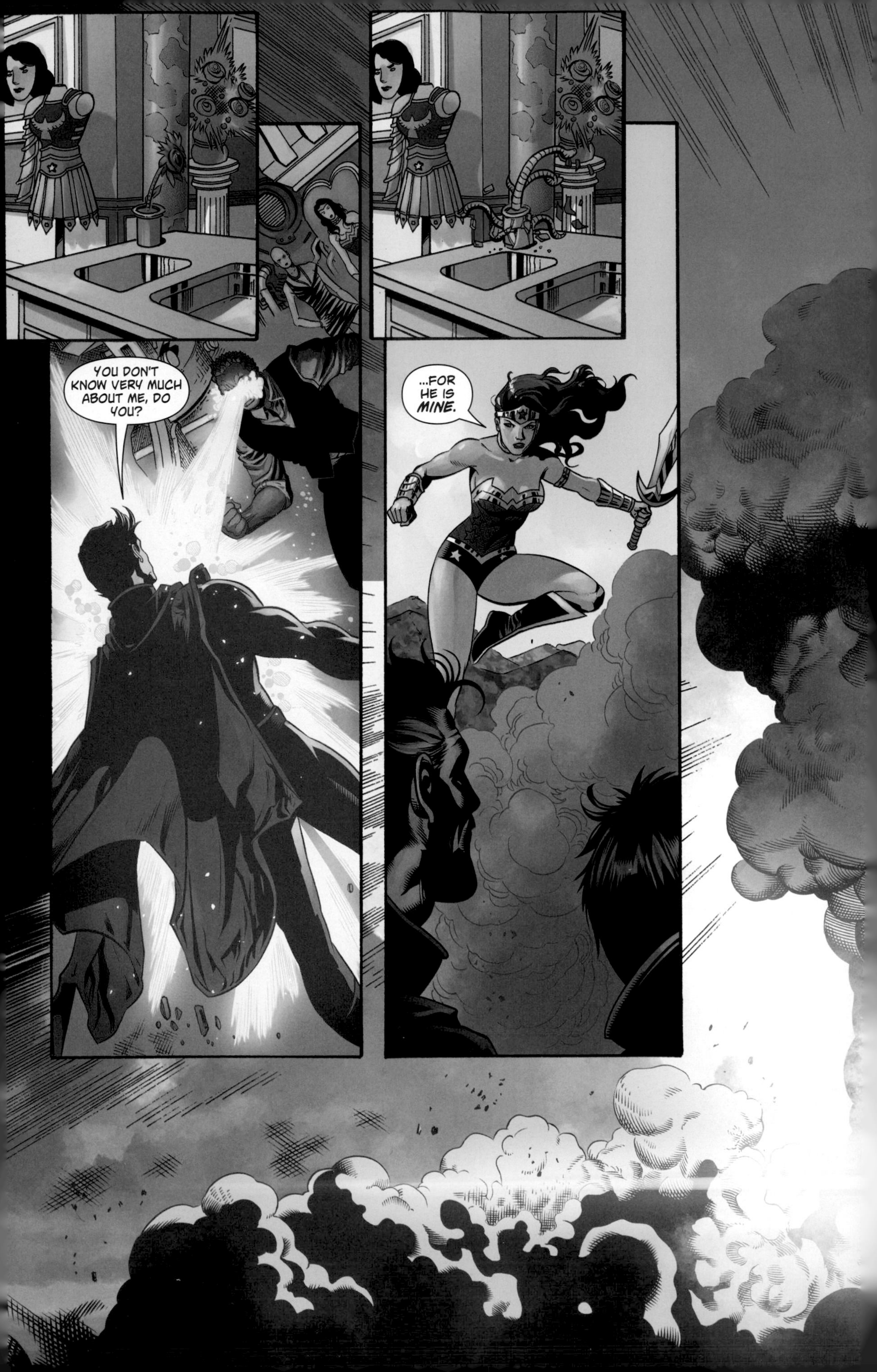
YOU DON'T KNOW VERY MUCH ABOUT ME, DO YOU?
...FOR HE IS MINE.

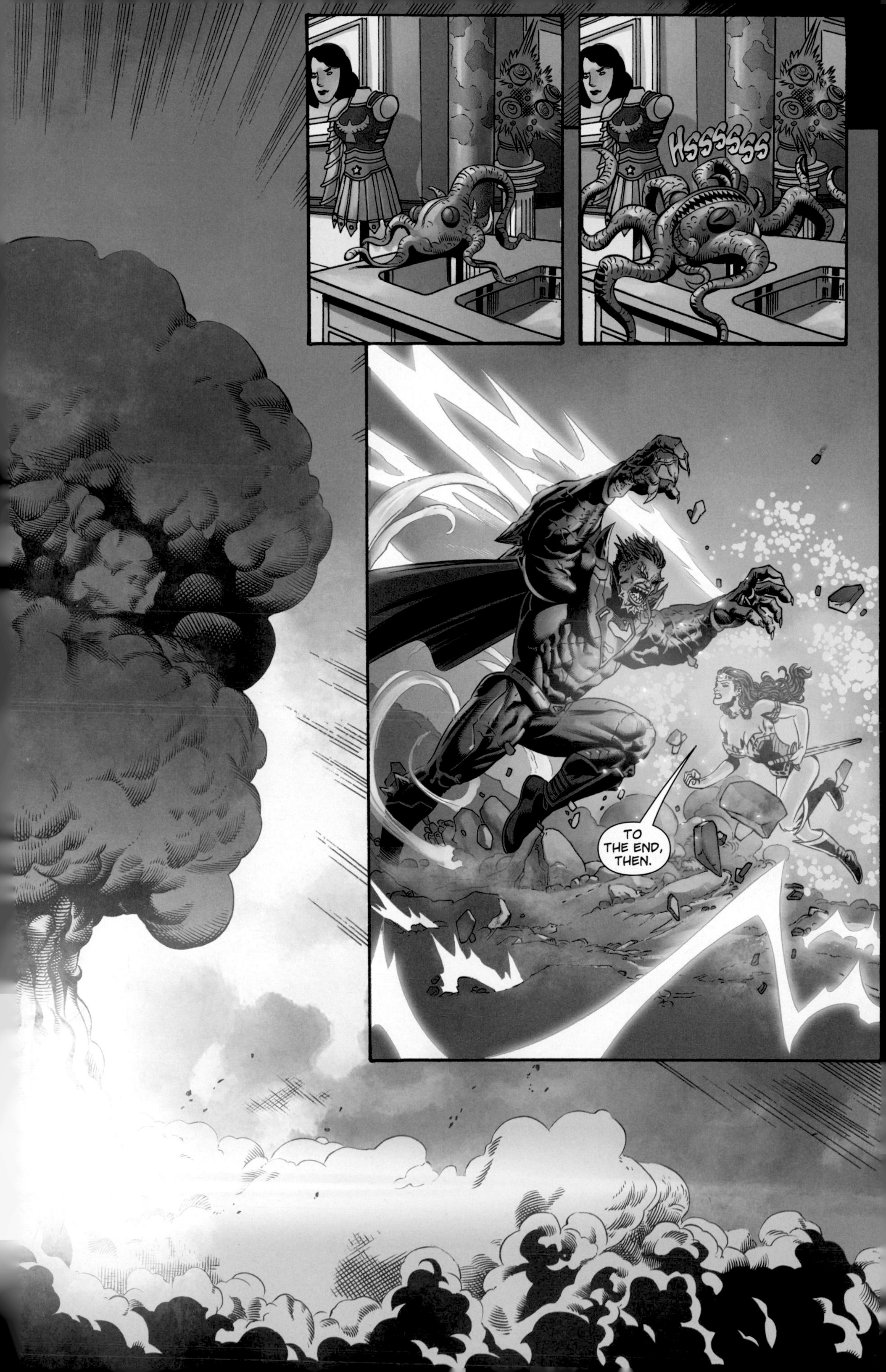
HSSSSSS
TO THE END, THEN.

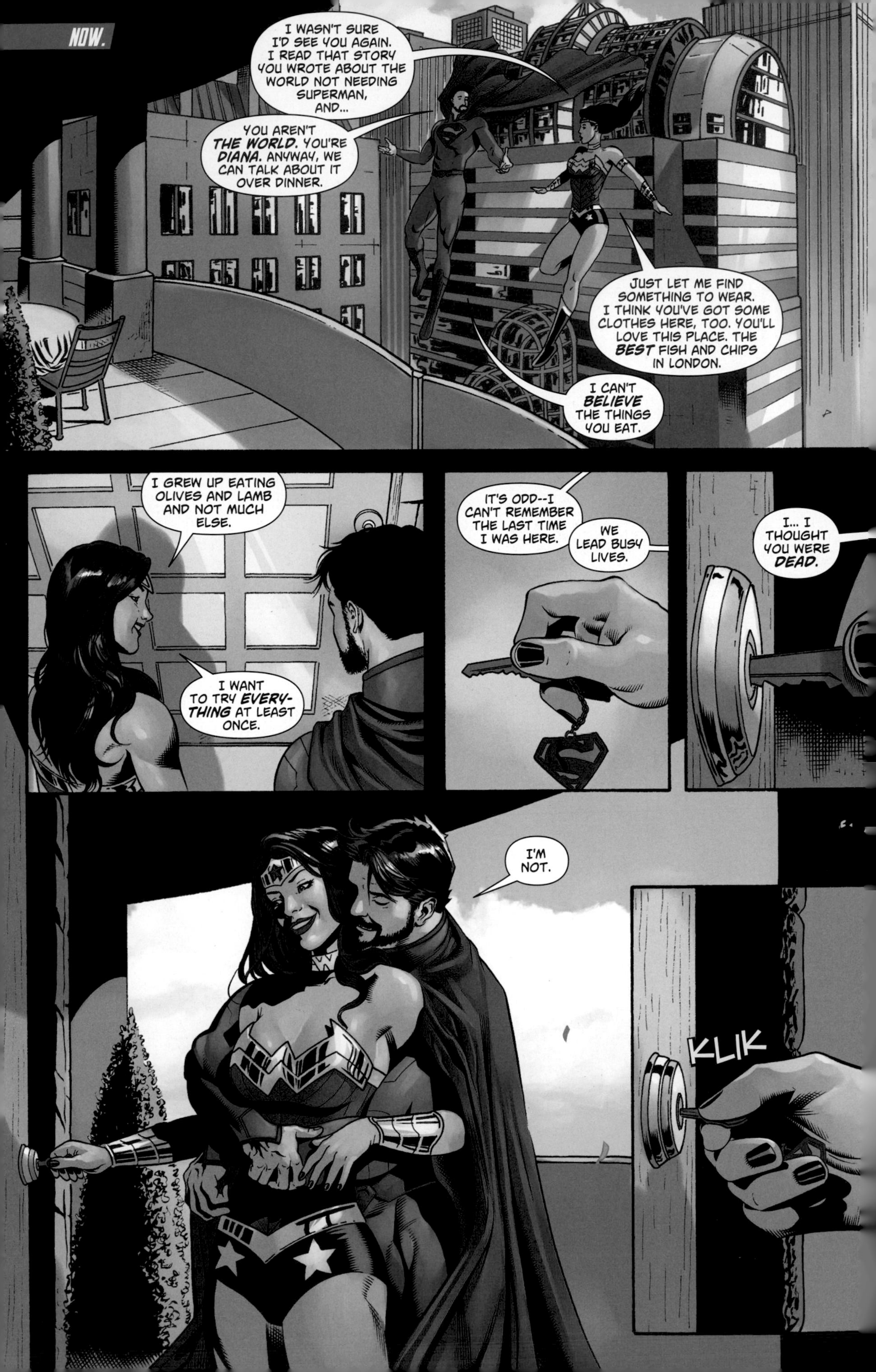
NOW.
I WASN'T SURE I'D SEE YOU AGAIN. I READ THAT STORY YOU WROTE ABOUT THE WORLD NOT NEEDING SUPERMAN, AND...
YOU AREN'T THE WORLD. YOU'RE DIANA. ANYWAY, WE CAN TALK ABOUT IT OVER DINNER.
JUST LET ME FIND SOMETHING TO WEAR. I THINK YOU'VE GOT SOME CLOTHES HERE, TOO. YOU'LL LOVE THIS PLACE. THE BEST FISH AND CHIPS IN LONDON.
I CAN'T BELIEVE THE THINGS YOU EAT.
I GREW UP EATING OLIVES AND LAMB AND NOT MUCH ELSE.
I WANT TO TRY EVERYTHING AT LEAST ONCE.
IT'S ODD--I CAN'T REMEMBER THE LAST TIME I WAS HERE.
WE LEAD BUSY LIVES.
I... I THOUGHT YOU WERE DEAD.
I'M NOT.
KLIK

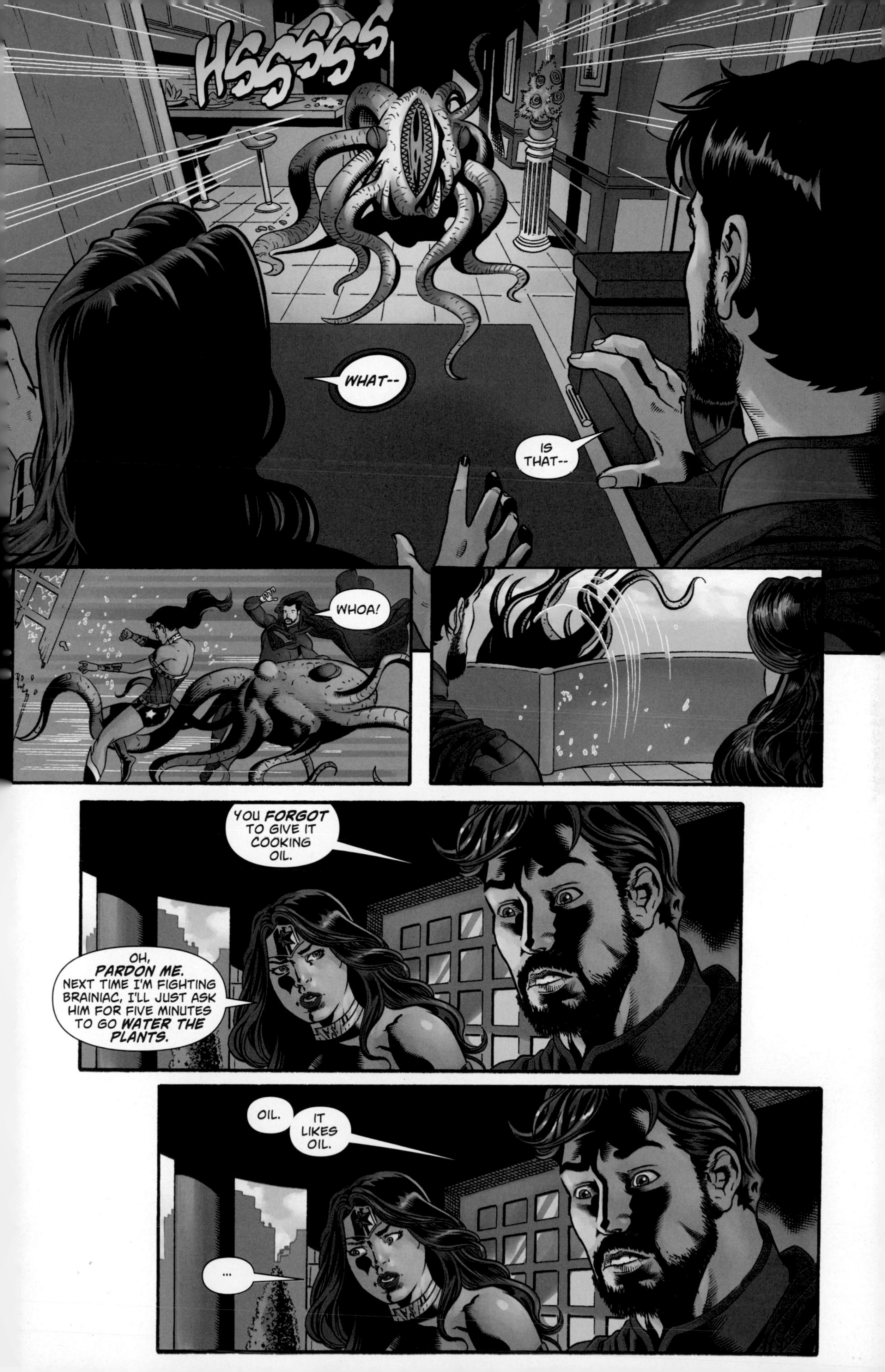
HSSSSS
WHAT--
IS THAT--
WHOA!
YOU **FORGOT** TO GIVE IT COOKING OIL.
OH, **PARDON ME.** NEXT TIME I'M FIGHTING BRAINIAC, I'LL JUST ASK HIM FOR FIVE MINUTES TO GO **WATER THE PLANTS.**
OIL.
IT LIKES OIL.
...

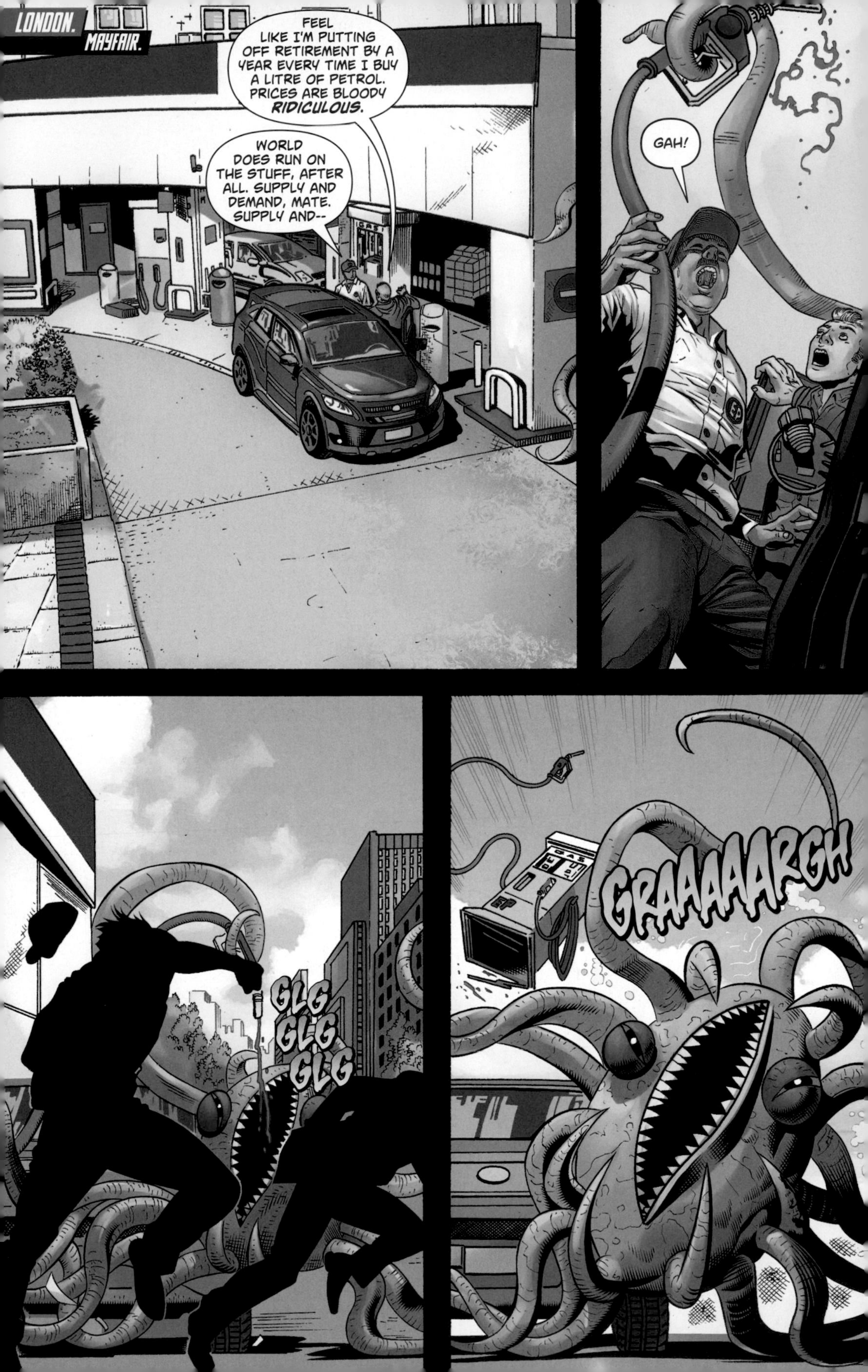
LONDON.
MAYFAIR.
FEEL LIKE I'M PUTTING OFF RETIREMENT BY A YEAR EVERY TIME I BUY A LITRE OF PETROL. PRICES ARE BLOODY RIDICULOUS.
WORLD DOES RUN ON THE STUFF, AFTER ALL. SUPPLY AND DEMAND, MATE. SUPPLY AND--
GAH!
GLG GLG GLG
GRAAAAARGH

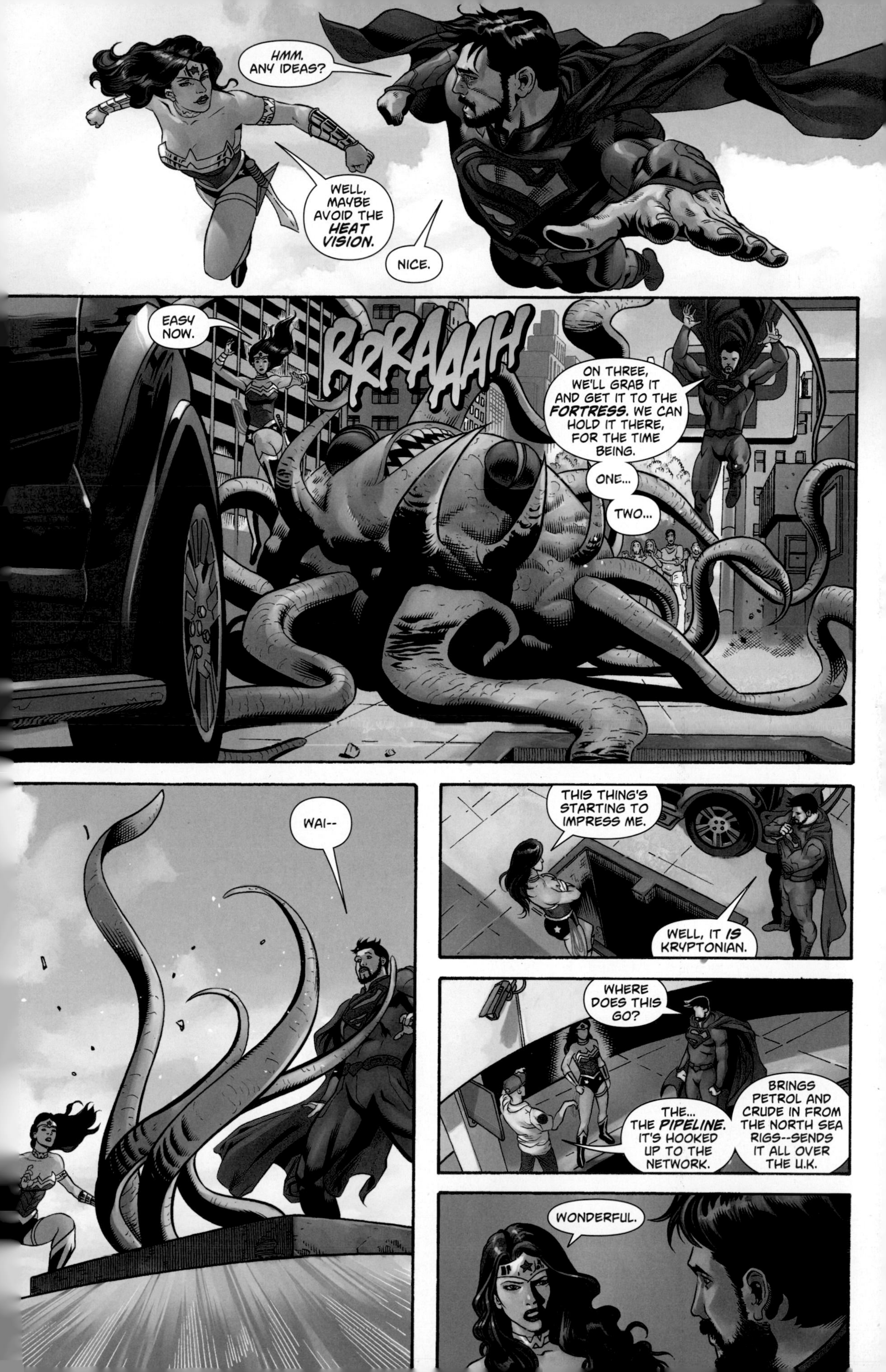
HMM. ANY IDEAS?
WELL, MAYBE AVOID THE HEAT VISION.
NICE.
EASY NOW.
RRRAAAAH
ON THREE, WE'LL GRAB IT AND GET IT TO THE FORTRESS. WE CAN HOLD IT THERE, FOR THE TIME BEING.
ONE...
TWO...
WAI--
THIS THING'S STARTING TO IMPRESS ME.
WELL, IT IS KRYPTONIAN.
WHERE DOES THIS GO?
THE... THE PIPELINE. IT'S HOOKED UP TO THE NETWORK.
BRINGS PETROL AND CRUDE IN FROM THE NORTH SEA RIGS--SENDS IT ALL OVER THE U.K.
WONDERFUL.

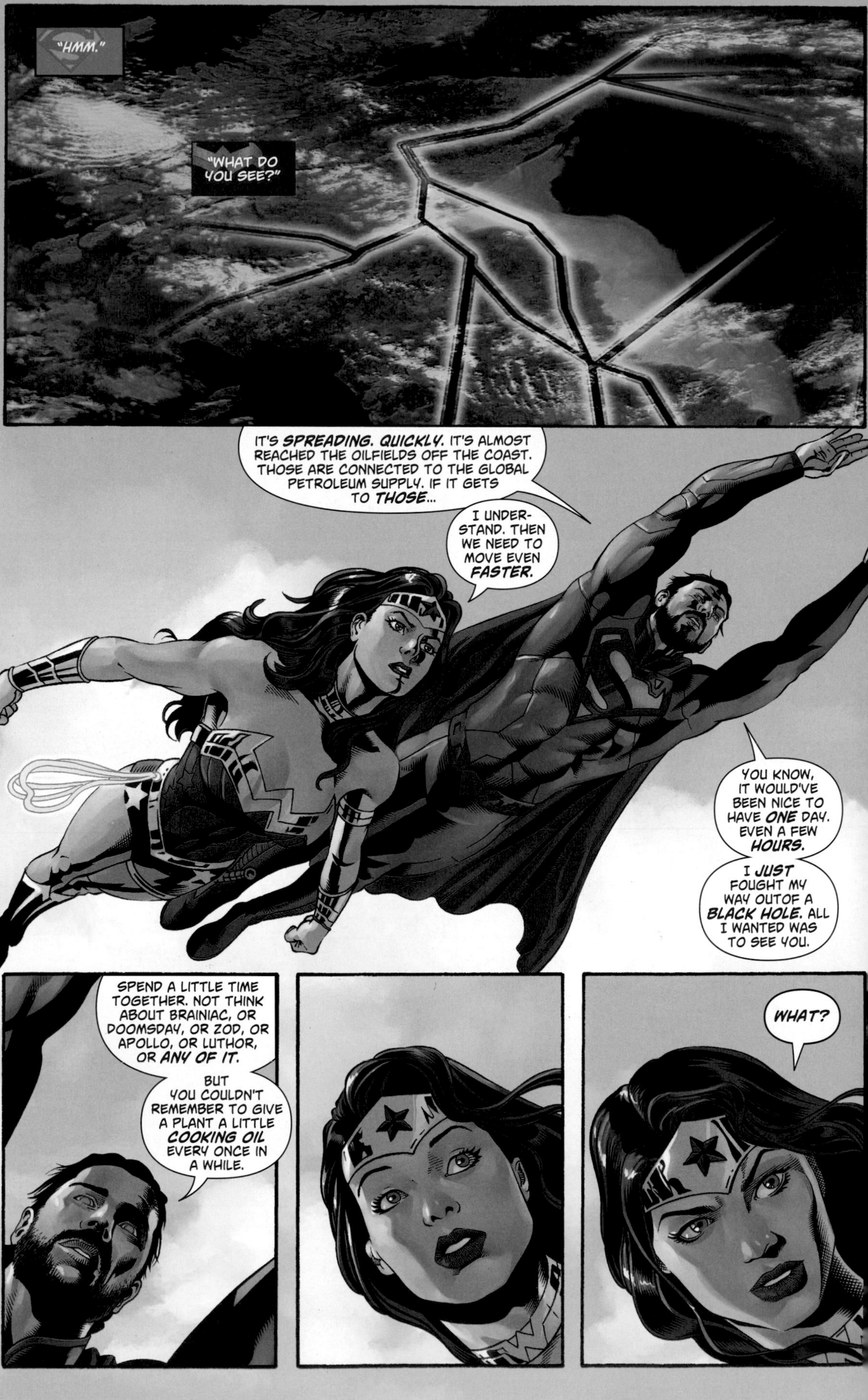
"HMM."
"WHAT DO YOU SEE?"
IT'S SPREADING. QUICKLY. IT'S ALMOST REACHED THE OILFIELDS OFF THE COAST. THOSE ARE CONNECTED TO THE GLOBAL PETROLEUM SUPPLY. IF IT GETS TO THOSE...
I UNDERSTAND. THEN WE NEED TO MOVE EVEN FASTER.
YOU KNOW, IT WOULD'VE BEEN NICE TO HAVE ONE DAY. EVEN A FEW HOURS.
I JUST FOUGHT MY WAY OUTOF A BLACK HOLE. ALL I WANTED WAS TO SEE YOU.
SPEND A LITTLE TIME TOGETHER. NOT THINK ABOUT BRAINIAC, OR DOOMSDAY, OR ZOD, OR APOLLO, OR LUTHOR, OR ANY OF IT.
BUT YOU COULDN'T REMEMBER TO GIVE A PLANT A LITTLE COOKING OIL EVERY ONCE IN A WHILE.
WHAT?

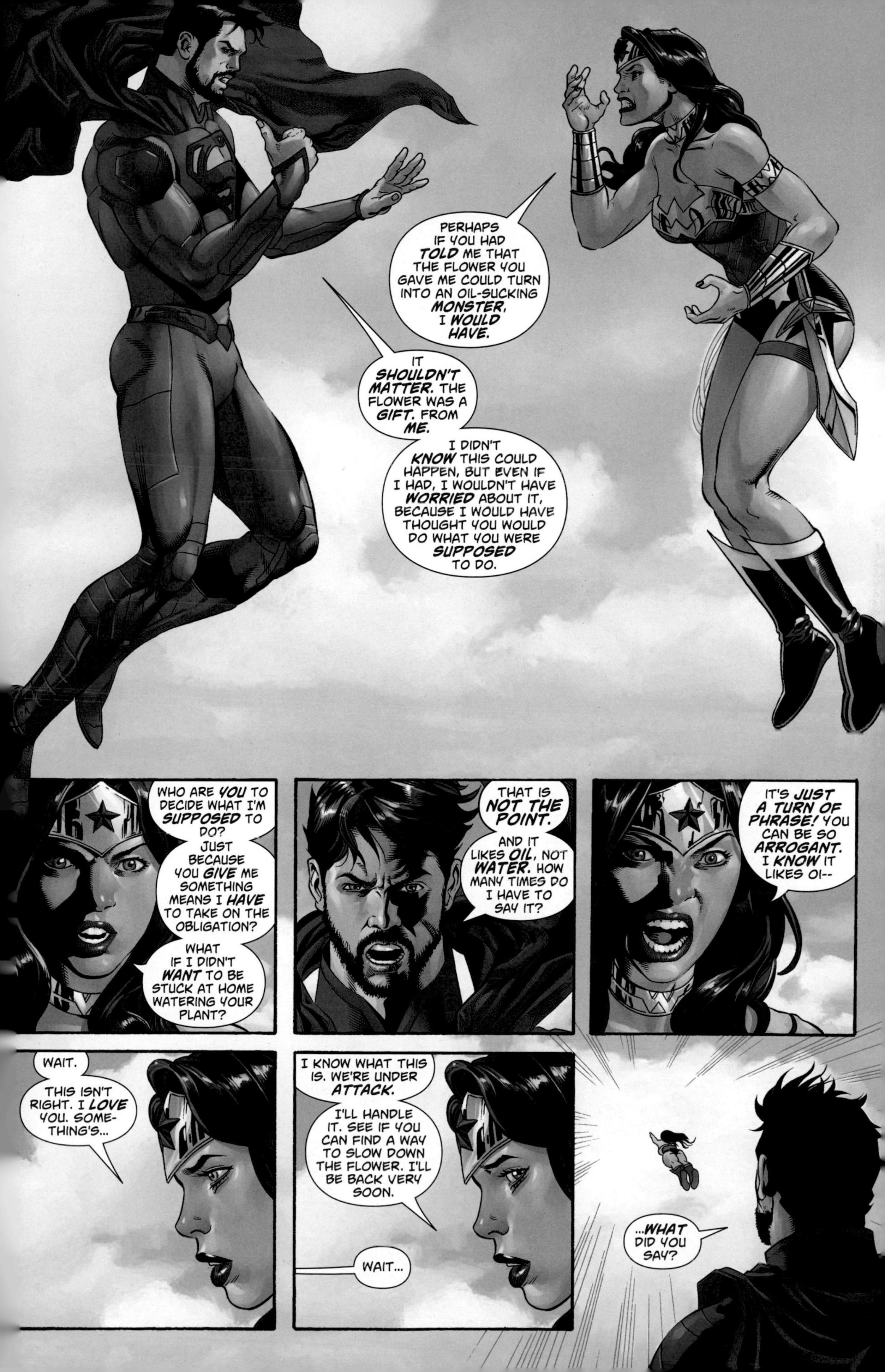
PERHAPS IF YOU HAD TOLD ME THAT THE FLOWER YOU GAVE ME COULD TURN INTO AN OIL-SUCKING MONSTER, I WOULD HAVE.
IT SHOULDN'T MATTER. THE FLOWER WAS A GIFT. FROM ME.
I DIDN'T KNOW THIS COULD HAPPEN, BUT EVEN IF I HAD, I WOULDN'T HAVE WORRIED ABOUT IT, BECAUSE I WOULD HAVE THOUGHT YOU WOULD DO WHAT YOU WERE SUPPOSED TO DO.
WHO ARE YOU TO DECIDE WHAT I'M SUPPOSED TO DO?
JUST BECAUSE YOU GIVE ME SOMETHING MEANS I HAVE TO TAKE ON THE OBLIGATION?
WHAT IF I DIDN'T WANT TO BE STUCK AT HOME WATERING YOUR PLANT?
THAT IS NOT THE POINT.
AND IT LIKES OIL, NOT WATER. HOW MANY TIMES DO I HAVE TO SAY IT?
IT'S JUST A TURN OF PHRASE! YOU CAN BE SO ARROGANT. I KNOW IT LIKES OI--
WAIT.
THIS ISN'T RIGHT. I LOVE YOU. SOME-THING'S...
I KNOW WHAT THIS IS. WE'RE UNDER ATTACK.
I'LL HANDLE IT. SEE IF YOU CAN FIND A WAY TO SLOW DOWN THE FLOWER. I'LL BE BACK VERY SOON.
WAIT...
...WHAT DID YOU SAY?

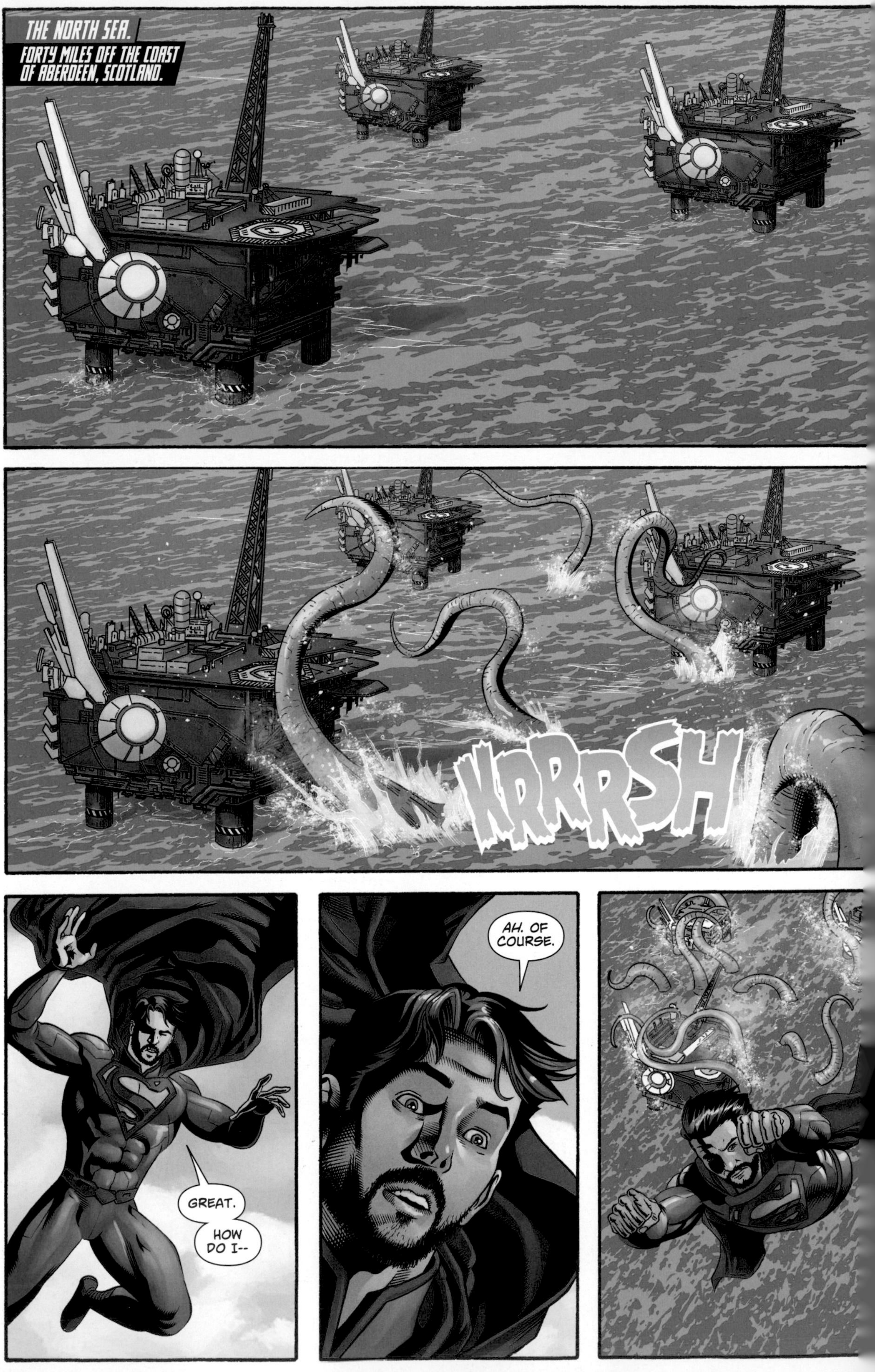
THE NORTH SEA.
FORTY MILES OFF THE COAST OF ABERDEEN, SCOTLAND.
KRRRSH
GREAT.
HOW DO I--
AH. OF COURSE.

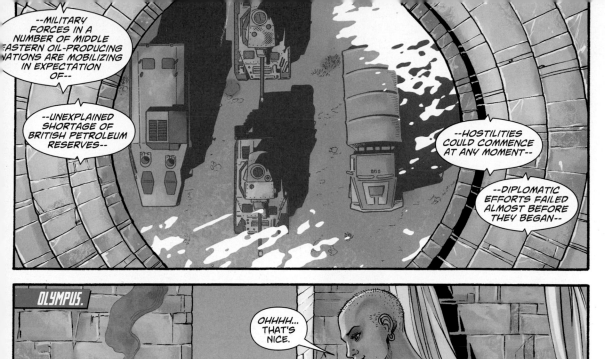

--MILITARY FORCES IN A NUMBER OF MIDDLE EASTERN OIL-PRODUCING NATIONS ARE MOBILIZING IN EXPECTATION OF--

--UNEXPLAINED SHORTAGE OF BRITISH PETROLEUM RESERVES--

--HOSTILITIES COULD COMMENCE AT ANY MOMENT--

--DIPLOMATIC EFFORTS FAILED ALMOST BEFORE THEY BEGAN--

OLYMPUS.

OHHHH... THAT'S NICE.

STRIFE.

UH-OH.

WHAT ARE YOU DOING?

COME ON, DIANA. I'VE ALWAYS FOUND THAT A RELATIONSHIP WITHOUT THE OCCASIONAL ARGUMENT LACKS PASSION.

JUST IMAGINE HOW FUN IT'LL BE WHEN YOU AND CLARK MAKE UP.

AND AS FOR THE REST OF IT... IF PEOPLE WANT TO GET UPSET ABOUT LOSING ALL THEIR PRECIOUS OIL AND GO TO WAR AND ALL THEY NEED IS A LITTLE NUDGE IN THE RIGHT DIRECTION... WELL...

...ISN'T THAT MY JOB?

WILL YOU KILL ME JUST FOR DOING WHAT I'M MADE TO DO?

NO.

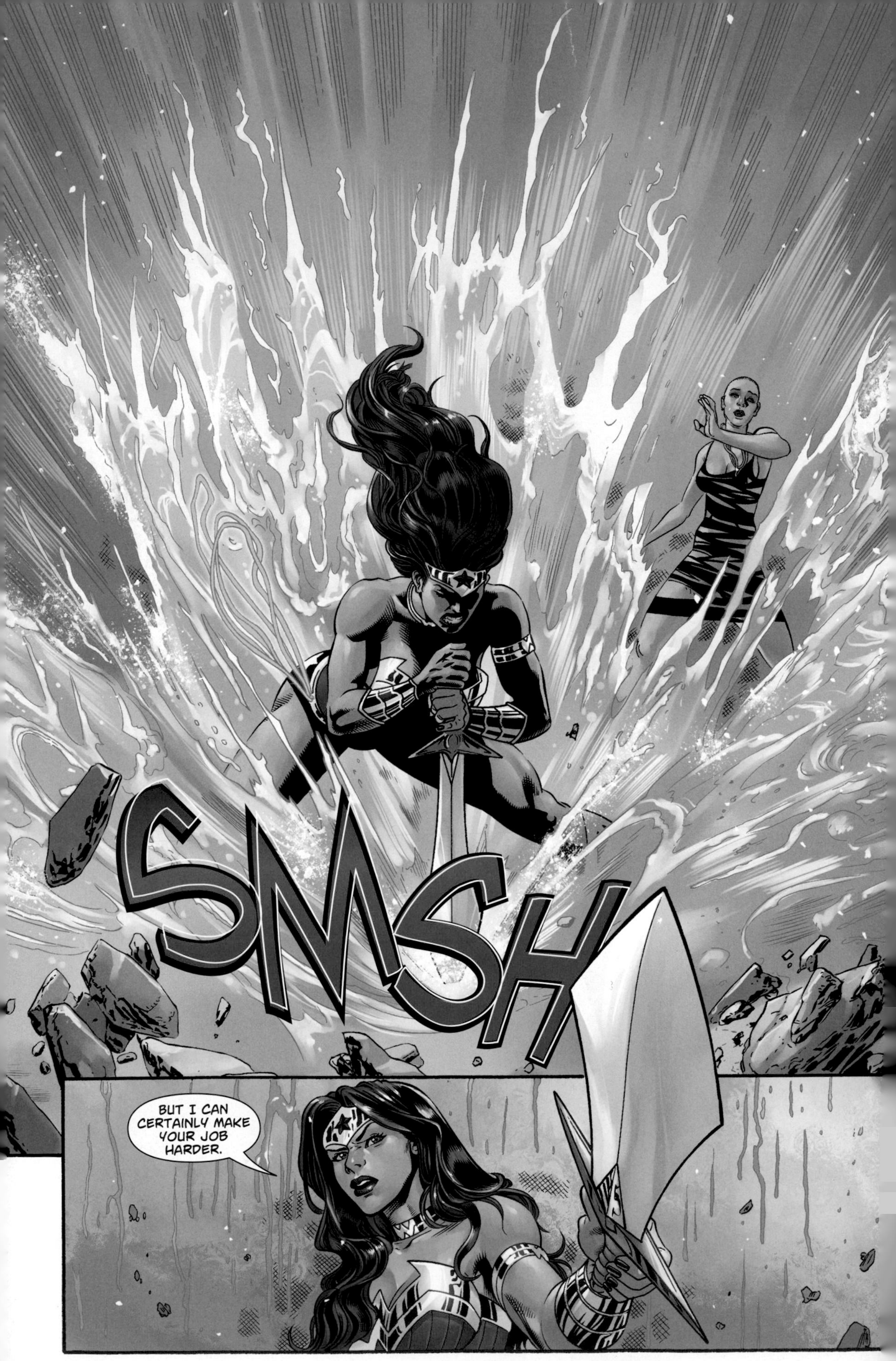
SMSH
BUT I CAN CERTAINLY MAKE YOUR JOB HARDER.

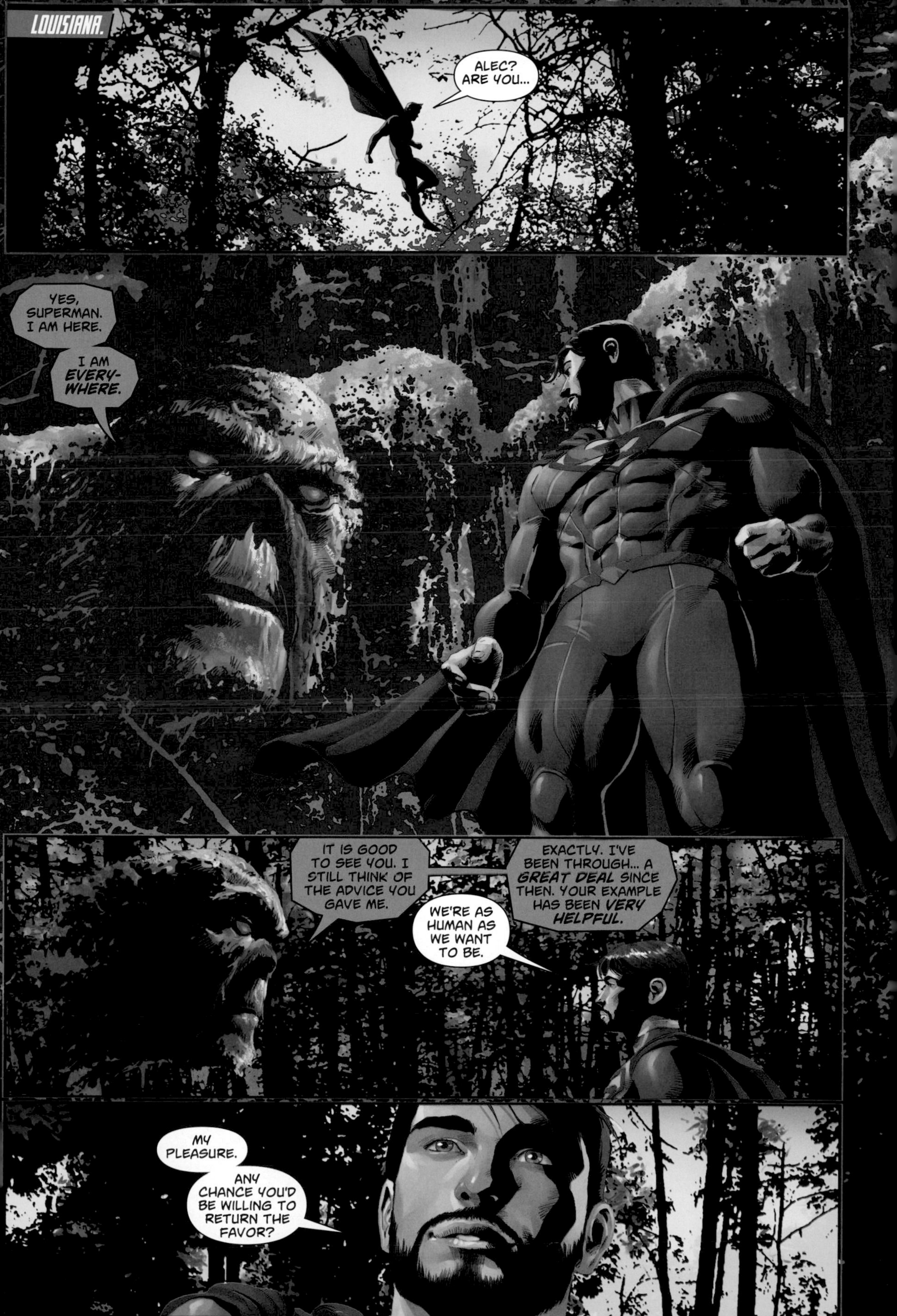

LOUISIANA.
ALEC? ARE YOU...
YES, SUPERMAN. I AM HERE.
I AM EVERY-WHERE.
IT IS GOOD TO SEE YOU. I STILL THINK OF THE ADVICE YOU GAVE ME.
WE'RE AS HUMAN AS WE WANT TO BE.
EXACTLY. I'VE BEEN THROUGH... A GREAT DEAL SINCE THEN. YOUR EXAMPLE HAS BEEN VERY HELPFUL.
MY PLEASURE.
ANY CHANCE YOU'D BE WILLING TO RETURN THE FAVOR?

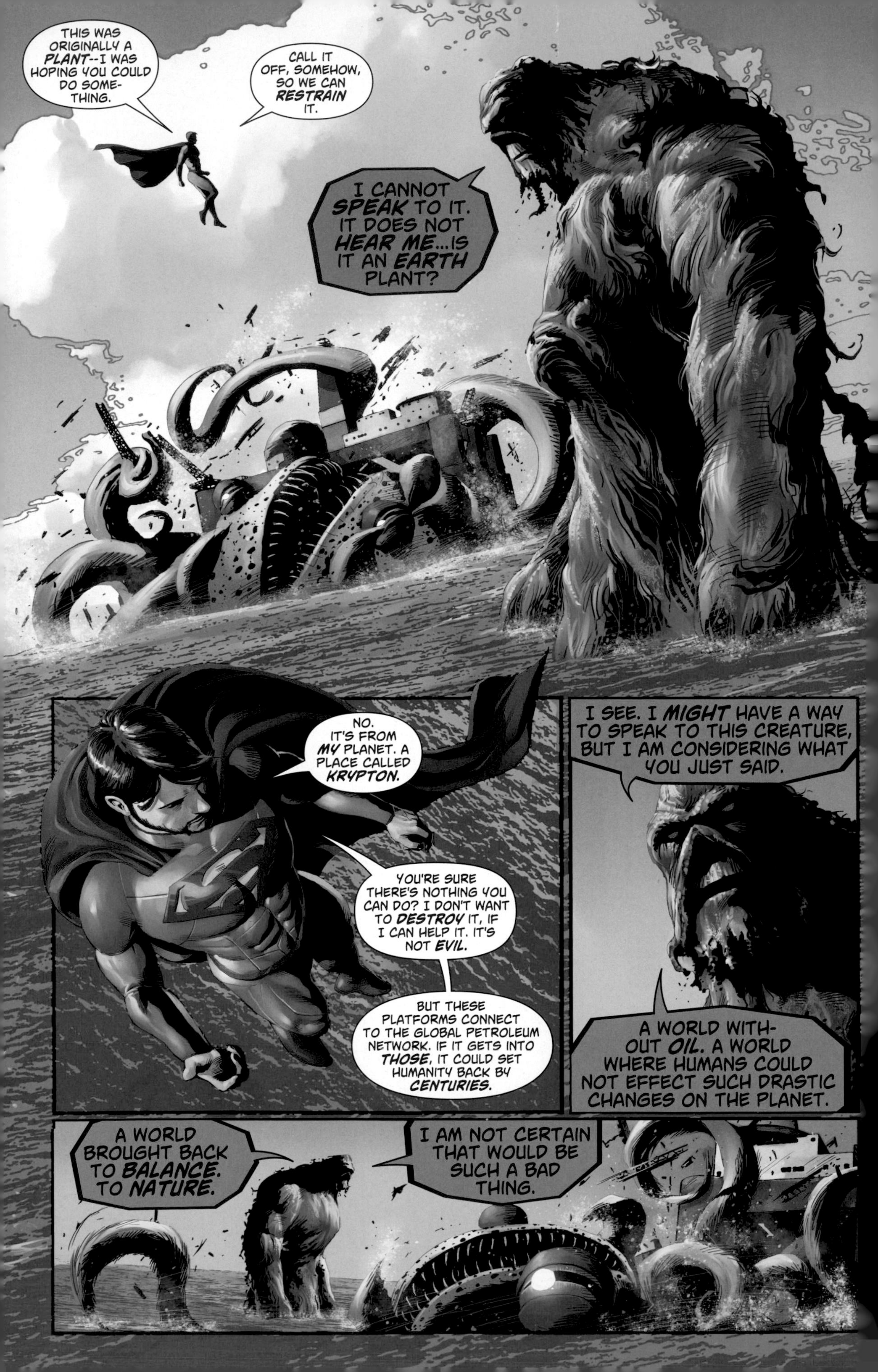
THIS WAS ORIGINALLY A PLANT--I WAS HOPING YOU COULD DO SOMETHING.
CALL IT OFF, SOMEHOW, SO WE CAN RESTRAIN IT.
I CANNOT SPEAK TO IT. IT DOES NOT HEAR ME...IS IT AN EARTH PLANT?
NO. IT'S FROM MY PLANET. A PLACE CALLED KRYPTON.
YOU'RE SURE THERE'S NOTHING YOU CAN DO? I DON'T WANT TO DESTROY IT, IF I CAN HELP IT. IT'S NOT EVIL.
BUT THESE PLATFORMS CONNECT TO THE GLOBAL PETROLEUM NETWORK. IF IT GETS INTO THOSE, IT COULD SET HUMANITY BACK BY CENTURIES.
I SEE. I MIGHT HAVE A WAY TO SPEAK TO THIS CREATURE, BUT I AM CONSIDERING WHAT YOU JUST SAID.
A WORLD WITHOUT OIL. A WORLD WHERE HUMANS COULD NOT EFFECT SUCH DRASTIC CHANGES ON THE PLANET.
A WORLD BROUGHT BACK TO BALANCE. TO NATURE.
I AM NOT CERTAIN THAT WOULD BE SUCH A BAD THING.

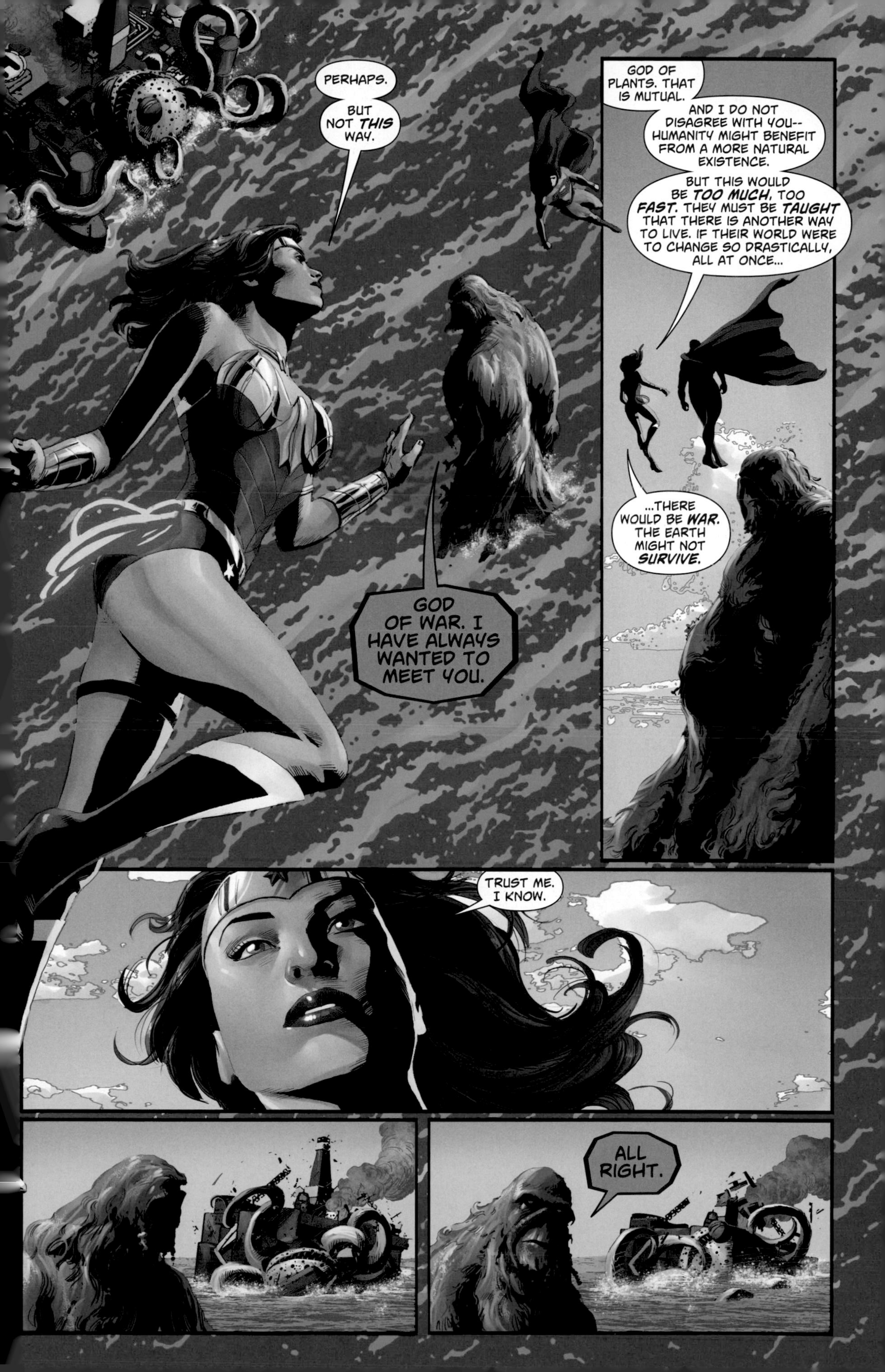
PERHAPS.
BUT NOT THIS WAY.
GOD OF WAR. I HAVE ALWAYS WANTED TO MEET YOU.
GOD OF PLANTS. THAT IS MUTUAL.
AND I DO NOT DISAGREE WITH YOU-- HUMANITY MIGHT BENEFIT FROM A MORE NATURAL EXISTENCE.
BUT THIS WOULD BE TOO MUCH, TOO FAST. THEY MUST BE TAUGHT THAT THERE IS ANOTHER WAY TO LIVE. IF THEIR WORLD WERE TO CHANGE SO DRASTICALLY, ALL AT ONCE...
...THERE WOULD BE WAR. THE EARTH MIGHT NOT SURVIVE.
TRUST ME. I KNOW.
ALL RIGHT.

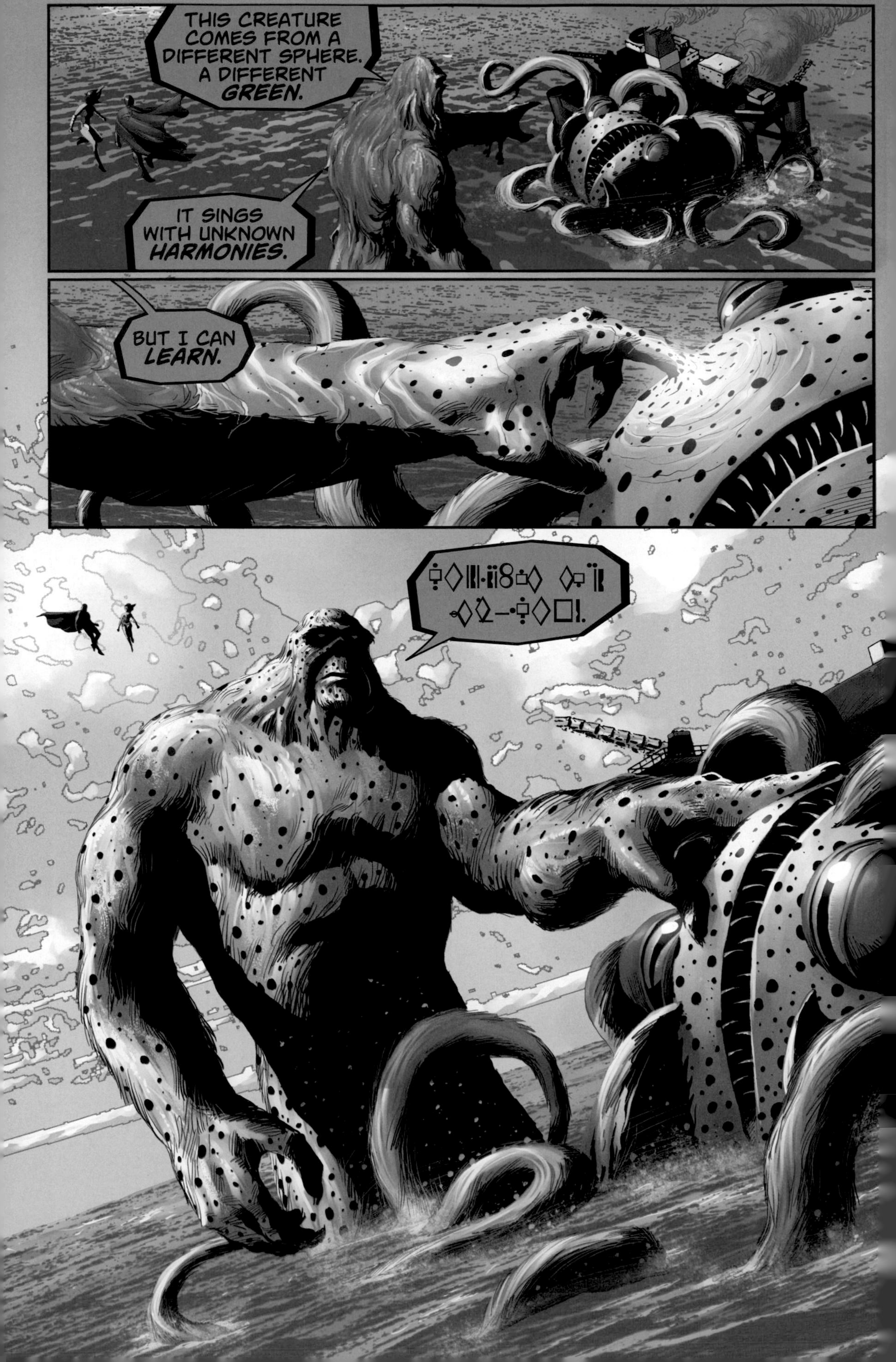
THIS CREATURE COMES FROM A DIFFERENT SPHERE. A DIFFERENT GREEN.
IT SINGS WITH UNKNOWN HARMONIES.
BUT I CAN LEARN.

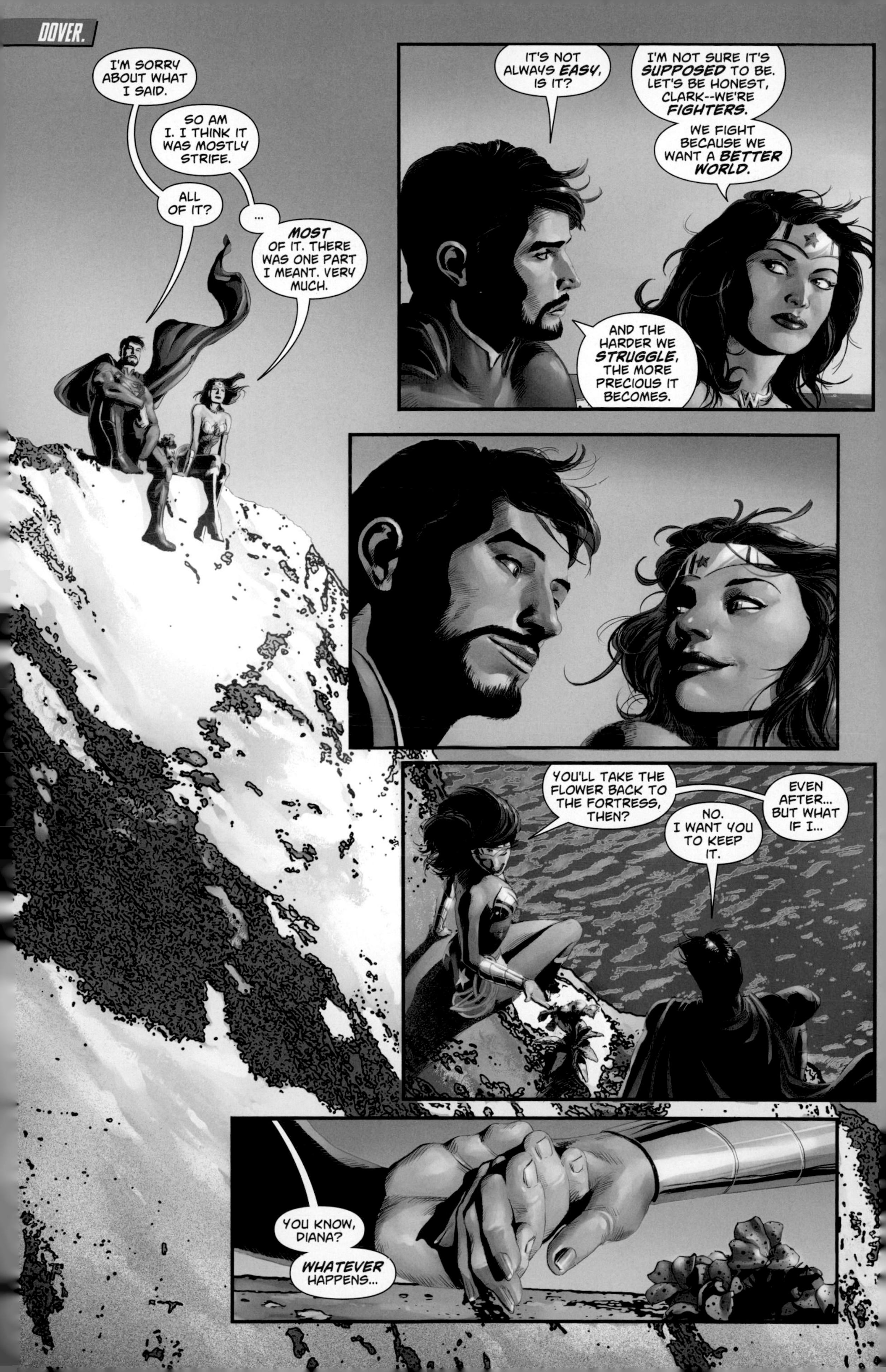
DOVER.
I'M SORRY ABOUT WHAT I SAID.
SO AM I. I THINK IT WAS MOSTLY STRIFE.
ALL OF IT?
...
MOST OF IT. THERE WAS ONE PART I MEANT. VERY MUCH.
IT'S NOT ALWAYS EASY, IS IT?
I'M NOT SURE IT'S SUPPOSED TO BE. LET'S BE HONEST, CLARK--WE'RE FIGHTERS.
WE FIGHT BECAUSE WE WANT A BETTER WORLD.
AND THE HARDER WE STRUGGLE, THE MORE PRECIOUS IT BECOMES.
YOU'LL TAKE THE FLOWER BACK TO THE FORTRESS, THEN?
NO. I WANT YOU TO KEEP IT.
EVEN AFTER... BUT WHAT IF I...
YOU KNOW, DIANA?
WHATEVER HAPPENS...

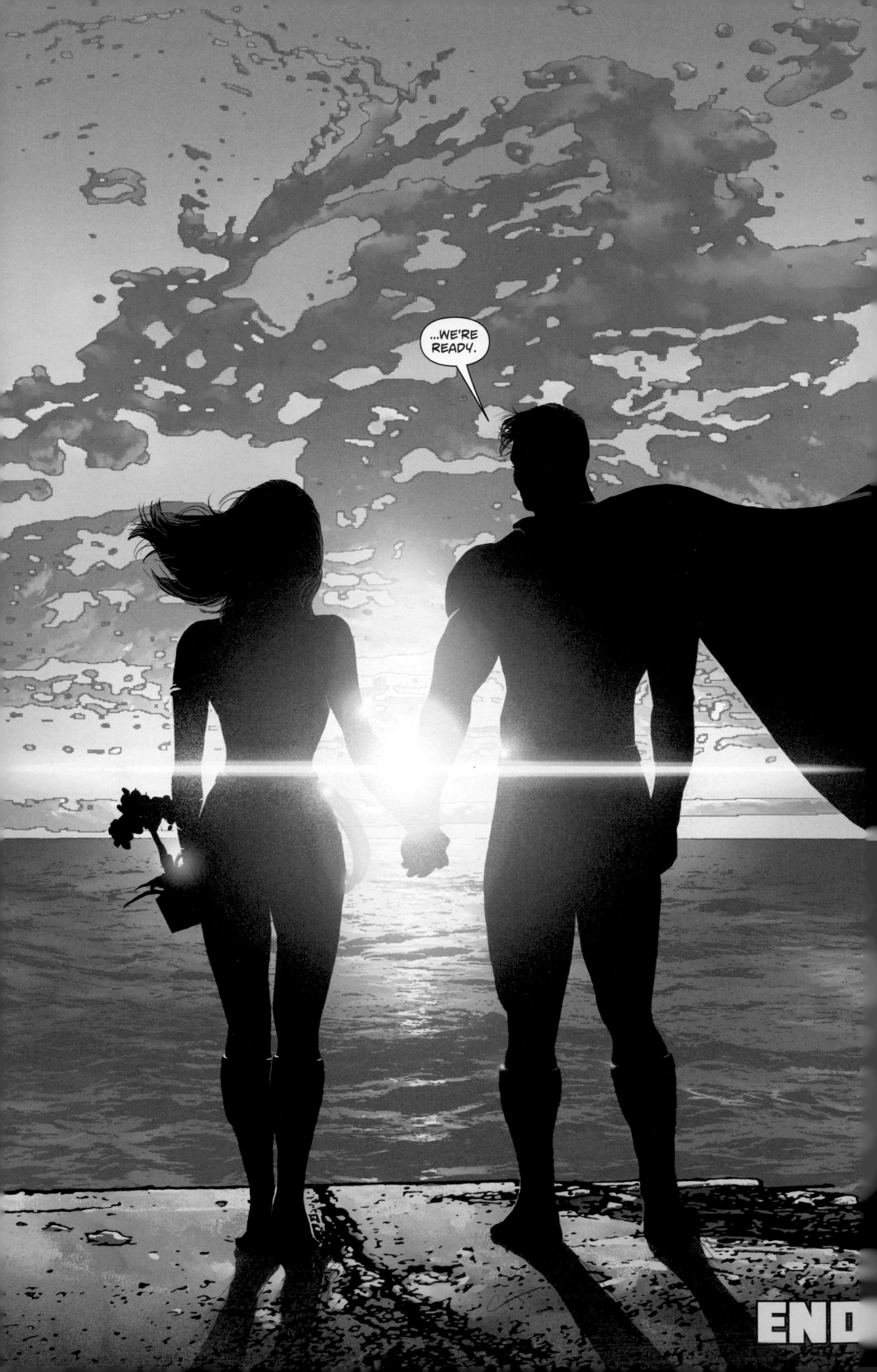
...WE'RE READY.
END

OLD SOLDIERS
RAGS MORALES JOSÉ MARZAN JR. BATT artists
cover by TOM RANEY & PETE PANTAZIS

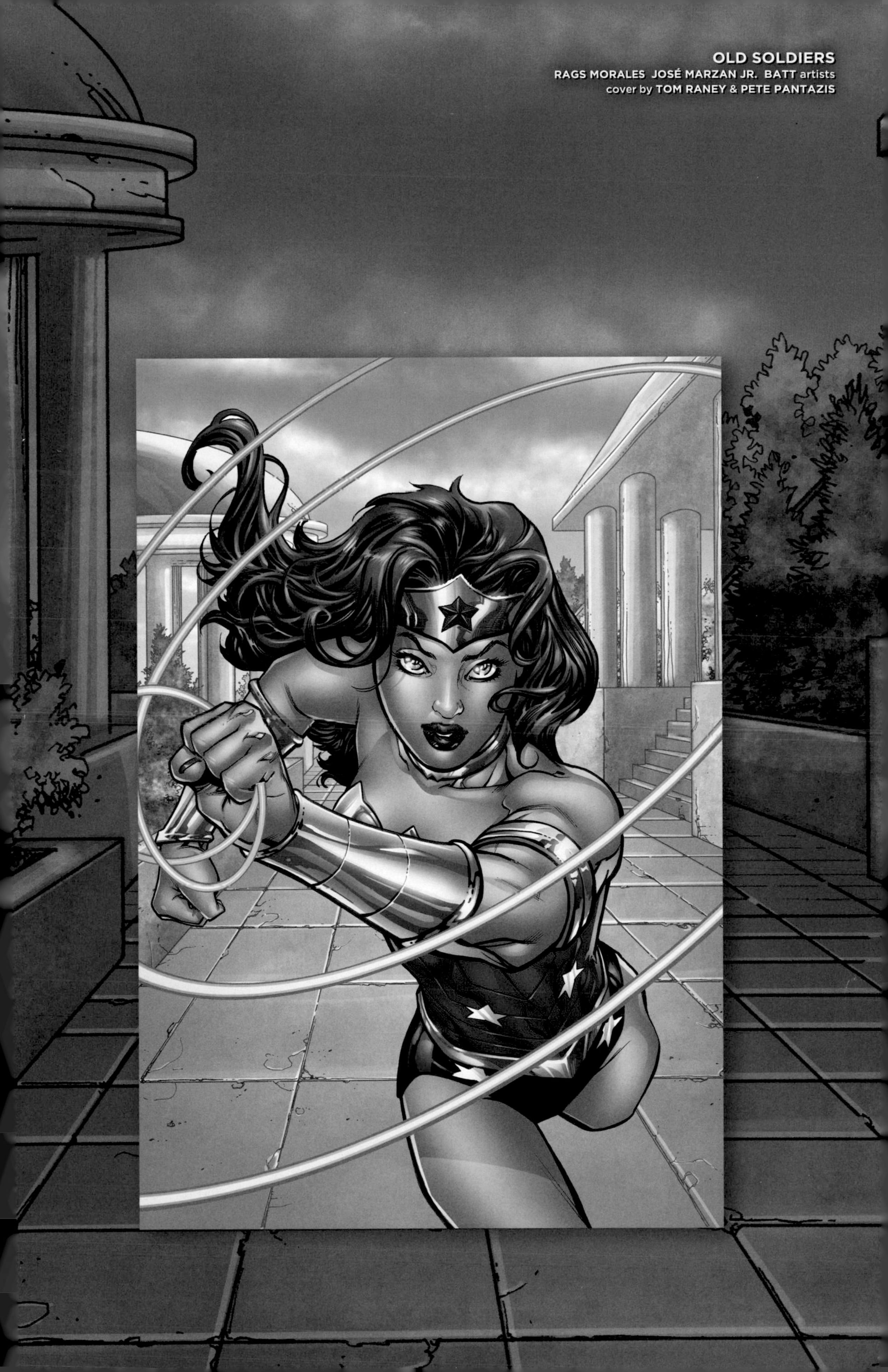

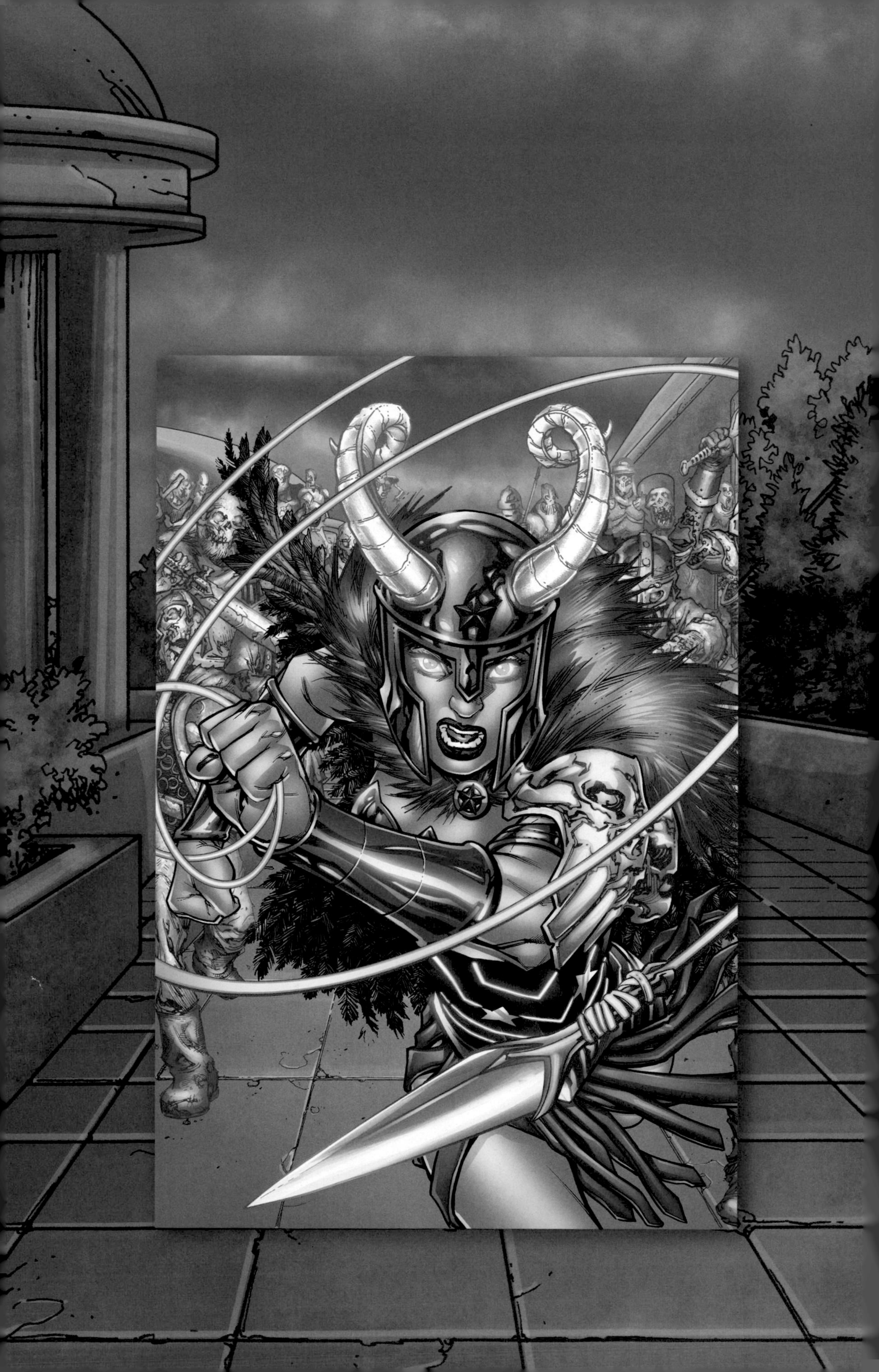

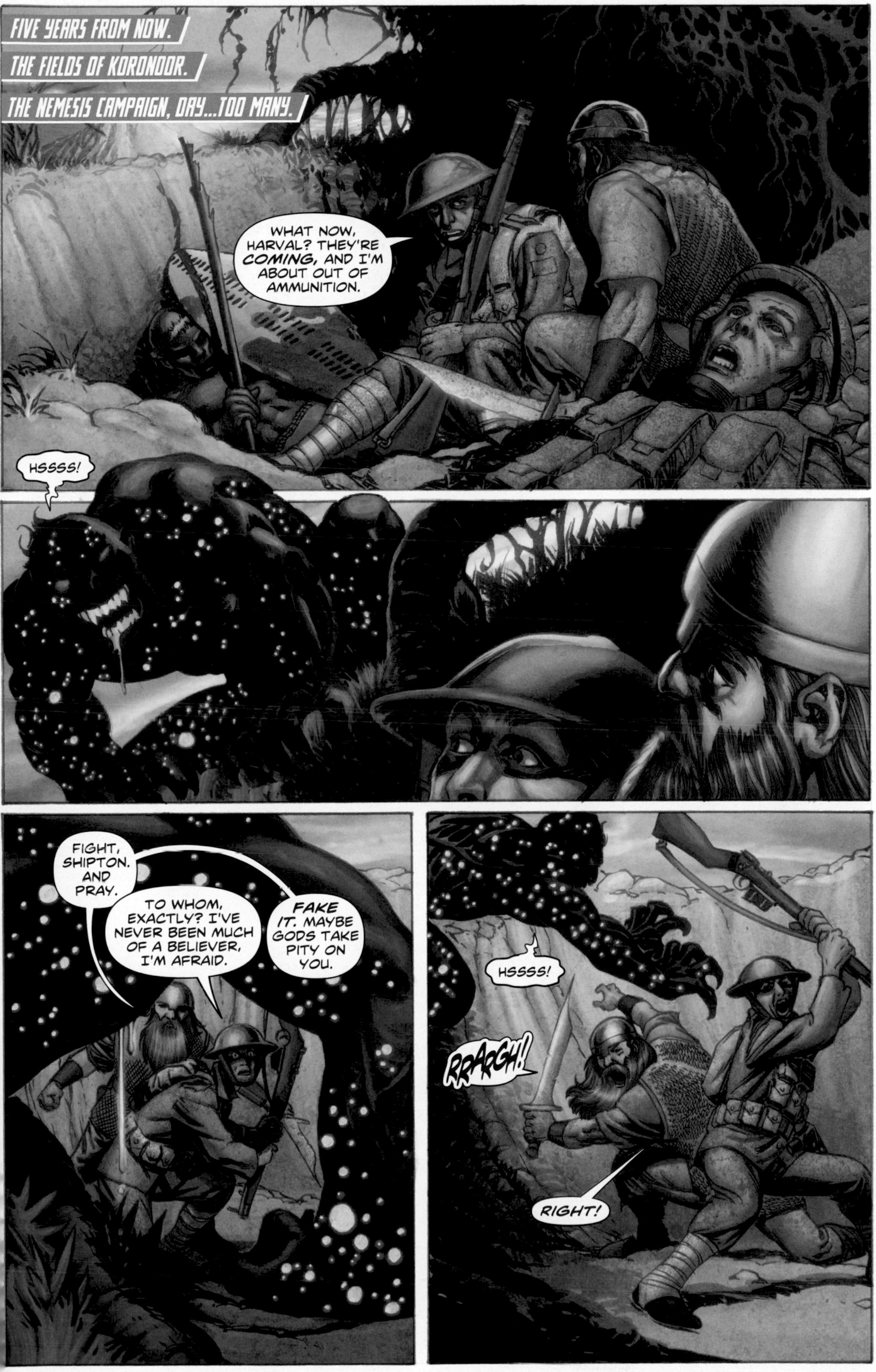
FIVE YEARS FROM NOW.
THE FIELDS OF KORONDOR.
THE NEMESIS CAMPAIGN, DAY...TOO MANY.
WHAT NOW, HARVAL? THEY'RE COMING, AND I'M ABOUT OUT OF AMMUNITION.
HSSSS!
FIGHT, SHIPTON. AND PRAY.
TO WHOM, EXACTLY? I'VE NEVER BEEN MUCH OF A BELIEVER, I'M AFRAID.
FAKE IT. MAYBE GODS TAKE PITY ON YOU.
HSSSS!
RRRARGH!
RIGHT!

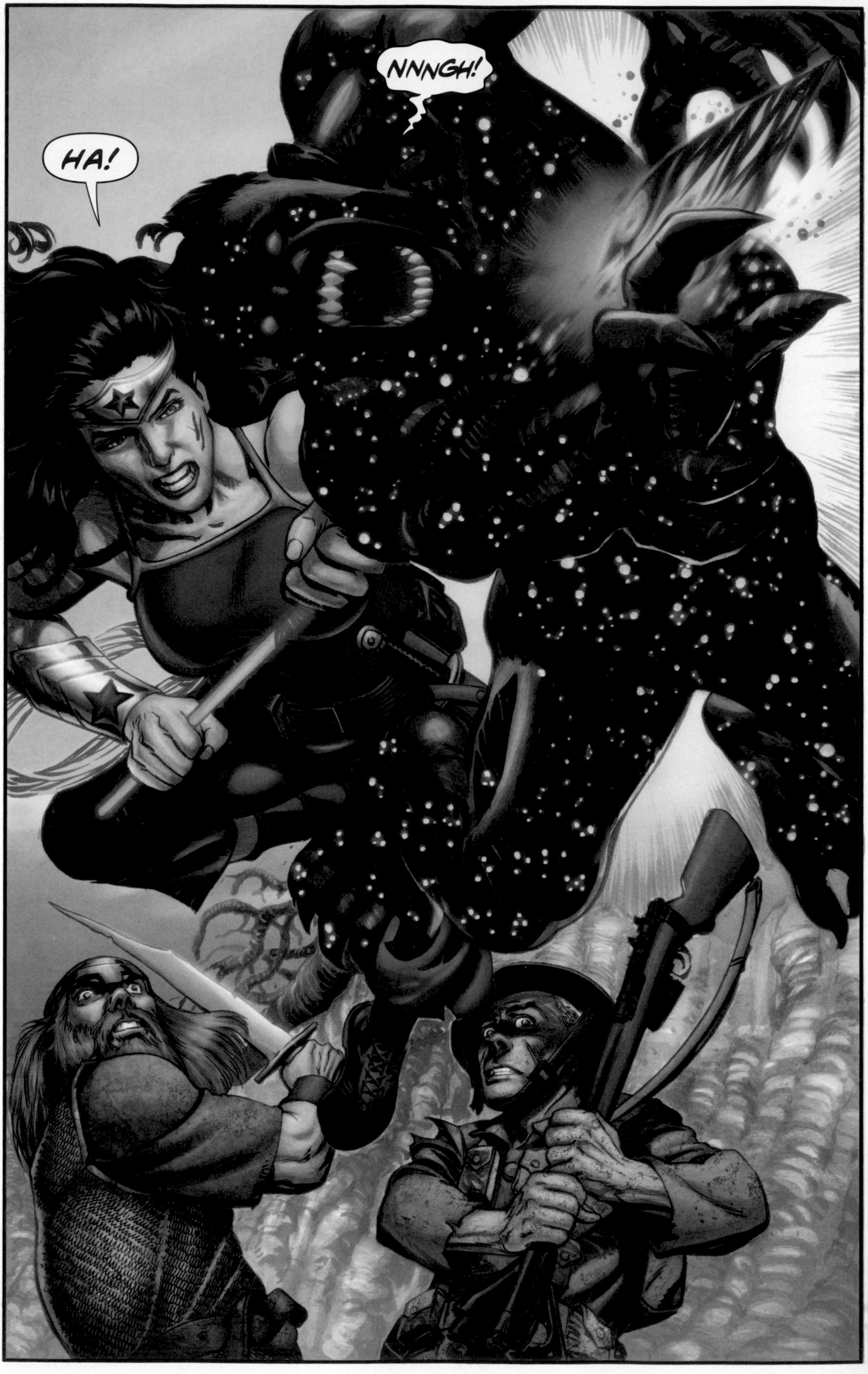
NNNGH!
HA!

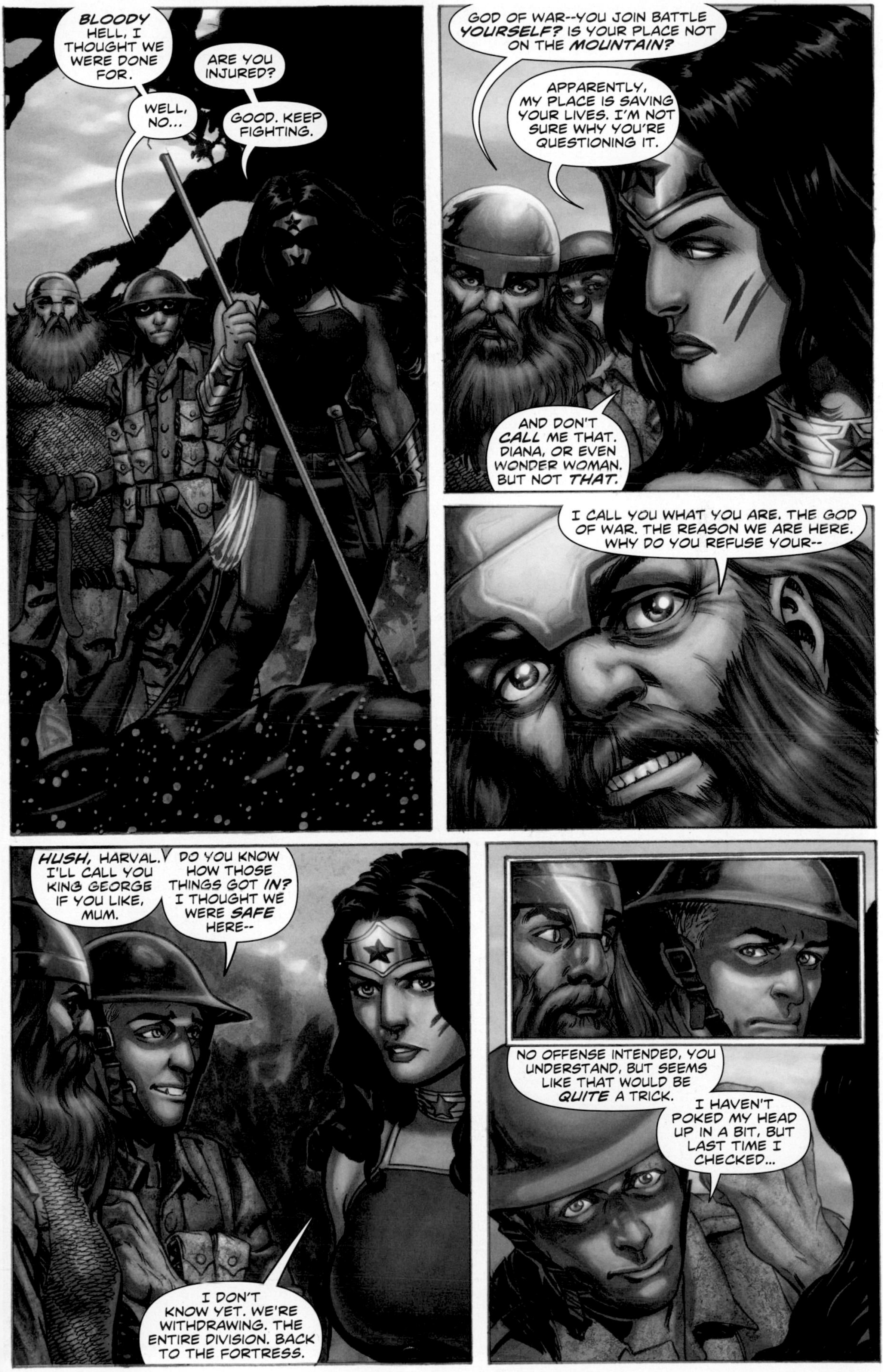
BLOODY HELL, I THOUGHT WE WERE DONE FOR.
ARE YOU INJURED?
WELL, NO...
GOOD. KEEP FIGHTING.
GOD OF WAR--YOU JOIN BATTLE YOURSELF? IS YOUR PLACE NOT ON THE MOUNTAIN?
APPARENTLY, MY PLACE IS SAVING YOUR LIVES. I'M NOT SURE WHY YOU'RE QUESTIONING IT.
AND DON'T CALL ME THAT. DIANA, OR EVEN WONDER WOMAN. BUT NOT THAT.
I CALL YOU WHAT YOU ARE. THE GOD OF WAR. THE REASON WE ARE HERE. WHY DO YOU REFUSE YOUR--
HUSH, HARVAL. I'LL CALL YOU KING GEORGE IF YOU LIKE, MUM.
DO YOU KNOW HOW THOSE THINGS GOT IN? I THOUGHT WE WERE SAFE HERE--
I DON'T KNOW YET. WE'RE WITHDRAWING. THE ENTIRE DIVISION. BACK TO THE FORTRESS.
NO OFFENSE INTENDED, YOU UNDERSTAND, BUT SEEMS LIKE THAT WOULD BE QUITE A TRICK.
I HAVEN'T POKED MY HEAD UP IN A BIT, BUT LAST TIME I CHECKED...

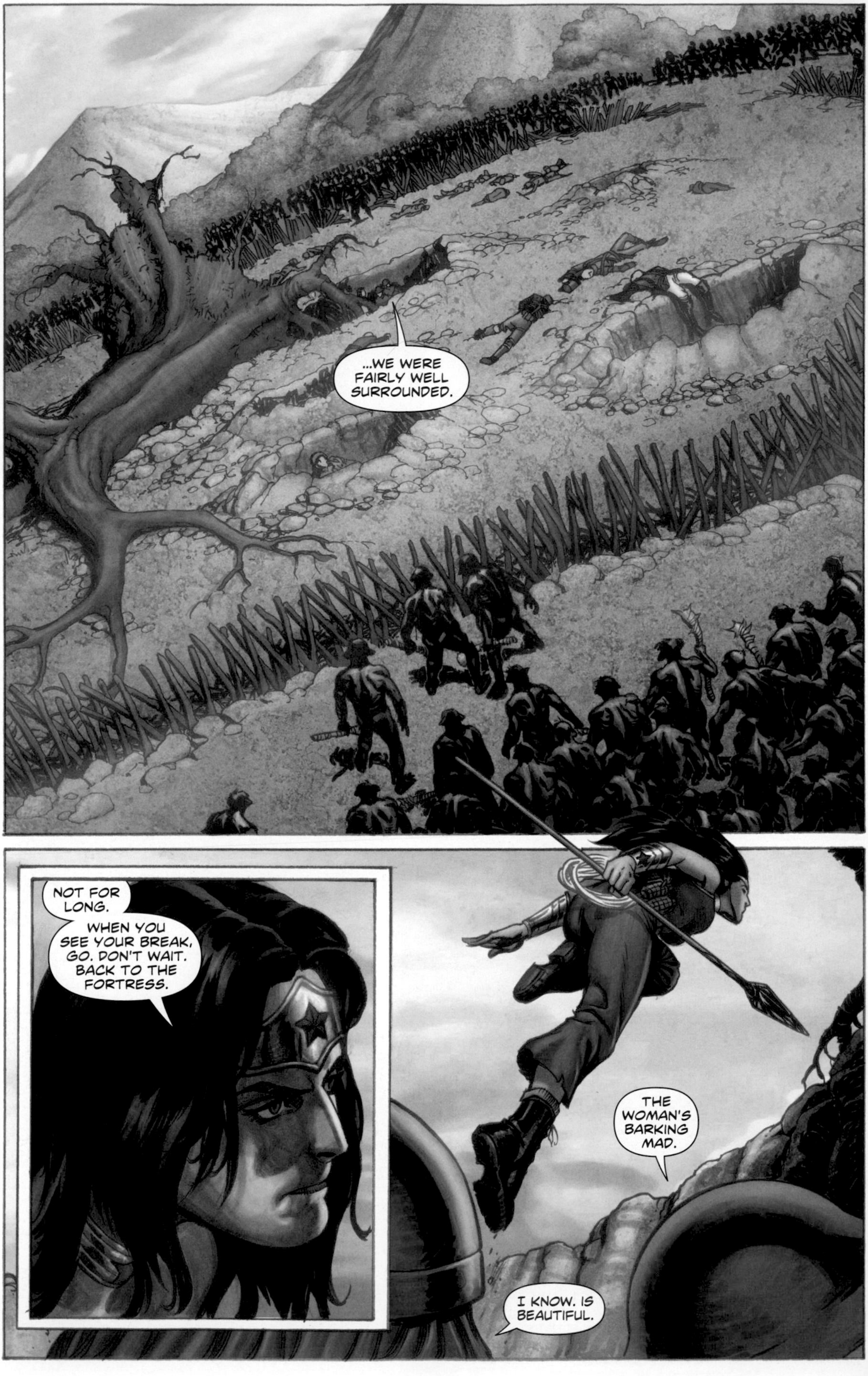
...WE WERE FAIRLY WELL SURROUNDED.
NOT FOR LONG.
WHEN YOU SEE YOUR BREAK, GO. DON'T WAIT. BACK TO THE FORTRESS.
THE WOMAN'S BARKING MAD.
I KNOW. IS BEAUTIFUL.

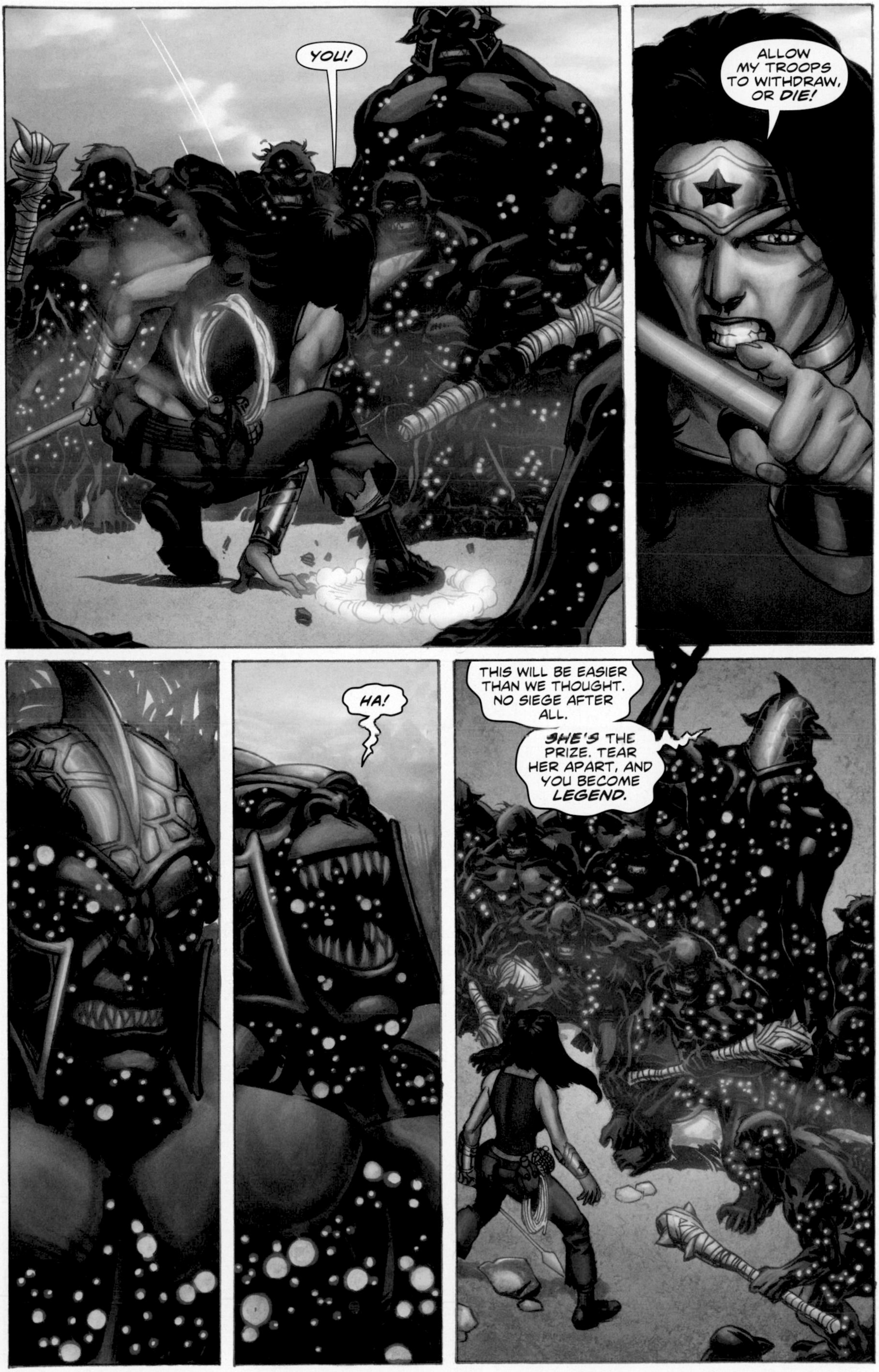
YOU!
ALLOW MY TROOPS TO WITHDRAW, OR DIE!
HA!
THIS WILL BE EASIER THAN WE THOUGHT. NO SIEGE AFTER ALL.
SHE'S THE PRIZE. TEAR HER APART, AND YOU BECOME LEGEND.

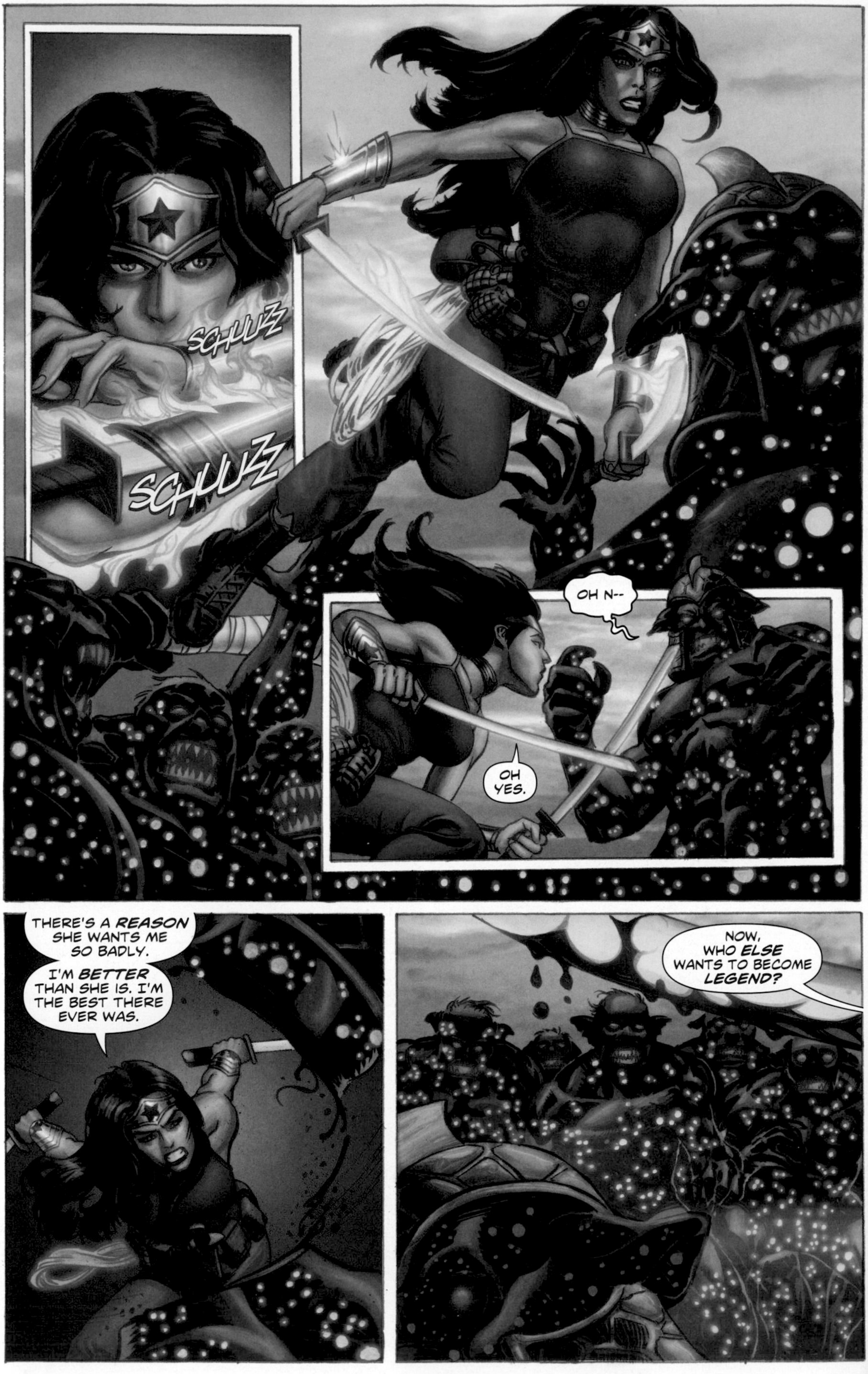
SCHUUZZ
SCHUUZZ
OH N--
OH YES.
THERE'S A REASON SHE WANTS ME SO BADLY.
I'M BETTER THAN SHE IS. I'M THE BEST THERE EVER WAS.
NOW, WHO ELSE WANTS TO BECOME LEGEND?

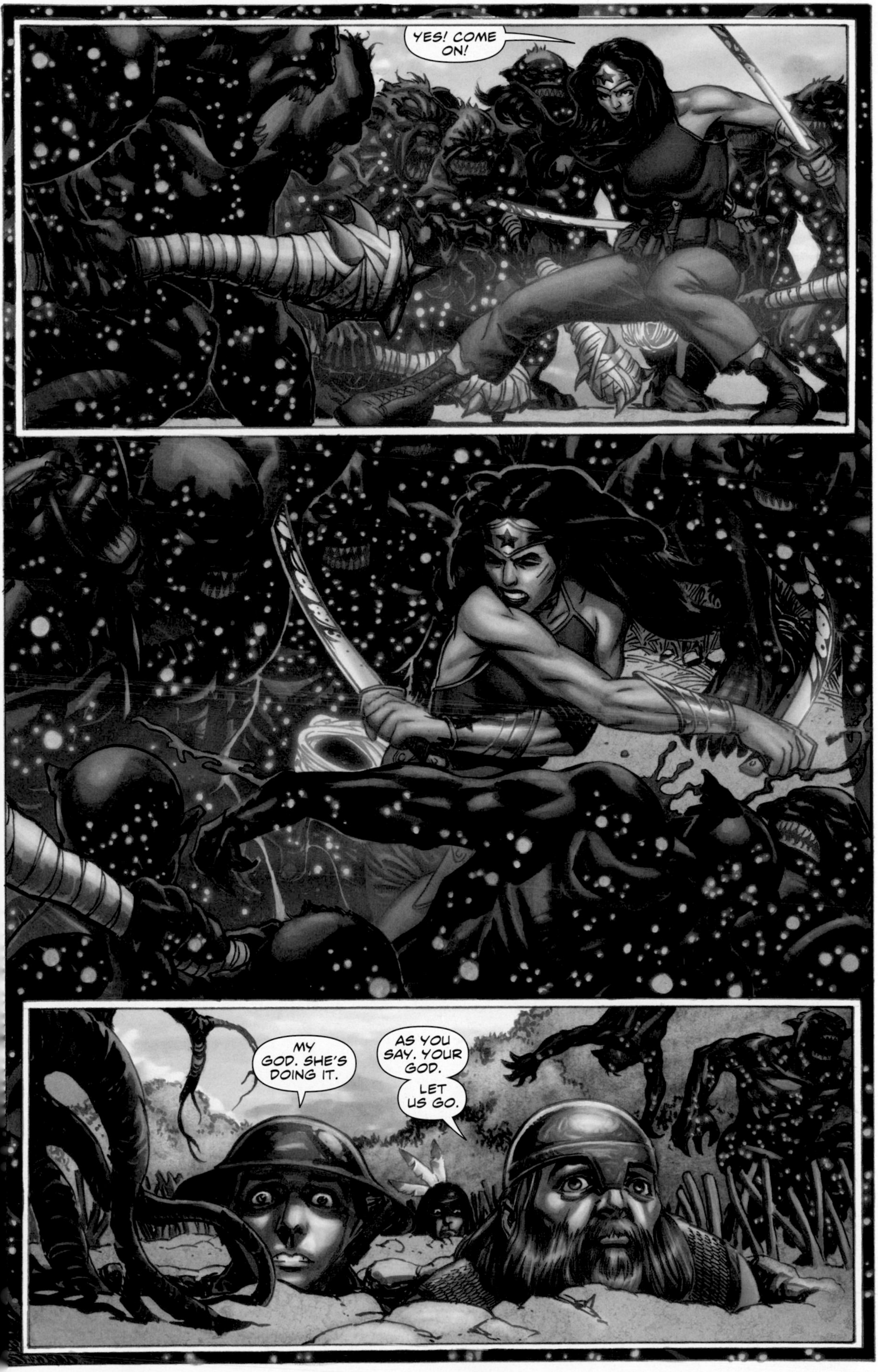
YES! COME ON!
MY GOD. SHE'S DOING IT.
AS YOU SAY. YOUR GOD.
LET US GO.

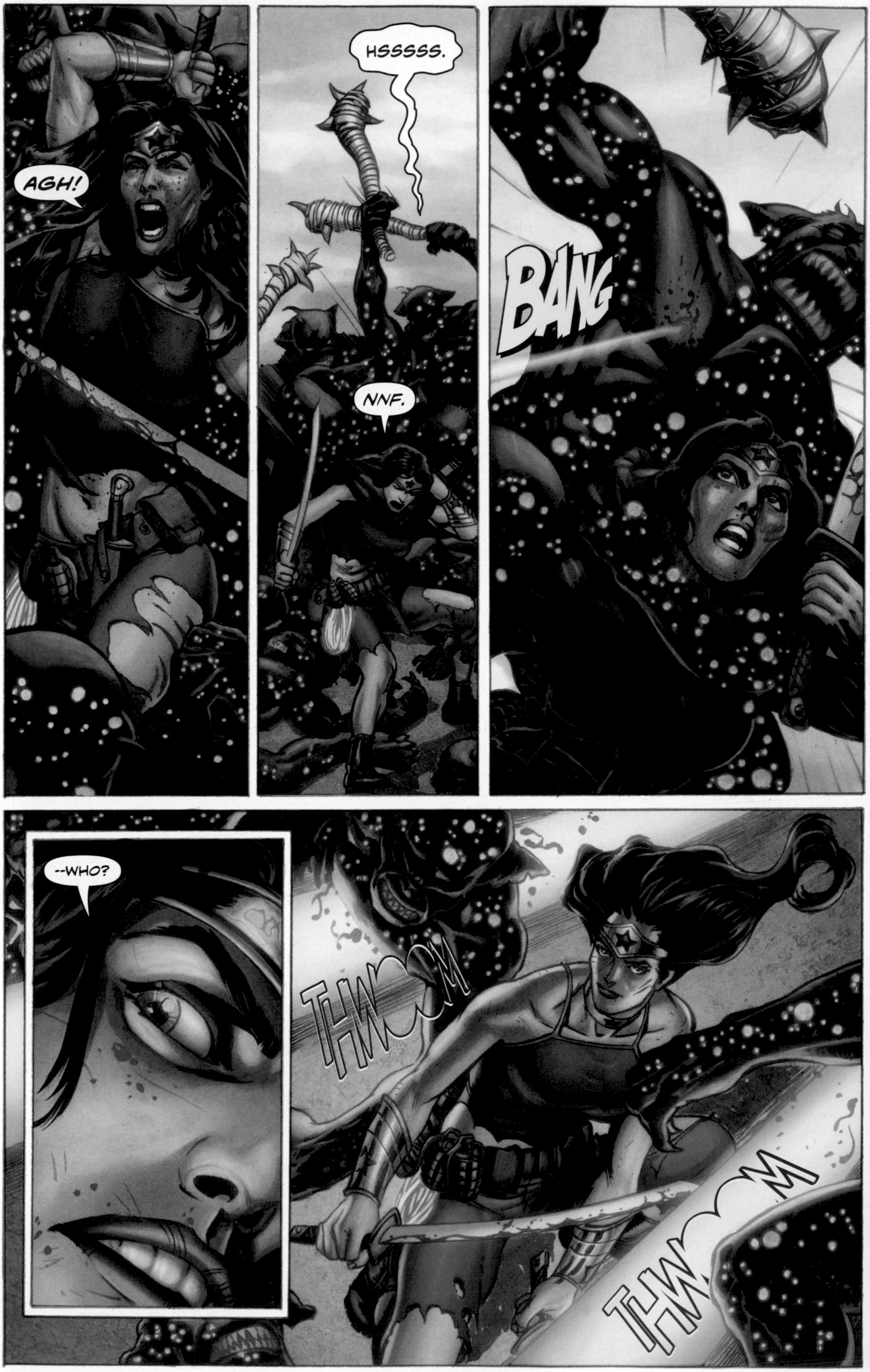
AGH!
HSSSSS.
NNF.
BANG
--WHO?
THWOOM
THWOOM

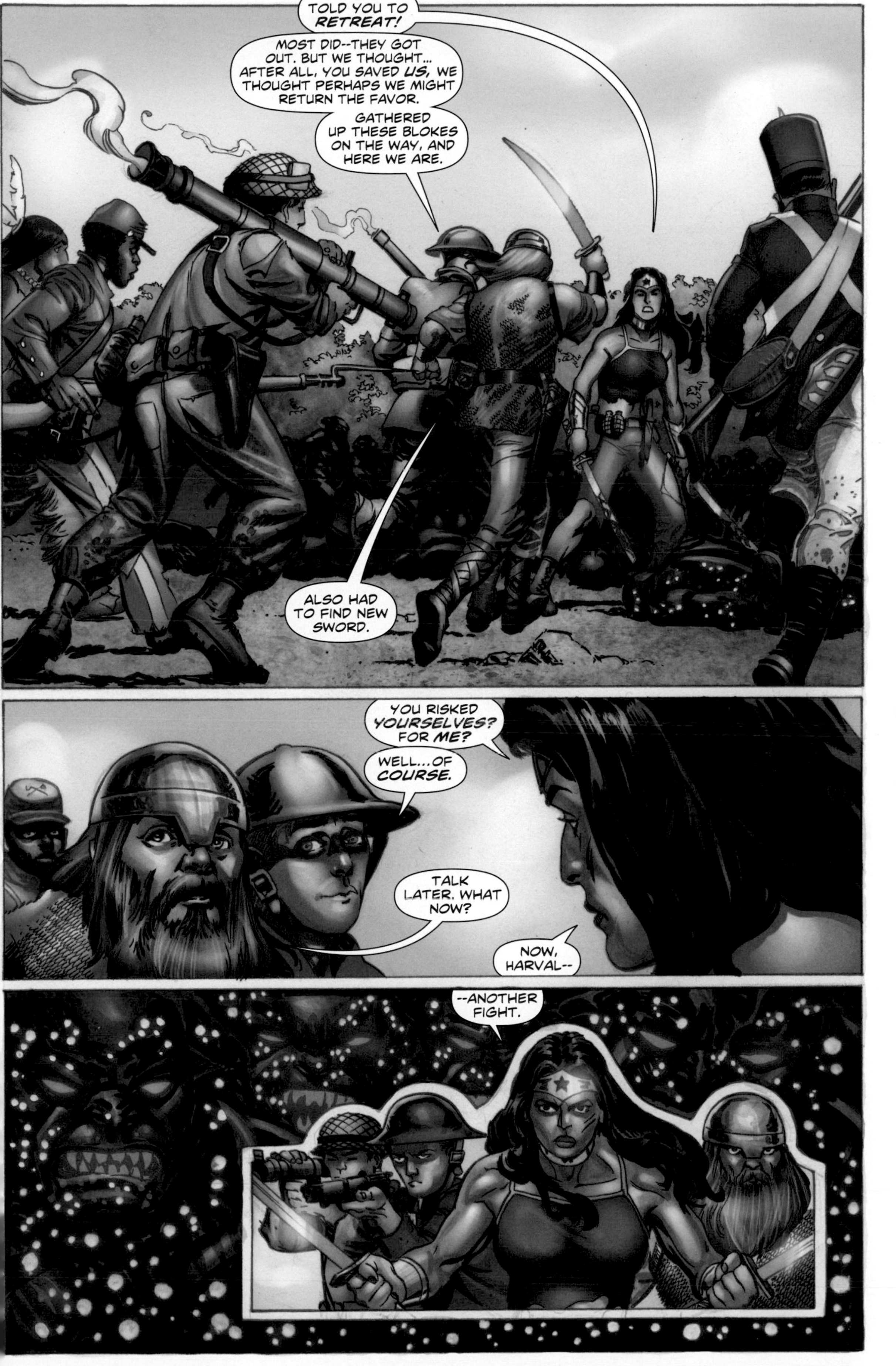
I TOLD YOU TO RETREAT!
MOST DID--THEY GOT OUT. BUT WE THOUGHT... AFTER ALL, YOU SAVED US, WE THOUGHT PERHAPS WE MIGHT RETURN THE FAVOR.
GATHERED UP THESE BLOKES ON THE WAY, AND HERE WE ARE.
ALSO HAD TO FIND NEW SWORD.
YOU RISKED YOURSELVES? FOR ME?
WELL...OF COURSE.
TALK LATER. WHAT NOW?
NOW, HARVAL--
--ANOTHER FIGHT.

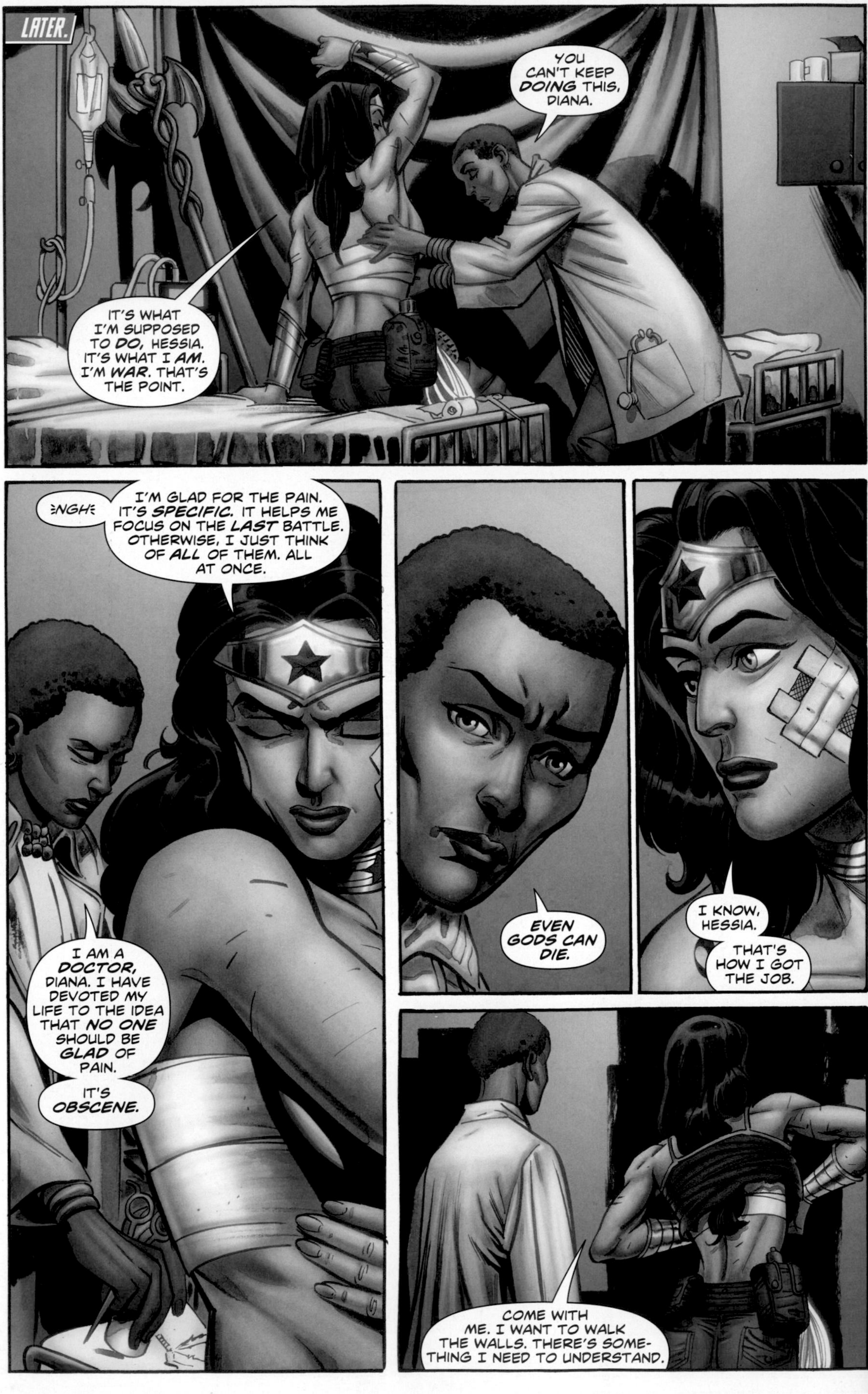

LATER.
YOU CAN'T KEEP DOING THIS, DIANA.
IT'S WHAT I'M SUPPOSED TO DO, HESSIA. IT'S WHAT I AM. I'M WAR. THAT'S THE POINT.
NGH
I'M GLAD FOR THE PAIN. IT'S SPECIFIC. IT HELPS ME FOCUS ON THE LAST BATTLE. OTHERWISE, I JUST THINK OF ALL OF THEM. ALL AT ONCE.
I AM A DOCTOR, DIANA. I HAVE DEVOTED MY LIFE TO THE IDEA THAT NO ONE SHOULD BE GLAD OF PAIN.
IT'S OBSCENE.
EVEN GODS CAN DIE.
I KNOW, HESSIA.
THAT'S HOW I GOT THE JOB.
COME WITH ME. I WANT TO WALK THE WALLS. THERE'S SOMETHING I NEED TO UNDERSTAND.

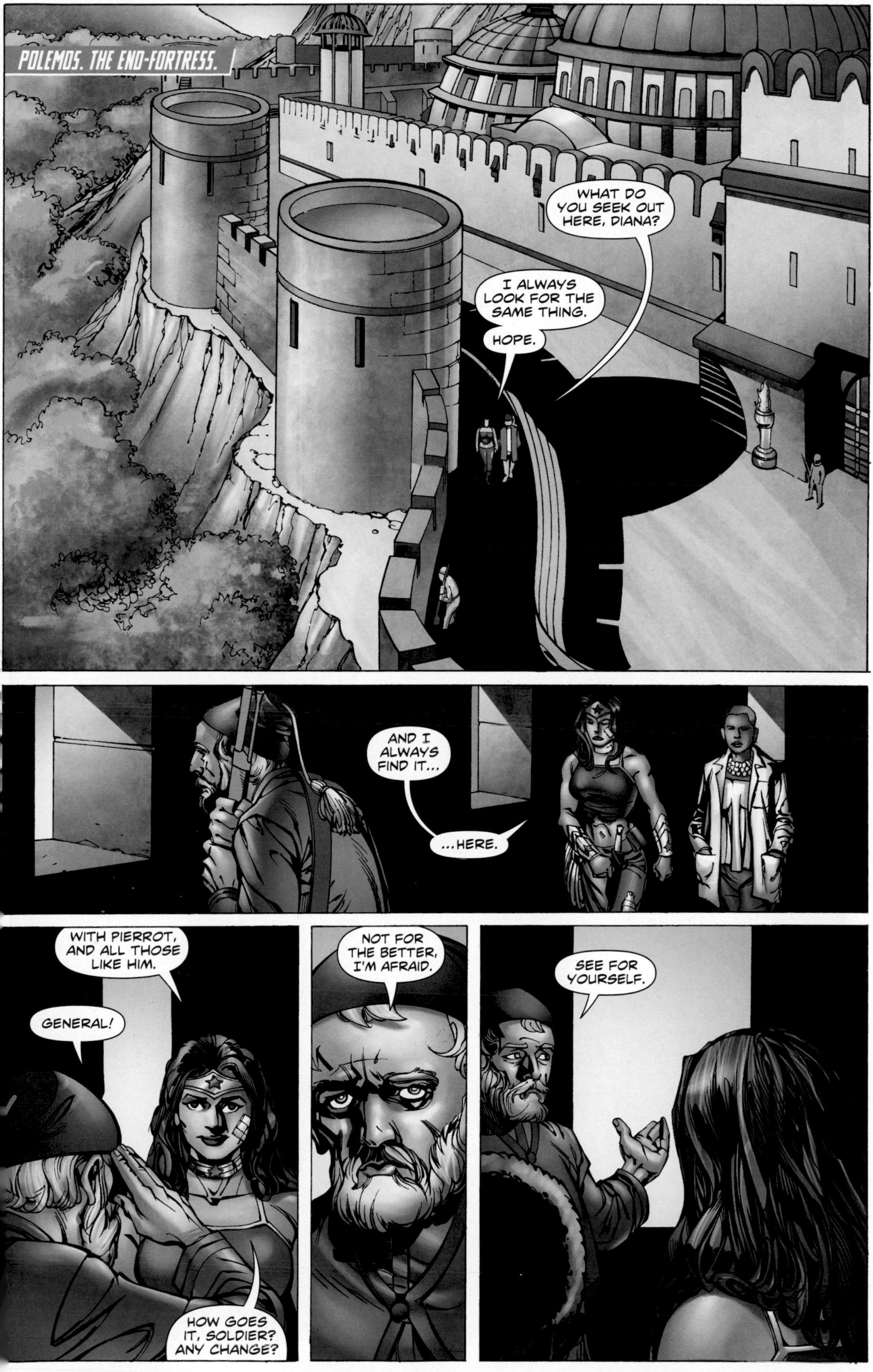
POLEMOS. THE END-FORTRESS.
WHAT DO YOU SEEK OUT HERE, DIANA?
I ALWAYS LOOK FOR THE SAME THING.
HOPE.
AND I ALWAYS FIND IT...
...HERE.
WITH PIERROT, AND ALL THOSE LIKE HIM.
GENERAL!
HOW GOES IT, SOLDIER? ANY CHANGE?
NOT FOR THE BETTER, I'M AFRAID.
SEE FOR YOURSELF.

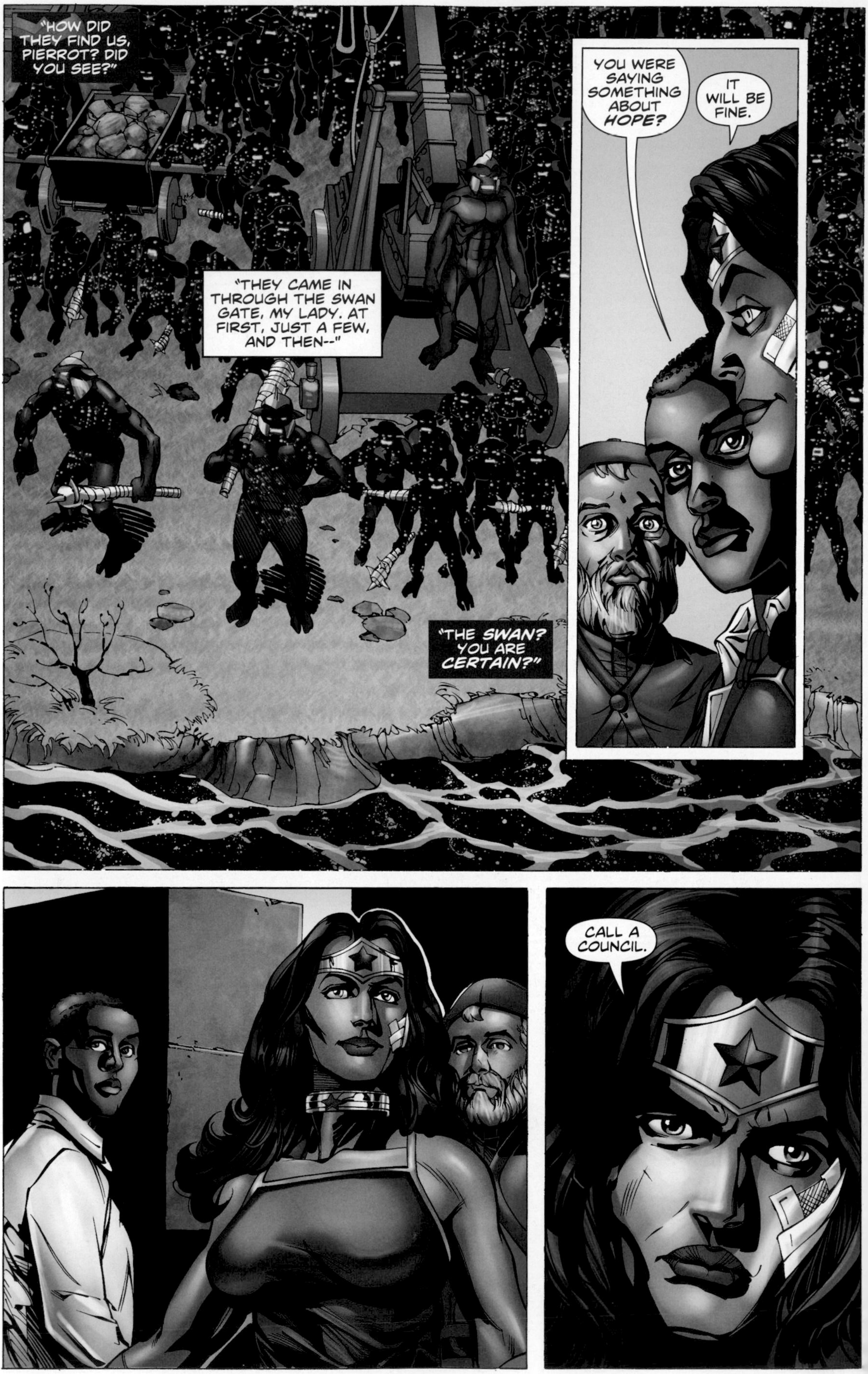
"HOW DID THEY FIND US, PIERROT? DID YOU SEE?"
"THEY CAME IN THROUGH THE SWAN GATE, MY LADY. AT FIRST, JUST A FEW, AND THEN--"
"THE *SWAN*? YOU ARE *CERTAIN*?"
YOU WERE SAYING SOMETHING ABOUT *HOPE*?
IT WILL BE FINE.
CALL A COUNCIL.

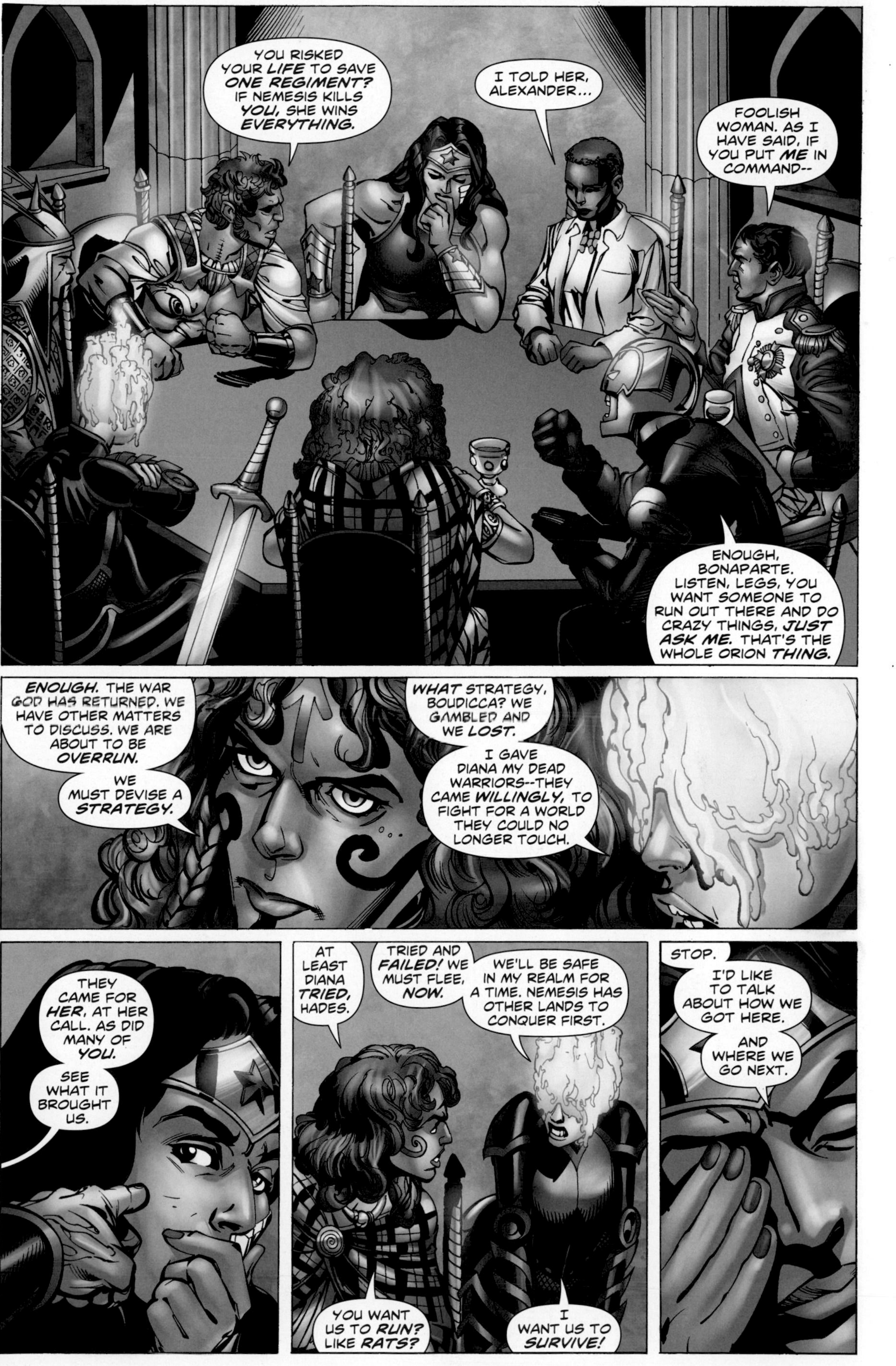
YOU RISKED YOUR LIFE TO SAVE ONE REGIMENT? IF NEMESIS KILLS YOU, SHE WINS EVERYTHING.
I TOLD HER, ALEXANDER...
FOOLISH WOMAN. AS I HAVE SAID, IF YOU PUT ME IN COMMAND--
ENOUGH, BONAPARTE. LISTEN, LEGS, YOU WANT SOMEONE TO RUN OUT THERE AND DO CRAZY THINGS, JUST ASK ME. THAT'S THE WHOLE ORION THING.
ENOUGH. THE WAR GOD HAS RETURNED. WE HAVE OTHER MATTERS TO DISCUSS. WE ARE ABOUT TO BE OVERRUN.
WE MUST DEVISE A STRATEGY.
WHAT STRATEGY, BOUDICCA? WE GAMBLED AND WE LOST.
I GAVE DIANA MY DEAD WARRIORS--THEY CAME WILLINGLY, TO FIGHT FOR A WORLD THEY COULD NO LONGER TOUCH.
THEY CAME FOR HER, AT HER CALL. AS DID MANY OF YOU.
SEE WHAT IT BROUGHT US.
AT LEAST DIANA TRIED, HADES.
TRIED AND FAILED! WE MUST FLEE, NOW.
WE'LL BE SAFE IN MY REALM FOR A TIME. NEMESIS HAS OTHER LANDS TO CONQUER FIRST.
YOU WANT US TO RUN? LIKE RATS?
I WANT US TO SURVIVE!
STOP.
I'D LIKE TO TALK ABOUT HOW WE GOT HERE.
AND WHERE WE GO NEXT.

"NEMESIS. THE ENEMY.

"FEAR OF THE OTHER, STEALING EVERYTHING YOU HAVE EVER LOVED.

"FEAR OF THE NEMESIS. IT IS PRIMAL.

"IT IS THE SOURCE OF HER POWER.

"AS GOD OF WAR, I HAVE WORKED TO DIMINISH THIS SENSE OF OTHER. I BELIEVE, I HAVE ALWAYS BELIEVED, THAT SOMEDAY THERE MIGHT BE NO MORE WAR.

"NO MORE ENEMIES.

"I REACHED OUT TO NEMESIS, ASKED HER TO HELP ME. I EXPLAINED WHAT I WAS TRYING TO DO.

"I... MISJUDGED HER.

"SHE BELIEVED THAT IF I ENDED WAR, THERE WOULD BE NO MORE NEMESIS. I THOUGHT THERE COULD BE LIFE FOR BOTH OF US...A NEW LIFE...BUT SHE COULD NOT SEE IT.

"SHE WANTS A WORLD CONVULSED BY HATRED AND FEAR, AND I AM IN HER WAY."

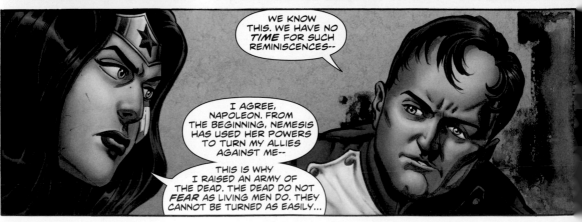

WE KNOW THIS. WE HAVE NO TIME FOR SUCH REMINISCENCES--

I AGREE, NAPOLEON. FROM THE BEGINNING, NEMESIS HAS USED HER POWERS TO TURN MY ALLIES AGAINST ME--

THIS IS WHY I RAISED AN ARMY OF THE DEAD. THE DEAD DO NOT FEAR AS LIVING MEN DO. THEY CANNOT BE TURNED AS EASILY...

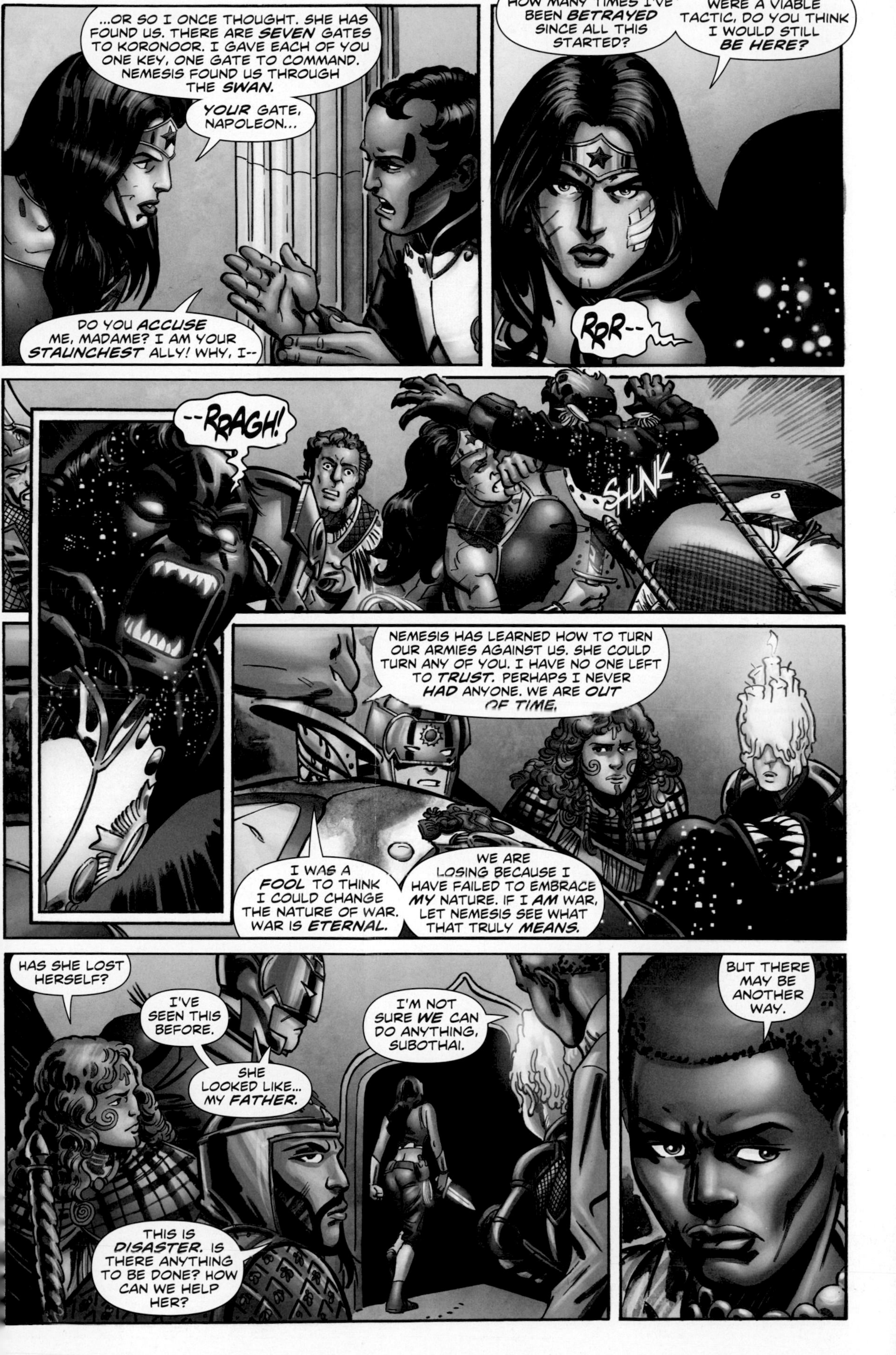
...OR SO I ONCE THOUGHT. SHE HAS FOUND US. THERE ARE SEVEN GATES TO KORONOOR. I GAVE EACH OF YOU ONE KEY, ONE GATE TO COMMAND. NEMESIS FOUND US THROUGH THE SWAN.
YOUR GATE, NAPOLEON...
DO YOU ACCUSE ME, MADAME? I AM YOUR STAUNCHEST ALLY! WHY, I--
DO YOU KNOW HOW MANY TIMES I'VE BEEN BETRAYED SINCE ALL THIS STARTED?
IF BETRAYAL WERE A VIABLE TACTIC, DO YOU THINK I WOULD STILL BE HERE?
RRR--
--RRAGH!
SHUNK
NEMESIS HAS LEARNED HOW TO TURN OUR ARMIES AGAINST US. SHE COULD TURN ANY OF YOU. I HAVE NO ONE LEFT TO TRUST. PERHAPS I NEVER HAD ANYONE. WE ARE OUT OF TIME.
I WAS A FOOL TO THINK I COULD CHANGE THE NATURE OF WAR. WAR IS ETERNAL.
WE ARE LOSING BECAUSE I HAVE FAILED TO EMBRACE MY NATURE. IF I AM WAR, LET NEMESIS SEE WHAT THAT TRULY MEANS.
HAS SHE LOST HERSELF?
I'VE SEEN THIS BEFORE.
SHE LOOKED LIKE... MY FATHER.
I'M NOT SURE WE CAN DO ANYTHING, SUBOTHAI.
THIS IS DISASTER. IS THERE ANYTHING TO BE DONE? HOW CAN WE HELP HER?
BUT THERE MAY BE ANOTHER WAY.

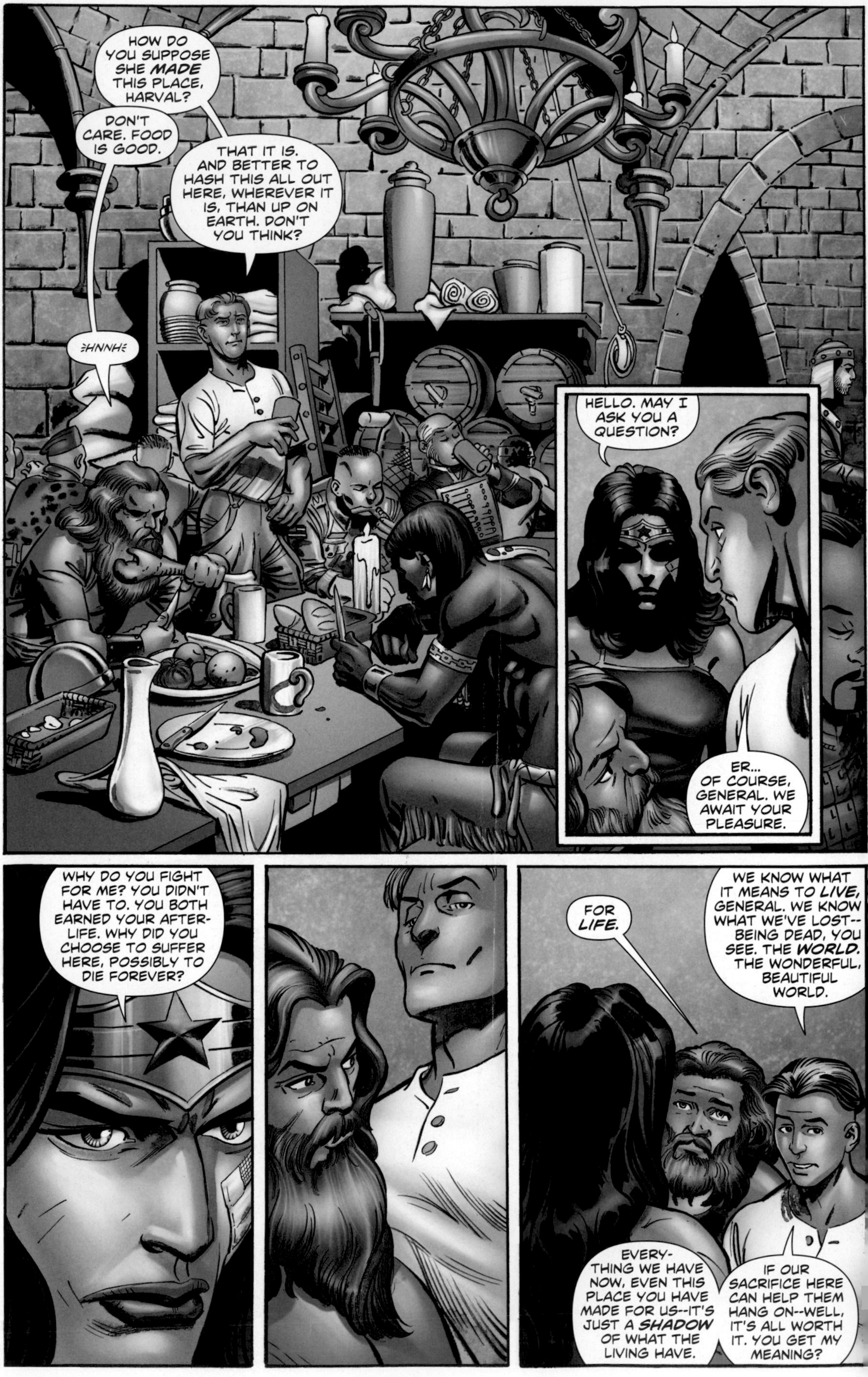

HOW DO YOU SUPPOSE SHE MADE THIS PLACE, HARVAL?
DON'T CARE. FOOD IS GOOD.
THAT IT IS. AND BETTER TO HASH THIS ALL OUT HERE, WHEREVER IT IS, THAN UP ON EARTH. DON'T YOU THINK?
HNNH
HELLO. MAY I ASK YOU A QUESTION?
ER... OF COURSE, GENERAL. WE AWAIT YOUR PLEASURE.
WHY DO YOU FIGHT FOR ME? YOU DIDN'T HAVE TO. YOU BOTH EARNED YOUR AFTER-LIFE. WHY DID YOU CHOOSE TO SUFFER HERE, POSSIBLY TO DIE FOREVER?
FOR LIFE.
WE KNOW WHAT IT MEANS TO LIVE, GENERAL. WE KNOW WHAT WE'VE LOST--BEING DEAD, YOU SEE. THE WORLD. THE WONDERFUL, BEAUTIFUL WORLD.
EVERY-THING WE HAVE NOW, EVEN THIS PLACE YOU HAVE MADE FOR US--IT'S JUST A SHADOW OF WHAT THE LIVING HAVE.
IF OUR SACRIFICE HERE CAN HELP THEM HANG ON--WELL, IT'S ALL WORTH IT. YOU GET MY MEANING?

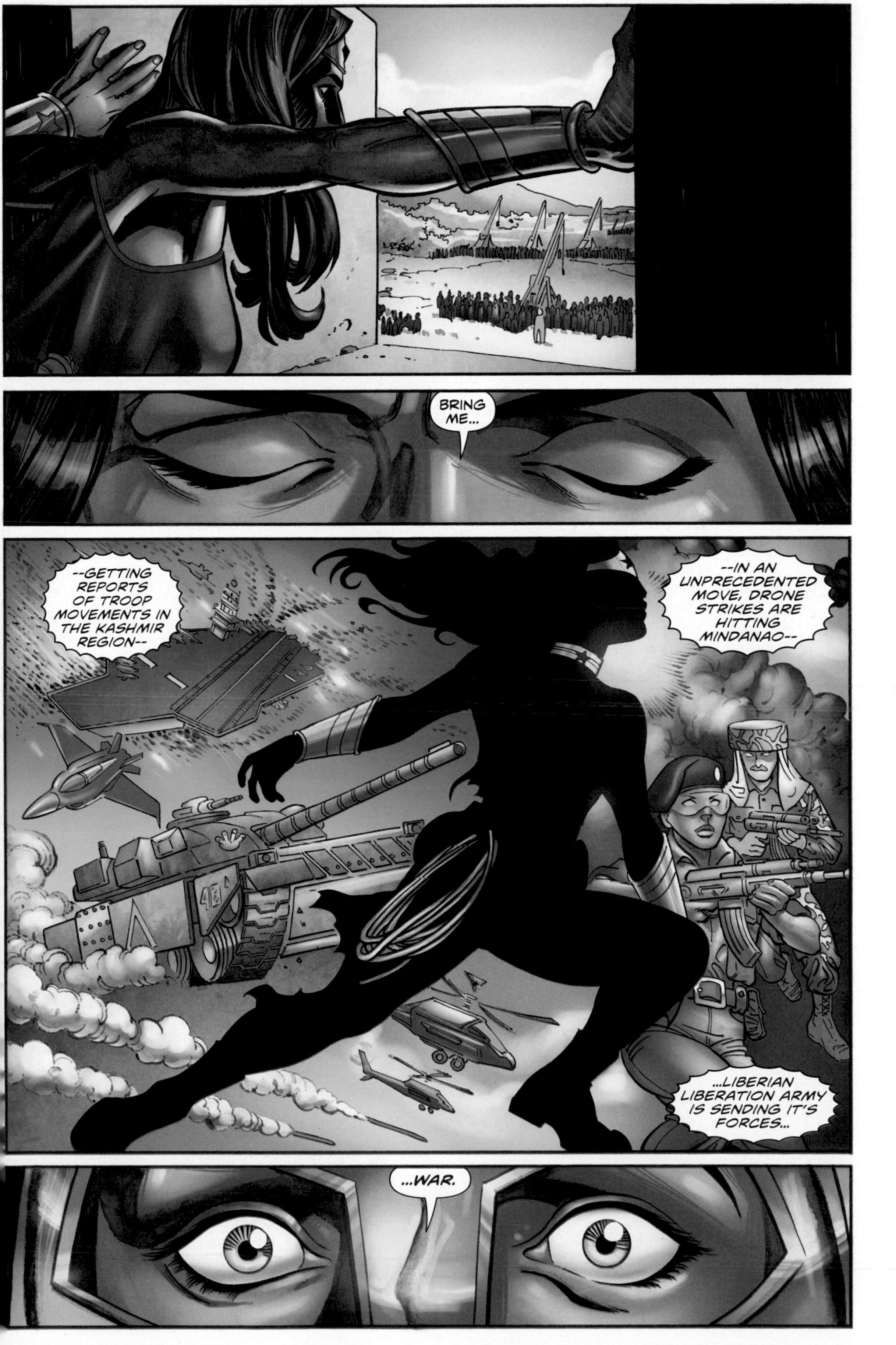
BRING ME...
--GETTING REPORTS OF TROOP MOVEMENTS IN THE KASHMIR REGION--
--IN AN UNPRECEDENTED MOVE, DRONE STRIKES ARE HITTING MINDANAO--
...LIBERIAN LIBERATION ARMY IS SENDING IT'S FORCES...
...WAR.

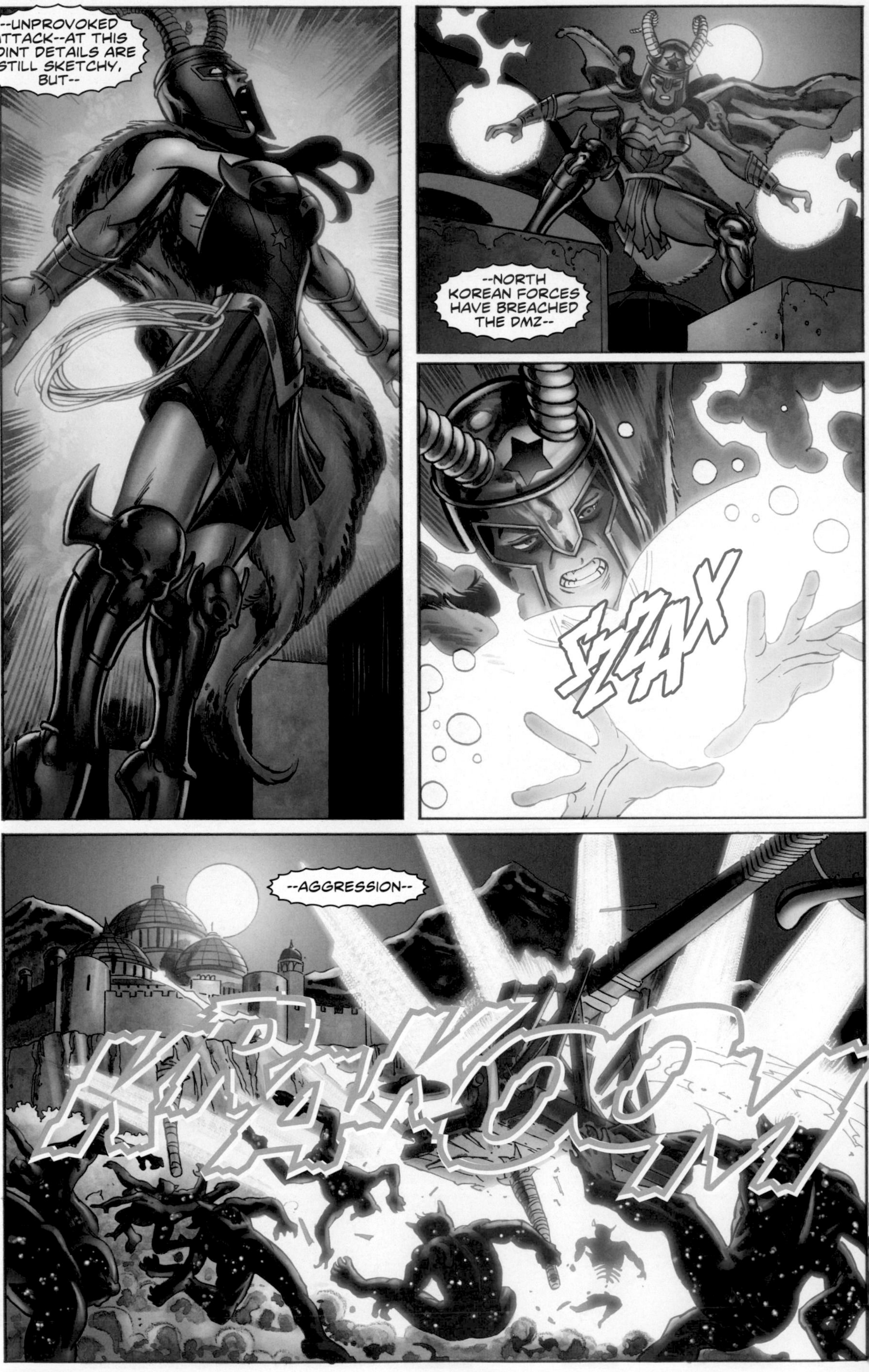
--UNPROVOKED ATTACK--AT THIS POINT DETAILS ARE STILL SKETCHY, BUT--
--NORTH KOREAN FORCES HAVE BREACHED THE DMZ--
SZZAK
--AGGRESSION--
KRAKOOM

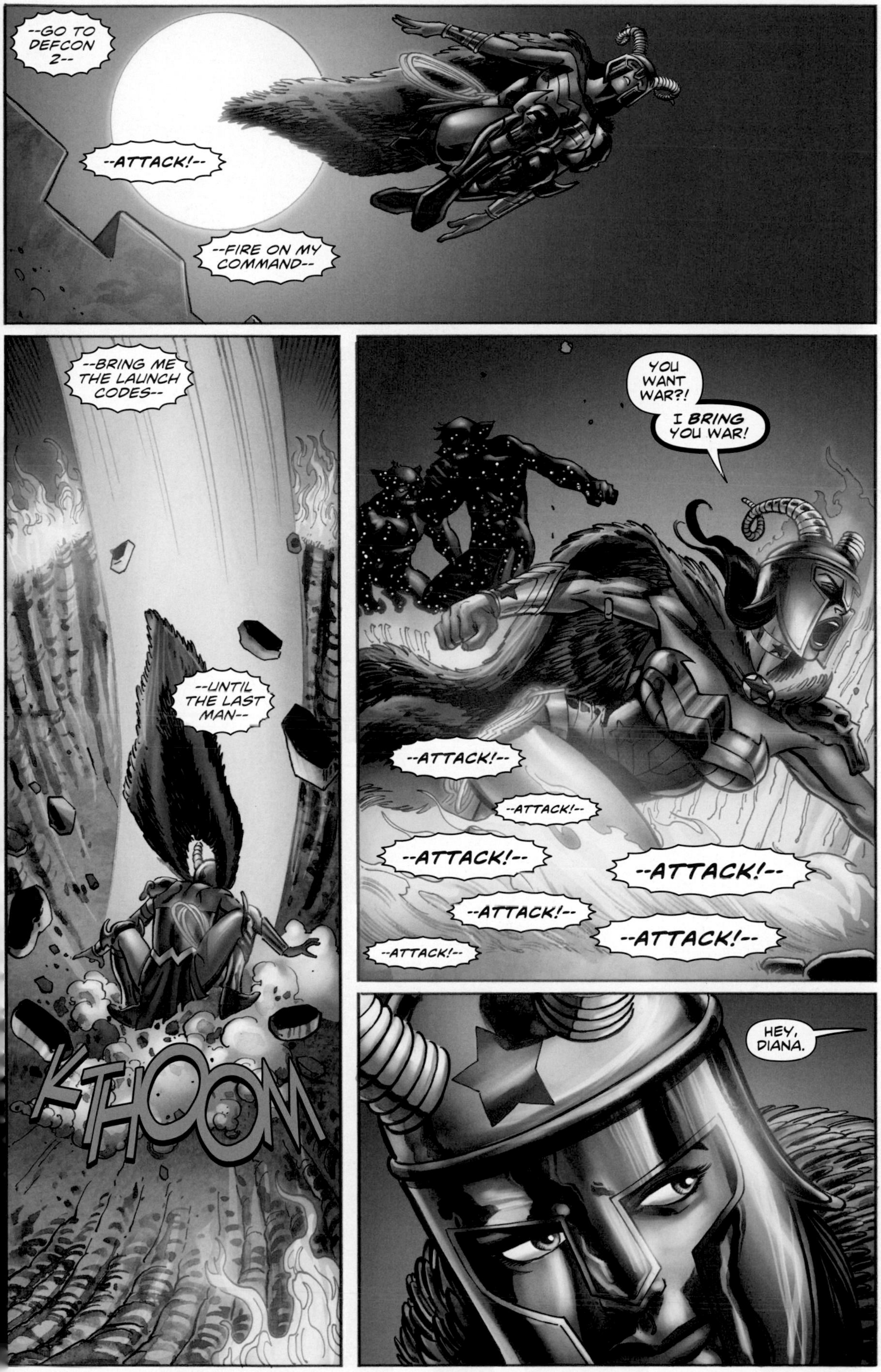

--GO TO DEFCON 2--
--ATTACK!--
--FIRE ON MY COMMAND--
--BRING ME THE LAUNCH CODES--
--UNTIL THE LAST MAN--
KTHOOM
YOU WANT WAR?!
I BRING YOU WAR!
--ATTACK!--
--ATTACK!--
--ATTACK!--
--ATTACK!--
--ATTACK!--
--ATTACK!--
--ATTACK!--
HEY, DIANA.

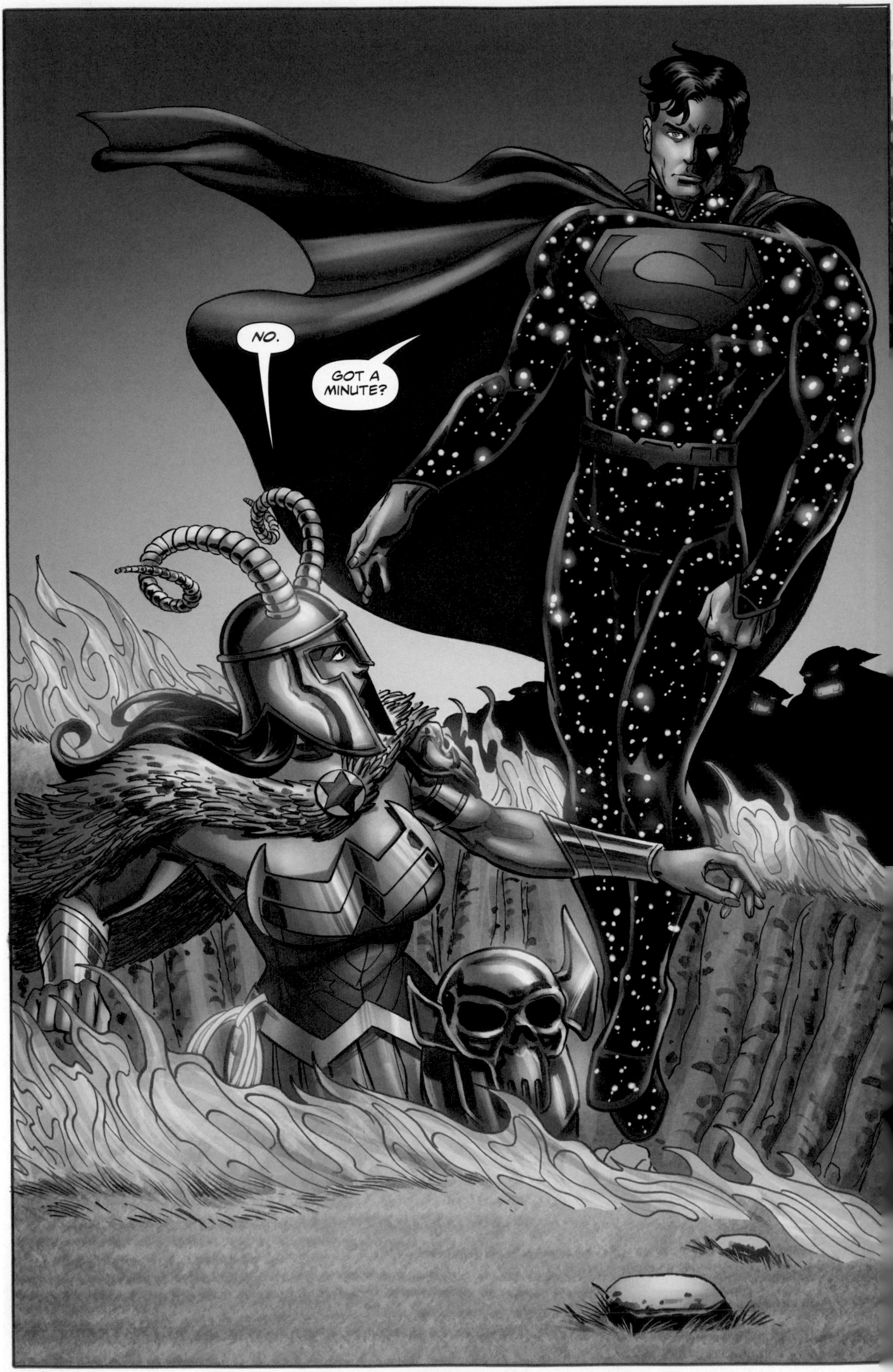
GOT A MINUTE?
NO.

WAR AND PEACE
BART SEARS artist
cover by **TOM RANEY** with **PETE PANTAZIS**

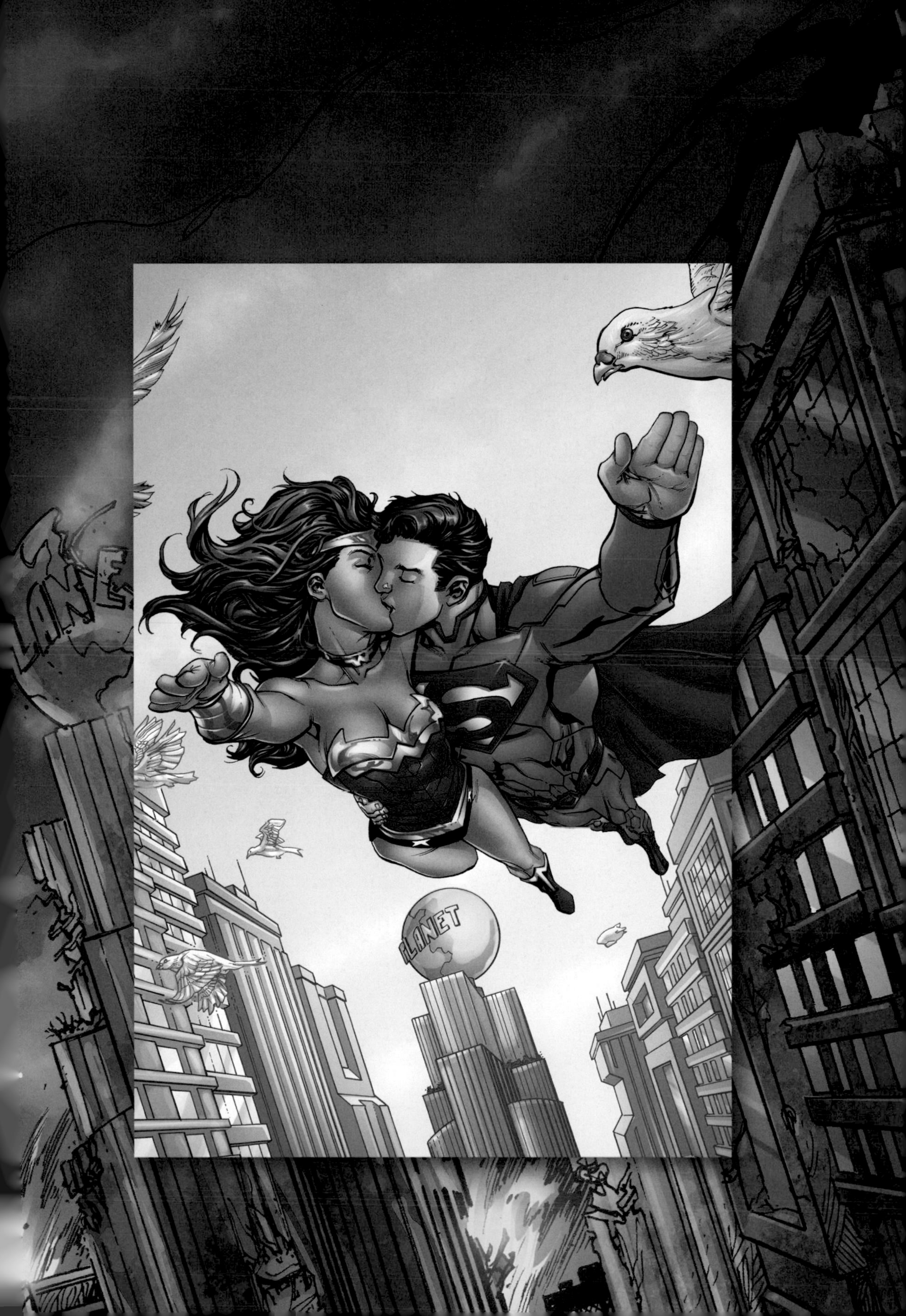
PLANET

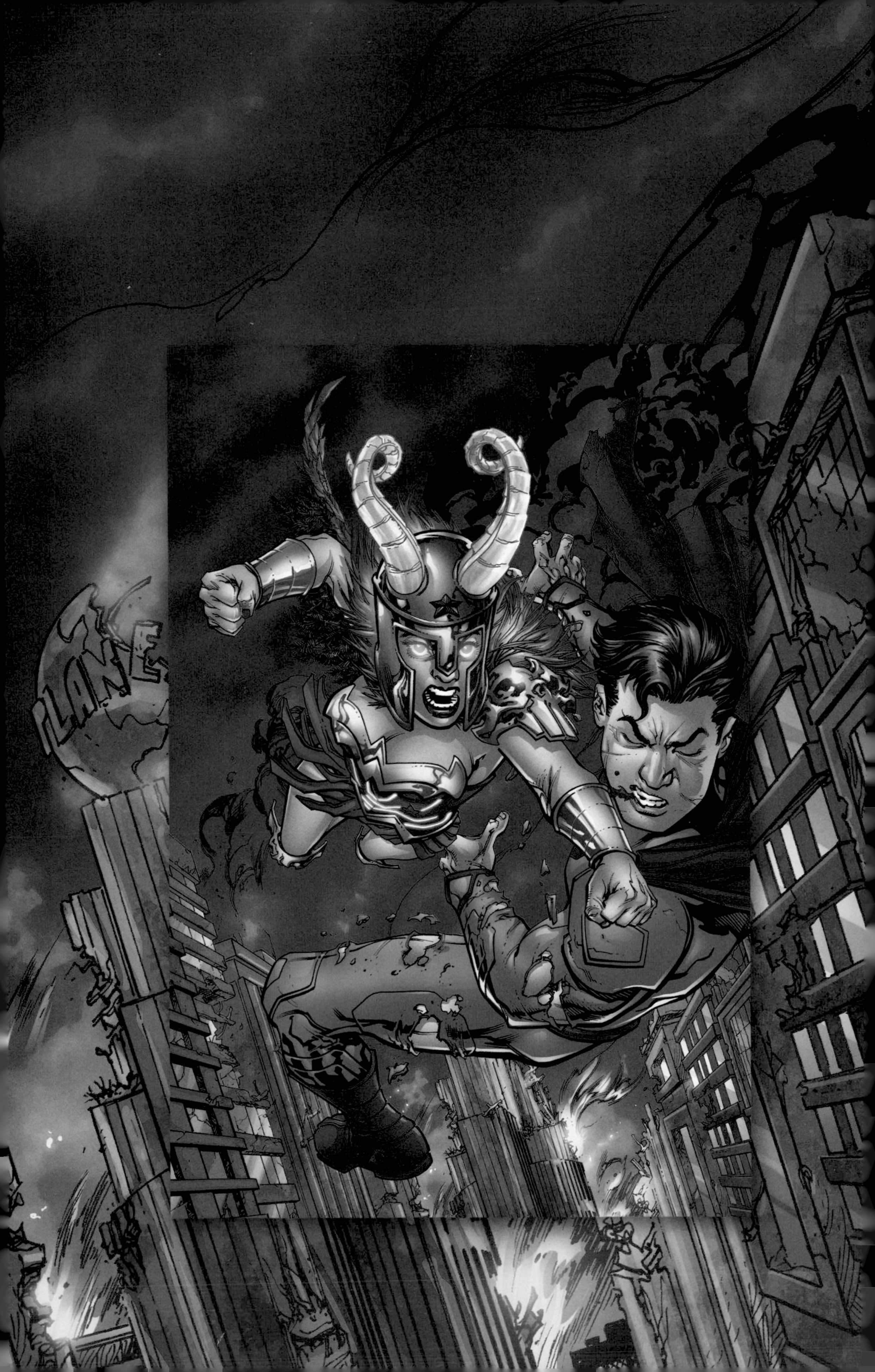

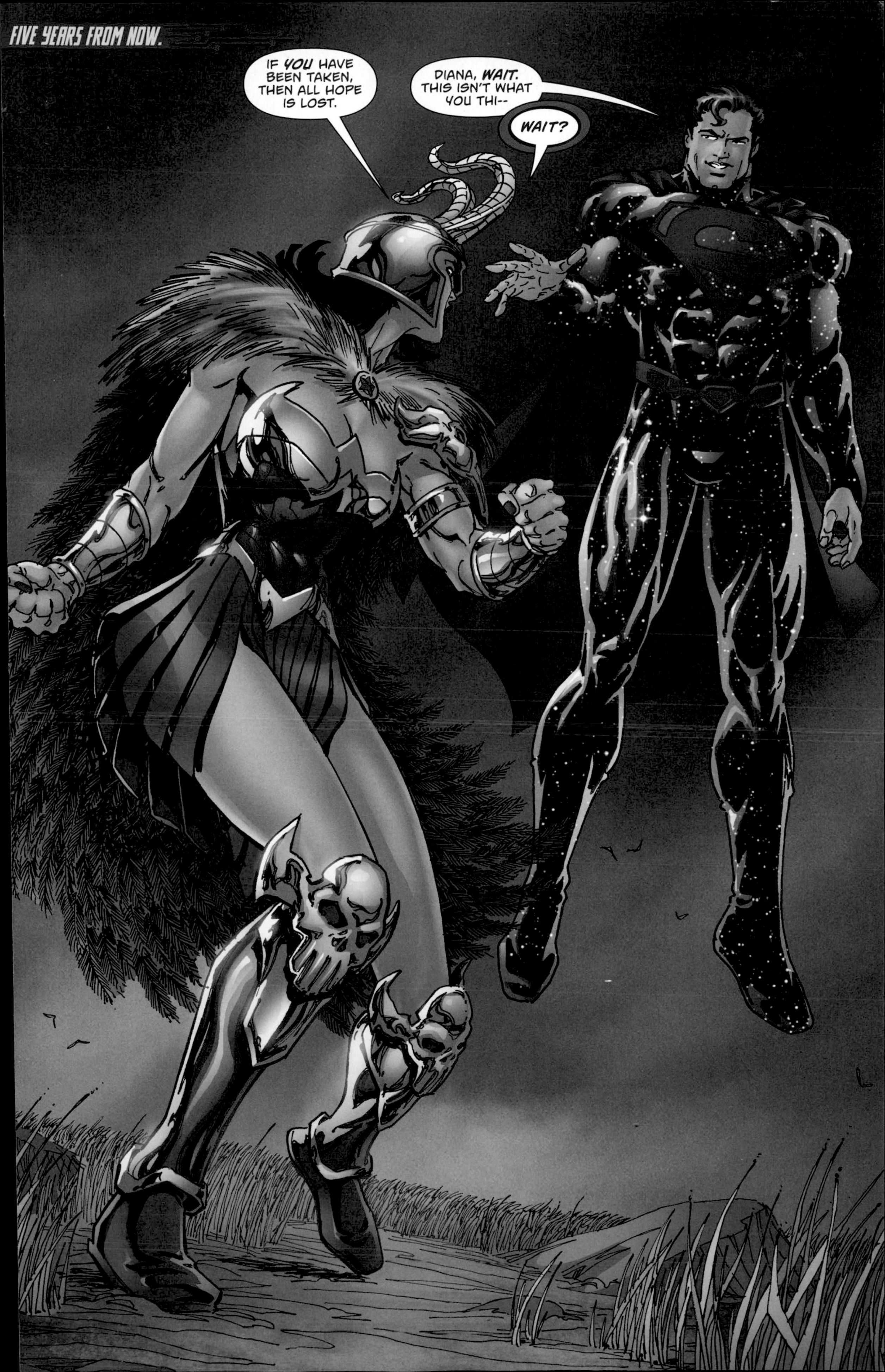
FIVE YEARS FROM NOW.
IF YOU HAVE BEEN TAKEN, THEN ALL HOPE IS LOST.
DIANA, WAIT. THIS ISN'T WHAT YOU THI--
WAIT?

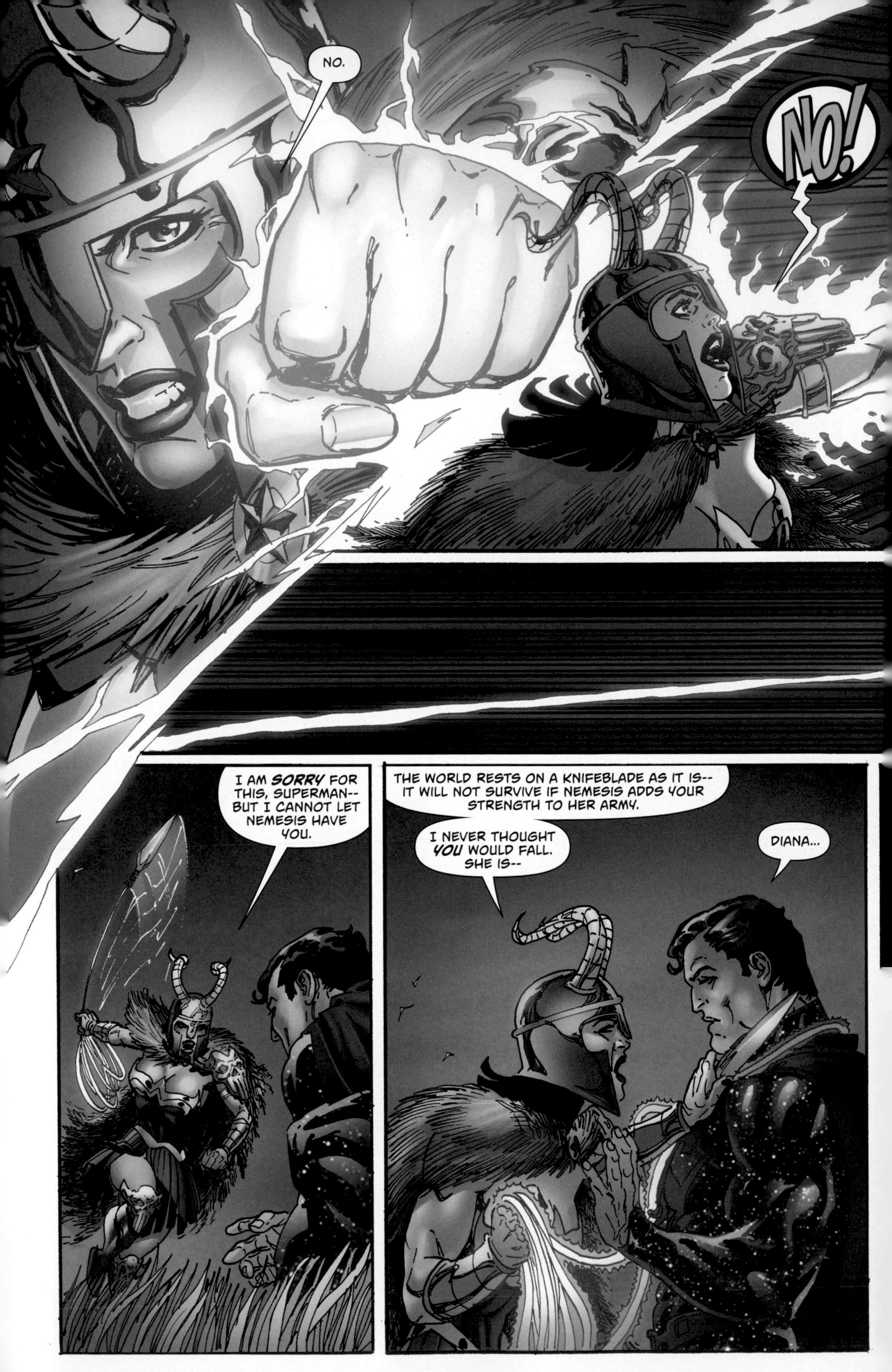
NO.
NO!
I AM SORRY FOR THIS, SUPERMAN-- BUT I CANNOT LET NEMESIS HAVE YOU.
THE WORLD RESTS ON A KNIFEBLADE AS IT IS-- IT WILL NOT SURVIVE IF NEMESIS ADDS YOUR STRENGTH TO HER ARMY.
I NEVER THOUGHT YOU WOULD FALL. SHE IS--
DIANA...

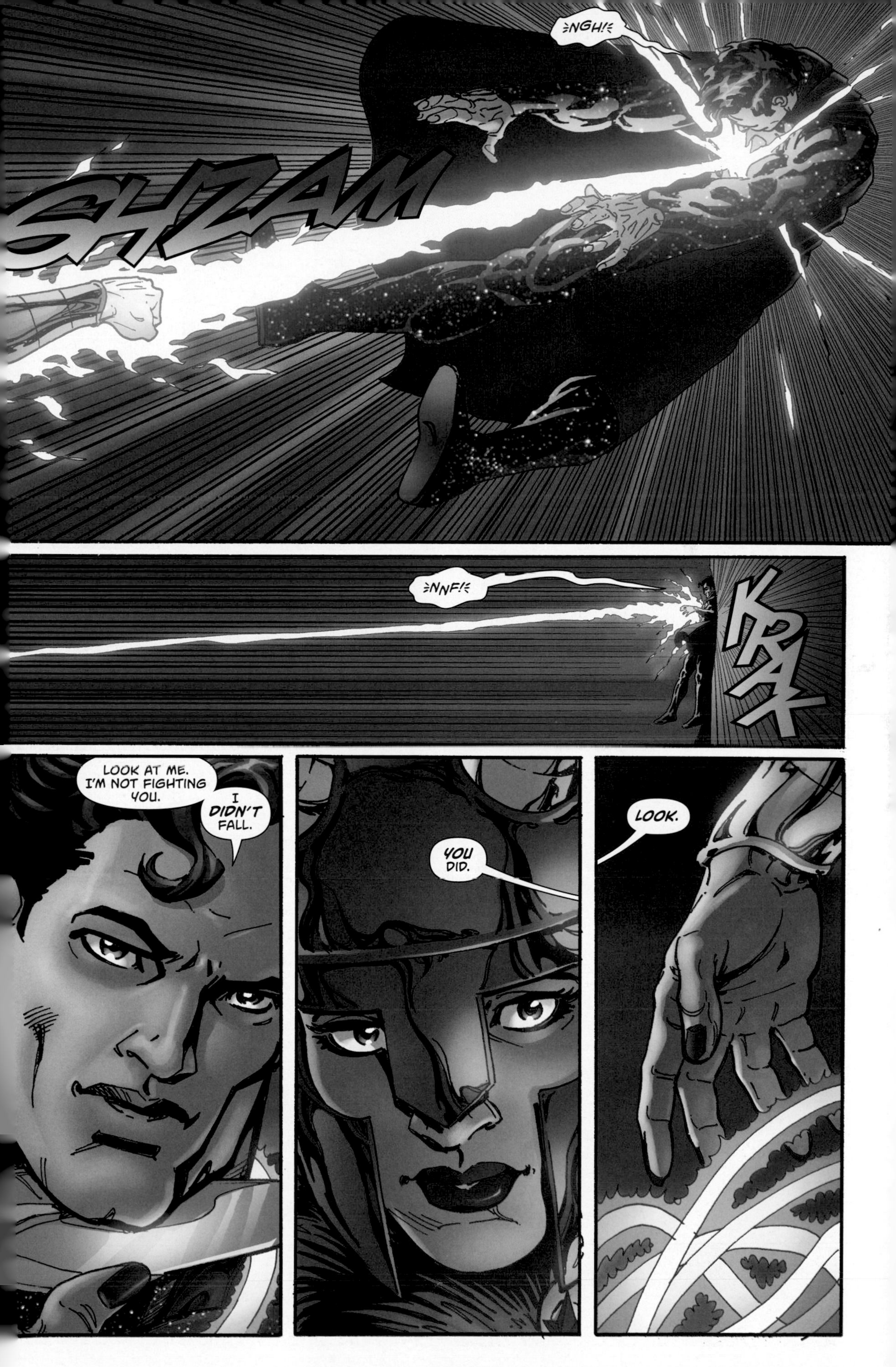
NGH!
SHZAM
NNF!
KRAK
LOOK AT ME. I'M NOT FIGHTING YOU.
I DIDN'T FALL.
YOU DID.
LOOK.

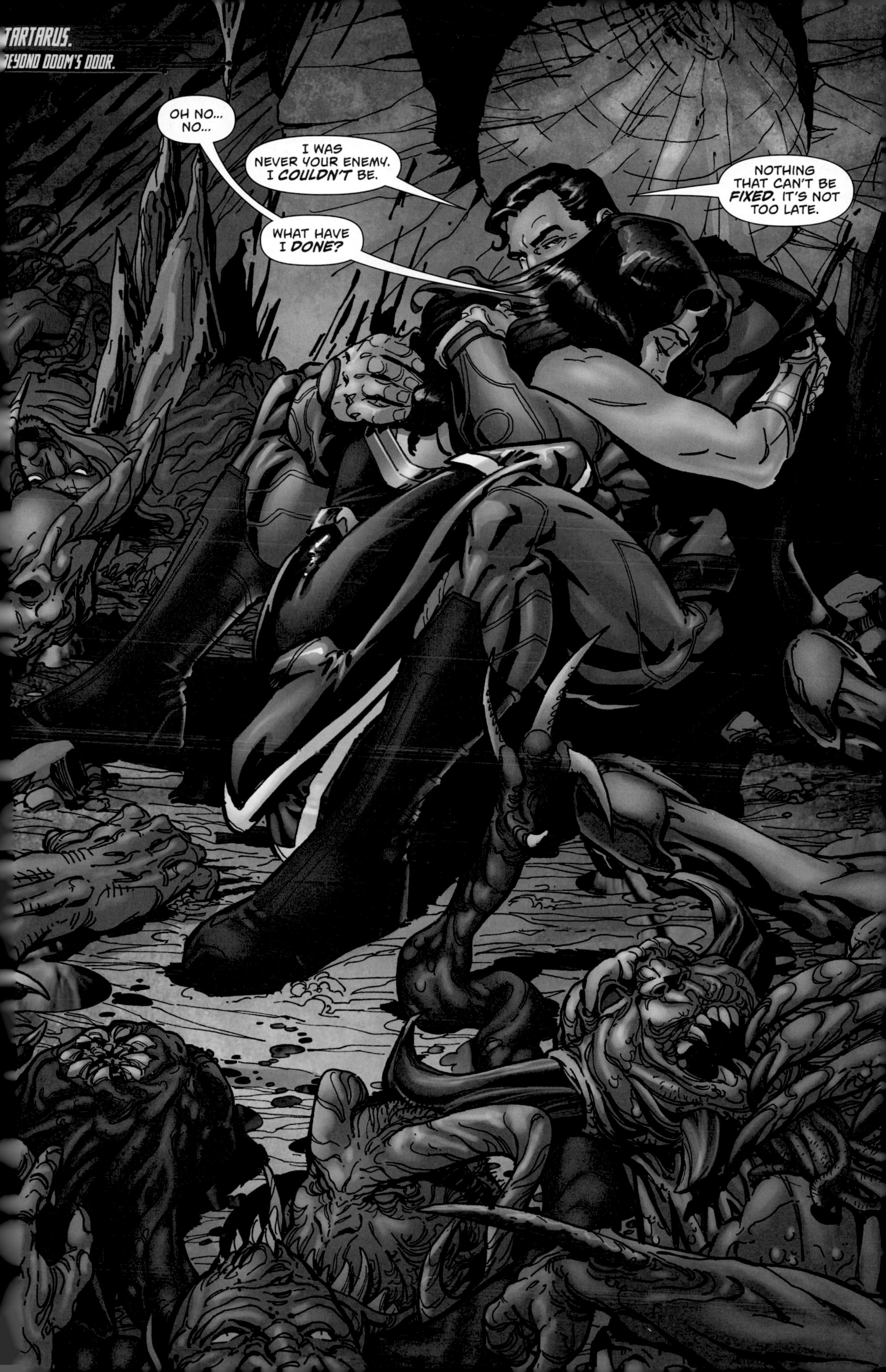
TARTARUS.
BEYOND DOOM'S DOOR.
OH NO... NO...
I WAS NEVER YOUR ENEMY. I *COULDN'T* BE.
NOTHING THAT CAN'T BE *FIXED.* IT'S NOT TOO LATE.
WHAT HAVE I *DONE?*

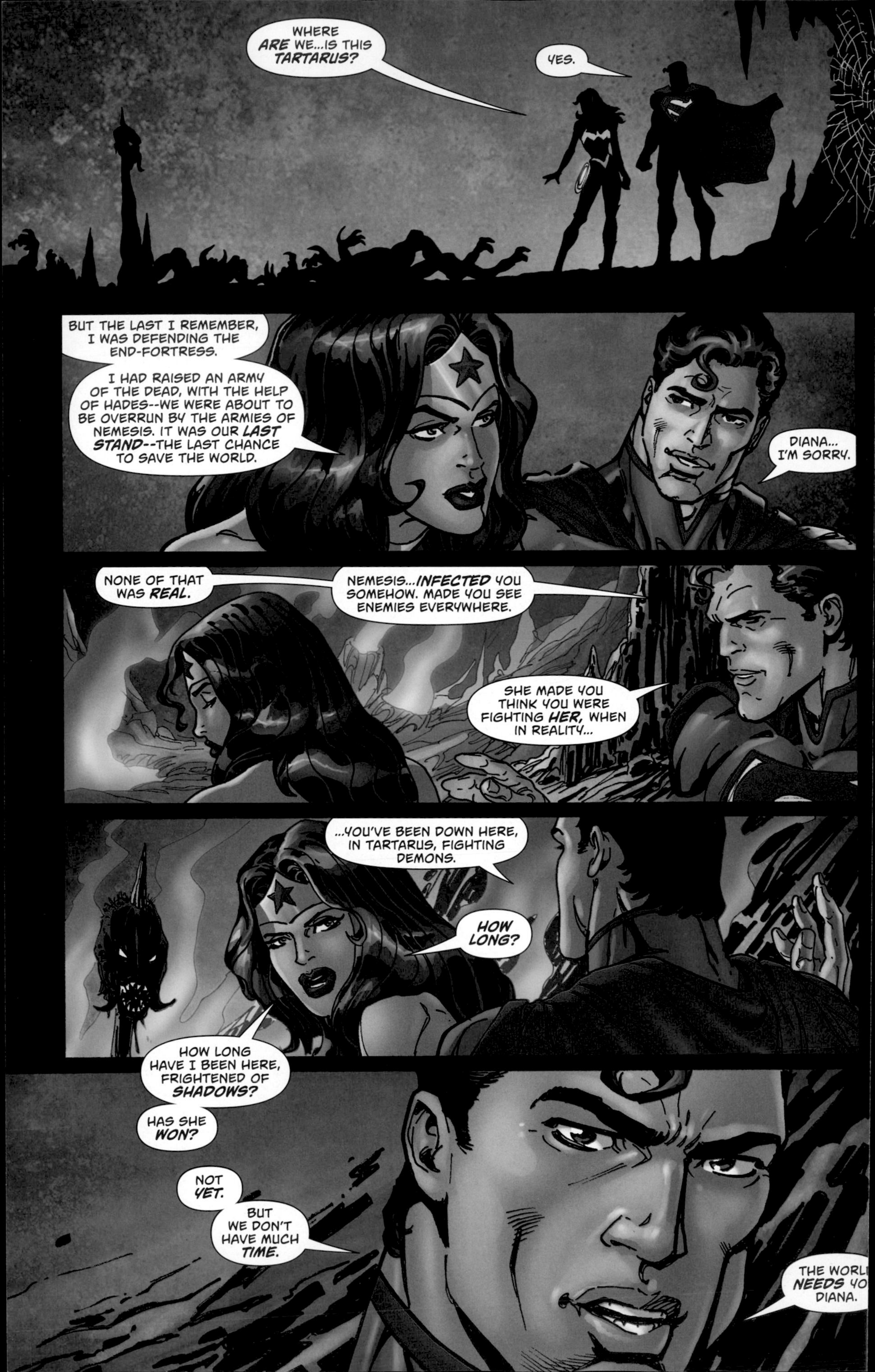

WHERE ARE WE...IS THIS TARTARUS?
YES.
BUT THE LAST I REMEMBER, I WAS DEFENDING THE END-FORTRESS.
I HAD RAISED AN ARMY OF THE DEAD, WITH THE HELP OF HADES--WE WERE ABOUT TO BE OVERRUN BY THE ARMIES OF NEMESIS. IT WAS OUR LAST STAND--THE LAST CHANCE TO SAVE THE WORLD.
DIANA... I'M SORRY.
NONE OF THAT WAS REAL.
NEMESIS...INFECTED YOU SOMEHOW. MADE YOU SEE ENEMIES EVERYWHERE.
SHE MADE YOU THINK YOU WERE FIGHTING HER, WHEN IN REALITY...
...YOU'VE BEEN DOWN HERE, IN TARTARUS, FIGHTING DEMONS.
HOW LONG?
HOW LONG HAVE I BEEN HERE, FRIGHTENED OF SHADOWS?
HAS SHE WON?
NOT YET.
BUT WE DON'T HAVE MUCH TIME.

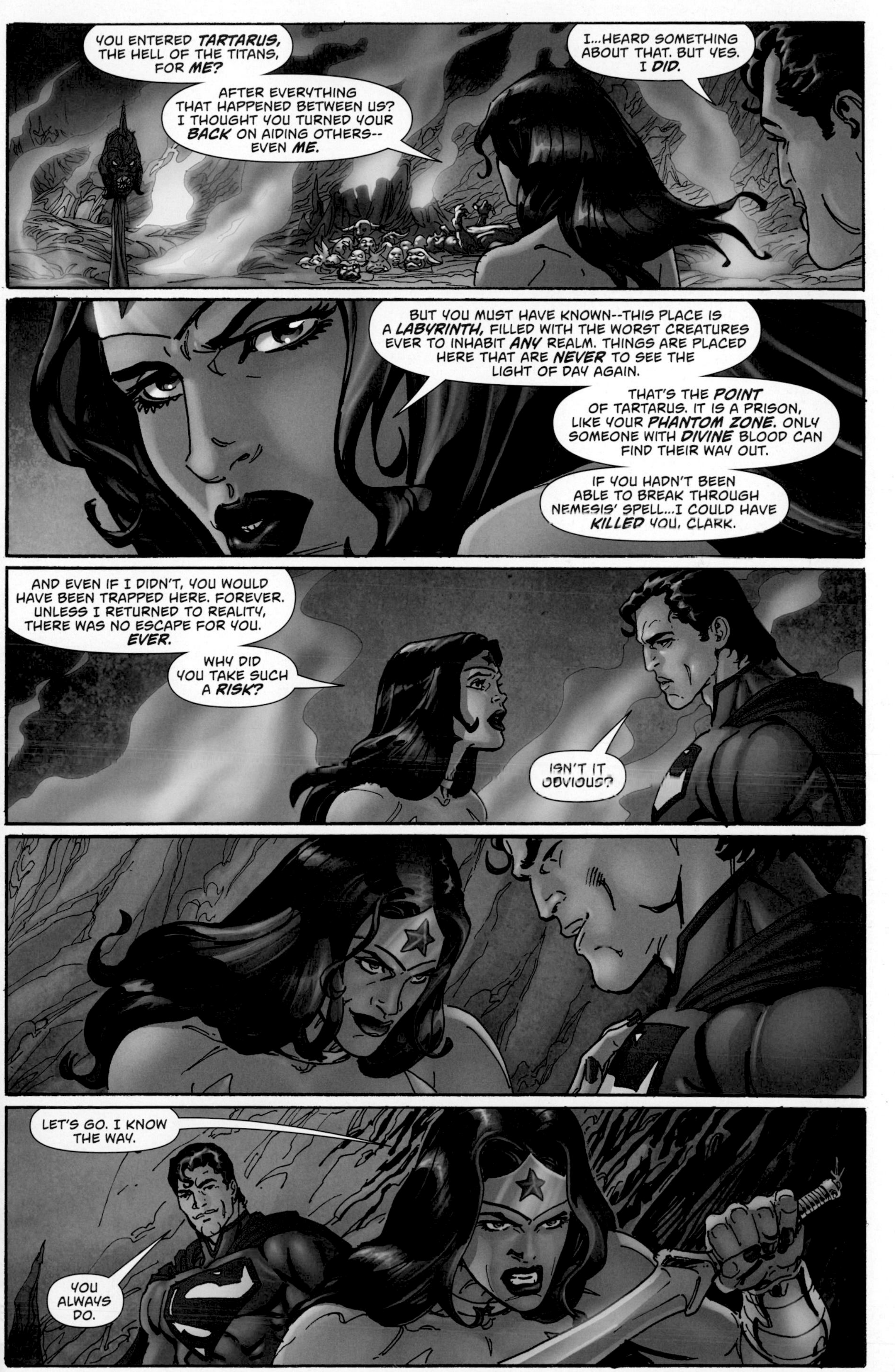
YOU ENTERED TARTARUS, THE HELL OF THE TITANS, FOR ME?
AFTER EVERYTHING THAT HAPPENED BETWEEN US? I THOUGHT YOU TURNED YOUR BACK ON AIDING OTHERS-- EVEN ME.
I...HEARD SOMETHING ABOUT THAT. BUT YES. I DID.
BUT YOU MUST HAVE KNOWN--THIS PLACE IS A LABYRINTH, FILLED WITH THE WORST CREATURES EVER TO INHABIT ANY REALM. THINGS ARE PLACED HERE THAT ARE NEVER TO SEE THE LIGHT OF DAY AGAIN.
THAT'S THE POINT OF TARTARUS. IT IS A PRISON, LIKE YOUR PHANTOM ZONE. ONLY SOMEONE WITH DIVINE BLOOD CAN FIND THEIR WAY OUT.
IF YOU HADN'T BEEN ABLE TO BREAK THROUGH NEMESIS' SPELL...I COULD HAVE KILLED YOU, CLARK.
AND EVEN IF I DIDN'T, YOU WOULD HAVE BEEN TRAPPED HERE. FOREVER. UNLESS I RETURNED TO REALITY, THERE WAS NO ESCAPE FOR YOU. EVER.
WHY DID YOU TAKE SUCH A RISK?
ISN'T IT OBVIOUS?
LET'S GO. I KNOW THE WAY.
YOU ALWAYS DO.

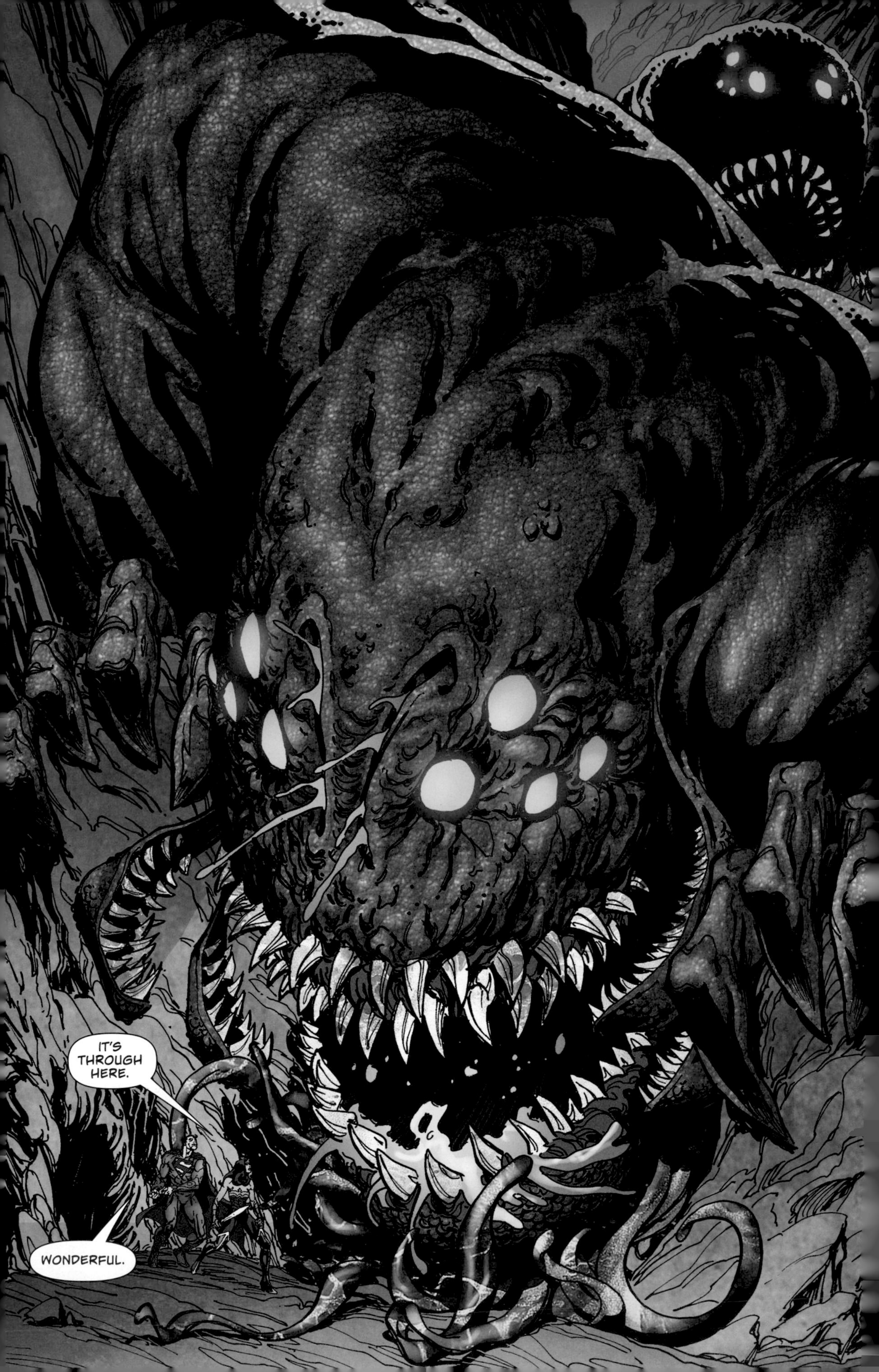
IT'S THROUGH HERE.
WONDERFUL.

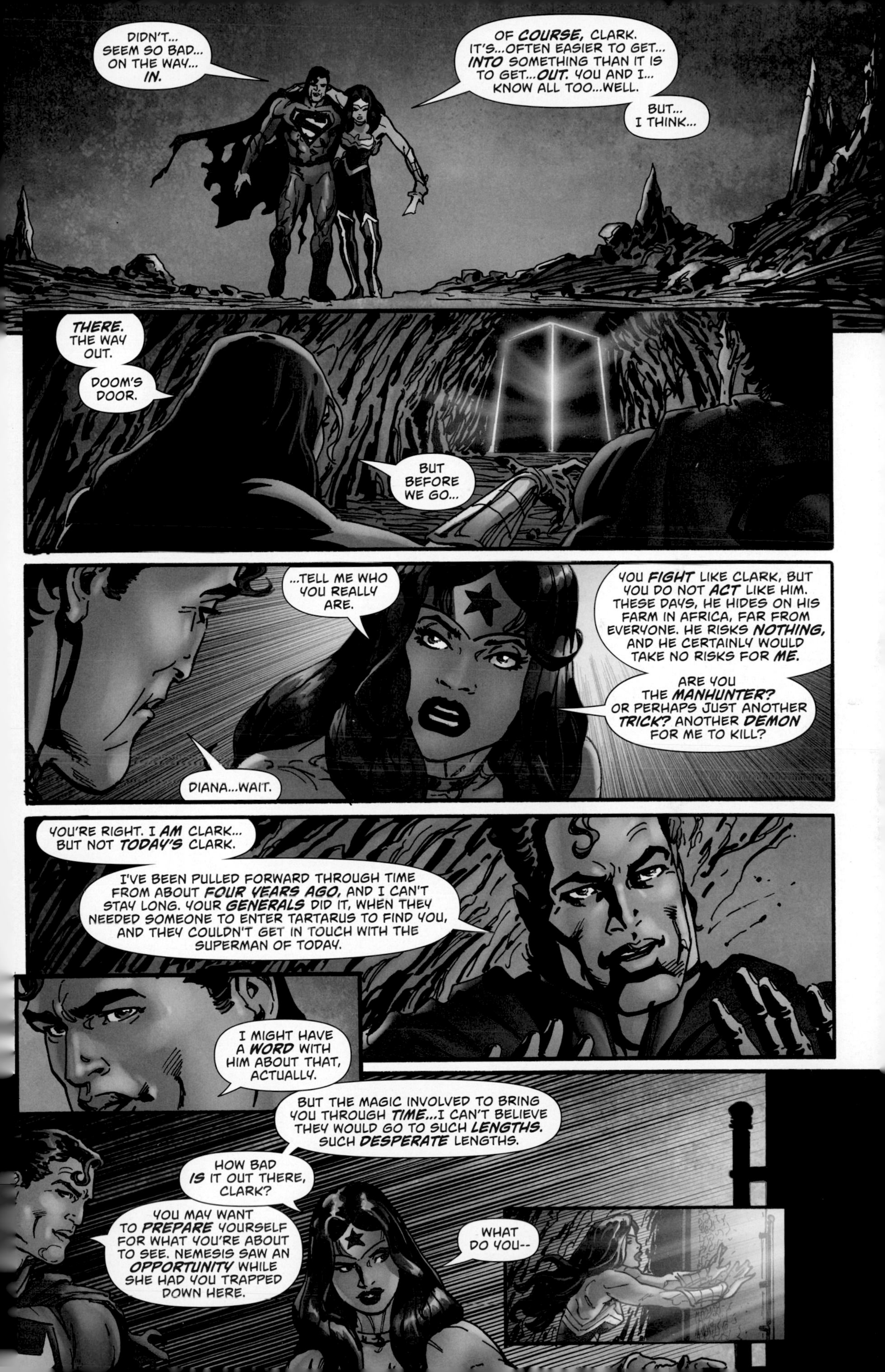
DIDN'T... SEEM SO BAD... ON THE WAY... IN.
OF COURSE, CLARK. IT'S...OFTEN EASIER TO GET... INTO SOMETHING THAN IT IS TO GET...OUT. YOU AND I... KNOW ALL TOO...WELL.
BUT... I THINK...
THERE. THE WAY OUT.
DOOM'S DOOR.
BUT BEFORE WE GO...
...TELL ME WHO YOU REALLY ARE.
YOU FIGHT LIKE CLARK, BUT YOU DO NOT ACT LIKE HIM. THESE DAYS, HE HIDES ON HIS FARM IN AFRICA, FAR FROM EVERYONE. HE RISKS NOTHING, AND HE CERTAINLY WOULD TAKE NO RISKS FOR ME.
ARE YOU THE MANHUNTER? OR PERHAPS JUST ANOTHER TRICK? ANOTHER DEMON FOR ME TO KILL?
DIANA...WAIT.
YOU'RE RIGHT. I AM CLARK... BUT NOT TODAY'S CLARK.
I'VE BEEN PULLED FORWARD THROUGH TIME FROM ABOUT FOUR YEARS AGO, AND I CAN'T STAY LONG. YOUR GENERALS DID IT, WHEN THEY NEEDED SOMEONE TO ENTER TARTARUS TO FIND YOU, AND THEY COULDN'T GET IN TOUCH WITH THE SUPERMAN OF TODAY.
I MIGHT HAVE A WORD WITH HIM ABOUT THAT, ACTUALLY.
BUT THE MAGIC INVOLVED TO BRING YOU THROUGH TIME...I CAN'T BELIEVE THEY WOULD GO TO SUCH LENGTHS. SUCH DESPERATE LENGTHS.
HOW BAD IS IT OUT THERE, CLARK?
YOU MAY WANT TO PREPARE YOURSELF FOR WHAT YOU'RE ABOUT TO SEE. NEMESIS SAW AN OPPORTUNITY WHILE SHE HAD YOU TRAPPED DOWN HERE.
WHAT DO YOU--

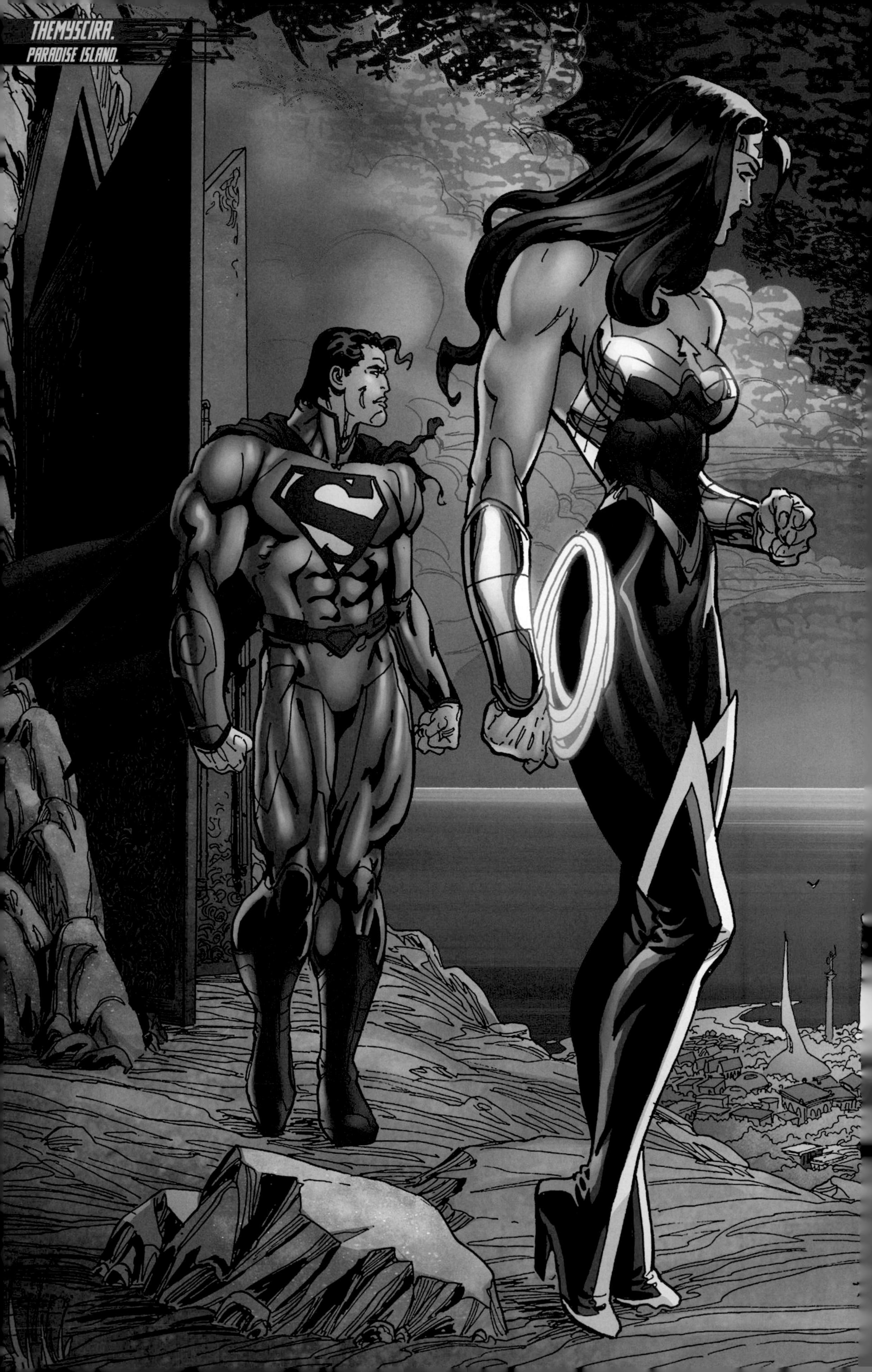
THEMYSCIRA.
PARADISE ISLAND.

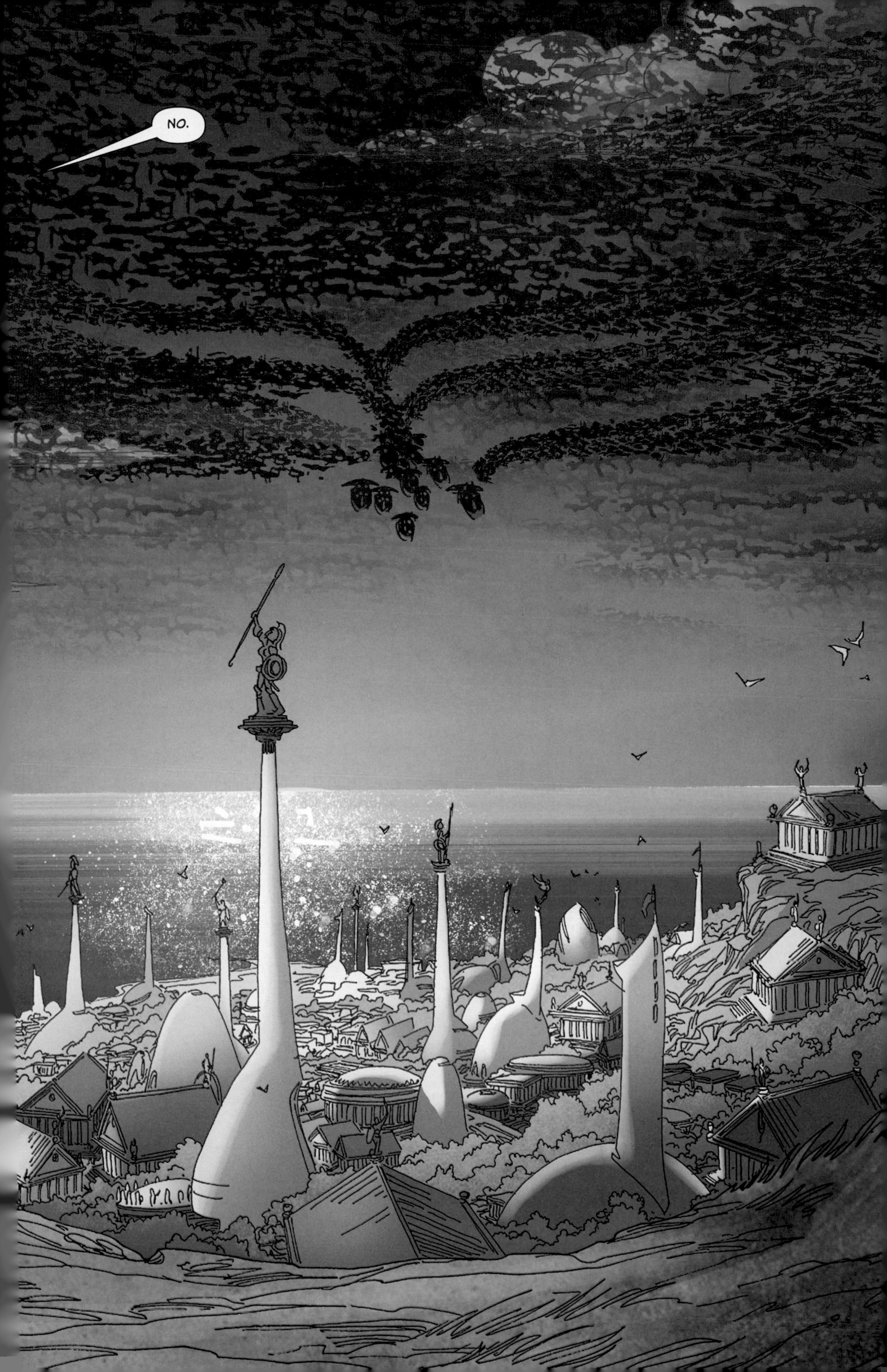
NO.

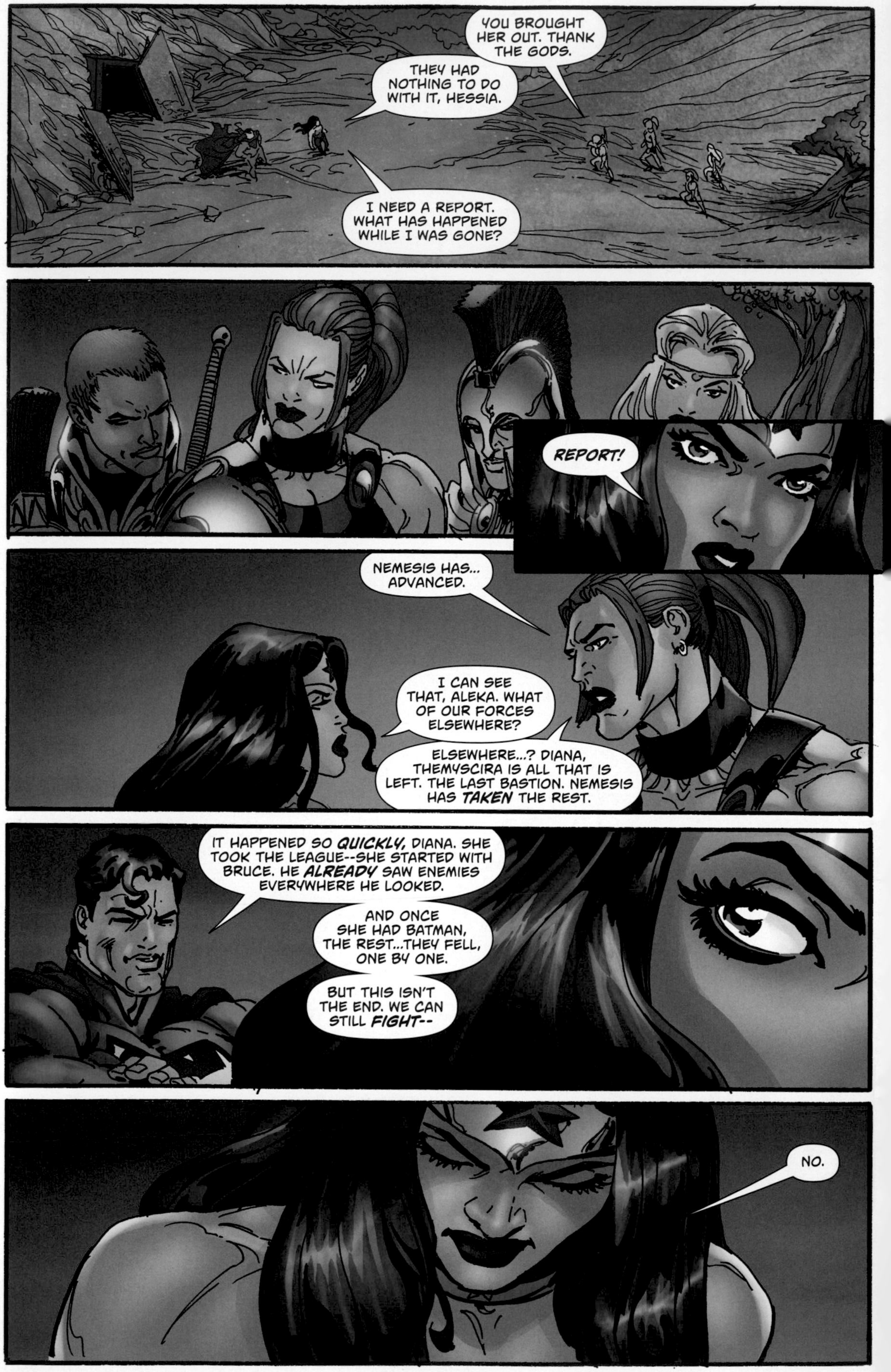
YOU BROUGHT HER OUT. THANK THE GODS.
THEY HAD NOTHING TO DO WITH IT, HESSIA.
I NEED A REPORT. WHAT HAS HAPPENED WHILE I WAS GONE?
REPORT!
NEMESIS HAS... ADVANCED.
I CAN SEE THAT, ALEKA. WHAT OF OUR FORCES ELSEWHERE?
ELSEWHERE...? DIANA, THEMYSCIRA IS ALL THAT IS LEFT. THE LAST BASTION. NEMESIS HAS TAKEN THE REST.
IT HAPPENED SO QUICKLY, DIANA. SHE TOOK THE LEAGUE--SHE STARTED WITH BRUCE. HE ALREADY SAW ENEMIES EVERYWHERE HE LOOKED.
AND ONCE SHE HAD BATMAN, THE REST...THEY FELL, ONE BY ONE.
BUT THIS ISN'T THE END. WE CAN STILL FIGHT--
NO.

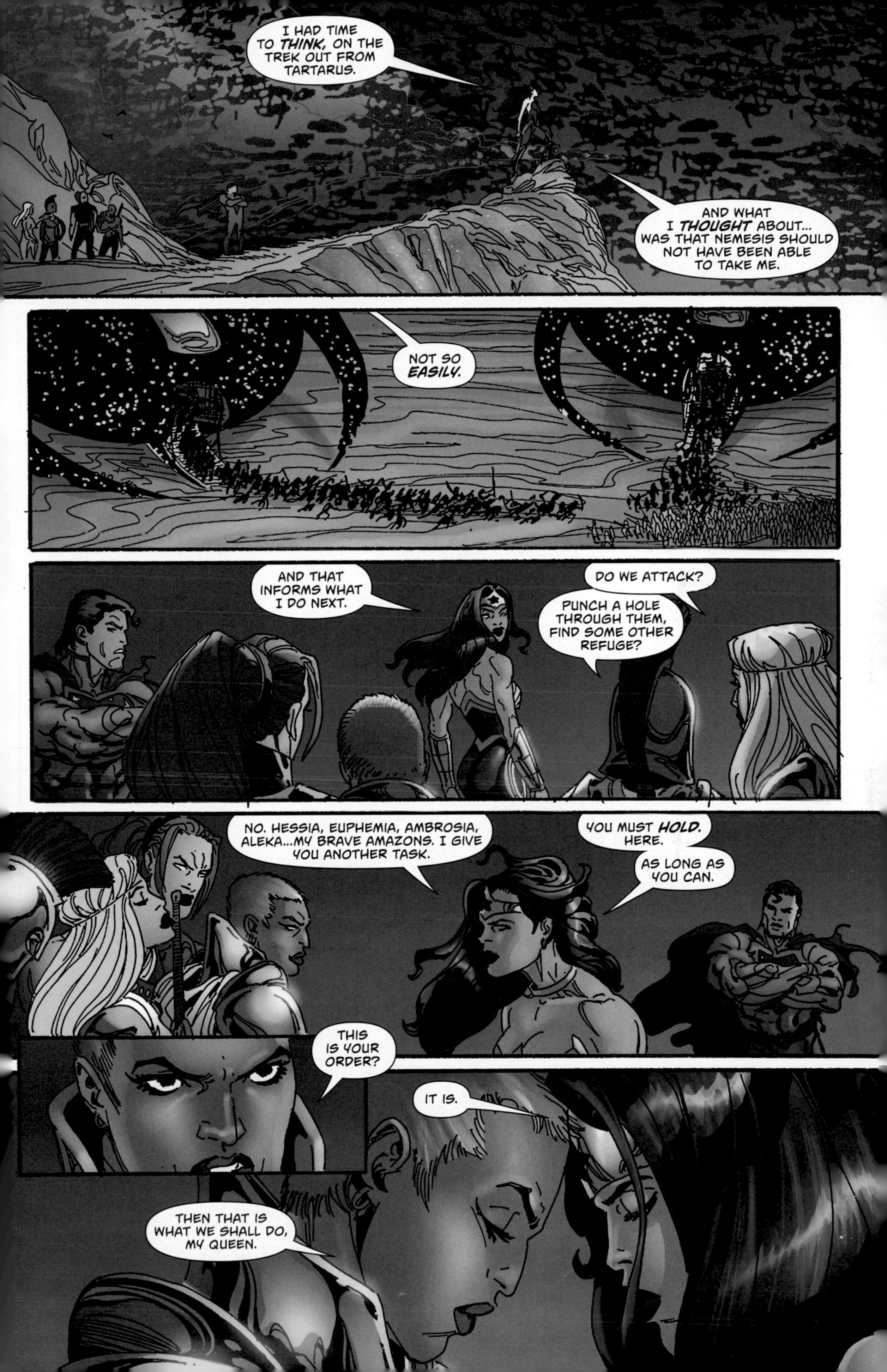
I HAD TIME TO THINK, ON THE TREK OUT FROM TARTARUS.
AND WHAT I THOUGHT ABOUT... WAS THAT NEMESIS SHOULD NOT HAVE BEEN ABLE TO TAKE ME.
NOT SO EASILY.
AND THAT INFORMS WHAT I DO NEXT.
DO WE ATTACK?
PUNCH A HOLE THROUGH THEM, FIND SOME OTHER REFUGE?
NO. HESSIA, EUPHEMIA, AMBROSIA, ALEKA...MY BRAVE AMAZONS. I GIVE YOU ANOTHER TASK.
YOU MUST HOLD. HERE.
AS LONG AS YOU CAN.
THIS IS YOUR ORDER?
IT IS.
THEN THAT IS WHAT WE SHALL DO, MY QUEEN.

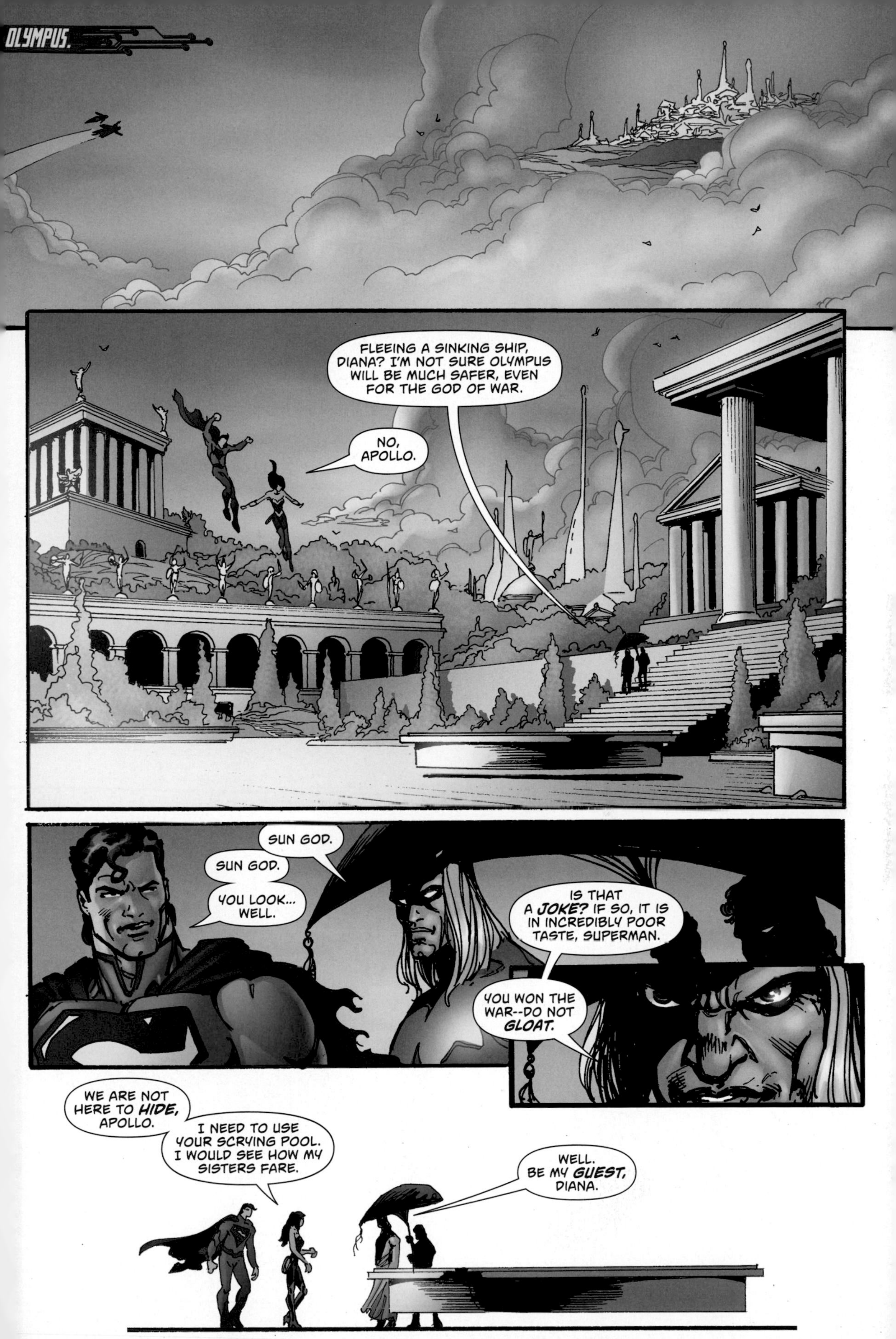
OLYMPUS.
FLEEING A SINKING SHIP, DIANA? I'M NOT SURE OLYMPUS WILL BE MUCH SAFER, EVEN FOR THE GOD OF WAR.
NO, APOLLO.
SUN GOD.
SUN GOD.
YOU LOOK... WELL.
IS THAT A JOKE? IF SO, IT IS IN INCREDIBLY POOR TASTE, SUPERMAN.
YOU WON THE WAR--DO NOT GLOAT.
WE ARE NOT HERE TO HIDE, APOLLO.
I NEED TO USE YOUR SCRYING POOL. I WOULD SEE HOW MY SISTERS FARE.
WELL. BE MY GUEST, DIANA.

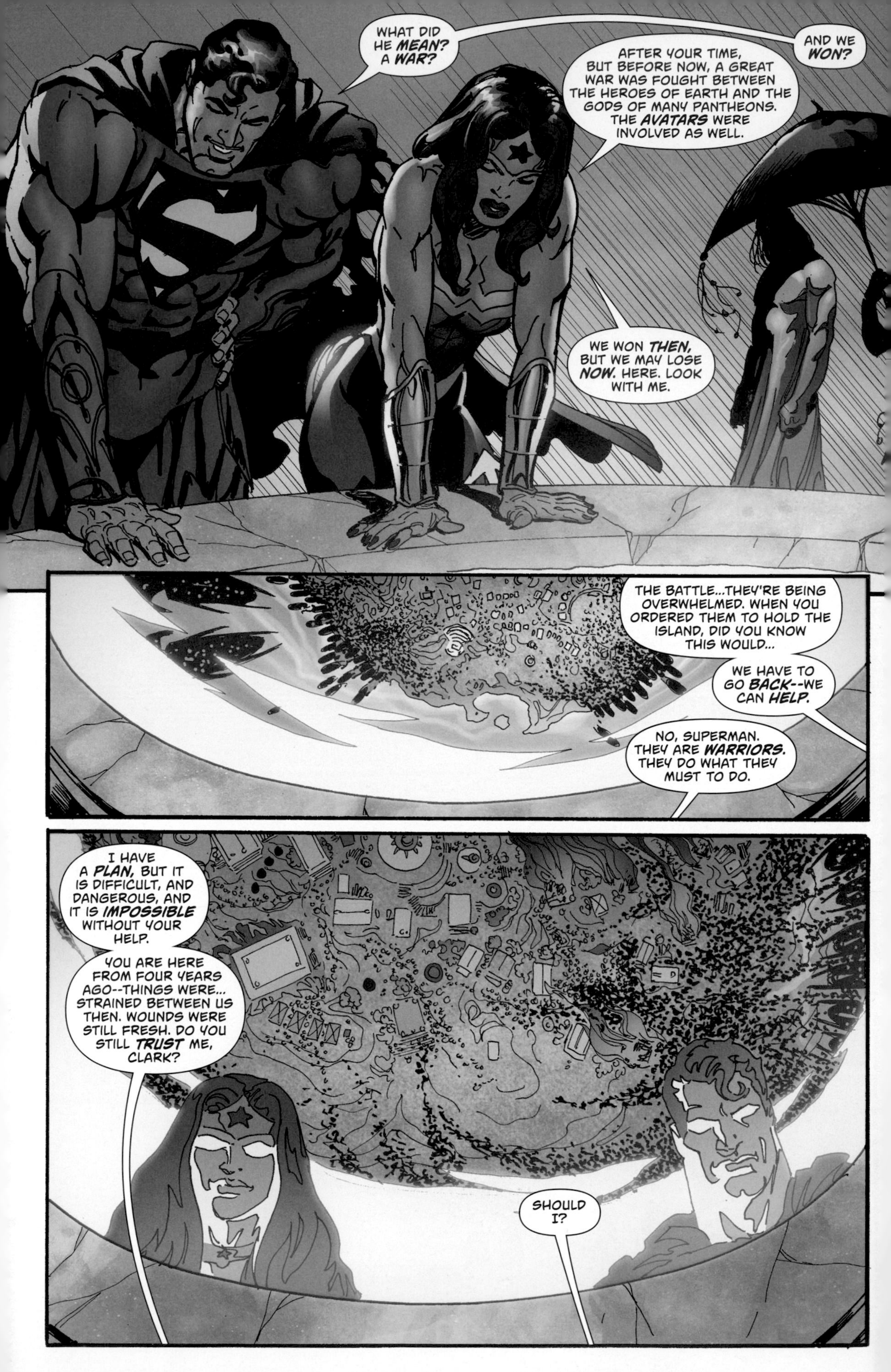
WHAT DID HE MEAN? A WAR?
AND WE WON?
AFTER YOUR TIME, BUT BEFORE NOW, A GREAT WAR WAS FOUGHT BETWEEN THE HEROES OF EARTH AND THE GODS OF MANY PANTHEONS. THE AVATARS WERE INVOLVED AS WELL.
WE WON THEN, BUT WE MAY LOSE NOW. HERE. LOOK WITH ME.
THE BATTLE...THEY'RE BEING OVERWHELMED. WHEN YOU ORDERED THEM TO HOLD THE ISLAND, DID YOU KNOW THIS WOULD...
WE HAVE TO GO BACK--WE CAN HELP.
NO, SUPERMAN. THEY ARE WARRIORS. THEY DO WHAT THEY MUST TO DO.
I HAVE A PLAN, BUT IT IS DIFFICULT, AND DANGEROUS, AND IT IS IMPOSSIBLE WITHOUT YOUR HELP.
YOU ARE HERE FROM FOUR YEARS AGO--THINGS WERE... STRAINED BETWEEN US THEN. WOUNDS WERE STILL FRESH. DO YOU STILL TRUST ME, CLARK?
SHOULD I?

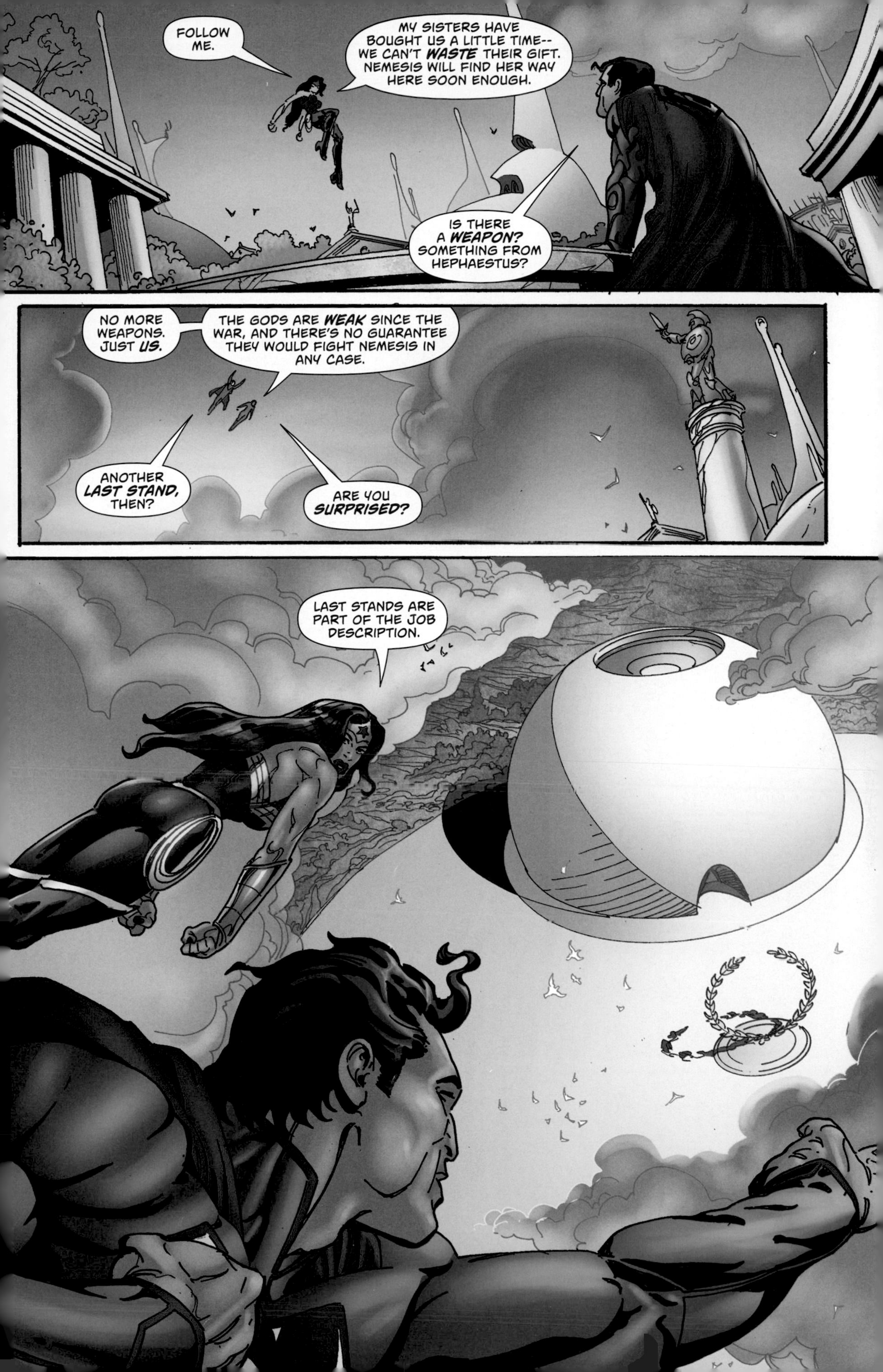

FOLLOW ME.
MY SISTERS HAVE BOUGHT US A LITTLE TIME-- WE CAN'T WASTE THEIR GIFT. NEMESIS WILL FIND HER WAY HERE SOON ENOUGH.
IS THERE A WEAPON? SOMETHING FROM HEPHAESTUS?
NO MORE WEAPONS. JUST US.
THE GODS ARE WEAK SINCE THE WAR, AND THERE'S NO GUARANTEE THEY WOULD FIGHT NEMESIS IN ANY CASE.
ANOTHER LAST STAND, THEN?
ARE YOU SURPRISED?
LAST STANDS ARE PART OF THE JOB DESCRIPTION.

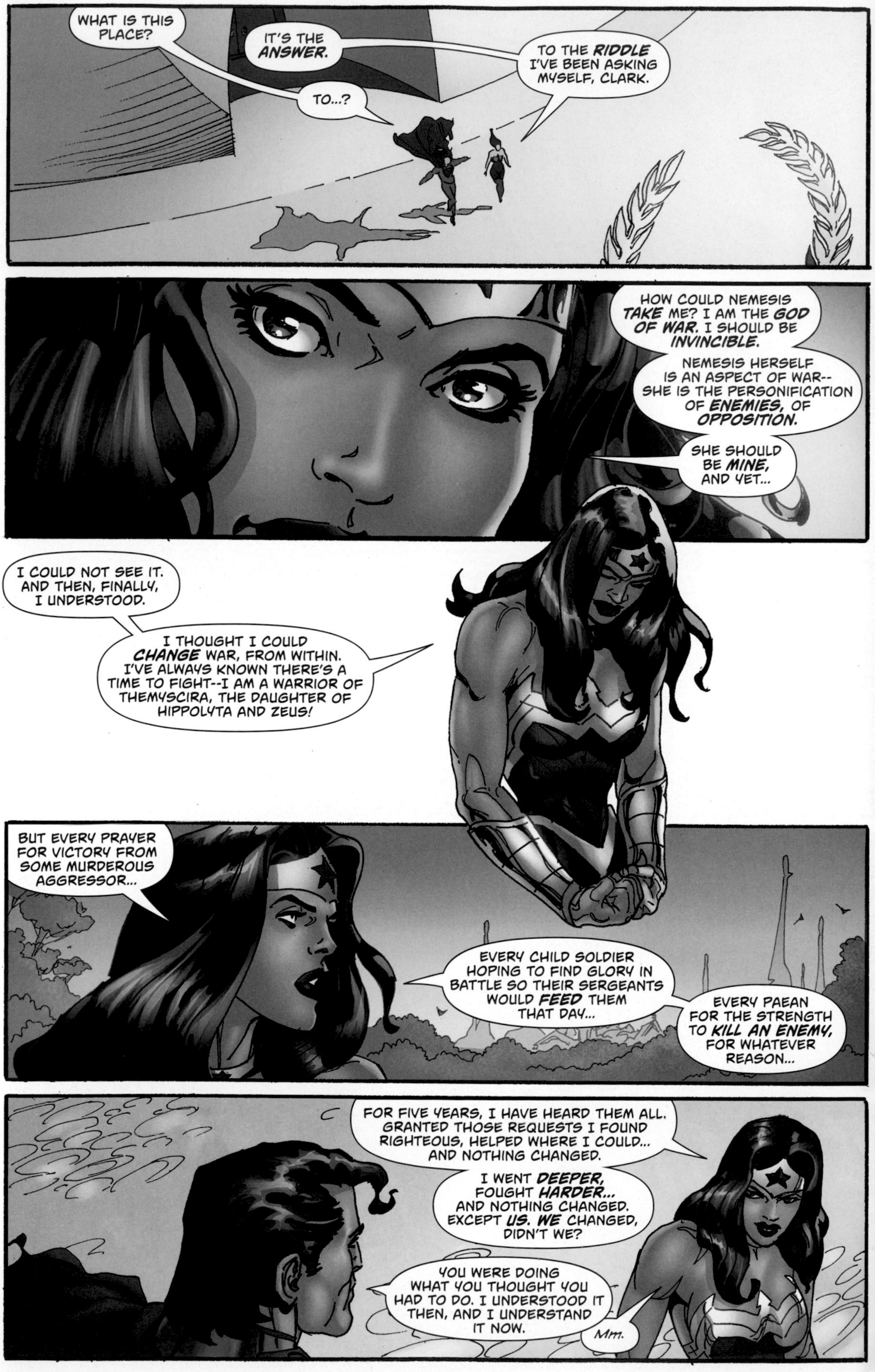
WHAT IS THIS PLACE?
IT'S THE ANSWER.
TO...?
TO THE RIDDLE I'VE BEEN ASKING MYSELF, CLARK.
HOW COULD NEMESIS TAKE ME? I AM THE GOD OF WAR. I SHOULD BE INVINCIBLE.
NEMESIS HERSELF IS AN ASPECT OF WAR-- SHE IS THE PERSONIFICATION OF ENEMIES, OF OPPOSITION.
SHE SHOULD BE MINE, AND YET...
I COULD NOT SEE IT. AND THEN, FINALLY, I UNDERSTOOD.
I THOUGHT I COULD CHANGE WAR, FROM WITHIN. I'VE ALWAYS KNOWN THERE'S A TIME TO FIGHT--I AM A WARRIOR OF THEMYSCIRA, THE DAUGHTER OF HIPPOLYTA AND ZEUS!
BUT EVERY PRAYER FOR VICTORY FROM SOME MURDEROUS AGGRESSOR...
EVERY CHILD SOLDIER HOPING TO FIND GLORY IN BATTLE SO THEIR SERGEANTS WOULD FEED THEM THAT DAY...
EVERY PAEAN FOR THE STRENGTH TO KILL AN ENEMY, FOR WHATEVER REASON...
FOR FIVE YEARS, I HAVE HEARD THEM ALL. GRANTED THOSE REQUESTS I FOUND RIGHTEOUS, HELPED WHERE I COULD... AND NOTHING CHANGED.
I WENT DEEPER, FOUGHT HARDER... AND NOTHING CHANGED. EXCEPT US. WE CHANGED, DIDN'T WE?
YOU WERE DOING WHAT YOU THOUGHT YOU HAD TO DO. I UNDERSTOOD IT THEN, AND I UNDERSTAND IT NOW.
Mm.

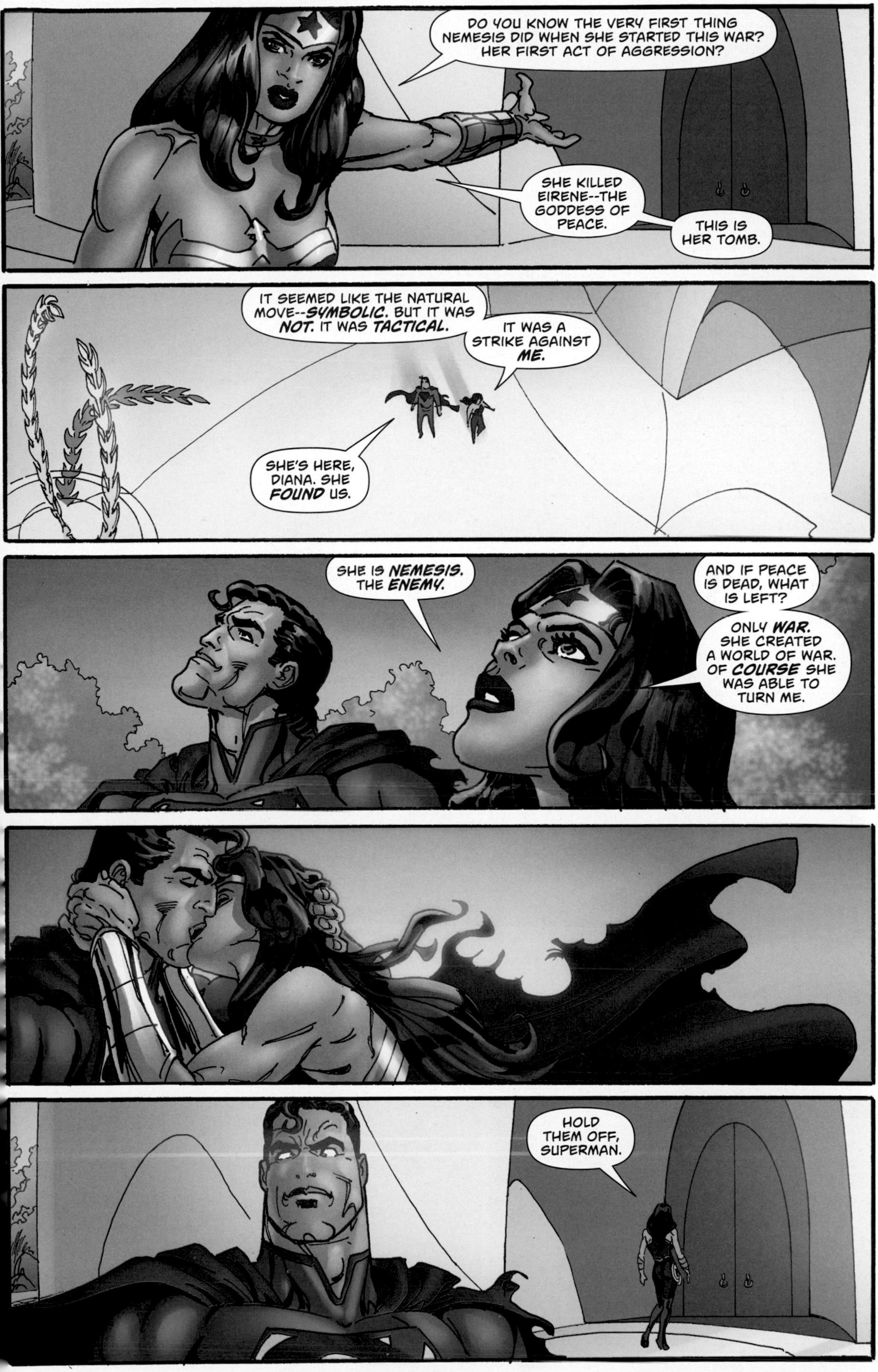
DO YOU KNOW THE VERY FIRST THING NEMESIS DID WHEN SHE STARTED THIS WAR? HER FIRST ACT OF AGGRESSION?
SHE KILLED EIRENE--THE GODDESS OF PEACE.
THIS IS HER TOMB.
IT SEEMED LIKE THE NATURAL MOVE--SYMBOLIC. BUT IT WAS NOT. IT WAS TACTICAL.
IT WAS A STRIKE AGAINST ME.
SHE'S HERE, DIANA. SHE FOUND US.
SHE IS NEMESIS. THE ENEMY.
AND IF PEACE IS DEAD, WHAT IS LEFT?
ONLY WAR. SHE CREATED A WORLD OF WAR. OF COURSE SHE WAS ABLE TO TURN ME.
HOLD THEM OFF, SUPERMAN.

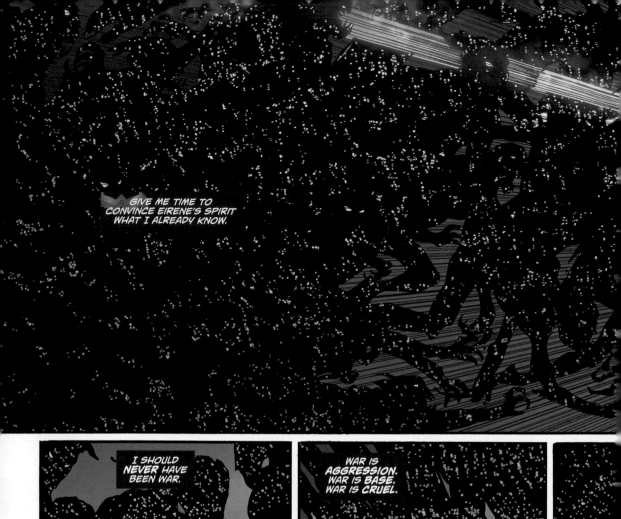

GIVE ME TIME TO CONVINCE EIRENE'S SPIRIT WHAT I ALREADY KNOW.

I SHOULD NEVER HAVE BEEN WAR.

WAR IS AGGRESSION. WAR IS BASE. WAR IS CRUEL.

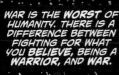

WAR IS THE *WORST* OF HUMANITY. THERE IS A DIFFERENCE BETWEEN FIGHTING FOR WHAT YOU *BELIEVE*, BEING A *WARRIOR*, AND *WAR*.

WAR IS *DEATH*.

AH. WONDERFUL.

I LOVE *LIFE*.

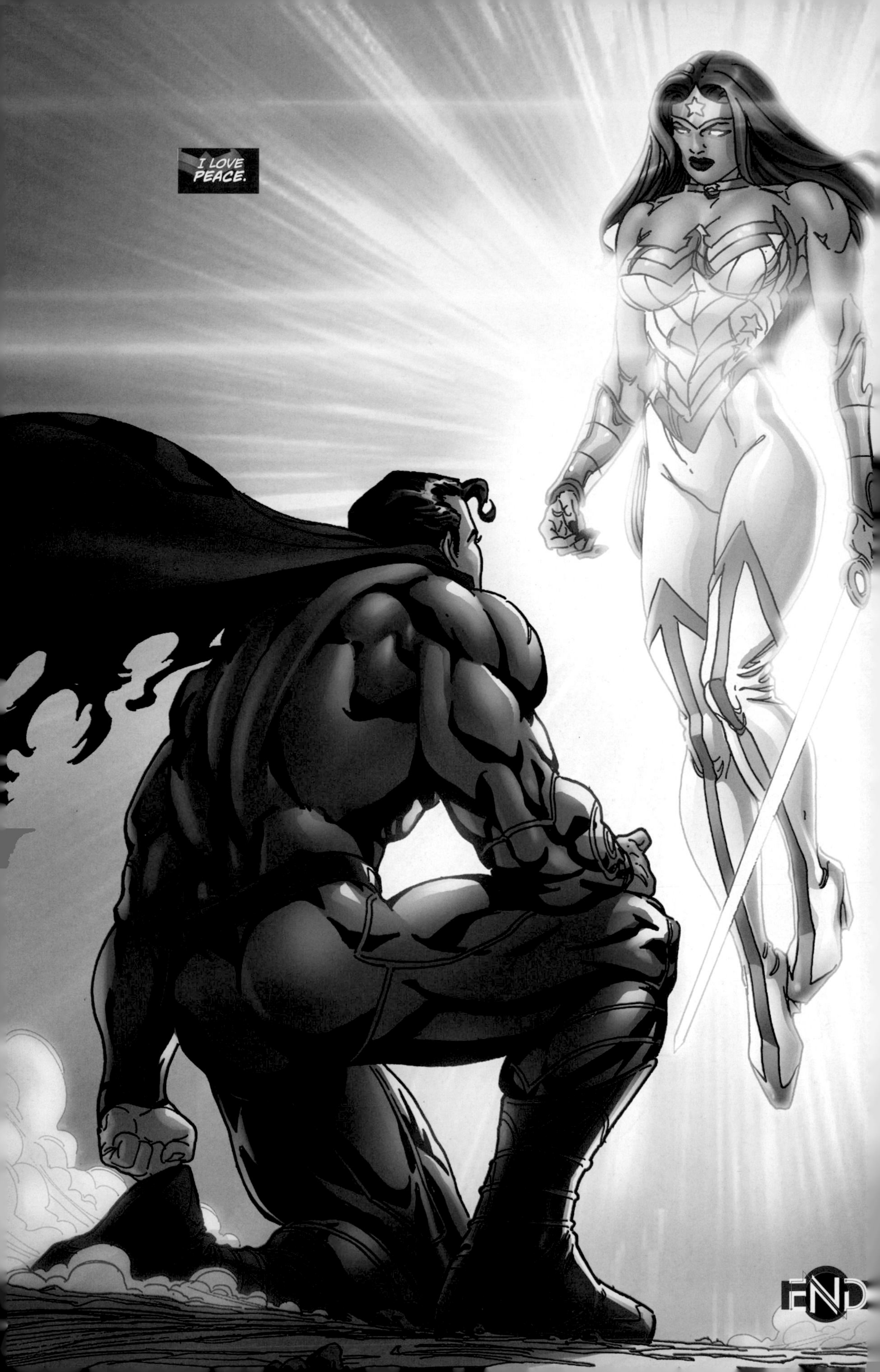
I LOVE PEACE.
END

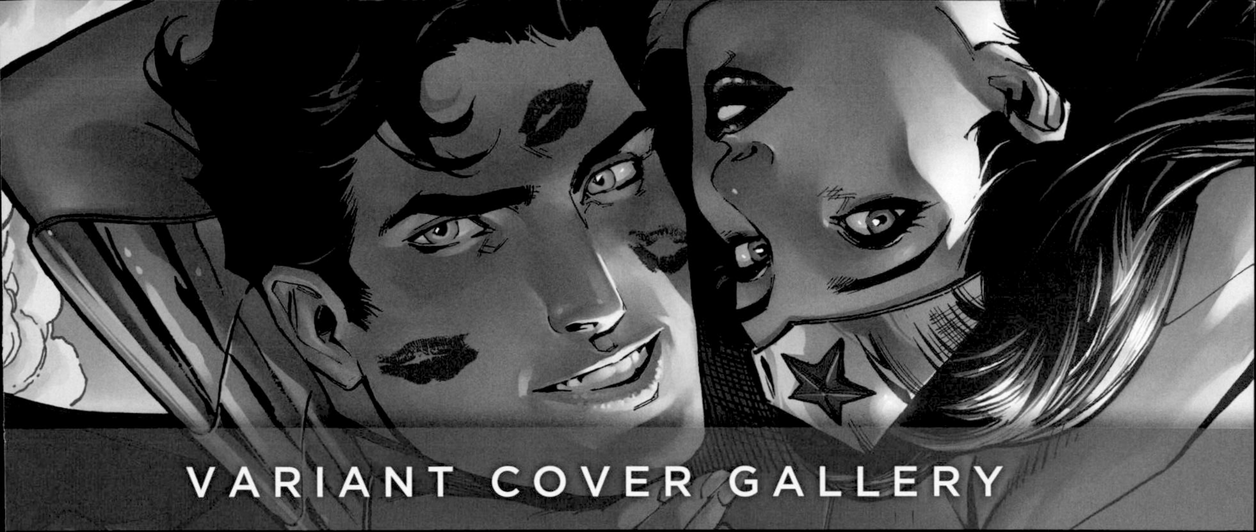

VARIANT COVER GALLERY

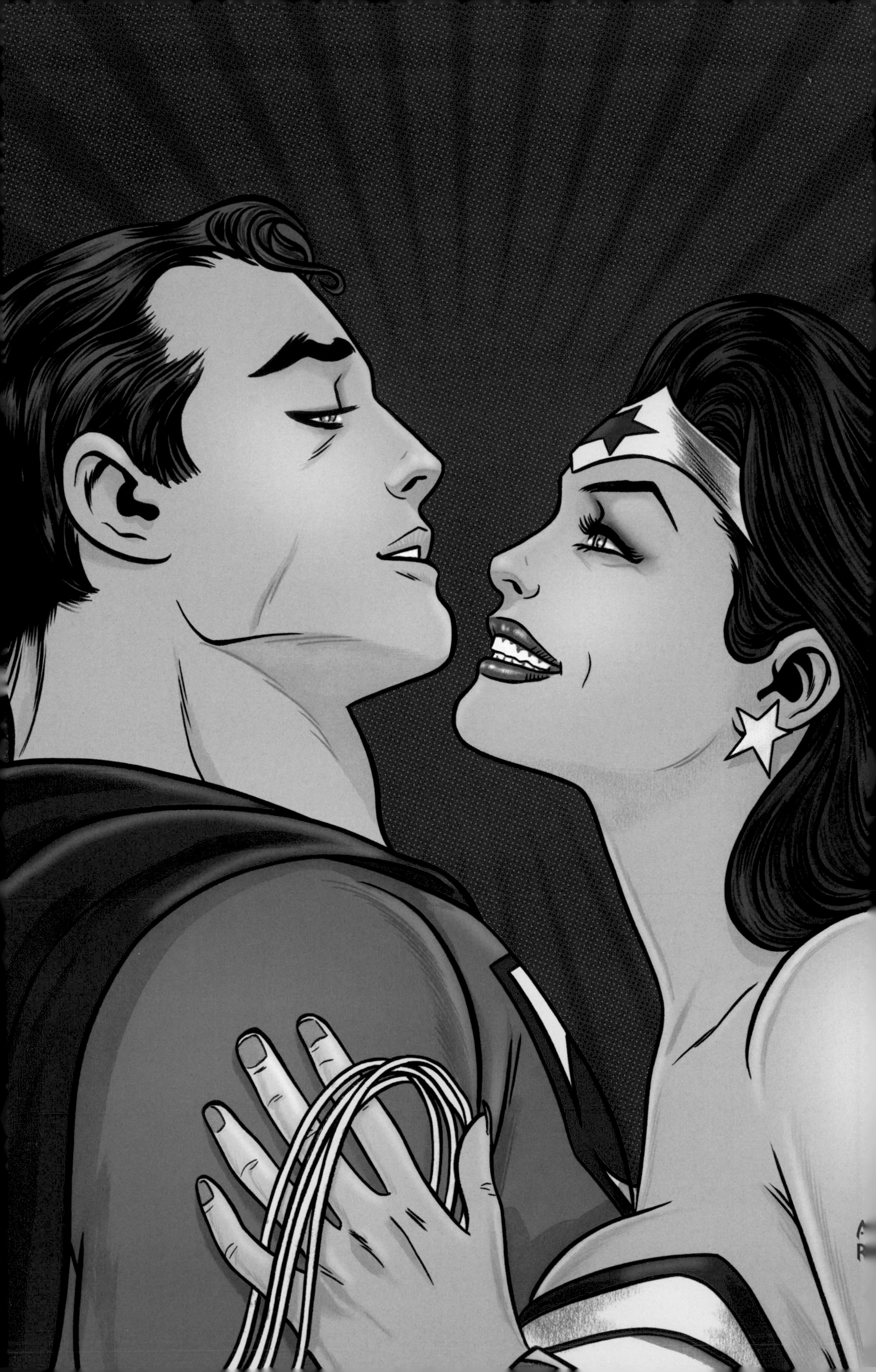

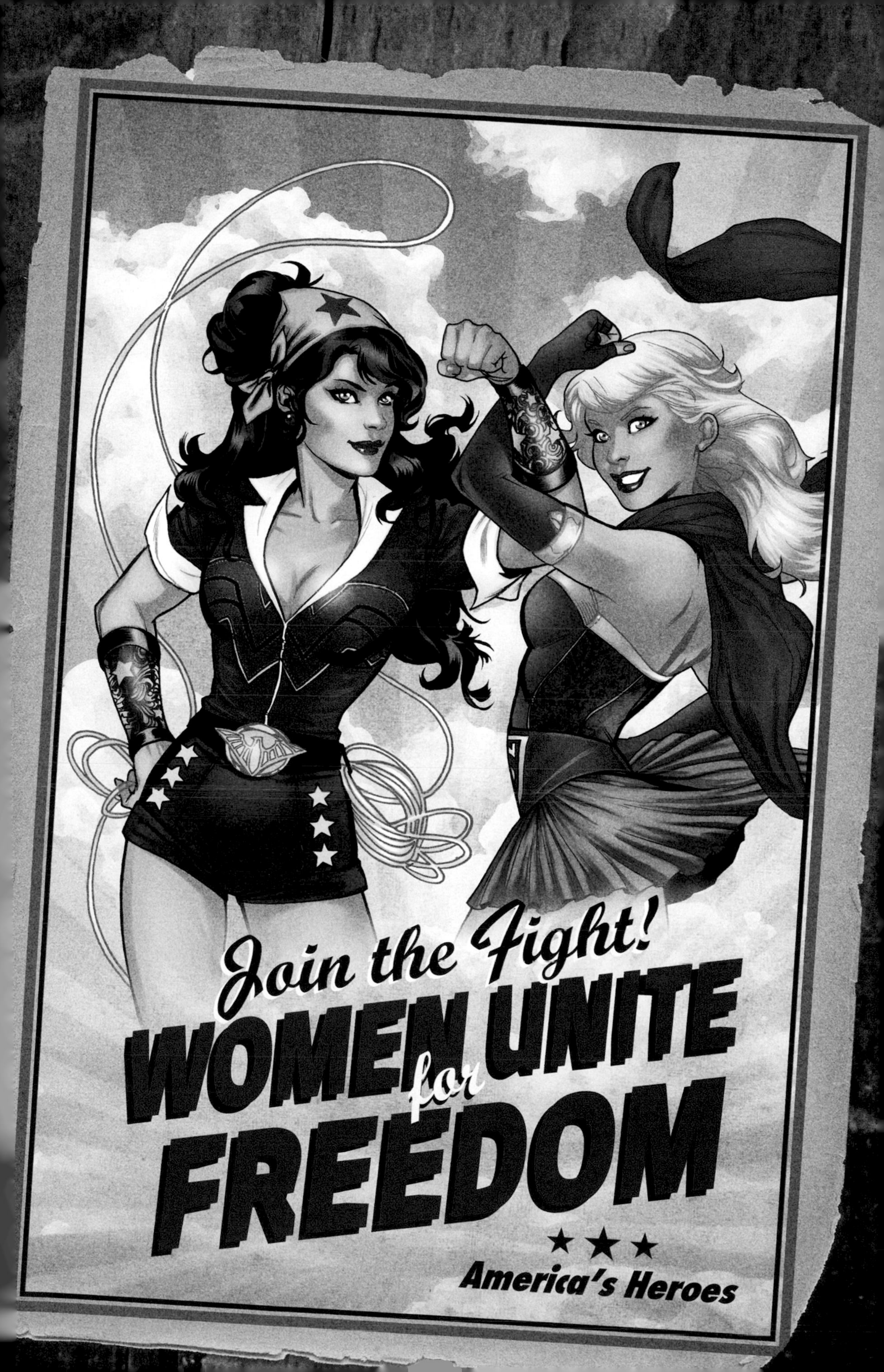
Join the Fight!
WOMEN UNITE for FREEDOM
America's Heroes

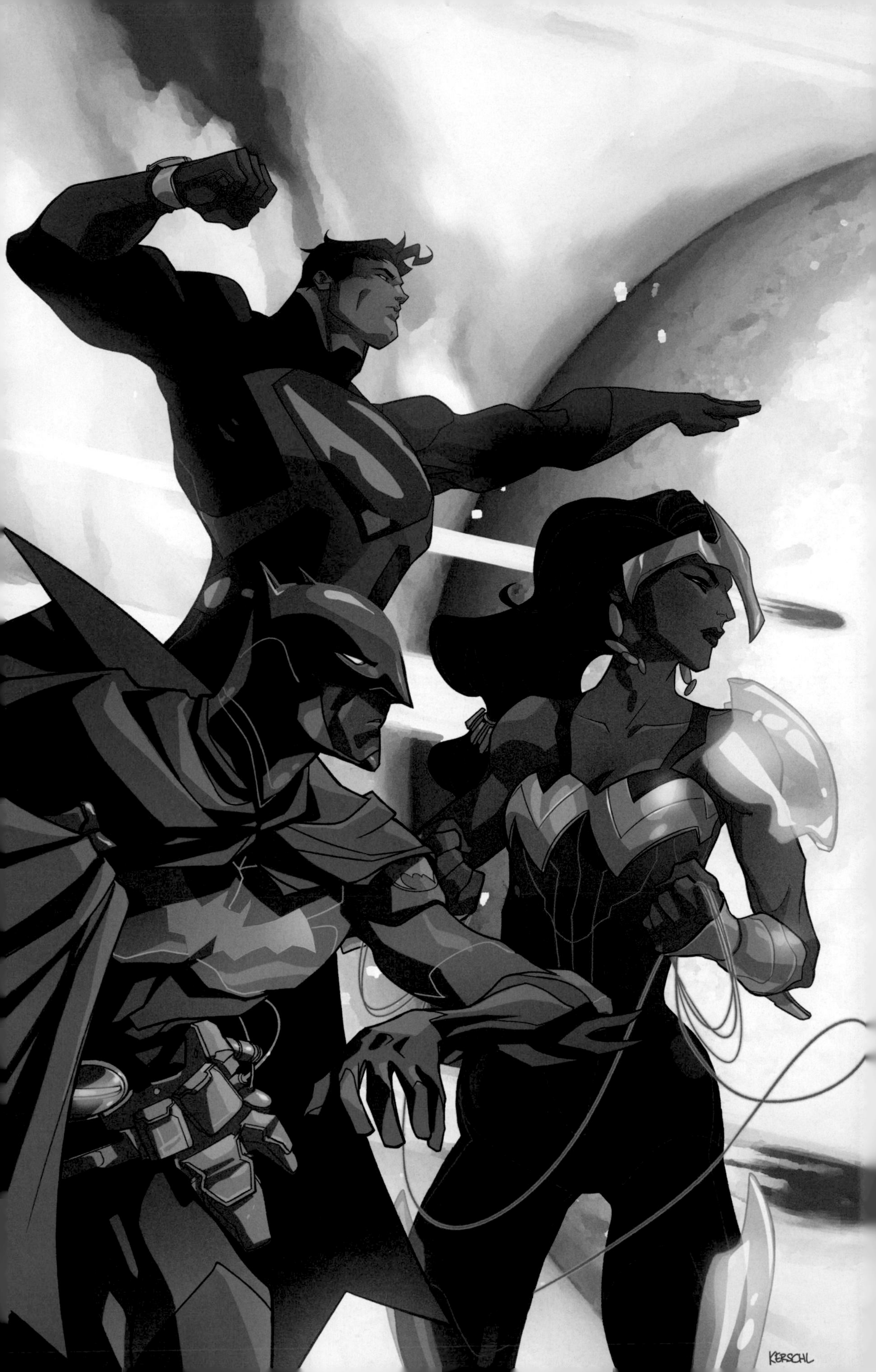
KERSCHL

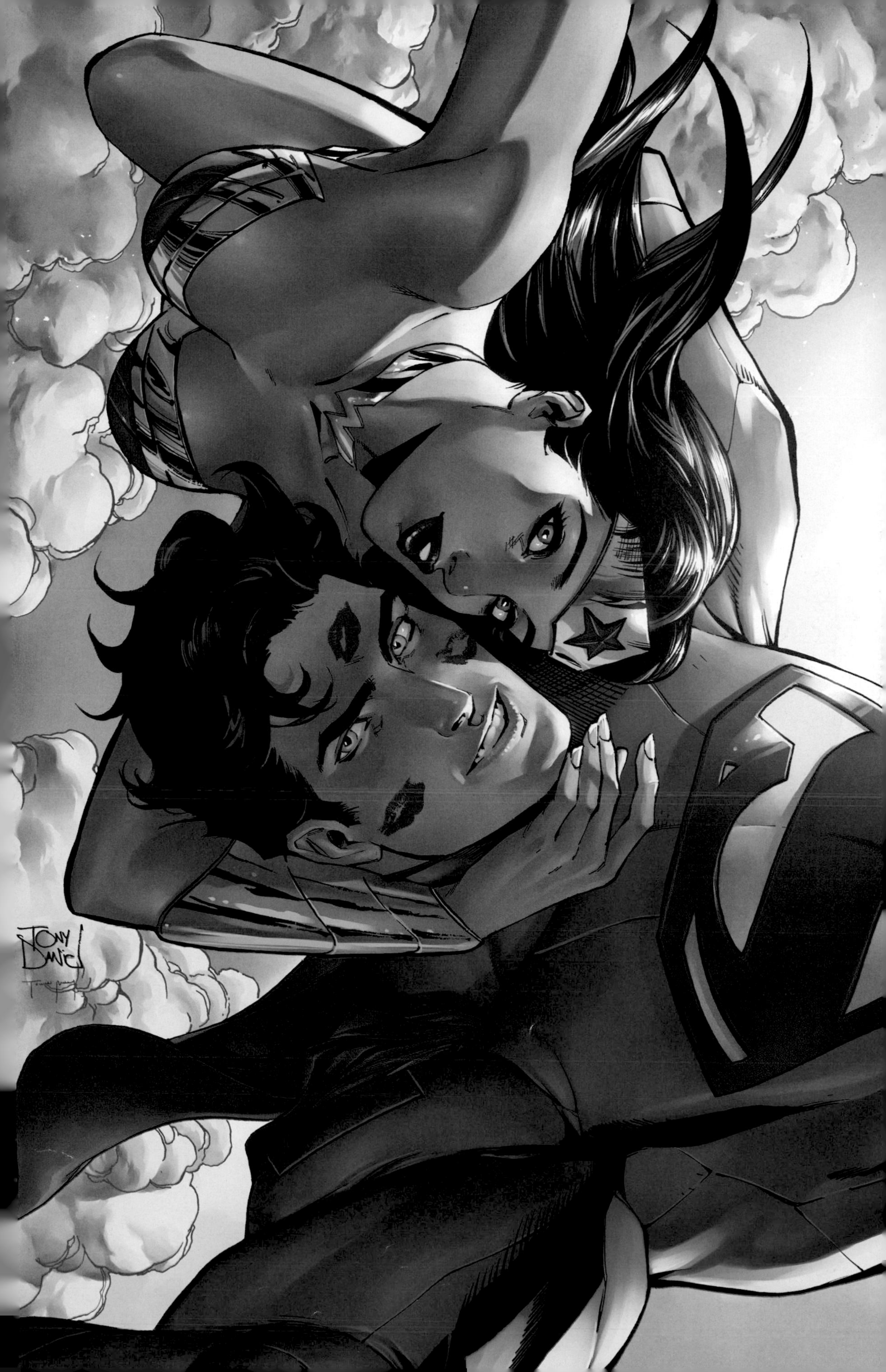

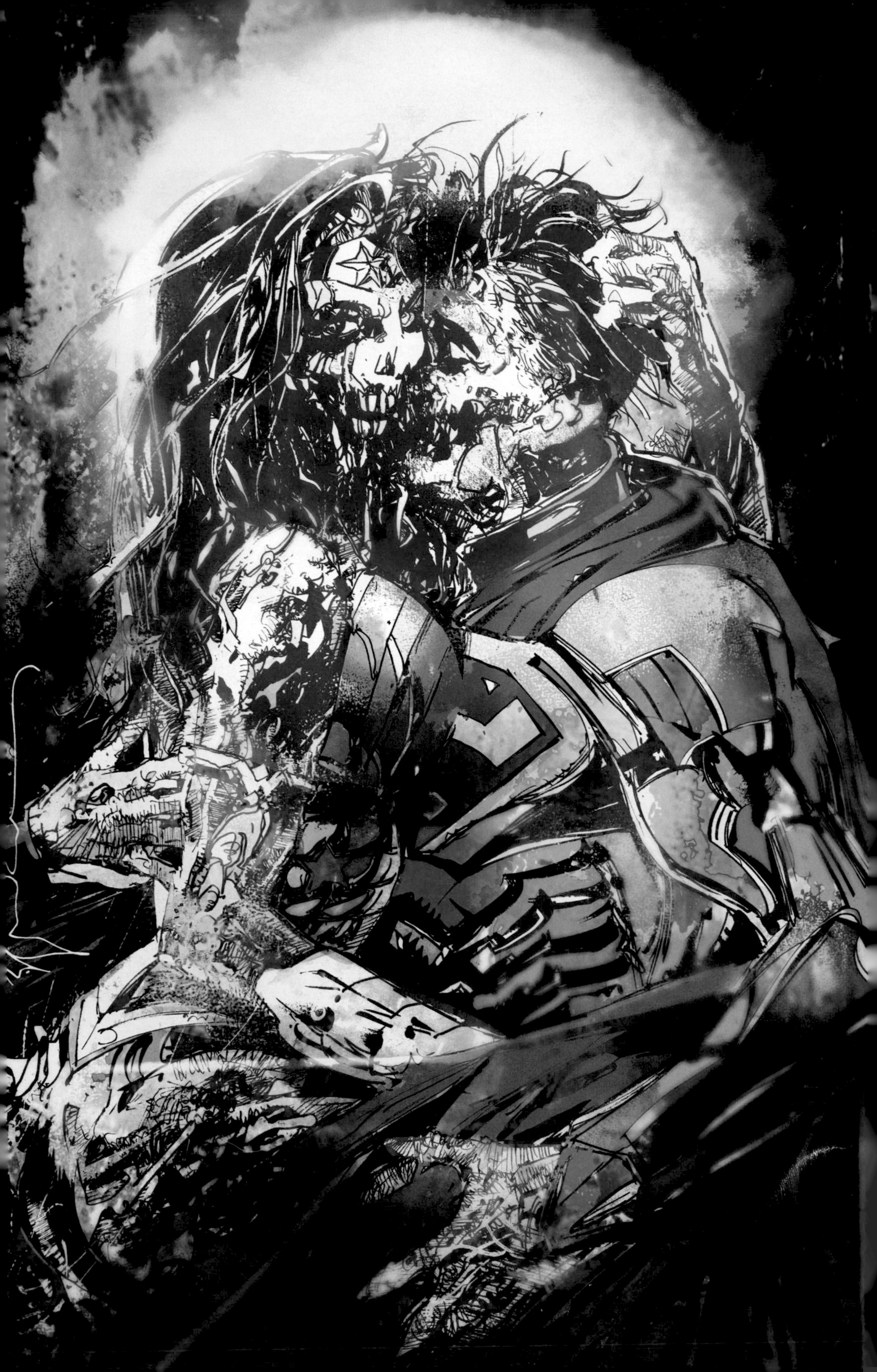

"Clear storytelling at its best. It's an intriguing concept and easy to grasp."—THE NEW YORK TIMES

"Azzarello is rebuilding the mythology of Wonder Woman."
—CRAVE ONLINE

START AT THE BEGINNING!

WONDER WOMAN VOLUME 1: BLOOD

THE NEW 52!
DC COMICS
WONDER WOMAN
VOLUME 1 BLOOD
"EXPECT A LOT MORE WONDER WOMAN FANS AFTER A FEW ISSUES OF THIS BOOK."
— USA TODAY
BRIAN AZZARELLO CLIFF CHIANG TONY AKINS

WONDER WOMAN VOL. 2: GUTS

THE NEW 52!
WONDER WOMAN
BRIAN AZZARELLO CLIFF CHIANG TONY AKINS

by BRIAN AZZARELLO and CLIFF CHIANG

WONDER WOMAN VOL. 3: IRON

THE NEW 52!
WONDER WOMAN
BRIAN AZZARELLO CLIFF CHIANG

by BRIAN AZZARELLO and CLIFF CHIANG

SUPERGIRL VOL. 1: LAST DAUGHTER OF KRYPTON

THE NEW 52!
SUPERGIRL
MICHAEL GREEN MIKE JOHNSON MAHMUD ASRAR

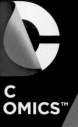

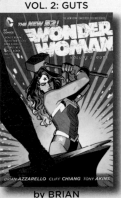

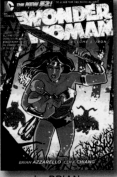

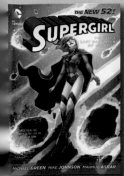

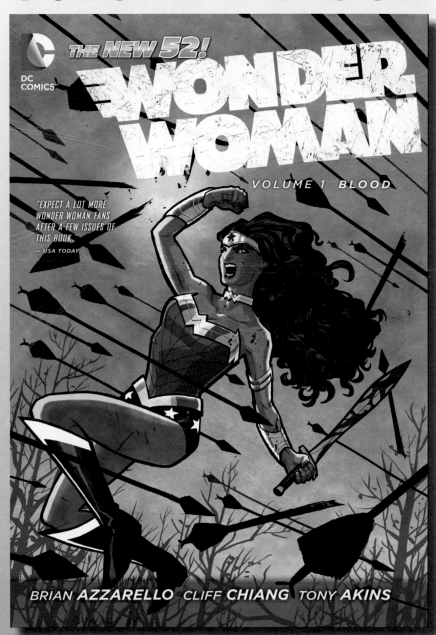

DC
COMICS™

"ACTION COMICS has successfully carved it
own territory and continued exploring Morrison'
familiar themes about heroism and ideas."—IG

"Casts the character in a new light, opens up fresh storytell
ing possibilities, and pushes it all forward with dynamic Rag
Morales art. I loved it."—THE ONION/AV CLU

START AT THE BEGINNING!

SUPERMAN: ACTION COMICS VOLUME 1: SUPERMAN AND THE MEN OF STEEL

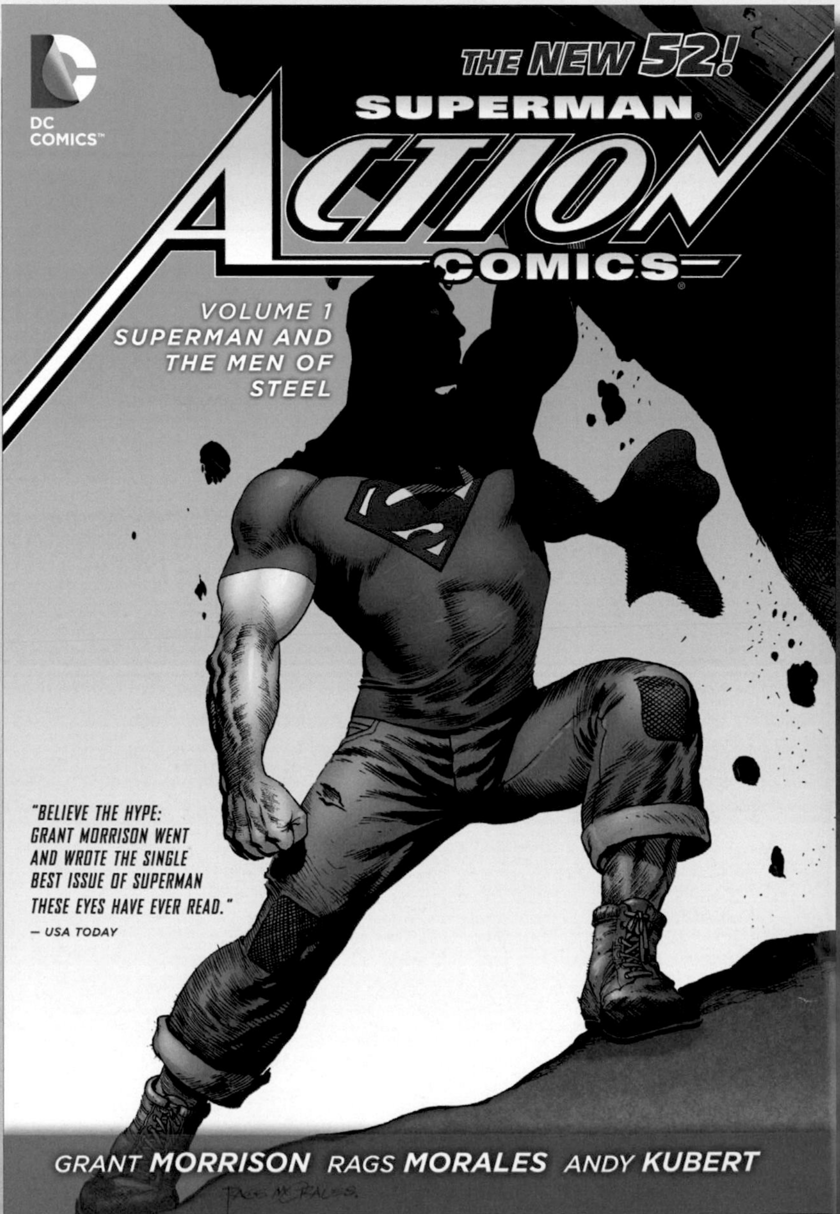
DC
COMICS™
THE NEW 52!
SUPERMAN
ACTION
COMICS
VOLUME 1
SUPERMAN AND
THE MEN OF
STEEL
"BELIEVE THE HYPE: GRANT MORRISON WENT AND WROTE THE SINGLE BEST ISSUE OF SUPERMAN THESE EYES HAVE EVER READ."
— USA TODAY
GRANT MORRISON RAGS MORALES ANDY KUBERT

SUPERMAN: ACTION COMICS VOL. 2: BULLETPROOF

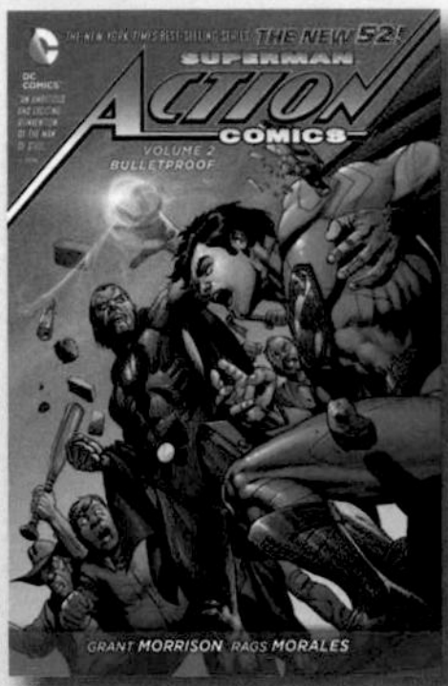
THE NEW 52!
SUPERMAN
ACTION
COMICS
VOLUME 2
BULLETPROOF
GRANT MORRISON RAGS MORALES

with GRANT MORRISON and RAGS MORALES

SUPERMAN: ACTION COMICS VOL. 3: AT THE END OF DAYS

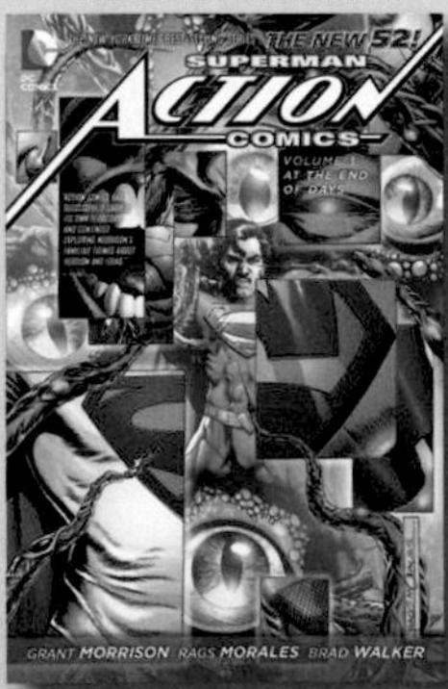
THE NEW 52!
SUPERMAN
ACTION
COMICS
GRANT MORRISON RAGS MORALES BRAD WALKER

with GRANT MORRISON and RAGS MORALES

SUPERBOY VOL. 1: INCUBATION

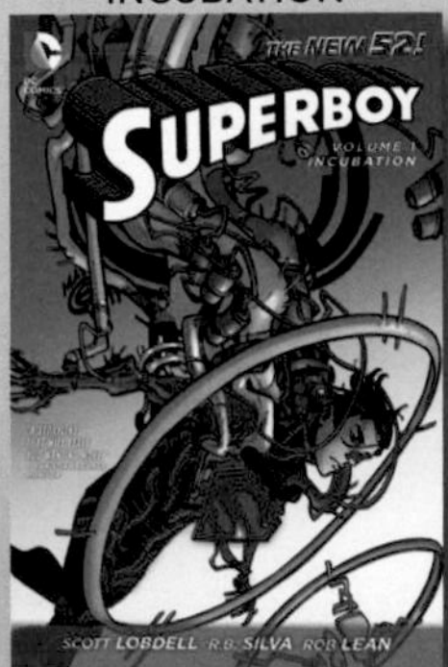
THE NEW 52!
SUPERBOY
VOLUME 1
INCUBATION
SCOTT LOBDELL R.B. SILVA ROB LEAN

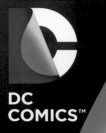

DC COMICS™

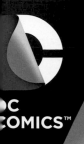

"Writer Geoff Johns and artist Jim Lee toss you–and their heroes–into the action from the very start and don't put on the brakes. DC's über-creative team craft an inviting world for those who are trying out a comic for the first time. Lee's art is stunning."—USA TODAY

"A fun ride."—IGN

START AT THE BEGINNING!

JUSTICE LEAGUE VOLUME 1: ORIGIN

GEOFF JOHNS and JIM LEE

THE NEW 52!
DC COMICS
JUSTICE LEAGUE
VOLUME 1 ORIGIN
"WRITTEN BY GEOFF JOHNS, WITH ART BY THE GODLY JIM LEE, JUSTICE LEAGUE IS A MUST READ."
— COMPLEX MAGAZINE
GEOFF JOHNS JIM LEE SCOTT WILLIAMS

JUSTICE LEAGUE VOL. 2: THE VILLAIN'S JOURNEY

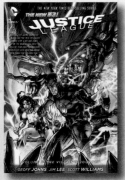

JUSTICE LEAGUE
GEOFF JOHNS JIM LEE SCOTT WILLIAMS

JUSTICE LEAGUE VOL. 3: THRONE OF ATLANTIS

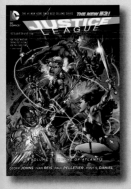

THE NEW 52!
JUSTICE LEAGUE
GEOFF JOHNS IVAN REIS PAUL PELLETIER TONY S. DANIEL

JUSTICE LEAGUE OF AMERICA VOL. 1: WORLD'S MOST DANGEROUS

JUSTICE LEAGUE OF AMERICA
VOLUME 1 WORLD'S MOST DANGEROUS
GEOFF JOHNS DAVID FINCH BRETT BOOTH DOUG MAHNKE

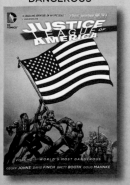

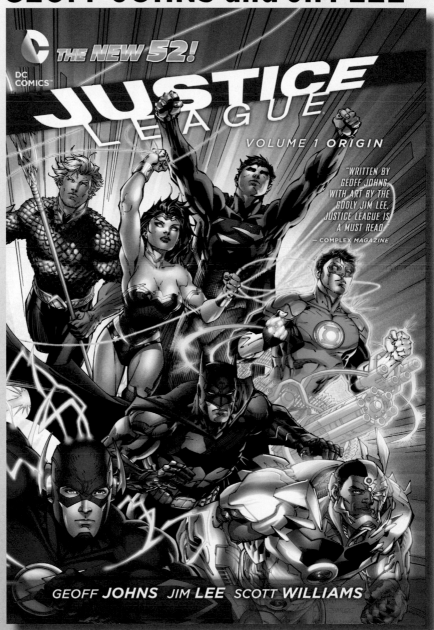

START AT THE BEGINNING!

SUPERMAN VOLUME 1: WHAT PRICE TOMORROW?

SUPERMAN VOL. 2: SECRETS & LIES

SUPERMAN VOL. 3: FURY AT WORLD'S END

SUPERMAN: H'EL ON EARTH

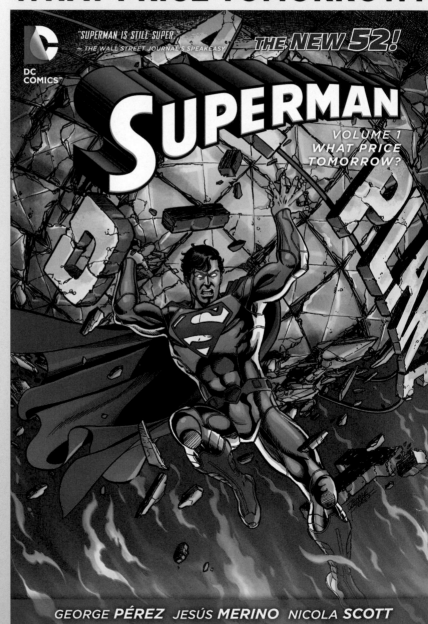

GEORGE **PÉREZ** JESÚS **MERINO** NICOLA **SCOTT**